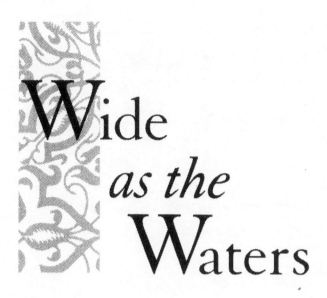

Wide as the Waters

THE STORY OF THE ENGLISH BIBLE AND THE REVOLUTION IT INSPIRED

Benson Bobrick

SIMON & SCHUSTER
NEW YORK   LONDON
TORONTO   SYDNEY   SINGAPORE

SIMON & SCHUSTER
Rockefeller Center
1230 Avenue of the Americas
New York, NY 10020

SIMON & SCHUSTER and colophon are registered trademarks
of Simon & Schuster, Inc.

Designed by Deirdre C. Amthor

Manufactured in the United States of America

10   9   8   7   6   5   4   3   2

Library of Congress Cataloging-in-Publication Data
Bobrick, Benson, date.
    Wide as the waters : the story of the English Bible and the revolution it inspired
Benson Bobrick.
    p.   cm.
    Includes bibliographical references (p.   ) and index.
    1. Bible. English—Versions—History.   2. Bible—England—History.   I. Title.
BS455.B62 2001
220.5'2'009—dc21   00-066174
ISBN 978-1-4516-1360-5

The Gospell off Sancte Jhon.
The fyrst Chapter.

In the begynnynge was that worde/and that worde was with god: and god was thatt worde. The same was in the begynnynge wyth god. All thyngs were made by it/and wyth out it/was made noo thinge/that made was. In it was lyfe/And lyfe was the light of men/And the light shyneth in darcknes/and darcknes comprehended it not.

There was a man sent from god/whose name was Jhon. The same cam as a witnes/to beare witnes of the light/that all men through him myght beleve. He was nott that light: but to beare witnes of the light. That was a true light/which lighteneth all men that come into the worlde. He was in the worlde/and the worlde by him was made: and the worlde knewe hym not.

ALSO BY BENSON BOBRICK

Angel in the Whirlwind: *The Triumph of the American Revolution*
Knotted Tongues: *Stuttering in History and the Quest for a Cure*
East of the Sun: *The Epic Conquest and Tragic History of Siberia*
Fearful Majesty: *The Life and Reign of Ivan the Terrible*
Labyrinths of Iron: *Subways in History, Myth, Art, Technology and War*

In Memory of My Grandfather

JAMES CHAMBERLAIN BAKER

Classical Scholar,
Bishop of the Methodist Church,
and a Founder of the World Council of Churches

Contents

Prologue

The first question ever asked by an Inquisitor of a "heretic" was whether he knew any part of the Bible in his own tongue. It was asked in 1233 of a man who belonged to a dissident religious sect known as the Waldensians, which emphasized Bible study and lay preaching; and it would be asked again of thousands of others before the course of history would render its dark implications null and void.

☍

In the beginning was the Word, and that word was Hebrew and Greek. In the fourth century, it was translated by St. Jerome into Latin, where in the form of manuscript copies it was reserved unto the medieval clergy to dispense as they saw fit. That period of scriptural exclusion endured for a thousand years, until it was shattered by the translation of the Bible into the vernacular. Of the vernacular translations, none would compare to the English in moral stature or literary power.

Next to the Bible itself, the English Bible was (and is) the most influential book ever published. It gave every literate person complete access to the sacred text, which helped to foster the spirit of inquiry through reading and reflection. These in turn accelerated the growth of commercial printing and the ever-widening circulation and production of books. Books "formerly imprisoned in the libraries of monasteries" were, as one contemporary put it, "redeemed from bondage, obtained their enlargement, and freely walked about in the light."

Once the people were free to interpret the Word of God according to the light of their own understanding, they began to question the authority of their inherited institutions, both religious and secular, which led to reformation within the Church, and to the rise of constitutional government in England and the end of the divine right of kings. Although the vernacular Bible had begun as a pillar of support for England's monarchical authority and independence from the pope, in the end it contributed to and justified defiance of the monarchy itself.

Only in England was the Bible in any sense a "national possession," in that it seemed to exist apart in English as an original work of art. Indeed, not even Luther's version (despite its impact on the development of the German language) may be compared to the English Bible in this way. Englishmen carried their Bible with them—as the rock and foundation of their lives—overseas, even as it came to live in their own language with more abiding force "than the greatest works to which their authors were giving birth." In some indefinable way, it managed to incorporate into their own history "a living memory of the central past of the world," so that, over time, "the deeds and thoughts of men who had lived thousands of years before in the eastern Mediterranean came to color the everyday thought and speech of Britons to the same degree," wrote the great historian G. M. Trevelyan, "as they are colored in our own day by the commonplaces of the newspaper press." Beyond the shores of Albion, it fortified the spirit of the pioneers of New England, helped to shape the American psyche, and through its impact on thought and culture eventually spread the world over, "as wide as the waters be."

The Christian Bible is made up of two Testaments, the Old and the New. The Old Testament, or Hebrew Bible, is the sacred Scripture of the Jews, and recounts in thirty-nine books in poetry, prophecy, story, and song the history of a people from the Creation of the World. Its profoundly theological understanding of all Creation as proceeding from one God is, for both Christians and Jews, the ground of their faith. The New Testament, which complements or (as some would say) fulfills the Old, is a compendium of twenty-seven books in Greek which represent the testimony of those who witnessed and sustained the ministry of Christ.

The Old Testament is commonly divided into three parts: the Law or Torah (sometimes called the Pentateuch, made up of the first five books of Moses—Genesis, Exodus, Leviticus, Numbers, and Deuteronomy); the Prophets (Joshua, Judges, 1 and 2 Samuel, 1 and 2 Kings, Isaiah, Jeremiah, Ezekiel, and the Twelve minor prophets); and the Writings (Psalms, Proverbs, Job, Song of Songs, Ruth, Lamentations, Ecclesiastes, Esther, Daniel, Ezra, Nehemiah, I and 2 Chronicles). Each part arose as a separate collection of sacred texts, with the Law in use as Scripture by 400 B.C.; the Prophets, by 200 B.C.; and the Writings by about 130 B.C. Through all the ravages of war and persecution, Hebrew scribes had labored to preserve copies of the texts intact, but it was not until after the Roman destruction of Jerusalem in A.D. 70—which completed the Diaspora, and scattered Jews from the Pillars of Hercules to the shores of the Euxine Sea— that Jewish scholars in Palestine established as canonical the Old Testament in its current form.

Well before that, however, in the wake of the stupendous conquests of Alexander the Great—which made Greek the common language of the eastern Mediterranean—the Hebrew Scriptures had been translated into Greek by elite Jewish scholars in Alexandria, Egypt, to serve the Greek-speaking Jewish communities of the Hellenistic world. Legend has it that in the third century B.C. seventy-two such chosen scholars (six from each of the twelve tribes of Israel) were dispatched by the high priest in Jerusalem to Alexandria at the request of King Ptolemy II Philadelphus, who wanted to include in his great library there a copy of the Torah in Greek. The scholars were royally received by the king, and then set to work in a quiet house on the island of Pharos, where they completed their translation in exactly seventy-two days. The remaining books of the Old Testament—as well as some fourteen others (called the Apocrypha and used by Jews outside Palestine)—were also translated in subsequent years and the whole became known as the Septuagint, meaning "seventy," after the round number of translators who had originally taken part.

The Septuagint was the Bible of the first apostles, and was afterward adopted as Scripture by the early Christian Church. But the more Christians embraced it as their own (and used it, in polemics, against Jews), the more Jewish scholars felt constrained to repudiate it as an imperfect translation and to enumerate its flaws. At just this time (in the second century A.D.) the New Testament also began to take shape as a collection of sacred texts. The story of the passion and the actual words of Jesus had originally been preserved by oral tradition, and it was from that tradition that the disciples had taught. St. Paul's letters to various churches in the Roman provinces were apparently the first New Testament texts to be accepted as inspired, but it was not until the middle of the fourth century A.D. that the twenty-seven books as we know them were established as canonical. These are: the thirteen epistles of Paul; the three synoptic Gospels of Matthew, Mark, and Luke; the Gospel According to John; the Epistles of James, Peter, John, and Jude; the Acts of the Apostles (written by Luke); and Revelation (written by John).

Meanwhile, the Roman empire had supplanted the empire of Alexander the Great, and imposed its language and culture on Christian communities throughout its vast domains. These adopted Latin for their ceremonies and rites, and in the second century A.D. an "Old Latin" translation of the Bible, made directly from the Greek by persons unknown, came into use as Scripture by the Latin-speaking Churches of North Africa, Italy, Spain, and Gaul. By the middle of the fourth century several variants were in circulation and the overall corruption of the text had become intolerable to Church authorities. About 382 A.D. Pope Damasus therefore invited Eusebius Hieronymus (afterward known as St. Jerome) to revise it. And this he undertook to do.

No one was more qualified. Born in northern Italy in 346, Jerome had been schooled in the classical rhetorical tradition of Rome, traveled through Gaul, Thrace, and Asia Minor, and for many years lived as a hermit in the Syrian desert, where he acquired a knowledge not only of Hebrew but of Chaldee, the Semitic language of southern Babylonia. At some point, he also studied in Byzantium with scholars of the Eastern Church. With his deep knowledge of all things biblical, he was the outstanding biblical scholar of his day.

Jerome began his revision at once, and the four Gospels appeared with "commendable promptness" in 383, followed almost immediately by a revision of the Psalter (the book of Psalms). In the fall of 386 Jerome left Rome for Bethlehem, where he carried his revisions through Ecclesiastes, Proverbs, the Song of Solomon, Chronicles, and Job, but then in 391 abandoned this procedure altogether and decided to translate directly from the original tongues. In 405, after many years of labor, he at last came forth with a substantially new and idiomatic Latin translation of the whole. Although a work of great magnitude, felicity, and skill, Jerome's translation was not accorded an immediate welcome by the Church. His enemies alleged that it was "tainted with Judaism," while conservatives automatically adhered to the older Greek and Latin versions which had "a halo of sanctity" about them from long and familiar use.

St. Jerome himself was exasperated by the calumnies which greeted his work. "If my occupation had been to plait rush baskets or to weave mats out of palm leaves," he wrote, "in order, by the sweat of my brow, to gain my daily bread, envy would have spared me. But since, in obedience to the precepts of the Savior, I have, for the good of souls, chosen to prepare the bread which perishes not and have wished to clear the path of truth of the weeds which ignorance has sown in it, I am accused of a twofold crime. If I correct errors in the Sacred Text, I am denounced as a falsifier; if I do not correct them, I am pilloried as a disseminator of error." At his death at Bethlehem in A.D. 420, his translation had yet to receive the recognition it deserved. But over time resistance gave way to admiration, and admiration to wonder, tinged with awe; by the early seventh century the Vulgate, or "common version," as his translation came to be known, was in general use by Churches throughout the Christian West. Eventually, it acquired that mystical aura of immutable perfection which for many Christians has enveloped it ever since.

Although the English Bible was destined to enjoy a comparable triumph, its story, like that of the Vulgate, is larger than the religious debate from which it arose. While in a sense it is a Protestant book, the story of its evolution has a decidedly Catholic side; and although the Catholic Church comes in for its usual Reformation drubbing (which, by its own later confession, it deserved), those who see the story through to the end will find that a Catholic has almost the last word. That is as it should be, if the tale is truly told. For all apparent opposites prove to be the heart of each other's life, and so it is with Scripture and Tradition, Faith and Works. The reader is asked only to set all assumptions aside, and to come to the story with an ecumenical mind.

⊗

I am grateful to Edward Hoagland for first turning my thoughts toward aspects of my subject; to the many scholars whose work prepared the way for my own, which is perhaps but a footnote to theirs; and to a number of friends and colleagues for helping to nudge the book along. Of these I must surely name: Paul Wharton Winthrop, Chelsea Forrest, Mark Souter, Shiloh Grey, Mary Hill, Jonathan Svensson, Matthew Drummond, Molly Spencer, Everett Finch, Samuel Rothberg, Penelope Wright, and Johanna Li. A memorable conversation I once had about etymology with Father Richard Adams helped refresh my study of Greek; to two great teachers in the Humanities—Hagop Missak Merjian and Edward W. Tayler—I owe an everlasting debt. May my labor find favor in their sight.

My agent, Russell Galen, gave the book an early lift; Margaret Crampton read over the first complete draft of the manuscript with immaculate care; with his usual patience, my editor, Bob Bender, allowed me to revise it through and through. Hilary's faith sustained.

As always, the New York Public Library and the Libraries of Columbia University were my rod and staff, in comforting assistance to my quest. I would also like to thank the Library of Congress; the

British Library; the Bodleian Library, Oxford; the Lambeth Palace Library, London; and the Union Theological Seminary in New York for material of use.

This book is dedicated to my grandfather, who knew the Bible by heart.

JOHN WYCLIFFE

Holy Scripture excels all branches of learning in the very way it speaks; for with one and the same expression, while it recounts history it utters a mystery.

—Gregory the Great

CHAPTER ONE

Morning Star

*he beginnings* of Christianity in Britain are wreathed with the mists of Avalon. According to an august and enduring tradition, Christian missionaries first arrived not long after the Crucifixion and settled as hermits at Glastonbury in Somersetshire, where they built a church of wattles, dedicated to the Virgin, and for a time lived in caves at the foot of Tor hill. Little else is known about their mission, except that they were twelve in number and "came in by way of Wales." But it is said they were sent by St. Philip, one of the twelve apostles, and led by Joseph of Arimathea, a member of the town council of Jerusalem and a secret disciple of Christ. It was Joseph who had persuaded Pilate to allow Christ an honorable burial, who took him down from the Cross, and laid him to rest in his own tomb. And it was Joseph (according to the Apocryphal Gospel of Nicodemus) who was the first to see Him risen from the dead. Later Joseph's story became entwined with that of the Holy Grail, and in Sir Thomas Malory's *Morte D'Arthur* he is the custodian of the sacred chalice from which Christ drank at the Last Supper and which was used to catch and preserve the blood flowing from Christ's wounds.

The founding of the church at Glastonbury made the British

Church the oldest in Western Christendom—older even than that of Rome. And in some sense its antiquity gave it priority, and represented an abiding challenge to Roman claims.

In the early Church every Christian was a potential evangelist, and after Christ commanded his apostles to "preach the Gospel to every creature," they reportedly dispersed to the ends of the known world. The message of redemption was spread throughout the Mediterranean basin, to the east into southern India and China, and to the north into England, where the faith at once took hold. As early as the beginning of the third century the African Church father Tertullian could refer to the Britons as a Christian people, and in 314 the British Church was recognized by the Council of Arles. In 432 St. Patrick, the son of a Roman deacon and minor official in Britain, crossed the seas to Ireland and eventually Church influence was extended throughout the British Isles.

That triumph was short-lived. Within two decades, the native Britons had been killed or driven westward by Germanic invaders, and thereafter Christianity was largely confined to the Celtic peoples of Ireland and Wales. The now dominant Germanic tribes of Angles, Saxons, and Jutes clung tenaciously to their Teutonic gods, and the worship of Christ seemed destined to yield before the altars of Woden, Freya, and Thor. Then in the spring of 597 Augustine of Canterbury (not to be confused with the famed North African saint) landed on the Isle of Thanet with forty monks on a mission from Pope Gregory the Great. King Ethelbert of Kent received him hospitably and promised not to interfere with his efforts to win converts, and before long a number of Ethelbert's subjects were swayed. As the year drew to a close, thousands more were reportedly baptized by Augustine himself on Christmas Day. A second wave of missionaries soon arrived, and in 602 Augustine founded Christ Church, Canterbury, as his episcopal see. The pope was overjoyed: "Behold, the tongue of Britain, which could only utter barbaric sounds, has lately learned to make the Hebrew Alleluia ring in God's praise."

Strangely enough, neither Pope Gregory nor Augustine seems to have been aware of the prior existence of the British (or Celtic) Church, but not long after his landing Augustine learned of other

Christian abbots presiding over the faithful in the western part of the isles. He arranged to meet with them on the banks of the Severn River (a stream of recurrent importance in our tale) in the interests of "Catholic unity," but the meeting turned sour. It was found that British liturgical practice differed from that of Rome in certain respects, and in particular that the two Church calendars did not coincide. The British saw no reason to alter their own calculations, but Augustine, who claimed to be their spiritual overlord, unwisely rebuked them for it and insisted on their immediate conformity to Latin norms. When they demurred, he resorted to threats and imprecations, which only served to confirm their distrust—a type and epitome of later tensions between the English Church and Rome.

The two Church missions were eventually joined (if not quite reconciled) by the Synod of Whitby in 664, and Britain was thereby incorporated into the universal Holy Roman Catholic Church. That Church had long since inherited the mantle of the Empire. A succession of remarkable popes with imperial (if godly) ambitions increasingly centralized Church authority under their own aegis, and gave it the complex hierarchical structure it ultimately retained. This process culminated in the theory of papal monarchy as definitively stated in the eleventh century by Pope Gregory VII:

> The pope can be judged by no one; the Roman church has never erred and never will err till the end of time; the Roman church was founded by Christ alone; the pope alone can depose and restore bishops; he alone can make new laws, set up new bishoprics, and divide old ones; he alone can translate [transfer] bishops; he alone can call general councils and authorize canon law; he alone can revise his judgments; his legates, even though in inferior orders, have precedence over all bishops; an appeal to the papal courts inhibits judgment by all inferior courts; a duly ordained pope is undoubtedly made a saint by the merits of St. Peter.

Twelfth-century popes carried on in the Gregorian spirit, which received a new infusion of grandiloquence from the pronouncements of Pope Innocent III, who adopted the title "Vicar of Christ," and by his involvement in the politics of Europe made himself the arbiter of its affairs. Papal monarchy had its day. In a disorderly and lawless time it represented order, stability, and righteousness, while "the example it presented of a spiritual authority uniting all nations" stood in dramatic contrast to the anarchy that feudalism produced in the temporal sphere.

Yet in the manner in which the Church had created (or recreated) itself, in the unassailable form it assumed, which emphasized unquestioning conformity and external compliance within a structure that had attained enormous worldly wealth and power, something indefinably essential had been lost. And that something might best be described as the "still, small" apostolic voice. A terrible decay for the lack of it had begun to subvert the Church from within, and by the middle of the fourteenth century had led to the decline of papal authority and ecclesiastical disgrace. Meanwhile, almost the entire progress of Christianity throughout Great Britain had originally come about through the active preaching of the Gospel. And that is the sacred tradition into which the heroes of our story were born.

∽

If the birth of religious inquiry and spiritual freedom can be traced (within the Protestant tradition) to one man in England, that man is John Wycliffe, the son of a squire, who was born in the North Riding of Yorkshire about 1328. A philosopher, theologian, and Church reformer, Wycliffe sponsored the first complete translation of the Bible into English, and made evangelization of the common folk his creed. "The preaching of the Word of God," he wrote, "is an act more solemn than the making of the sacrament."

Although we know almost nothing about his childhood, tradition gives his birthplace as Wycliffe-on-Tees, and the hilltop estate to which he was apparently heir encompassed some 720 acres of arable land. Eleven miles to the south stood the parish town of Richmond, organized around a stately Norman castle, while the great city of York, with its even mightier battlements, archepiscopal palace, abbey, and future cathedral was a two days' ride away.

In September 1345, Wycliffe was admitted to Merton College, Oxford, and made his way down the old Roman road from Yorkshire to the university in the company of a "fetcher" or official escort. The town of Oxford—originally built as a fortress settlement to defend Wessex from Danish attack—offered few creature comforts, and Wycliffe would have found life there far more spartan than in the manor to which he was born. At Merton, students were housed in thatched cottages with scant furniture, mud floors, and unheated rooms; and at meals they could seldom expect anything better than bread, beer, soup thickened with oatmeal, and one serving of meat a day. Books were scarce and laboriously made, and the college library at the time was kept under St. Mary's Church in a large chest. Several of the departments had no buildings of their own, and most of the lectures were held in churches or hired halls.

But Oxford of late had been attracting ambitious minds. By Wycliffe's day, it also consisted of a number of different colleges—Balliol, St. Edmund Hall, University, Exeter, Queens, as well as Merton—and had long since come to occupy an independent place in English life and thought. Its faculties of law, theology, medicine, and the arts surpassed even those of the University of Paris in esteem; and among its recent illuminati it could boast such immortal scholars as Roger Bacon ("Doctor Mirabilis"), Duns Scotus ("Doctor Subtilis"), William of Ockham ("Doctor Invincibilis"), Thomas Bradwardine ("Doctor Profundus"), and (fully their equal) Robert Grosseteste, whom some revered as a saint. Wycliffe himself would one day be honored among them as "Doctor Evangelicus," because of the stress he laid on the authority of Scripture above all other sources of the truth.

Oxford became Wycliffe's life. He remained at the university as a student and teacher for some thirty-five years; acquired degrees from three of its colleges (Merton, Balliol, and Queens); survived the Black Death of 1349 and other calamities which struck the community; and witnessed the Great Slaughter on St. Scholastica's Day in 1355—a "town and gown" dispute that went awry. This last began after a student got into an argument with a local tavern keeper over the quality of his wine. After a brief but bloodless confrontation, eighty men from town armed with long bows assembled at the gates of St. Giles on the following day, and by nightfall the campus lay littered with the dead.

Wycliffe also involved himself in university politics. At the time, Oxford was aswarm with friars. Some of her greatest scholars had been Franciscans (Scotus, Bacon, and Grosseteste, among them), but most of their brethren disparaged the prescribed course of study with its emphasis on the liberal arts and sought to give the curriculum a more theological stamp. Passions were especially aroused by their attempt to take advantage of the younger students—some as young as twelve—whose matriculation at Oxford often took them far from home. One official university pronouncement charged the friars with luring children "by apples and drinks" into their establishments where they were indoctrinated with the order's teaching and kept from contact with family or friends. "Once he had taken his vows," wrote G. M. Trevelyan, "the novice was caught, and a temporary convenience became a life-long bond." The secular clergy (those not under a monastic order or rule) regarded this practice as poaching, and it brought the university into discredit with parents, who had entrusted their children to its schools.

Wycliffe made the issue his own, led the fight to exclude friars from university honors and degrees, and tried to protect undergraduates from their snares. Meanwhile, sometime prior to May 14, 1361 (when he was appointed rector of Fillingham in Lincolnshire), he was ordained to the priesthood, and in November 1362 was provided with the prebend (or collegiate living) of Aust at the church of Westbury-on-Trym near Bristol. The combined income of the two appointments enabled Wycliffe to continue his Oxford studies, and three years later, in 1365, he also became warden of Canterbury Hall. The archbishop commended him at the time as one "on whom we have fixed our eye, both because of our confidence in thy fidelity, circumspection and industry, as also by reason of thy knowledge of letters and the laudable conversation and honesty of thy life." During his brief tenure (in which he came into conflict with the resident monks), Wycliffe emulated the evangelical poverty of the Franciscans, going about in a long russet gown with naked feet and carrying a simple staff. Years later opponents claimed this had been an affectation of humility in an effort to win unsuspecting converts to his views. Then in the fall of 1368 he exchanged his Fillingham parish for that of Ludgershall, nearer to Oxford; became a bachelor of divinity in 1369; and a doctor of divinity in 1372.

Wycliffe's course of study was standard for the time. In addition to the Seven Liberal Arts—Grammar, Rhetoric, Logic (the Trivium), Music, Arithmetic, Geometry, and Astronomy (the Quadrivium)—he studied the Three Philosophies (natural, moral, and metaphysical), Latin literature, and Aristotelian philosophy. His theological courses took another eight years. Four were spent on the Latin Vulgate Bible of St. Jerome; two more on the *Sentences* of Peter Lombard, a medieval textbook on Scripture; and two in lecturing on parts of the Old and New Testaments, one chapter at a time. Finally, he engaged in numerous public disputations and debates. Along the way, having been "reared on the syllogisms and hair-splitting quibbles of the medieval schoolmen," he acquired that bent for subtle disquisition and logic which characterized his mind.

He made his mark. Even his later enemies agreed (as one confessed) that he was "second to none in philosophy, unrivalled in the Schools, and the flower of Oxford. Many divines esteemed him little less than a god." He wrote many works in Latin as well as English—some scholars regard him as the last of the great scholastic philosophers—and his theological tomes were as knotty and learned as those by any scholiast. One weary Czech scribe, copying out a section, exclaimed in the margin, "Dear God, help me to finish this work as quickly as I can."

But his speculative ruminations had more than an academic cast. While a number of his colleagues were content to discuss at unending length such questions as: "Does the glorified body of Christ stand or sit in Heaven? Is the body of Christ, which is eaten in the sacrament, dressed or undressed? Were the clothes in which Christ appeared to his disciples after his resurrection, real or only apparent?" Wycliffe was interested in the living truth. "He had an eager hatred of what was wicked," noted Trevelyan, "and could never be kept from denouncing what he regarded as such. Similarly, in matters of belief he invariably exposed what he thought was false." In the course of his life, his views on various points of Church doctrine—the Lord's Supper, the papacy, Church-state relations, and so on—evolved or changed, and (though a dogmatic man) he was not unwilling to acknowledge his faults. On more than one occasion, for example, he admitted that he brought a certain "vindictive zeal" to debate, and that his motives in seeking victory were not always pure.

Deeply versed in all things theological, Wycliffe had the deepest reverence for St. Augustine (the Church father he most admired), but his three more contemporary heroes were Robert Grosseteste, Thomas Bradwardine, and Richard Fitzralph. All three were distinguished public figures—Grosseteste had been chancellor of Oxford and Bishop of Lincoln; Bradwardine, Archbishop of Canterbury and confessor to Edward III; Fitzralph, chancellor of Oxford and Bishop of Armagh—but their prominence as thinkers had been greater still, and their ideas were all woven together with those of Augustine himself in Wycliffe's thought. From Augustine he derived his theory of predestination and the difference between the visible and invisible Church; from Bradwardine, the notion of God's prevenient Grace; from Fitzralph the doctrine of dominion; and from Grosseteste, his sense of his own mission, as "a Doctor who praised Bible study, a reformer who resisted Papal pretensions, and a Bishop who devoted himself to pastoral care." Grosseteste, not incidentally, was a remarkable polymath who knew Hebrew and Greek (rare in his day) as well as Latin, compiled an encyclopedia of all known knowledge, wrote commentaries on Aristotle's *Posterior Analytics* and *Physics,* was the first to translate Aristotle's *Ethics,* and prepared editions of a number of Arab philosophical and scientific works.

But Fitzralph and Bradwardine more clearly shaped Wycliffe's thought. In a huge work of one thousand pages called *De Causa Dei* (*Of the Cause of God*), Bradwardine had argued that "all human activity was worthless, even impossible, without God's ineffable and gratuitous gift of grace." This was diametrically opposed to the notion that man can earn his salvation through acts of free will. For man needs grace even to repent: he can do nothing on his own. "Let a man repent and forsake past sins, and by virtue of the merits of Christ and through His mercy, his sins shall be blotted out."

Fitzralph's correlative idea of dominion (which became the

basis for two of Wycliffe's works) was essentially that God, as the ruler of the universe, apportions out His rule on loan to rulers in their various stations in tenure to obedience to Himself. Mortal sin was a breach of such tenure, and from this it followed that a sinful priest could be deprived of his benefice, a bishop of his estates, the pope himself of all authority, if he failed to acquit himself in a manner befitting his duty and rank.

Behind such ideas, which animated Wycliffe's work, it is hard to get much of a sense of his private concerns. As a result, he lives more "as a force than as a man." His published writings—some forty works in scholastic Latin and a lesser number in English—are impersonal throughout, though here and there we get a glimpse of his affections. He loved, for example, the Yorkshire downs of his youth, and the simple working folk who inhabited the hamlets of the dales. Above all, he loved Oxford, where he spent the majority of his days. "The house of God and the gate of heaven," he called it, and eulogized its meadows, streams, and balmy air. "Not without reason is it called the Vineyard of the Lord. . . . [It] is a place gladsome and fertile, suitable for a habitation of the gods." But letters to friends and other personal documents have vanished without a trace.

The earliest portrait we have of him—a half-length woodcut prefixed to John Bale's *Summary of Famous Writers of Great Britain* printed at Basel in 1558—shows a middle-aged cleric preaching from a stone pulpit with one hand raised, the other holding a book. Another appeared in the first French edition of Theodore Beza's *Icones,* or *Images of Reformers of Religion and Letters* (printed at Geneva in 1581), and shows him as an old man with a long flowing gown, white beard, and simple staff. A third, a mezzotint engraving, resembles the latter and was published in Richard Rolle's *Lives of the Reformers* in 1759. None is from life. But we know from the testimony of one of his followers that he was "spare, frail, and [in his later years] of emaciated frame," deemed a holy man, much loved by his disciples and an inspiration to them in their lives.

The Oxford historian Anthony à Wood once claimed that while Wycliffe was at Canterbury Hall he had taught Geoffrey Chaucer. It may be so. The Oxford philosopher Ralph Strode, who wrote a treatise on scholastic logic and to whom Chaucer dedicated *Troilus and Criseyde,* was apparently a friend of Wycliffe during the 1360s, and both Wycliffe and Chaucer had the same patron, John of Gaunt. It is not impossible that Chaucer's "pore Parson" in the *Canterbury Tales* is a partial portrait of Wycliffe as well:

A good man was ther of religioun,
And was a pore Parson of toun,
But riche he was of holy thought and werk.
He was a learned man, a clerk
That Christ's gospel gladly would preche,
His parishioners devoutly would he teche.
Benign he was and wondrous diligent,
And in adversity ful pacient,
And such he was approved oft times.
Ful loth were him to curse for his tithes,
But rather would he give them out of doute
Unto his pore parishioners about
Of his offrynge, and eke of his substaunce.
He could in little thing have suffisance.

"There are several features of this portrait which agree with the character of Wycliffe," one early biographer wrote, "and not a single trait can be detected in it which does not suit him." All his admirers extolled his personal virtue. Even Archbishop Thomas Arundel (a later adversary) admitted that Wycliffe was not only a great scholar but widely held to have been "a perfect liver," that is, irreproachable in the conduct of his life. Certainly, he was a great and compelling university teacher and an outstanding preacher who attracted many to his fold.

He was also a bold reformer, and about the time he earned his doctorate, he began to get into trouble with the Church. In 1371, he supported a parliamentary initiative to exclude the clergy from secular office because they monopolized so many places of honor and profit in the state; and in 1374 (upon his appointment as rector of Lutterworth) he was attached to a government embassy sent to

Bruges to negotiate with papal representatives about differences between England and Rome.

Those differences were of a potentially drastic kind. Long before the Reformation came about—before German princes assumed the right to name their own bishops, or Luther tacked up his famous theses on the door of a Wittenberg church—secular authorities had begun to insist on sharing in ecclesiastical revenues, on filling high Church offices with their own appointees, and on giving national security precedence over international religious crusades. It was in Wycliffe's day that the challenge to the pope's authority by the rising power of the national monarchies seemed to be coming to a head. Along their path of self-aggrandizement and self-assertion, those monarchies were aided, abetted, and to some degree justified not only by the prerogatives of their own national aspirations but by the numerous ways in which the Church seemed determined to discredit itself. All Catholic historians today acknowledge the manifold corruptions of the medieval Church. Despite many attempts at reform from within—by individual popes, Church councils, enlightened bishops, grassroots spiritual movements, and so on—"at every level of Church life," as Pope Adrian VI later acknowledged to the Diet of Nuremberg in 1522, "there were signs of grave disorganization and decay." Though numerous priests and bishops ministered devoutly to their flocks, lived exemplary lives, and sought to renew the spiritual life of the Church, "everything could be obtained for money," confessed an independent papal commission, "however hurtful it might be to the general welfare of the Church."

The trouble had begun in 1293, when a bitterly divided College of Cardinals gathered to elect a new pope. Some of the cardinals were allied to the French descendants of Charles of Anjou; others to the Spanish House of Aragon. "The deadlock was finally broken," writes one Church historian, "by one of the strangest occurrences in the history of papal elections: Someone shouted the name of Peter Morrone, a barely educated Benedictine hermit famed for holiness; all present felt inspired by the Holy Spirit, and suddenly and enthusiastically responded to the weird suggestion. The startled monk was brought from his mountain retreat on a donkey and crowned Pope Celestine V. He proved totally unequal to the demands of the office, disgusting the cardinals with his eccentricities, ineptitude, and subservience to Charles of Naples, who practically held him in captivity." After less than a year, he voluntarily relinquished his office, and the cardinals elected Benedetto Gaetani (Boniface VIII), an outstanding jurist and experienced legate of noble birth.

Few popes had a more exalted sense of their own authority, or were more energetic in its exercise. His first act was to place his predecessor under house arrest, then proceeded to annul most of the privileges Celestine had granted and the officials he had hired. He reorganized the Curia and Vatican archives, catalogued the papal library, made a lasting contribution to the field of canon law by publishing the works of Gregory XI, and founded a university in Rome. On the other hand, he sponsored so many statues of himself that he was accused of encouraging idolatry. Most of his pontificate was taken up with politics. He involved himself in disputes between Venice and Naples, England and Scotland, France and England, and matters bearing on the Hungarian succession, and for a short time acted as the unchallenged arbiter of European affairs. But then his ambitions collided with those of Philip the Fair, the most powerful of the medieval French kings.

The conflict began over the issue of clerical taxation. Philip, coveting the wealth of the Church, had levied a heavy tax on the French clergy; Boniface declared it unlawful and threatened to excommunicate anyone who tried to implement it; Philip retaliated by cutting off the pope from most of his sources of revenue in France. After a truce, Boniface plotted Philip's demise, but the king, anticipating this, had already dispatched his own henchmen, who captured the pope on September 3, 1303, at his summer residence at Anagni near Rome and beat him almost to death. Local residents freed him, but a few weeks later he died.

The next pope was served a dish of poisoned figs before he could make an impression; he was followed by Bertrand de Got, a native of Aquitaine and Archbishop of Bordeaux, who was crowned Clement V in Lyons. In 1305, at Philip's behest, Clement transferred the papal court to Avignon in southern France. And there it was destined to remain for seventy years. Its long spiritual confinement would afterward be compared in Church history to the seventy-year Babylonian Captivity of the Jews. As long as the popes had maintained their court in the Eternal City, they had been clothed in the universality which the idea of Rome evoked. At Avignon this vanished, and "the tacit renunciation by the papacy of its autonomy meant nothing less than its spiritual collapse." This sad state of affairs was compounded by the work of Clement's successor, John XXII, who assumed the office in 1316, and gave the papacy a thoroughly materialistic cast.

It was John who developed, if he did not devise, the widespread system of remitting sins by the sale of indulgences, which allowed anyone with money to sin with impunity, so long as he could pay the "fine." Such fines (as a commutation of punishment) were based in part on the doctrine of the superabundant merits of the saints, who were supposed to have been better than they needed to be for their own salvation. Their excess credits could therefore be stored in a celestial deposit box called the "Thesaurus meritorum sanctorum" (Compendium of the Merits of the Saints), and from this treasury "the pope could draw and make transfers to anyone whose account happened to be deficient." At the same time, this treasury could never be exhausted because its assets included the inexhaustible merits of Christ. So there was no end to the indulgences the pope could sell. In effect, he controlled "the central bank of salvation."

∽

John's whole tenure as pontiff was devoted to enriching the papal treasury. He extended the powers of his office over appointments, created a system that required the first year's revenues of a benefice to go to the pope, established a scale of fees for Church documents, and concentrated power in the hands of his relatives and friends. Upon his death the papal treasury was valued at twenty-five million gold crowns. But wealth did not confer moral authority, and other princes and monarchs were therefore emboldened to defy his power. In one celebrated instance, Louis of Bavaria annulled the marriage of one of his subjects so that the woman could marry his son. When the pope declared a crusade against him, Louis branded the pope a heretic. He also enlisted the aid of an Italian lawyer and theologian, Marsilio of Padua (formerly rector of the University of Paris), who set forth an anticlerical theory of Church-state relations which held that the Church had no right to own property of any kind, and that all it possessed was on loan from the state. Such ideas (in reaction to ecclesiastical munificence) soon came to be embraced by dissidents within the Church itself. It was under John that the famous dispute arose between the Spiritual Franciscans, who maintained that neither Christ nor His apostles owned property, and the Conventuals, who claimed they had. The two factions appealed to the pope for a judgment, but John was hardly fit to decide. He was (as one biographer of Wycliffe put it) "as far removed from apostolic poverty as the east is from the west." The Spiritual Franciscans were denounced, some imprisoned and burned, while the pope issued a bull stating that the right to own property predated the Fall of Adam and Eve.

John's policies were sustained by his successors, who came up with a vast array of ingenious taxes and fees to fuel their mighty fiscal machine. Deeming it necessary to live on a scale equal to their worldly estate, they also built for themselves at Avignon an enormous battlemented palace, aswarm with courtiers and attendants and furnished with luxuriously appointed rooms. The papal court was a veritable sink of vice and corruption, and the great Italian poet Francesco Petrarch (a devout Catholic) described it in a letter to a friend as "a receptacle of all that is most wicked and abominable. What I tell you is not from hearsay, but from my own knowledge and experience. In this city there is no piety, no reverence or fear of God, no faith or charity, nothing that is holy, just, equitable, or humane."

By means of a series of French popes, France now reaped the first fruits of Church income, even as the reach of the Church increased. In England and elsewhere, prelates enjoyed immense landed estates, princely revenues, and high civil and ecclesiastical powers. The lower clergy, which derived their parish livings from the people and were supported chiefly by tithes, were eventually transformed into an army of papal bailiffs, whose great business it was to enrich their masters and themselves. Sometimes terrible anathemas were launched from the pulpit against those who resisted their designs. The most ferocious were known as "general" or "greater" excommunications, and exceeded anything pronounced against those guilty of capital crimes:

> Let them be accursed eating and drinking; walking and sitting; speaking and holding their peace; waking and sleeping; rowing and riding; laughing and weeping; in house and in field; on water and on land, in all places. Cursed be their head and their thoughts; their eyes and their ears; their tongues and their lips; their teeth and their throats; their shoulders and their breasts; their feet and their legs; their thighs and their inwards. Let them remain accursed from the bottom of the foot to the crown of the head, unless they bethink themselves and come to satisfaction.

The prosperity of the Church even reached down to corrupt the ranks of the monks and mendicant friars. During the eleventh and twelfth centuries, monastic endowment had become a positive mania, as lands, buildings, precious stones, gold and silver were lavished upon cloisters with unsparing largess. At the same time, "the exhibition of relics, the performance of miracles, and above all the sale of indulgences and of Masses for the dead, formed an open sluice through which a steady golden stream poured into the monastic treasury." The modern idea of the monastery as "a gloomy, isolated residence, where emaciated anchorites wept and fasted, and prayed their lives away in holy conflict with sin" was not apt for the time. At least there were abundant exceptions to the rule. Meanwhile, the great orders of evangelical friars had been transformed into the pope's private army. After 1321 (thanks to a bull issued by Pope John XXII) they had full authority to exercise any sacerdotal function in any parish, and as such began to compete with the parish priest.

The friar had the pope's leave both to hear confession and give absolution, and he often did so with appalling alacrity. "He was an esy man to yeve penaunce," wrote Chaucer, "Ther as he wist to have a good pittaunce" (that is, his absolution depended on a fee). Most parishioners found this irresistible. "Ful swetely herde he confessioun,/And plesaunt was his absolucions." In time, wrote one historian the friars became "proverbial for their effrontery, their cupidity, and their capacity for unblushing imposture. They heard confessions, they preached, they administered the sacraments, they hawked about their cheap indulgences just as a strolling pedlar might hawk his wares. And they made their fortunes out of the ruin of the parochial priests whose tithes had been annexed by the regular monks." The private lives of some were scandalously free.

Round many a convent's blazing fire
Unhallowed threads of revelry are spun;
There Venus sits disguised like a Nun,—
While Bacchus, clothed in semblance of a Friar,
Pours out his choicest beverage. . . .
The arched roof, with resolute abuse
Of its grave echoes, swells a choral cheer
Whose votive burden is—OUR KINGDOM'S HERE!

There was enough truth to such otherwise scurrilous verses to give a church historian pause. Yet another scandal was the intrusion of foreign priests and prelates into English livings. At the time, the deaneries of Lichfield, Salisbury, and York, and archdeaconry of Canterbury (the wealthiest benefice in England), together with a host of other prebends and preferments, were held in absentia by foreign-born cardinals and priests, who collected through their London agent twenty thousand marks a year for the papal treasury. The clergy also exacted fees from every probated will, contract, and divorce, so that the pope's revenue from England alone was said to be comparable to that taken in by the king. "God gave his sheep to be pastured," one Parliament complained, "not to be shaven and shorn."

Wycliffe could find no warrant in Scripture for the organization of the Church as a feudal hierarchy, or for the rich endowments the Church enjoyed. From his study of the New Testament, he had concluded: First, that in the primitive Church or in the time of Paul, two orders of the clergy had been sufficient, that is, a priest and a deacon. All other degrees and orders (based on the Epistles of Timothy and Titus) had their origin in worldly pride. Second, that the legislative right claimed by popes, prelates, and councils, and the power of excommunication and absolution attributed to every member of the clergy, were impious invasions of the prerogatives of Christ. Third, that the priest's office was simply to preach the Word—"and for this reason, Christ occupied himself mostly in preaching, and thus did his apostles, and for this God loved them." And fourth, that the ministry of the Gospel was meant to be supported by voluntary contributions from the folk. "Men wonder highly," he wrote in a treatise entitled *The Curse Expounded,* "why curates are so severe in exacting tithes, since Christ and his apostles took no tithes, as men do now; nor even spoke of them, either in the Gospel or the Epistles. . . . Christ lived on alms, as the Gospel telleth; and the apostles lived sometimes by the labor of their hands, and sometimes took a poor livelihood and clothing, given of the people's free will."

Although Wycliffe admired the ideals of the mendicants (in particular the Spiritual Franciscans) and their life of poverty, he condemned the wealth and property the orders had amassed. He noted wryly that their great flowing gowns were unsuitable for manual labor (although monasteries had been founded for such work), and that "one cope and hood of a monk" contained enough cloth to clothe "four or five needy men." He criticized bishops for holding secular office, in neglect of their ecclesiastical appointments, and priests who preoccupied themselves with secular duties, to the neglect of those in their pastoral care. In his view, the Church should be stripped of its endowments and its wealth distributed among the poor.

Wycliffe also despised indulgences, and the whole notion of a storehouse of merit, or spiritual treasury, at the disposal of the pope. God alone could remit sin. And he gave no importance to canonization, maintaining that only God—not the pope and his cardinals—could know whether someone was a saint or not.

In adopting such ideas (though not yet ready to give them full voice) Wycliffe was expressing a point of view that—in England, at least—was widely held. And its prevalence was somewhat tied to a long war with the French. The Hundred Years' War, as it came to be called, had begun in 1338 ostensibly in support of the claim of England's King Edward III to the French throne. He marked that pretense by quartering the lilies of France beside the leopards of England on his coat of arms, and the fighting had begun with glorious English victories at Crécy, Poitiers, and Sluys. But then English land forces met a number of setbacks, while combined French and Spanish fleets swept English shipping from the sea. By 1374, the English were clinging to a few fortified cities along the Channel coast. The new might of French arms owed something to monies drawn from the papal treasury at Avignon, and to allow even a little of England's own wealth to enlarge that fund would be as if the country were funding a war against herself.

Meanwhile, every English Parliament since 1343 had tried to chip away at Church immunities; and in 1366, when Parliament had been called to consider a papal demand that England renew its payment of a feudal tribute (dating to 1213), Parliament treated the demand with contempt. The expropriation of Church property also came up for discussion—for why not force the Church to contribute its wealth to the war chest of the king? One member of Parliament drove the point home with a fable, which recounted the plight of an owl (representing the Church) who appealed for help to a conference of birds. The owl had lost its feathers and was suffering from the cold. She piteously appealed to the other birds to share their feathers with her, and in sympathy each bird gave her one. Suddenly a hawk appeared, in quest of prey. To escape its talons, each bird asked for its own feather back. But the owl, now handsomely plumed, refused. So the others proceeded to take them back by force. "Just so," said the peer in Parliament, "when war breaks out, we must take from the endowed clergy a portion of their temporal possessions, for that property belongs to us as well as to the kingdom in common, with which we must defend ourselves."

The alliance between king and Parliament, however, was a shaky one at best; nor was the Church to prove an acquiescent prey. For most of his reign, Edward III had been a vigorous, shrewd, and courageous king. His court had been regarded as the most brilliant in contemporary Europe, and he himself, as an exceptionally gallant knight, well fitted to be the head of it. As a tactical genius, he had ensured English military supremacy by coupling the firepower of the longbow to the skill of the dismounted man-at-arms; and at the Battle of Halidon Hill (the first of his many triumphs) had avenged the military failures of his father by crushing the Scots. But as the war with France faltered, his talents seemed to fail; he sank into a long dotage and lost the will to control his realm. Meanwhile, a power struggle had developed between the king's two most powerful sons, Edward the "Black Prince" and John of Gaunt. The true nature of that struggle has puzzled historians, but one thing it was *not* was a struggle between a clerical and an anticlerical party, since both were nationalists who also had churchmen in their pay. If anything can be said for certain about it, it was a struggle for power itself, and (in the long view) for the line of succession to the Crown.

Gaunt's faction for a time enjoyed the upper hand, but widespread discontent with high taxation and the government's mismanagement of the war found expression in 1376 in the so-called Good Parliament, which met at Westminster and indignantly demanded an overhaul of the administration, impeachment of a number of its officials, an end to the domination of high state offices by the clergy (including the Chancery, Treasury, and Privy Seal), and curtailment of Church taxes or tithes. In its reforming zeal, the Commons had the support of the Black Prince, but he died before Parliament adjourned, and his death brought an end to its designs.

Gaunt now took the reins of government and in January 1377 convened a new, "Bad," Parliament, which reversed all the work the Good Parliament had done. But he was no less covetous of Church wealth than his court rivals and by his support of Wycliffe and others had inspired hatred in some of the high churchmen of the land. Recently, in fact, he had invited Wycliffe up to London to evangelize in support of Church disendowment, provoking William Courtenay, the mighty Bishop of London and Gaunt's implacable foe. Courtenay was (in effect) head of the Church in England, since his nominal superior, Simon Sudbury, the Archbishop of Canterbury, was too diffident to wield his crozier with any force.

In the winter of 1377 a convocation of bishops assembled at St. Paul's Cathedral and summoned Wycliffe to appear before them on February 19 to answer charges of heresy. The exact charges are not known, but his prominence in the growing political movement against Church property made him a clear target of the bishops' ire. By 1377, he had also written several learned works attacking the temporal power and corruption of the Church, had boldly advised the government to reject the pope's demands for tribute, exalted the state above the Church in secular affairs, and was honored by the University of Oxford for his zeal against the friars. More recently, he had gained a considerable following for himself in the capital, where he had attracted large crowds. It was impossible for the Church hierarchy assembled in the city, writes Trevelyan, "to allow its authority to be so openly defied, or for a man as proud and fierce as Courtenay to hear himself and his order attacked in his own diocese by an unauthorized Oxford priest."

Other circumstances made Wycliffe's arraignment still more opportune. The political situation in London at that moment was confused. While the population had been stirred by Wycliffe's preaching, it had also been aroused against his patron and chief protector, Gaunt. As chairman of the Royal Council, Gaunt had recently introduced into Parliament a bill designed to wrest control of the city administration from the mayor and turn it over to the king's marshal, Lord Henry Percy, Gaunt's ally. This would have placed the city (literally) under martial law, and would have deprived its citizens of many of the time-honored civil liberties to which they had grown used.

February 19 arrived and the robed and mitered dignitaries gathered in the chapel behind the altar where Courtenay, seated on the episcopal throne, waited for the accused to appear. The great cathedral was filled with people, and when Wycliffe entered, flanked by Percy, Gaunt, and their retainers, an armed guard had to clear a passage through the crowd. When Courtenay saw the commotion, he rebuked Lord Percy for it, saying he would never have allowed him into the church if he'd known "what masteries he'd attempt." Gaunt disdainfully replied that they "would keep such mastery there" as they pleased. Then they took their chairs, and Percy also invited Wycliffe to sit, saying, "Since you have much to reply, you will need all the softer seat." A dispute now arose as to whether Wycliffe "should stand as a prisoner before the bar or sit as a doctor defending his arguments." Courtenay declared that it was "contrary to reason and law" that Wycliffe should sit and that he would have to stand as long as the trial might last. Unwilling to yield the bishop any ground, Gaunt rasped out with menace: "You put your trust in your parents [the Earl and Countess of Devon], but they will not be able to help you, for they will have enough to do to help themselves." Courtenay stood up: "I do not trust in my parents, nor in you, nor in any man, but in my God, who is not one who 'trusts in Himself.' " Gaunt sprang up in turn and threatened to drag the bishop out of the church by his hair. That created an uproar, and fighting broke out in the nave. As the melee spread, the assembly scattered, as all the principals sought safety for themselves.

The following day, an armed mob stormed Lord Percy's residence and, failing to find him (since he was elsewhere at dinner with Gaunt), broke into Gaunt's palace, plundered and set it ablaze. A messenger, "wild with fear and haste," finally located the two men "at their oysters" and bursting in upon them "told them to fly for their lives." Gaunt stood up from the table with such violence that he smashed one of his shins. With some difficulty, they made their way down to the waterfront and hastily crossed the Thames.

Three months later, on May 22, 1377, the pope issued five bulls against Wycliffe, variously addressed to the Archbishop of Canterbury, the Bishop of London, the king, and the chancellor of Oxford. "We have learned to our extreme sorrow," wrote the pope "that John Wycliffe, rector of the church at Lutterworth, of the diocese of Lincoln, a professor of holy writ—would he were not a master of errors!—has been impugning received doctrine." He then berated the English churchmen as "slothfully negligent" for having allowed him to flourish unrestrained, and said that the propositions he had been promulgating "tended to the entire subversion of the Church." The prelates were ordered to investigate all the errors and heresies with which Wycliffe had been charged and, if he were found guilty, to clap him in irons and compel him to confess.

The pope also demanded that Oxford cooperate with the authorities and not allow any of Wycliffe's theories to be taught. Of the nineteen propositions listed, the most irksome to the pope were the eighth, ninth, seventeenth, and nineteenth. The eighth and ninth together stated that the pope had no power to excommunicate anyone, because each person could only excommunicate himself by living an unholy life. The seventeenth recognized the right of kings to deprive bishops and other ecclesiastics of their worldly wealth if they failed to conduct themselves in a manner befitting their office; and the nineteenth held that any ecclesiastic, including the pope, could be arraigned and tried for his misdeeds.

Wycliffe first learned of the charges against him that fall. Meanwhile, King Edward III had died and all public interest had since been absorbed by new reversals in the war and the accession of Richard II. Richard, the son of Edward the Black Prince, was but "a lad of eleven years, fair as Absalom," when he was crowned in splendor on a midsummer's day. The Church came under renewed attack as the problem of raising war supplies was once more thrust to the fore, and when Parliament convened that fall, it called Wycliffe as an expert witness as to whether England could "lawfully, in its own defense" reject papal demands for any part of the kingdom's wealth. Since the pope, in the view of the English, was a puppet of the French, money channeled to the papal treasury at Avignon might also be thought to enlarge the war chest on which the French relied. Wycliffe testified that not only was it right to reject the pope's demands, but it would be immoral not to. And he gave three grounds. By the law of nature, he said, England had an inherent right to defend herself; by the law of the Gospel, the Church could only accept money in the form of alms; and by the law of conscience, it would be "asinine stupidity" for England to destroy herself by her own gold. Then he exhorted the council to ignore any threat of excommunication the pope might make. That, however, went beyond his brief and "silence was imposed upon him by our Lord the King with the Council of the Realm."

Meanwhile, Oxford University had refused to condemn him. The vice-chancellor considered it unwise to imprison an Englishman (who was also a royal servant) at the pope's command because this would seem "to give the pope lordship and regal authority in England." On the other hand, he wanted to appear cooperative, and so arranged with Wycliffe's consent to place him at Black Hall under house arrest. There he was snugly confined, while the vice-chancellor empaneled a group of theologians to scrutinize the propositions the pope had condemned. All were judged orthodox, though it was admitted some of them "sounded poorly to the ears."

Nevertheless, in March 1378 Wycliffe was again summoned before the bishops—this time at Lambeth Palace—to answer for his views. Once more the government was on his side. In the previous trial at St. Paul's, the clerics had been acting within the acknowledged rights of the English Church courts; but now they were sitting as papal commissioners and so seemed to challenge the sovereignty of English law. Scarcely had the proceedings begun when a message arrived from the Queen Mother sternly warning them not to take any harsh measures against the accused. This struck such fear into their hearts, according to one unhappy chronicler, that they began to tremble and were almost apologetic, "to the manifest forfeiture of their dignity and the injury of the whole Church." The trial was transformed into a hearing, and as the demoralized clerics attempted to proceed, they were so often interrupted by hostile shouts from the audience that at length they thought it best to let Wycliffe go with a reprimand. "In this way," the chronicler tells us, "that slippery John Wycliffe deluded his inquisitors, mocked the Bishops, and escaped . . . although all his propositions are clearly heretical and depraved."

Brief though it was, the trial had lasting importance, for it prevented the inquisitorial powers of the pope from ever taking root on English soil. With the single exception of Mary Tudor's harsh reign, Church and state would never again proceed against heresy under papal authority, but only (when it did) according to English law.

A few days later, Pope Gregory XI died. With his death, the Captivity at Avignon came to an end. Such an auspicious event might have done much to resuscitate the Church, but instead it led to an even more bizarre development that compounded its decline.

For a number of years the papacy had been trying to free itself from French control. On the 23rd of May 1365, the Emperor Charles IV of Bohemia had traveled to Avignon to see Pope Urban V (Gregory's predecessor) and had told him that only his return to Rome could repair papal prestige. After two years of vacillation, Urban at length agreed (despite thinly veiled threats of assassination by the French), and on the 30th of April 1367 left his stately French palace, "amid the wailing and gnashing of teeth of his cardinals." At Marseilles, the cardinals made a last effort to detain him, before he set sail on May 19 for Viterbo, Italy, where he arrived on the 9th of June. There he lingered in agonized uncertainty for four months. Finally, on October 16, escorted by two thousand men-at-arms, he entered Rome and celebrated mass in St. Peter's Basilica, where no pope had set foot for sixty-three years. The city's cathedrals and churches were in ruins, "cattle wandered into the buildings and grazed at the foot of the altars," even the marble blocks of the Colosseum had been sold for lime. Amid such comfortless decay, the city's reduced population had long dragged out a pitiful, impoverished existence without hope of improvement in their lives. The former papal residence, the Lateran, was also in shambles, so Urban ensconced himself in the Vatican, under the protective shadow of the castle of St. Angelo, where the ramparts were manned by a frightened papal guard. Few of Urban's cardinals were willing to follow him, and at length, his own resolve failed. On April 17, 1370, he fled back to the safety of the Avignon court. There (in fulfillment of an angry prediction by St. Bridget, a Swedish mystic) he died before the end of the year.

When Gregory XI succeeded Urban, he tried to mitigate French influence, but ultimately proved captive to his own luxury and pride. St. Bridget excoriated him for allowing "insatiable avarice, execrable wantonness, and all-devouring simony" to run rampant at his court, which she compared to a brothel, and enjoined him to "arise and reform the Church." "If thou dost not obey," she warned, "know verily every devil in hell shall have a morsel of thy immortal and inconsumable soul." Still he refused to act, and after Bridget's death, the voice of doom was assumed by St. Catherine of Siena, who spent the summer of 1376 in Avignon uttering prophecies equally dire. At length the beleaguered pontiff yielded to her persuasions and on September 13, 1376, he set out for Rome. After a difficult journey, he entered the Eternal City on January 17, 1377, accompanied by a crowd of mountebanks, "clothed in white, clapping their hands and dancing before him." Late in the afternoon, he entered St. Peter's Basilica, illuminated for the occasion with eighteen thousand lamps, and knelt in prayer before the shrine.

One of his few notable acts as a Roman (not French) pontiff was to issue the five bulls against Wycliffe. But then he died; and Wycliffe had been glad to see him go—"an abiding heretic," he called him, "who died without any sign of penitence for his crimes and the slaughter of many thousands in war for temporal gain." At his death the French still dominated the College of Cardinals, but the people of Rome were determined not to let the papacy go. When the cardinals assembled on April 7, 1378, a huge mob gathered outside the Vatican and threatened to kill them if they didn't elect an Italian pope. The captain of the guard protecting them warned: "You will be torn to pieces if you don't do what the people expect." Even as they deliberated, part of the mob invaded the building and seized the papal wine cellars; without more ado, the cardinals hastily elected Bartholomew Prignano, Archbishop of Bari, and (as he was not himself then in Rome) dressed up a colleague in papal robes and pushed him out onto a balcony to pacify the crowd.

On Easter Sunday, April 18, the new pope was crowned Urban VI. Despite the circumstances of his election, everyone expected the best from him. He had a reputation for piety and justice, was a master of canon law, a diligent student of the Bible, and grave and austere. He hated worldliness and simony, and Wycliffe for one thanked God for "providing our mother church with a catholic head, an evangelical man," who had already given evidence that he would live "in conformity with the law of Christ." But Urban lacked diplomacy and tact. A fortnight after his election, he openly upbraided the cardinals for their immorality and insisted they learn to forgo the luxuries to which they had grown used. One of the cardinals, Robert of Cambray, Count of Geneva, promptly warned him (much like a great noble speaking to his king), "I tell you, if you diminish our honor, we shall diminish yours." But Urban continued to assault their character, and after two months the cardinals decided they had had enough. A majority decamped to Fondi, in the kingdom of Naples, and from there issued an encyclical that declared Urban's election invalid (as having occurred under duress) and denounced him as an apostate, tyrant, and the Antichrist. The three remaining Italian cardinals soon joined them, and the pope was left "like a sparrow on a house-top," without support. At first he repented his rashness and "wept bitter tears"; but then he grew irate. On November 28 he created twenty-four new cardinals to replace those who had defected. In response, the dissidents elected Robert of Cambray as their new pope.

The count took the name of Clement VII and almost at once Western Christendom was split into two camps. The Holy Roman Empire, England, most of Italy, the Netherlands, Scandinavia, Hungary, Poland, and Portugal (according to their own perceived political interests) recognized Urban, while France, Naples, Scotland, Luxembourg, Castile, Burgundy, Savoy, and Austria rallied to Clement, who set himself up in Avignon. Both popes promptly excommunicated each other, and accused each other of being imposters and of everything impious and vile. Thus arose the Great Schism, which was to divide (and rend) the Church for forty years.

The spectacle of two popes, each devoting his entire energies to the destruction of his rival, was appalling to every devout heart, and dealt a heavy blow to that idea of Church unity which had exercised such a great (and consoling) influence on the imagination of the Middle Ages. Wycliffe gave voice to a rising tide of disgust. "Many noble, catholic truths," he sarcastically wrote, "are made plain by this happy division," and compared the two popes to dogs snarling over a bone. Ultimately, he regarded the institution of the papacy as without scriptural foundation, and came to reject the doctrine of papal infallibility outright. "Some think that if the pope canonizes a man, he must needs be a saint in Heaven," but "how could the pope have the power to bind and to loose?" He also leveled increasing fire at such abuses as pluralism (holding more than one benefice at a time), absenteeism, the sale of indulgences, the politics of excommuniction, and even the veneration of saints. He had a puritanical dislike of any kind of opulence or show, disapproved of loud singing and intoning in Church, and regarded the worship of images and the adoration of relics as forms of idolatry. The notion that an image had miraculous powers he considered a diabolical deceit. Though he revered the Virgin Mary as "blessed in heaven" and "without sin," he thought Masses for the dead worthless. One small act of goodness, he wrote, was of more use to a man than thousands of gold crowns spent after his death for the repose of his soul. In some measure, his critique was shared by others. In *Piers the Plowman,* William Langland exalted the integrity of a simple peasant's heart over ecclesiastics in their pride; and Chaucer's "gorge rose at the Pardoner and his relics of 'pigge's bones.' "

The tone of defiance in Wycliffe's polemical writing, however, grew ever more pronounced, and from the seclusion of his study in Lutterworth, he began a systematic attack on the beliefs and practices of the Church. It has sometimes been claimed that his onslaught had its source in some early, bitter disappointment—for example, his ouster as warden of Canterbury Hall in 1365, or his failure to secure a bishopric upon his return from Bruges in 1374. But by that time some of his controversial views had already been formed, and incorporated into a number of tracts. Between 1378 and 1380, he wrote several new works (afterward deemed heretical)—among them, the *De Veritate Sacrae Scripturae (On the Truth of Holy Scripture)*, *De Ecclesia (On the Church)*, *De Apostasia (On Apostasy)*, *De Eucharistia (On the Eucharist)*, *De Potestate Papae (On the Power of the Pope)*, and *De Officio Regis (On the Office of the King)*.

In all of these tracts, Wycliffe argued strongly that the Church had been corrupted by worldly possessions and should return to its apostolic ideals. He also articulated his own idea (derived from Augustine, Bradwardine, and others) of what the true Church was. When men speak of it, he said, they usually mean prelates, priests, monks, canons, and friars—members of the acknowledged Church community. Not so: the Church, said Wycliffe, was the whole body of the elect. Who were they? God had foreordained some to salvation and glory, by virtue of His election; others, to everlasting punishment by virtue of His foreknowledge of their sin. The former Wycliffe called *praedestinati* ("predestinated"), the latter *praeciti* ("foreknown"). Only true believers—the elect—belonged to the Church in the proper sense; but they were mixed with the unconverted, "as wheat and chaff are mixed together on the threshing floor." In the present life, many reprobate sinners, apparent Christians, and unconverted souls formed part of the visible Church. Only God could know who a true member of His congregation was. Membership in the visible Church was therefore no guarantee of election. Even the pope himself could not count on it: "For no pope that now lives knows whether he is of the Church or a limb of the fiend."

No one could be sure of his own standing in grace. Only a life of piety, morality, and good works in imitation of Christ could provide possible reassurance of one's fate. At the same time, Wycliffe fought shy of the conclusion that people were damned beyond all possible hope of recovery. "Who knows the measure of God's mercy?" he wrote; since no one knows for sure whether another is damned or saved, no man (not even the pope) could pronounce a judgment either way. The true source of all authority and truth was in one place only—the Bible, God's Word.

This was at variance with Church doctrine, which recognized Tradition as equal to Scripture yet (by its priority) above it in authority. By Tradition was meant all those teachings that could be traced back to the time of Christ and the Apostles, and were afterward expressed in the conclusions of Church councils, pronouncements of the Fathers, and decrees of the popes. Such Traditions could therefore be said to justify doctrines not found in Scripture itself.

But for Wycliffe, the Bible, in particular the Gospels, was the supreme standard by which even Church doctrine must be tried. "Were there a hundred popes and all the friars turned to cardinals," he wrote, "their opinions in matters of faith should not be accepted except in so far as they are founded on Scripture itself." Again, whereas the Church maintained that Scripture itself was not doctrine, but must be interpreted for the doctrine it contains, Wycliffe held that one passage explained another better than any gloss could. Each verse was to be understood in the light of the whole truth of the text. On that ground, he dismissed the papal doctrine of the two swords, the spiritual and the temporal, as given to Peter (and the pope as his successor) based on Luke 22:38: since the doctrine was not corroborated by anything else the Bible said.

Others before Wycliffe (among them Grosseteste and William of Ockham) had stressed the authority of Scripture, but Wycliffe's emphasis was different and "added a new doctrine, the right of every man, whether cleric or layman, to examine the Bible for himself." At the heart of biblical truth was the story of the Savior, who was the "Book of Life," and whose actions embodied the meaning of His words. There could be no better way to educate a Christian, or Christianize a pagan, than to place the Bible—and in particular the Gospels, with the life of Christ—before the eyes of all for "it is a life which comes home to every man. Christ is our sinless Abbot; whereas the saints, even the Apostles Peter, Paul, and John, and the rest, were not free from sin, and error, and foolishness, as we know from Scripture itself."

He contrasted the institution of the papacy with the life of the apostles, and noted that Christ Himself had "claimed no authority in this world for Himself. The primacy of Peter in the New Testament had been in faith, humility, and meekness, not in worldly dignity, might, and renown." The Church could be reformed only by a return to the apostolic poverty of New Testament times; and "a knowledge of those times could best be acquired through a knowledge of the New Testament books."

In Wycliffe's day, Bible reading, even among the clergy, was surprisingly rare. As one of his disciples put it, it was thought sufficient if the priest knew the Ten Commandments, the Paternoster (Our Father), the Creed and Ave (Hail Mary), "with common parts of holy Writ." The ordinary Christian knew even less—often no more than "some jingle picked up from a passing friar." The focus of popular interest was the cult of the saints, and the great national shrines—Canterbury, where Thomas à Becket had been martyred; the Abbey of Haile, which claimed to have a miraculous vial of Christ's blood; the shrine of St. Cuthbert of Durham; and, of course, Glastonbury Abbey, where the remains of St. Joseph of Arimathea were said to be interred. The tendency of Church ritual, moreover, was to subordinate the written word to pictorial and ceremonial forms of worship—especially in the liturgical dramas of Christmas and Easter—while biblical stories were mostly gleaned from miracle and morality plays.

The pulpit fashion of the time was also, largely, to draw material from civil and natural history, fable, and mythology. Ovid's *Metamorphoses,* for example, was culled for this purpose almost as much as the Bible itself. Wycliffe faulted the clergy in general for not preaching from Scripture (when they preached at all) and friars in particular for packing their sermons with unscriptural anecdote and story for entertainment instead of calling the people to reform their lives. He himself saw no need to embellish biblical quotation with extraneous material, and often quoted St. Augustine's remark that God's Word had a peculiar and incomparable eloquence all its own.

Wycliffe's own works are full of biblical quotation—over seven hundred in one tract alone—and his insistence on the authority of Scripture was more emphatic than that of any other figure of his time. Although he acknowledged that some passages might be hard to construe, "the New Testament is . . . open to the understanding of simple men," he insisted, "as to the points most needful to salvation. . . . [For] Christ did not write His laws on tables, or on skins of animals, but in the hearts of men." Meaning was revealed by "the Holy Ghost." The paramount responsibility of the priest was therefore "to address himself to the heart, so as to flash the light of the Gospel into the spirit of the hearer, and to bend his will . . . to the truth."

But if people lacked access to the Word, what good could it do? In Church teaching it was axiomatic that Christ had given the Scriptures to the clergy that they "might sweetly minister to the laity and to weaker persons, according to the message of the season, the wants of men, and the hunger of their souls." But they were not for general consumption. Wycliffe, however, held that the only way to free the minds of Christians from the corrupt tyrannies of papal rule was to make the text of Scripture available to them directly, so they could judge controversial matters for themselves. Besides, if everyone was supposed to obey the Bible, as God's law, then everyone ought to know what it said. The whole Bible should therefore be accessible to all in a form they could understand. That meant a full and literal translation of the text. Moreover, since Christ and his apostles had taught the people in their own tongue, why should men not do so now? Even St. Jerome's Vulgate had been a vernacular translation in origin, prepared for the Latin-speaking communities of the Western Church. In that capacity, it had superseded the older Latin version (done by persons unknown), and the Greek Septuagint, the third-century B.C. translation of the Hebrew Scriptures that had served the Greek-speaking Jewish communities of the Mediterranean world.

By the beginning of 1380, Wycliffe had involved himself in the preparation of the first English Bible, intended to meet the general need. The extent of his contribution is not known, but it is accepted that the translation was begun under his direction and done at his behest. Some of his contemporaries condemned him for it, maintaining that he had made the Scriptures "more open to the reading of laymen and women," as one unhappy chronicler put it, "than it had previously been to the best instructed among the clergy; and thus the jewel of clerics is turned to the sport of the laity, and the pearl of the Gospel is scattered abroad and trodden underfoot by swine."

Such fears, of course, were not unfounded, as ignorant, confused, and twisted interpretations can be imposed on any text. A vernacular translation might be thought to increase the danger, since Latin remained the language of the universal Church and stood for Catholic unity (or the unity of truth) as against the parochial claims of local tongues. But at times the Church also spoke in a confused or muddled voice. Thomas Arundel, who succeeded William Courtenay as Archbishop of Canterbury, evidently did not object in principle to Bible translations, for in his funeral tribute to Anne of Bohemia, Richard II's queen, he noted that "notwithstanding that she was an alien born she had in English all the four gospellers with the doctors upon them." And these she had submitted to Arundel for his inspection and he had found them "good and true."

Before Wycliffe, there had been partial translations or paraphrases of parts of the Bible into Old and Middle English (including two by near contemporaries, William of Shoreham and Richard Rolle) but none was complete. A few, hallowed by legend or story, had entered into the fabric of national consciousness and pride. There was Caedmon, an untutored and speechless youth whose tongue had been freed by an angel who appeared to him in a dream; King Alfred the Great, who had placed the Ten Commandments at the head of his code of Saxon laws; and the work of St. Aldhelm, Aelfric, and the Venerable Bede—the last an eighth-century monk of Jarrow and the brightest light in Western Europe in his day. His entire life had been dedicated to Christian learning, and one of his followers tells us that toward the end Bede translated into English both the Apostles' Creed and the Lord's Prayer. He had also been working on a translation of St. John's Gospel, and dictated the final chapters on the last day of his life—Ascension Eve, 735. As evening fell, his sobbing scribe reportedly leaned over and whispered, "Master, there is but one sentence left." When that was written down, the boy said, "It is done." "Thou hast said the truth," Bede replied. "Take my head in thy hands. I would sit in the holy place in which I was wont to pray." And while he chanted the *Gloria*, his life passed away.

By Wycliffe's day, the push for a complete translation had acquired a nationalistic as well as a religious cast. English patriotism was on the rise. It was reflected in the increased scope and powers of the Commons, the transfer of certain cases from Church to civil courts, growing resentment at the interference of the pope in the kingdom's affairs, and—as manifest in the works of Langland, Chaucer, Gower, and others—the rebirth of English literature. As a result of the long war with France, French, the language of the court, was also in decline. In 1347, it was dropped from the curriculum of many schools, and in 1362 its use forbidden in courts of law. In 1363 (the year Langland's *Piers the Plowman* appeared), Parliament was opened for the first time with an English speech. By 1370, even upper-class children, who had once been taught French "in the cradle," were said to know no more of it "than their left heels." Wycliffe was allied to all these trends, and in his English sermons, tracts, and Bible translations the people were at last addressed in their own tongue.

The translations associated with Wycliffe have come down to us in two versions. Both were translations of Jerome's Latin Vulgate, and the first was evidently done between 1380 and 1382 under the supervision of Nicholas Hereford, a Wycliffe disciple and sometime bursar and fellow of Queens College, Oxford. Hereford carried the work through from the beginning of Genesis to Baruch 3:20, before he was obliged to break it off and let others take up the task.

To render the text into readable English was a tremendous challenge, for the language itself was then in transition and the whole vernacular vocabulary of theology had yet to form. In the course of English history, successive invasions had brought about the presence of three distinct dialects on English soil: Old English or Anglo-Saxon, Old Norse, and Anglo-Norman. Old English was Germanic; Old Norse Scandinavian; Anglo-Norman French. By Wycliffe's day, the three had somewhat blended together and the "great vowel shift" to Modern English had begun. At the same time, the acquisition of French words with different sounds (such as "j" and "oi") had begun to create a "warmer and more exotic" tonality. Still, England had almost as many regional dialects as it had counties, and before there could be an English Bible there had to be something like a common English speech. The inevitable unifying center proved to be central England. It so happened that Wycliffe's Midland dialect was akin to that of Chaucer, at the right linguistic crossroads when English began to assume a standard form.

The translation made by Hereford and his associates took less advantage of this than it might. To its general credit, it showed a complete respect for the authority of the Vulgate, but its word-for-word rendering often followed the Latin syntax so closely that the awkward result was impractical for popular use. It was soon decided to revise it, and the task was now assigned to John Purvey, Wycliffe's personal secretary, confidant, and fellow priest. Purvey proved to have a much better feel for English idiom. He occasionally gave the phrasing a simple dignity and grace, and furnished a helpful prologue and epilogue for each book. In place of Hereford's earlier glosses, he introduced marginal notes—principally from Nicholas of Lyra, an outstanding fourteenth-century Franciscan scholar with an expert knowledge of Hebrew, as well as from various Church fathers, including St. Augustine. In his notes for the New Testament, Purvey also drew upon Robert Grosseteste.

Some 170 manuscripts of the Wycliffe Bibles (most in Purvey's version) still survive.

In his General Prologue, Purvey explained that his first task had been, with the help of "good and cunning fellows," to collect "many old bibles" and expository works, and by their collation and study to authenticate the Latin text. Most of the Latin Bibles then available, he noted, were riddled with scribal error and so only with "much travail" had he and his colleagues managed "to make one Latin Bible some deal true." They consulted the work of other scholars, combed through commentaries on the Old Testament that "helped full much," and conferred with a number of grammarians and divines as to how "hard words and hard sentences . . . might best be understood." With this information in hand, he had translated "with many at the correcting" in order to render not just the words but the sense or meaning of the text. "For the words ought to serve to the intent . . . else they be superfluous and false."

In Purvey's revision, such awkward English sentences as "I forsoothe am the Lord Thy God, strong jealous," became "For I am thy Lord God, a strong jealous lover"; or "Lord, go from me, for I am a man sinner" became "Lord, go from me, for I am a sinful man." Great care was also taken with ambiguous terms—in Acts 2:2, for example, *spiritus* was correctly translated "wind" and not "spirit," as in the earlier version—and decidedly Latinate constructions like the ablative absolute were turned into subordinate clauses, according to English usage already established at that time.

Even so, it is a pity Wycliffe did not undertake the translation himself. He wrote about three hundred sermons in English (which Purvey evidently consulted), and all contain passages from the Gospels that on the whole are more idiomatic and have an energy, vividness, and wit that both Hereford and Purvey lacked. Had the Bible been truly his, he might, as one biographer remarks, "have left behind a monument more lasting than brass."

Here is a comparative translation of Luke 5:1–8—

First Version

Christ stood beside the standing water of Gennesaret, and saw two boats standing beside the standing water; and the fishers had gone down and washed nets. And he went into a boat, that was Simon's, prayed him to lead again a little from the land; and he sitting taught the companies from the boat. And as he ceased to speak he said to Simon, Lead thou into high, and slacken ye your nets into the taking. And Simon answering said to him, Commander, we travailing by all the night took we nothing, but in thy word I shall lay out the net. And when they had done this thing, they closed together a plenteous multitude of fishes; forsooth their net was broken. And they beckoned to fellows, that were in another boat, that they should come, and help them. And they came, and filled both little boats, so that they were all most drenched. Which thing when Simon Peter saw, he fell down to the knees of Jesus, saying, Lord, go from me, for I am a man sinner.

Second Version

He stood beside the pool of Gennesaret, and saw two boats standing beside the pool; and the fishers were gone down, and washed their nets. And he went up to a boat, that was Simon's, and prayed him to lead it a little from the land; and he sat, and taught the people out of the boat. And as he ceased to speak, he said to Simon, Lead thou into the depth, and slacken your nets to take fish. And Simon answered, and said to him, Commander, we travailed all the night, and took nothing, but in thy word, I shall lay out the net. And when they had done this thing, they closed together a great multitude of fish; and their net was broken. And they beckoned to fellows, that were in another boat, that they should come, and help them. And they came, and filled both the boats, so that they were almost drenched. And when Simon Peter saw this thing, he fell down to the knees of Jesus, and said, Lord, go from me, for I am a sinful man.

Wycliffe

Christ stood by the river of Gennesaret . . . and fishers came down to wash therein their nets; and Christ went up into a boat that was Simon's, and prayed him to move it a little from the land, and he sat and taught the people out of the boat. And when Christ ceased to speak, he said to Simon, Lead the boat into the high sea, and let out your nets to taking of fish. And Simon answering said to him, Commander, all the night travailing took we naught; but in thy word shall I loose the net. And when they had done this, they took a plenteous multitude of fish, and their net was broken. But they beckoned to their fellows that were in the other boat, to come and help them; and they came and filled both boats of fish, so that both were well nigh sunk. And when Peter had seen this wonder, he fell down to Jesus' knee, and said, Lord, go from me for I am a sinful man.

Although later partisans (most notably, Sir Thomas More) condemned the Wycliffe translations as heretical, they were never so judged—or even denounced as erroneous—by the Church, but suppressed only because they were unauthorized, and because their polemical notes called some Church teachings into doubt.

Of all such teachings, that pertaining to the Eucharist aroused the most debate. The doctrine then obtaining (and still held by the Catholic Church today) was of comparatively recent origin and could be dated to the time of Pope Innocent III. In a sense, it was a scholastic doctrine—at least, it was heavily defended by scholastic arguments—and Wycliffe came by his own critique of it in a scholastic way. Known as transubstantiation, the doctrine held that the substance of the bread or Host of Communion was transformed by the priest's consecration into the body of Christ. What then sustained the "accidents" or visible appearance of the bread? Why did the bread appear to be the same? Some said it was a "phantasm," others a "quantity," a "quality," or a "weight." The scholastic theologian Duns Scotus said simply the accidents were sustained by the will of God.

Although theologians of the early Church had assumed the supernatural presence of Christ in the Sacrament, they had not tried to give it a name. Irenaeus had said the Sacrament combined both an earthly and a heavenly thing; Tertullian, that the bread was a figure of the Body; this was the understanding, too, of both St. Augustine and St. Jerome. But with Cyril of Jerusalem (a fourth-century theologian of the East) the notion began to take hold that the bread was actually "changed" in substance by the words of the priest.

Wycliffe regarded the doctrine of "accidents without subject" (or substance) as absurd. "Of all the heresies that have ever sprung up in the Church," he wrote in his *Trialogus,* "I think there is not one more artfully introduced, or imposing such manifold fraud."

His analysis of the matter was deeply rooted in contemporary thought. That thought was caught up in a great scholastic controversy that pitted the Nominalists against the Realists. Wycliffe was a Realist, which in his day meant that he believed in the objective reality of Universal Ideas. Ideas (in this Platonic sense) are the eternal paradigms or exemplars emanating from God by which He produces realities outside Himself. As such, they are both beyond and (essentially) inherent in all individual things. Nominalists, on the other hand, held that only individual things are real, and that what we call Universals are nothing but mental concepts which we designate by a term, or name.

To a Realist, Universal Ideas were coeternal with, created by, and shared their being with God. As all individual things shared in the being of their Idea or Archetype, the annihilation of anything (for example, the bread of the Host) was impossible because that meant a partial destruction of the mind of God. While upholding a "real Presence" of Christ's body in the Host, Wycliffe therefore objected to the Nominalist assertion that the bread was annihilated, leaving accidents without a subject, or the appearance of bread without the bread itself. That, he thought, invested the priest with supernatural powers, and enabled him "to make the Body of Christ." This in turn exposed Christ's body to accidental indignities, was contrary to the plain sense of the Gospels, and promoted idolatry. "Who could set limits to the spiritual power of one who could thus 'make his Maker?' " wrote one Church historian. "The simple minister of the word thus rose into the dignity of a sacrificing priest, whose consecrated hands offered the atonement, without which there was no remission of sins."

Wycliffe regarded his own view—that the substance of material bread remained in the Host—as orthodox. "I believe as Christ and his apostles have taught us, that the sacrament is truly God's body in the form of bread. . . . And just as it is heresy to believe that Christ is a spirit and no body, so it is heresy to believe that this sacrament is God's body and no bread; for it is both." He tried to clarify his own understanding by a series of intelligible analogies. He compared the Host and the presence of Christ to paper, ink, and the content of what was written; or to a live coal that is wood, united with fire; or to a broken glass in which "thou mayst see thy face, and thy face not parted" in every fragment—"as a man may light many candles at one candle and the light of that candle never the less": just so is Christ in every fragment of the bread. He quoted St. Augustine. "What we see is the bread and the chalice that the eyes announce, and faith receives that the bread is the body and that in the chalice is the blood of Our Lord." Wrote Wycliffe: "Yea! even irrational animals, such as mice, when they eat a lost consecrated wafer, know better than these unbelievers do, that the host is bread, just as it was before!"

All doctrines of the Eucharist (including those to which the Reformation gave rise) may fairly be called elusive, and toward the end of his life Wycliffe grew impatient with subtle arguments about a matter which, he believed, defied definition. His final position was: "Let us accept the unexplained phrases of Scripture and receive this sacrament to freshen within our hearts the image of Christ."

Along with his Bible translation and polemical teaching, Wycliffe began to organize and train what amounted to a new religious order of itinerant preachers, "animated by something like the culture and spirit of the Franciscans." By the end of 1377 several had already embarked on their mission, and in the highways and byways, taverns, inns, and village greens, they denounced abuses, proclaimed Wycliffe's doctrine of the Eucharist, and taught the apostolic way of charity, hope, and faith. Their typical garb was a long russet-colored robe of undressed wool, without purse or scrip, and a long staff, much like the Franciscan attire Wycliffe had worn at Canterbury Hall. Although many from among the low-born would eventually join their ranks, the core of Wycliffe's new unbeneficed order of "poor priests" (as he called them) were Oxford scholars; and their avowed inspiration were the seventy evangelists whom

Jesus had sent out to convert the world. In after years, all Wycliffites came to be called Lollards, a term some derived from "lolia," meaning tares or weeds (as mingled with the pure grain of truth); others, from the Old Dutch or German "lollen," meaning "to sing softly," "to mutter," or "to hum." John Purvey, Wycliffe's assistant, wore the name proudly, saying that "the most blessed loller that ever shall be/ Was our Lord Jesus lolling on the rood tree." The Lollards themselves preferred to be known by such epithets as Christian Brethren or "true men."

The established Church, of course, abhorred their views, although in the beginning at least they were able to evangelize with relative impunity. Then in 1381, the whole political landscape changed when a great Peasants' Revolt shook England to its roots.

The large agrarian population had long been oppressed by a manorial system based on serfdom, as well as by heavy taxes, including a particularly ill-advised poll tax passed by Parliament the year before. But as often happens on the cusp of social unrest, the laboring classes had recently become more conscious of their power. Wages had risen (with the scarcity of labor, created by the decimations of the Black Death), while workers felt increasingly free to abandon conditions they judged too harsh. Parliament responded with legislation to contain wages, but failed to impose price controls to any degree. The result was "a vast floating population in and out of employment," runaway peasants, parasites, criminals, and vagrants roaming the land.

Toward the end of May, resistance to the tax collectors broke out spontaneously in various localities, spread throughout East Anglia, and eventually engulfed twenty-eight counties in all. Men of local responsibility—reeves, bailiffs, constables—assumed direction of the rising and before long the rebels began to gather themselves into a body for a coordinated march on London.

On Wednesday, June 12, they assembled on Blackheath, where John Ball, a country priest and one of the principal leaders of the revolt, along with Jack Straw and Wat Tyler, delivered a stirring sermon to the multitude, taking for his text the famous couplet about Adam and Eve—"When Adam delved and Eve span/Who was then a gentleman?" He urged his listeners to remember that all men had been created equal, and that manorial serfdom was an evil creation devised by the rich and powerful purely to benefit themselves. For twenty years Ball had been preaching a kind of communism throughout the north of England, before he carried his message to London and its suburbs, where, according to the chronicler Froissart,

> he was accustomed every Sunday after Mass, as the people were coming out of the church, to preach to them in the market-place and assemble a crowd around him, to whom he would say, "My good friends, things cannot go well in England, nor ever will until everything shall be in common; when there shall be neither vassal nor lord and all distinctions levelled, when the lords shall be no more masters than ourselves. How ill have they used us? And for what reason do they thus hold us in bondage? Are we not all descended from the same parents, Adam and Eve? And what can they show or what reasons give, why they should be more masters than ourselves? They are clothed in velvets and rich stuffs, ornamented with ermine and other furs, while we are forced to wear poor cloth. They have handsome seats and manors, when we must brave the wind and rain in our labors in the field; but it is from our labor that they have the wealth with which to support their power."

The rebels invaded London, destroyed Marshalsea prison, gutted Lambeth Palace, ransacked the estate of John of Gaunt, and beheaded numerous victims in spasms of random violence in Cheapside. A number of high officials took refuge in the Tower, which also served as the king's headquarters in the rebellion's last turbulent days. Outside, a great mob "encamped on St. Catherine's Hill, over against the Tower, howled for blood, and their horrible cry ever and again penetrated into the chambers of the Tower where prelates and nobles 'sat still with awful eye.' " Many mansions throughout the city, in Westminster, Highbury, and elsewhere, were set ablaze, and "the young king Richard, from a high turret window, watched the conflagrations reddening the sky." A number of his advisers rashly urged him to muster his retainers for a direct counterattack, but he heeded the sage advice instead of William Montague, Lord Salisbury, the most experienced soldier present, who told him: "Sire, if you can appease them by fair words and grant them what they wish, it will be so much the better; for should we begin what we cannot go through, we shall never be able to recover it. It will be all over with us and our heirs, and England will be a desert."

The king agreed to meet and negotiate with the rebel leaders at Mile End, where he affected wholesale concessions—nothing less than the complete abolition of serfdom with a "commutation of all servile dues for a rent of fourpence an acre." He also promised a general pardon, and thirty clerks were at once set to work to draw up the charters of liberation and pardon in the proper legal form for every village, manor, and shire. The exulting peasants then poured back into town through Aldgate. But the king and his advisers did not proceed in good faith. "If they had," remarked G. M. Trevelyan, "they would have haggled more over the terms. They regarded it only as a means of freeing themselves from the present situation, as King John had regarded Magna Carta, and as Charles I later regarded the Petition of Right." Meanwhile, part of the mob had broken into the Tower and butchered a number of officials (including the relatively moderate Simon Sudbury, Archbishop of Canterbury), even as violence continued in London. One xenophobic rampage was directed against Belgian and Flemish mercers who lived in the foreign quarter by the Thames. (Chaucer later recalled the incident obliquely in his description of farm servants chasing a fox in the "Nun's Priest's Tale.")

Although thousands of rebels, trusting to the king's concessions, had left London, those that remained made other demands—for the disendowment of the Church (with a redistribution of its wealth), abolition of the game laws, free use of the woods, and so on. This led to a final confrontation between them and the king's men. In the market square of Smithfield outside London, the mayor of London, flanking King Richard, got into an altercation with Wat Tyler and stabbed him to death. When Tyler's men saw him fall, they began to string their bows; but the young king, still no more than a boy, rode straight toward them, and bravely called out, "Sirs, will you kill your own king? I am your captain and your leader. Follow me." And as he rode out of the square, they followed him, in a kind of dumbfounded awe, through the fields to Clerkenwell.

In the end, the privileges which had been wrung from the king by the rebels were revoked, hundreds were tried and executed as traitors, and when challenged about his promises at Mile End, the king replied: "Villeins ye are and villeins ye shall remain."

Where would the revolt have ended had it not been suppressed? With rough justice for some, no doubt, but with atrocities for more. Jack Straw evidently testified before he died that "we would have ended by taking the life of the king, and by exterminating from the face of the earth all landholders, bishops, landed monks, endowed canons, and parish priests. Only the Begging Friars would have been spared, and these would have been sufficient to keep up divine service throughout the land."

Some of the responsibility for the revolt was laid at Wycliffe's feet. His natural sympathies lay with the oppressed, and the preaching of his "Poor Priests" had probably contributed to an awareness of injustice in the land. Like Wycliffe, they decried the exploitation of the poor by their lords and overseers, the "wrongs [done to them] by extortions and unreasonable amercements and taxes," and the nobles' predatory consumption of goods "in gluttony and waste and pride," leaving the poor to perish in hunger, thirst, and cold. "And if their rent be not readily paid . . . they [are] pursued without mercy, though they be never so poor and needy. . . . And so in a manner the [rich] eat and drink their flesh and blood."

But Wycliffe himself was not a social revolutionary. He upheld the power of the state, and (with some reservations) accepted a class society. "Oh how happy," he exclaimed, "would England be if every parish had as of yore a saintly Rector residing with his people, every manor a just lord living with his wife and children! Arable land would not then lie fallow, as now it does, but the realm would have abundance sure." And he cited St. Paul in support of the obligation of all to obey the ruling powers.

But in the aftermath of the rebellion, Church and state closed ranks. On May 17, 1382, a special council, made up of eight bishops including Courtenay, now Archbishop of Canterbury, various masters of theology, doctors of canon and civil law, friars, and so on (forty-five in all) met in Blackfriars, London, to examine the orthodoxy of twenty-four "conclusions" drawn from Wycliffe's works. Their own conclusion was preordained, and just two days into their meeting they began to draft a statement by which all of Wycliffe's pronouncements would be condemned. In mid-afternoon, the proceedings were interrupted by an earthquake and some of the frightened members quickly moved to adjourn. Courtenay, however, insisted they all resume their seats, and tried to reassure them that the quake was to be looked upon as a sign from God portending a cleansing of the realm. Nevertheless, the council accelerated its deliberations and by the end of the day found fourteen of Wycliffe's conclusions "erroneous" and ten heretical. Those judged to be heretical concerned his doctrine of the Eucharist (specifically "That the substance of the material bread and wine remains in the sacrament of the altar after consecration"); Church-state relations; and his disparagement of auricular confession as superfluous.

On May 21, 1382, Courtenay also secured a formal condemnation of some of Wycliffe's associates, including Nicholas Hereford, and five days later, having "learnt by bitter experience that unless the King's arm is stretched against the heretic, the Bishop curses but in vain"—sponsored a parliamentary statute (confirmed by the king without consent of the Commons) authorizing the arrest and prosecution of itinerant preachers throughout the land. On May 30 Courtenay instructed every diocese to publish the verdict against Wycliffe's conclusions, while at Oxford the chancellor prohibited anyone in the university under threat of suspension, excommunication, and imprisonment from presenting, defending, or even attending a lecture or discussion in which the banned theses were set forth. Then on July 13, the king sent down to Oxford a peremptory mandate that Hereford and two of his colleagues, John Aston and Philip Repyngdon, be banished from its halls.

Only the year before, the former chancellor, Robert Rigge, had invited Hereford to deliver the Ascension Day sermon to the student body in English, and Repyngdon the Latin sermon on Corpus Christi Day. But times had changed. Wycliffe's own position at Oxford had become untenable and he withdrew to his parish of Lutterworth. On May 10, 1381, he published a *Confessio,* or Latin defense of his views. In the following year he was partially paralyzed by a stroke. Two years later, on the Day of Holy Innocents (December 28, 1384) "at the time of the elevation of the Host" in the Mass, he collapsed, and died on the last day of the year. A few days later, he was buried in the parish churchyard, in consecrated ground. There were those who rejoiced in his demise. One of them, Thomas Walsingham, chronicler of the Abbey of St. Albans, wrote: "John Wycliffe, that instrument of the Devil, the enemy of the Church, the confusion of men, the idol of heresy, the mirror of hypocrisy, the nourisher of schism, was, by the rightful doom of God, smitten with a horrible paralysis [before he] breathed out his malicious spirit into the abodes of hell." But even before he died, attempts were made to hunt down some of his disciples, including Nicholas Hereford, Philip Repyngdon, John Aston, and John Purvey, who were all eventually arraigned. Both Repyngdon and Purvey were taken into custody and excommunicated on July 1, 1382. Aston and Hereford at first eluded the Church's grasp.

It may be remembered that Hereford had carried his translation of the First Wycliffe Version of the Bible as far as Baruch 3:20. Then he stopped and turned it over to others when he learned that he had been condemned with Wycliffe by the Blackfriars Synod in May 1382. Convinced that Courtenay and his fellow bishops would not accord him a fair trial (but supposing the pope and his cardinals might), Hereford slipped out of England, made his way to Rome, and appealed to Urban VI, who flung him into St. Angelo's prison. A few years later (1385), he was freed during a night of anarchic rioting in the streets, returned to England, found shelter for a time at Sir John Montague's manor in Hertfordshire, then moved north into the Midland shires at the close of 1386, preaching as he went. He got as far as Nottingham, where the law finally caught up with him.

The following year he escaped and took part with John Aston in a preaching campaign in the west of England. There he was caught again, imprisoned, "grievously tormented," and in 1390 recanted at St. Paul's Cross. His recantation seems to have been sincere, for in later years he became the Lollards' implacable foe. Ecclesiastical rank was bestowed on him as a result, and he became treasurer of

Hereford Cathedral. In 1417, at the age of eighty, he resigned his preferments and entered the Charterhouse of St. Anne at Coventry founded in honor of Anne of Bohemia, Richard II's queen. He died in 1419.

Like Hereford, Philip Repyngdon was also induced to recant, joined in campaigns against the Lollards by the Church, and rose from abbot of St. Mary de Pre in Leicester to become confessor to King Henry IV, Bishop of Lincoln, and ultimately, "wearied of honors," died a cardinal in 1424. In his will he asked to be interred "naked in a sack" in a churchyard under the open sky, but instead he was buried in Lincoln Cathedral with all the honors befitting his rank.

John Aston was eventually arrested and recanted, but soon repented having done so and with evangelical zeal endeavored to make amends. According to one angry chronicler, he "went every where on foot with no horse to delay him, regardless of toil, able to take the road like a bee and ready to bark like a dog, pouring out the poisons of Wycliffe to which he did not blush to add new ones of his own." His fellow Lollards thought otherwise of his diligence, and esteemed him constant and "right perfect unto life's end."

As for Purvey, the best of the Wycliffe translators, he gave all his energy to itinerant preaching, and like Aston "despised comfort and rest." For many years he eluded the authorities, but in 1401 he was captured and together with William Sawtrey (a Lollard parish priest) hauled before the bishops and exhorted to recant. Sawtrey, who had previously recanted but since relapsed, was condemned, degraded from his office, and in early March met a martyr's end. Purvey was tortured in the archbishop's prison at Saltwood, recanted on March 6, and read a contrite statement at St. Paul's Cross. For doing so, he was rewarded with the parish living of West Hythe in Kent, but his heart was not in it, and two years later he resigned and returned "to the only life he knew, that of the Lollard underworld," where he vanished forever from sight.

Meanwhile, on November 2, 1389, Archbishop Courtenay had come down to Leicester near Lutterworth to celebrate High Mass in full pontificals, and in the course of the service denounced those sympathetic to Wycliffe's views. The next day he specifically named nine people of the town as excommunicate and accursed. Then he placed the whole town under interdict so long as the nine remained at large. Four of them (one a priest) were soon rounded up, forced to recant, and humiliated in the public square.

The king gave Courtenay support, though the government was not of one mind. On May 20, 1394, Richard II renewed and strengthened measures for the arrest of unlicensed preachers, but the following January Lollard sympathizers in Parliament, led by Sir Thomas Latimer, Sir Lewis Clifford (who had delivered the Queen Mother's stern warning to the bishops at Wycliffe's second trial), Sir Richard Stury, and Sir John Montague (third Earl of Salisbury, deputy marshal of England, and a member of the Privy Council) asked for a full discussion of Church reform. One of their adherents (presaging Luther) also nailed to the doors of St. Paul's Church and Westminster Hall a paper setting forth Twelve Conclusions drawn from Wycliffe's work. Like Luther's more famous theses, these questioned clerical celibacy, transubstantiation, Masses for the dead, pilgrimages, confession, and indulgences.

Courtenay sent a copy to the pope, who complained to the king. The king compelled the Lollard knights to disavow their views, while the Church mounted a counterattack by introducing a parliamentary ban on all English Bible translations. But there a line of sorts was briefly drawn. John of Gaunt (the king's dread uncle) reportedly swore on that occasion: "By God, we will not be the refuse of all men, for since other nations have God's law, which is law of our belief, in their own mother tongue, we will have ours in English, who will ever it begrudge."

The following year, Archbishop Courtenay died and was buried with much fanfare at Canterbury under an alabaster monument before the king and court. He was duly praised as "a fruitful tree in the house of the Lord, diligent in extirpating heresies and errors which the Enemy had sown in his diocese," and posthumously assured that his zeal would be sustained. Indeed, his successor, Thomas Arundel, formerly Archbishop of Ely, proved even more ardent for the Church than he. As soon as he took office, he petitioned the king and Parliament for the power to burn heretics at the stake. While the matter was under consideration, Richard II was deposed by

Henry Bolingbroke, John of Gaunt's son, and the latter was enthroned in October 1399 as Henry IV. Two years later, in 1401, the enabling and infamous statute, *De Haeretico Comburendo* (*Concerning the Burning of Heretics*), was passed.

Sir John Montague (a Wycliffe ally) had proved faithful to King Richard to the last. Convicted of conspiring to restore him to the throne, he was beheaded and dismembered by a mob on January 8, 1400, and his salted remains, "welcomed in London by Arundel and thirty-two mitred Abbots, with music and trumpets at St. Paul's." Afterward, his remains were exposed on London Bridge. A Chronicle tells us disdainfully that as a friend of Lollards he "died miserably, refusing the sacrament of confession, if the common account be true." But his friend, Christine de Pisan (the celebrated French poet), more poignantly mourned his loss: "He was humble, sweet, and courteous in all his ways, loyal in all places and right prudent. He was brave and fierce as a lion. Ballads and songs and lays and roundels right beautiful he made. Though but a layman his deeds were all so gracious that never, I think, shall his country produce a man in whom God put so much good. May his soul be set in Paradise forever among the saints."

Thereafter Lollards were at constant risk of their lives. They met in hidden places, in the deep forests and dells of Hereford and Monmouth, and in the mountains and moss hags on the border with Wales. In one way or another, they managed to elude the agents of the Church, preserve their congregations, and keep their faith alive. Indeed, well into his tenure, Archbishop Arundel could complain that Lollard preachers were still going "from county to county and from town to town . . . preaching daily," winning converts, and receiving food and shelter from the folk. They generally drew their preaching texts from some part of Purvey's translation, or from the three hundred short English sermons Wycliffe had written that had been organized into an annual homiliary cycle for the Church year. A number of manuscripts of the cycle survive—"costly volumes of large size intended for use in church"—written on parchment and bound between leather-covered boards. Rooms in manor houses were turned into scriptoria for their production, and copies continued to be produced even after 1401, when it became mortally dangerous to own any of Wycliffe's works. In addition to the sermon cycle, the Lollards compiled Latin commonplace books with "flowers of learning," containing quotations from Wycliffe and various Church fathers—St. Augustine, St. Ambrose, St. Jerome, Origen, Cyprian, Peter Lombard, St. Bernard, Nicholas of Lyra, St. Thomas Aquinas, Richard Fitzralph, and Robert Grosseteste.

Conditions in the west of England seem to have been especially favorable for the Lollard movement, with centers of influence also in Leicester, Northampton, Nottingham, Gloucester, Reading, Salisbury, London, and Bristol. One contemporary chronicler claimed that "every second man" he met was a Lollard, and that they "went all over England luring great nobles and lords to their fold." One such preacher, William Swinderby, known as William the Hermit, was an earnest, fearless priest so charismatic in denouncing luxury and worldliness that even "honest men," we are told, "were wellnigh driven to despair." Barred by his bishop from church, he reportedly made a pulpit of two millstones in High Street in Leicester and there regularly preached to crowds who came from far and wide.

Arundel, however, did not let up. Among his most punitive measures were the so-called Constitutions of Oxford of 1408, designed to suppress freedom of thought in the schools. Any unauthorized person caught with a Wycliffe Bible could be tried for heresy, and all speculation on the Sacraments or other articles of faith, as well as disputations about crosses, saints, images, pilgrimages, and so on were proscribed. University officials were to ascertain, by monthly inquiries, whether anyone was guilty of violating such guidelines, and if so they were to be expelled or dismissed. The seventh of the thirteen Constitutions also read: "We therefore command and ordain that henceforth no one translate on his own authority any text of Holy Scripture into English . . . and that no one read anything of this kind lately made in the time of the said John Wycliffe . . . either publicly or privately, whole or in part" unless it was first "approved and allowed" by the local bishop of the diocese.

Arundel also leveled a stern rebuke at Oxford itself: "This University which once was a juicy vine, and brought forth its branches for the glory of God and the advancement of His Church, now brings forth wild grapes; and so it comes to pass that the unfruitful doctrines of the Lollards increase in the land."

Oxford intellectual life was shattered. The century that followed was the most barren in its annals, as the number of students declined to a fifth of their former number and "Oxford Latin" became proverbial for a scholarship in which even the knowledge of grammar had been lost. Eventually, when the Reformation flooded in, "it was at Cambridge that the main current flowed." Meanwhile, the university, wrote one scholar, "devoted its enfeebled scholarship to defacing its former star." Many copies of Wycliffe's works were destroyed, and those who secretly kept them erased his name from their pages out of fear. When a bursar's list for Merton College was drawn up in 1411, its compiler scrawled beside Wycliffe's name: "Doctor in theology. He trusted too much to his own wit, as is said. He was neither a fellow of the College, nor had he a full year of probation in it." But such attempts to falsify or abridge his affiliation could not be sustained. Other records showed that Wycliffe had obtained both his bachelor's and master's degrees at Merton, was a fellow of the college, a member of the ruling faculty, and had taught philosophy for five years in the Faculty of Arts before completing his work for his doctorate in theology at Queens in 1372.

Meanwhile, Arundel had ordered Wycliffe's works to be burnt, and in 1412, in a letter to the pope enclosed a list of 267 heresies and errors "worthy of the fire" which he claimed to have culled from their pages. His accompanying remarks were harsh. "That wretched and pestilent fellow, son of the Serpent, herald and child of Antichrist, John Wycliffe," he wrote, "filled up the measure of his malice by devising the expedient of a new translation of Scripture into the mother tongue."

The number of martyrs grew. One was John Badby, a tailor of Evesham in Worcester, and as low-born as Sir John Montague was high. He was arraigned for heresy in London in 1410, confronted with the whole majesty of Church and state (two archbishops, eight bishops, the Duke of York, and the chancellor of England), but did not swerve from his conviction that "Christ sitting at supper could not give his disciples his living body to eat." A more severe trial lay before him, as he was led out to Smithfield and placed on a funeral pyre. The Prince of Wales (Shakespeare's Prince Hal, afterward Henry V) attempted unsuccessfully to persuade him to recant, and when the local prior displayed the Host, Badby exclaimed, "It is consecrated bread, and not the body of God." The pyre was lit. Badby cried "Mercy!" and the prince immediately doused the fire and offered not only to pardon him but to sustain him with an annual stipend if he would only recant. But Badby had been calling out not to Henry, but to God.

A few years later, the most famous of all the Lollard martyrs met his end. In the autumn of 1413, Sir John Oldcastle, Lord Cobham—a man of rank, wealth, honor, and long public service, and a friend and soldier of the king—was charged with heresy for having aided Lollard preachers and advanced their views. Brought before the bishops at St. Paul's, he made a bold confession of faith, denounced the worship of images, and rejected transubstantiation and auricular confession. The king clapped him in the Tower and gave him forty days to recant. On October 19, 1413, he escaped, organized an abortive assault on the capital (supported by scattered sympathizers in the Midlands and the south), and colluded with a picked band of conspirators, disguised as mummers, who planned to kidnap the royal family at Eltham. Their plot was betrayed, and Oldcastle's supporters were dispersed by royal troops. Thirty-seven were afterward executed, while Oldcastle took refuge in the hills of West Herefordshire, where he hid for three years until the king tracked him down. Indicted before Parliament, he was sentenced to be hanged as a traitor and burned as a heretic; and this double sentence was literally carried out. Brought to St. Giles's Fields, he was suspended over a flaming pyre between two gallows by chains.

After Oldcastle's execution, the movement lost what support it had among the nobility and gentry and upper classes and became a secret sect to which mostly commoners belonged. Many of its adherents earned an independent living in the burgeoning new cloth industry, as weavers, wool combers, winders, fullers, dyers; others—smiths, carpenters, masons—belonged to the building trades.

In 1414, Arundel died. The obituary notice in the register at Christ Church, Canterbury, praised him as "a man of great knowledge, of excellent ability, and in individual matter wise and circumspect; sedulous and most devoted in the execution of his pontifical office; and acceptable to kings for the maturity of his wise counsel." All this was doubtless so. Though a hunter of Lollards, it was said that he "preferred justice to gold," and the poet John Gower tells us that "he strove at all times not against the law but to divert the king from his wrath." But there was also something tragic about his life. One chronicler recorded a dream he had upon hearing of his death in which he saw Arundel dressed as if he were about to go on a long journey, "running very fast alone. And when I tried as hard as I could to catch up with him he handed me a wax candle saying, 'Divide this in the middle between us two.' And so he disappeared from my sight, and waking, I understood that henceforth we were divided, and sorrowfully I said a mass for his soul." England, indeed, was being split. Arundel's "diseased energy" for persecution (as G. K. Chesterton chose to phrase it) did much to create the conditions for anti-Catholic bigotry in England even as the fires he kindled under his victims helped in time to "put a torch to his own Church."

Throughout this period, the Great Schism had followed its own horrendous course. Pope Urban VI had proclaimed a crusade against Clement VII, tortured and killed five of his own cardinals, and led an army of mercenaries back and forth across Italy until in 1389 he died at Rome. The remaining cardinals immediately elected a successor, who took the name of Boniface IX. Five years later Clement died and was succeeded by Benedict XIII. At the beginning of the fifteenth century, some attempt was made to end the rift by the election of yet a third pope. Then on March 25, 1409, an imposing assembly of churchmen gathered at Pisa, and the two absent popes were declared contumacious and schismatical, notorious heretics, guilty of scandalizing the universal Church and therefore deposed. The townspeople reacted with wild joy and burned them in effigy. A new pope was elected: Peter Philargi, Cardinal of Milan, a seventy-year-old Venetian with an excellent reputation as a theologian, canonist, and diplomat. He took the name of Alexander V, but the other two popes repudiated his authority, and before he could establish it, he died at Bologna on May 3, 1410, on his way to Rome. His successor, Baldassare Cossa, took the name John XXIII. Cossa (later condemned by the Church as an antipope, and not to be confused with the twentieth-century pope of sanctified fame) was a soldier-prelate and entered Rome with an army on April 12, 1411. He immediately called a Church council, but even as he intoned the invocation, "Come, Holy Spirit," a screech owl reportedly landed on his head. He flinched and cried out, "A strange shape for the Holy Spirit to take!"

Finally, at the insistence of the Emperor Sigismund, King of Hungary and Rome, the more decisive Council of Constance was called in 1414. This council was the most imposing ever convoked by the Catholic Church. Among its members and attendees were a German emperor, twenty princes, one hundred and forty counts, a pope, seven patriarchs, twenty-nine cardinals, thirty-three archbishops, ninety-one bishops, six hundred other prelates, and about four thousand priests. Its deliberations also extended over four years until 1418. In his opening address, Pope John defined the council's objectives as union and reform. But the first question facing it was the fate of John himself. On March 1, 1415, he agreed to abdicate if the other two popes did also, at which the emperor knelt in gratitude and kissed his feet. But on March 20, under cover of night, the pope slipped out of town disguised as a valet and sought refuge with the Duke of Austria. The duke, however, could see no advantage in giving him protection, and turned him over to the council, which deposed him forthwith. The other two popes—Benedict XIII at Avignon, and Gregory XII at Rimini—were also disavowed. One "authentic and universal pope," Martin V, was at last elected in their place.

Before it disbanded, the assembly also decreed that councils received their authority directly from Christ and should be held at regular intervals in the interests of reform; condemned Wycliffe as a heretic; and ordered his bones to be exhumed and removed from consecrated ground. This last decree was finally (and reluctantly) carried out in the spring of 1428 by Richard Flemyng, then Bishop of Lincoln and a former Lollard, who acted on peremptory orders from the pope. With the new Primate of England looking on, Wycliffe's remains were disinterred and burned on a little arched bridge that spanned the river Swift (a tributary of the Avon), and his calcined ashes cast into the stream. From thence the prophecy arose:

The Avon to the Severn runs,
The Severn to the sea,
And Wycliffe's dust shall spread abroad,
Wide as the waters be.

And so it was. In England, the movement he had founded obstinately endured, even as his ideas spread almost within his own lifetime to Bohemia and took root overseas. In England, Purvey's English translation was prodigiously copied and circulated in whole or in part, often with a table of the Lessons, Epistles, and Gospels for Sundays appended to the text. As late as the 1520s Purvey's New Testament was also translated into Scots. John Foxe, the martyrologist, tells us that among the common folk, some paid whatever they could for the Scriptures in English, "to taste the sweetness of God's Holy Word. . . . Some paid more, some less: some gave a load of hay for a few chapters of St. Paul or St. James." Thousands (perhaps tens of thousands) read or went to secret readings of them, while publicly continuing to attend their local church. No one knows how many such "silent Protestants" there were.

A handful of openly defiant believers also went to the fire. In the spring of 1428, for example, sixty accused heretics (most of them artisans and their wives) were rounded up and tried. Of these, seven, including three priests, were burned.

From various urban centers the new Lollard teachings spread into the countryside, along natural routes of trade; found their way north and west into "the strange and independent world of the Forest of Dean"—a mining district; and especially infested the area around Lincoln, where, between 1509 and 1521 the bishop was kept constantly busy in attempting to repress the sect. One of those summoned before him apparently owned "a book of the Four Evangelists in English"; another "divers English books prohibited and damned by law: as the Apocalypse, the Epistles and the Gospels in English, Wycliffe's damnable books, and others containing infinite errors"; a third, "the Gospel of St. Luke, the Epistles of St. Paul, James and Peter in English, and the Wisdom of Solomon."

Manuscript Bibles were costly and scarce, so it was not uncommon for Lollards also to commit portions to memory. A certain Alice Collins of Burford was famed in this regard, and "could recite much of the Scriptures and other good books; and so when any conventicle did meet at Burford, commonly she was sent for, to recite unto them the declaration of the Ten Commandments, and the Epistles of Peter and James." Occasionally, her little daughter, Joan, would also recite, "for she knoweth the seven deadly sins, the seven works of mercy, the five wits bodily and ghostly, the eight blessings, and five chapters of the Epistle of James."

Wycliffe's views flourished abroad in Bohemia, thanks in part to Jerome of Prague, a reformer who attended Oxford on one of the scholarships established for Czech students in 1388. But of all the Czechs influenced by Wycliffe, the most important by far was Jan Hus, who translated Wycliffe's *Trialogus* into Czech, and incorporated much of the latter's tract *De Ecclesia* almost verbatim into his own work. At the same Church Council of Constance that ordered Wycliffe's remains exhumed, Hus had been arrested, imprisoned, and on July 6, 1415, burned at the stake. Afterward, his ashes, still smoking from the fire, were carefully scooped into a wheelbarrow and tipped into the Rhine. A century later (in February 1529) Martin Luther would write: "I have hitherto taught and held all the opinions of Hus without knowing it. . . . We are all of us Hussites. . . . I do not know what to think for amazement." In truth, they were all Wycliffites, if a forebear must be claimed. And this the Catholic Church in England knew. In 1523 the Bishop of London sized up the first great impact of Lutheranism on English life by declaring: "It is no question of some precocious novelty; it is only that new arms are being added to the great band of Wycliffite heretics." Many of the fundamental ideas of the Reformation, originally disseminated by the English, had merely returned home to Albion's shores in Germanic guise. And that is why they found such fertile ground. "England was not converted from Germany," wrote G. M. Trevelyan, "but changed her own opinion, and had begun that process long before Wittenberg or Geneva became famous in theological debate."

Wycliffe had lived in a period of transition, contributing much to the tide of change. He had allied himself with the widespread and growing demands of the people for social and economic justice, and his doctrine of dominion had given "the initial impetus to the movement in England which finally ended in the separation of Church and state." He dimly foresaw that political power would (and should) ultimately belong to the people, and in that prophetic vein (if he can be said to have possessed it) "was determined that before they came into control they should know God's law." He was the moving force behind the first translation of the whole Bible into English; and for that, and the tenets of his theology, has justly been called the "John the Baptist of the Reformation," and its brightly shining "Morning Star."

His critique of the Church was so thorough that the poet John Milton would later declare: "Why else was this Nation chosen before any other, that out of her, as out of Sion, should be proclaimed and sounded forth the first tidings and trumpet of Reformation to all Europe? And had it not been the obstinate perverseness of our prelates against the divine and admirable spirit of Wycliffe, to suppress him as a schismatic and innovator, perhaps neither the Bohemian Hus and Jerome [of Prague]—no, nor the names of Luther or of Calvin—had even been known: the glory of reforming all our neighbors had been completely ours."

That sure lineage, indeed, is emblematically expressed in a Bohemian Psalter of 1572, which contains a page, with a hymn to Hus, adorned with three medallion miniatures, arranged in a vertical row. The first depicts Wycliffe striking a spark; below him Hus lights a candle; while Luther, at the bottom, brandishes a blazing torch.

WILLIAM TYNDALE

Every sort of doctrine which is to be delivered to the faithful is contained in the Word of God, which is divided into Scripture and Tradition.

—Catechism of the Council of Trent

CHAPTER TWO

Martyr

 e have now to enter into the story of the good martyr of God, William Tyndale; who, as he was a special organ of the Lord appointed, and as God's mattock to shake the inward roots and foundation of the pope's proud prelacy, so the great prince of darkness, with his impious imps, having a special malice against him, left no way unsought how craftily to entrap him, and falsely to betray him, and maliciously to spill his life, as by the process of his story here following may appear."

Thus did John Foxe in his *Book of Martyrs* begin his brief but memorable biography of William Tyndale, the father of the English Bible as we know it, and in the pantheon of Protestant martyrs, one of its authentic saints.

Born of Northumberland parentage about 1495 in Slimbridge, Gloucestershire, not far from the border with Wales, Tyndale belonged to one of several families called Hutchyns living in hamlets tucked into the western folds of the Cotswold scarp overlooking the Vale of Berkeley. All the Hutchynses were said to be descended from Hugh de Tindale, baron of Langley Castle in Northumberland, who as a loyalist of the York faction in the Wars of the Roses fled south before the advance of Lancastrian arms to settle in Gloucestershire under his adopted name.

As an adolescent William Tyndale tramped about the "high wild hills and rough uneven ways" of the Slimbridge district, and from the summit of Stinchcombe Hill had a panoramic view of the rippling landscape as it stretched away to the horizon "like the garden of the Lord." Far in the distance he could also make out the tall menacing towers of Berkeley Castle, "right famous as the seat of barons bold," which had once held Edward II captive, and were stained with the blood of that king. The beauty of the local environment was matched by the vigor of its speech, and even today, it is said, "the thrilling poetic cadence of the united voices of a Welch choir singing old hymns in a thunder of feeling can make unbelievers weep."

Lollard sentiment was rife in the district. Langland's *Piers the Plowman,* with its stinging critique of clerical abuse, had been set in the Vale of Berkeley and the adjacent Malvern Hills; Wycliffe himself had held a prebend at Aust, not far from Tyndale's haunts; and just twenty miles away was the great port of Bristol, where Purvey had preached, Oldcastle's revolt had found support, and the ideas of the Reformation would soon come flowing in.

As a child, Tyndale was evidently taught at a special grammar school where he demonstrated an unusual aptitude for languages, and by the age of ten or so could read Latin with ease. He tells us that about that time he was deeply impressed by a passage in one of the Latin chronicles (probably the *Gesta Regum Anglorum* or *Great Deeds of the English Kings*) "how that King Athelstane, [King Alfred's grandson] caused [part of] the Holy Scripture to be translated" into English—a story that imprinted itself powerfully on his mind. At age twelve he went up to the University of Oxford, to Magdalen Hall, and there, Foxe tells us, "by long continuance he grew and increased in the knowledge of tongues and other liberal arts," and was "singularly addicted to the study of the Scriptures." His teachers included three great Humanists—William Grocyn, William Latimer, and Thomas Linacre—and after he earned his M.A. in 1515, Tyndale left Oxford for Cambridge, where Greek studies had recently received a tremendous boost from Erasmus, who had taught both Greek and divinity there from 1511 to 1514. Tyndale also devoured the works of the new Continental Reformers—Luther, Melanchthon and Zwingli—and before he left Cambridge at the end of 1521, the Reformation itself had begun to take hold.

☙

Between the death of Wycliffe and the advent of Luther the world had changed. And the manner of that change had coupled the Renaissance together with the printing press. Although the spirit of the Renaissance took many forms, its hallmark was the revival of classical learning and wisdom, which immensely enlarged the cultural horizons of contemporary thought. That thought was notably epitomized in the intellectual movement known as Humanism, which stressed the unity of truth and the dignity of man. Its broadly tolerant, generally optimistic and rational character stood in contrast to the formalistic pieties of an earlier age. If its human ideal of the "Renaissance Man," completely accomplished in all things, suggested a perfection beyond practical reach, it at least encouraged the fullest possible development of human capacities. Christian Humanists also hoped the Church could renew itself by direct contact with the best in classical and early Christian thought. The Dialogues of Plato, for example, gave access to the revelations of ancient wisdom, while the Epistles of St. Paul, read in the original Greek, freed the Gospel from "the arid and undiscerning commentaries" that for centuries had overlaid the text. The champions of this program (or cultural expectation) included the Italian Pico della Mirandola, the Frenchman Jacques Lefèvre d'Etaples, the Spaniard Luis Vives, Erasmus of Rotterdam, and the Englishman Sir Thomas More. All hoped to save Christendom through enlightened learning, and as G. K. Chesterton remarked of the revival of Greek, "for the man who got it, it is not too much to say that he felt as if he were in the open air for the first time. . . . When, therefore, we look at the world with his eyes we are looking from the widest windows of that time; looking over a landscape seen for the first time very equally, in the level light of the sun at morning." It was the printing press that caught and held that light to the widest possible surmise.

The development of movable type has generally been credited

to Johann Gutenberg, a Mainz goldsmith, who set up the first mechanized printing operation in Europe about 1450. His press was modeled on the screw press, which had long been used for "surfacing" paper, embossing patterns on textiles, and pressing grapes. But it wasn't until techniques of die-stamping and casting from molds had been perfected that the two could be combined to produce letters in relief. Few inventions (apart from the invention of writing itself) have had such an impact on human life and culture, and Sir Francis Bacon was surely right to identify it—along with gunpowder and the compass—as one of three that "changed the appearance and state of the whole world."

During medieval times, monasteries and other ecclesiastical establishments had enjoyed an almost complete monopoly of book production. Each abbey and monastery had its own scriptorium, where manuscripts were copied, decorated, and bound; but the work was laborious and even the most diligent copyist could seldom cover more than four leaves a day. The colophon of one twelfth-century Beatus manuscript from Silos tells us: "If you do not know what writing is, you may think it is not especially difficult. . . . Let me tell you that it is an arduous task: it destroys your eyesight, bends your spine, squeezes your stomach and your sides, pinches your lower back, and makes your whole body ache. . . . Like the sailor arriving at the port, so the writer rejoices arriving at the last line."

From the thirteenth century on, intellectual life increasingly centered on the university, where professional copyists (sometimes formed into guilds) copied course books, commentaries, and other works of reference; Bibles; scholastic treatises; prayer books (breviaries and Books of Hours); as well as works of practical piety. These often went out in quires or signatures for copying, which allowed several scribes to work on the same text at once. As demand increased, production diversified. Books of all sorts—cookbooks, medical manuals, educational treatises, tales of courtly love, and so on—appeared, variously illustrated and in a number of different calligraphic styles.

Gutenberg's invention was therefore launched on a rising tide. The wealthy could always hire scribes to copy books for their own collections, but by the early 1400s the demand had become so great that booksellers were making speculative commissions on even the most costly manuscripts. The Florentine Vespasiano da Bisticci, for example, employed up to fifty scribes.

The potential of the new technology was recognized at once, and other presses were soon established in most of the major cities of Europe, including Rome, Venice, Milan, Florence, Budapest, Cracow, and Cologne. It was at Cologne that William Caxton, "the father of English printing," learned his craft before establishing his own press at Westminster in 1476. In the prologue to the first book ever printed in English (*The Recuyell of the Historyes of Troye,* a work on the Trojan War), Caxton tells us: "I was born and learned my English in Kent in the Weeld, where I doubt not is spoken as broad and rude English as in any part of England." By "rude" he meant "natural," and his allegiance to the vernacular distinguished his work from the start.

During the remaining fourteen years of his life, Caxton printed nearly a hundred English books (many of his own translation) on morality, religion, social philosophy, fable, history, law, politics, science, and romance, as well as a number of vernacular classics, including works by Chaucer, John Gower, John Lydgate, and Sir Thomas Malory. He is thought to have been a man of Lollard sympathies, and might have printed an edition of Purvey's Bible, too, except that the ban instituted by the Constitutions of Oxford remained in force. In 1440, he had witnessed the burning of Richard Wyche, a Lollard priest, at Tavern Hill and remarked afterward that Wyche had died "a good Christian man."

As a publisher, Caxton was keenly aware of the impact of his work on English diction, then in considerable flux, and in his own translations tried not to overemphasize unusual words (or "curious terms," as he called them) while not wanting his language to seem too plain. He had no dictionaries to guide him or even, in fact, any means beyond his own judgment to discriminate between different dialects, at a time when English speech varied from shire to shire. Indeed, the residents of one county sometimes thought those of another spoke a foreign tongue. In that regard, he recounted the story of a company of Northumberland merchants who one morning sailed south along the coast and disembarked at the mouth of the Thames. As they wanted breakfast, they went straight to an inn. One of them asked for some "eggys." The landlady turned to his companions and said, "Please explain to him that I don't speak French." The hungry man cried out that he didn't speak French either but would still like some "eggys." It was then explained to her that he wanted a plate of "eyren," which meant "eggs" in the dialect of Kent. "What should a man in these days write," asked Caxton, " 'eggys' or 'eyren'?" He settled for "eggys"—and so we now settle for them too.

Although Chaucer and his linguistic confreres (Wycliffe among them) had helped to establish a dominant dialect, it was Caxton's publications that consolidated the gains. These would ultimately be made permanent by the English Bible and the Prayer Book, which in Tudor times, thanks to printing , reached everyone who could read.

Meanwhile, great strides had been made in biblical studies, with progress in Greek, Hebrew, and other languages, such as Aramaic and Chaldee. Throughout the Middle Ages, Hebrew and Greek had seldom, if ever, formed part of the university curriculum, although some scholars and monastics (including Roger Bacon and Robert Grosseteste) had taken them up.

Then in 1453, Constantinople fell to the Turks, and for classical scholarship, at least, this apparent catastrophe worked an unexpected gain. Greek exiles fleeing to Italy brought Greek manuscripts with them, and Pope Nicholas V, a true bibliophile, eagerly gathered them up and had them transcribed. Upon his death in 1455, he left behind a vast library of five thousand tomes. Meanwhile, many of the exiled scholars had begun to teach at European universities, as their knowledge spread. Greek was reintroduced into the curriculum of the University of Paris in 1458; a new Greek grammar published in 1476; a Greek lexicon in 1480; and from 1492, Greek studies became a fixture at Oxford under William Grocyn and Thomas Linacre, who had both studied in Florence with Greek tutors to the Medicis. More influential still was John Colet, who upon returning from his own Italian tour in 1497 delivered a series of momentous lectures at Oxford on St. Paul's Epistle to the Romans in which he made a clean break with the interpretive methods of the medieval scholastics, and expounded the text in accordance with the plain meaning of the words. In so doing, as one writer put it, "he swept away centuries of turgid and often fantastic pedantry and went directly to the text itself."

It was to hear Colet that Erasmus had come to England in 1499 in the first place, and the atmosphere of culture he found there moved him to rapturous praise. "When I listen to my friend Colet I seem to be listening to Plato himself," he wrote. "Who does not admire in Grocyn the perfection of his training? What can be more acute, more profound, or more refined, than the judgment of Thomas Linacre? When did nature ever fashion a disposition more sweet, more gentle, or more congenial than that of Thomas More? . . . Here I have met with humanity, politeness, and learning that is neither superficial nor trite, but deep, accurate, and true in the classical sense—and withal so much of it, that, but for mere curiosity, I can see no reason to return to Italy again." It was Colet who apparently inspired Erasmus to make a fresh Latin translation of the Greek New Testament (amending St. Jerome) as part of a new landmark edition of the Greek text prepared by Erasmus in 1516.

Meanwhile, Hebrew learning had also taken root. The first Hebrew grammar had appeared in 1503 and the first Hebrew lexicon in 1506. Part of the Old Testament or Hebrew Scriptures had already been printed in 1477, and the entire text, with vowel signs and accents, at Soncino, Italy, in February 1488. A fully annotated edition (on which all subsequent Hebrew Bibles would be based) was prepared by Jacob Ben Chayyim and published in 1525.

Before long, regius (royal) professorships in Hebrew would be founded at Oxford and Cambridge, with comparable positions at the universities of Paris, Wittenberg, and Louvain. So-called trilingual colleges—which taught Latin, Hebrew, and Greek—also "sprang up," in Germany, England, France, and Spain. The most famous was that founded by Fray Francisco Jiménez de Cisneros (Cardinal Ximénez) at Alcala, which produced the great Complutensian Polyglot edition of the Bible in 1517. On each page of the Old Testament portion, the Vulgate Latin was flanked by the Hebrew on the left and the Greek Septuagint on the right—like Christ, the editors remarked, crucified between two thieves. The New Testament appeared with the Greek text and the Latin Vulgate side by side. Various indices and study aids, including Hebrew and Aramaic dictionaries, and a Hebrew grammar, were also provided, along with interpretations of Greek, Aramaic, and Hebrew names.

Luther, of course, would publish his German translation of the New Testament in 1522; Lefèvre d'Etaples, a French translation of the New Testament in 1523; Luther a complete German Bible in 1534; and Pierre-Robert Olivetan, a complete French translation of the whole Bible from the original languages in 1535. Meanwhile, in 1528, Sanctus Pagninus had published the first complete Latin Bible since St. Jerome. Critical editions of the Vulgate and the Greek New Testament would also be prepared by the French scholar Robert Estienne at Paris in 1528 and 1550 respectively. Other important works that lay over the horizon were Sebastian Munster's Latin translation of the Hebrew Bible, with a critical edition of the text, published in 1534–35; Leo Juda's Latin Bible of 1543; the Latin translation of the Old and New Testaments by John Immanuel Tremellius, which appeared in 1579; and the Antwerp Polyglot, edited by Arias Montanus, which appeared in 1584.

Bible editions and translations, in fact, dominated sixteenth-century book production, and by the end of the century every European nation would have the Scriptures in its own tongue. The book-reading public became increasingly a lay public, and the form of the vernacular languages was to some degree fixed by such works as they appeared.

∽

If printing was allied to the revival of learning, it also proved to be the handmaid of the Reformation—indeed, the two were sometimes viewed as aspects of a single phenomenon.

In the beginning the Church had welcomed the new technology. The first complete book to be typeset, after all, had been the Gutenberg Latin Bible of 1455 at Mainz, and at the time the local archbishop had proclaimed printing "a divine art." That attitude changed, however, when printing began to disseminate ideas associated with reform. In 1491, the papal legate at Venice drew up a legal code under which no work on a religious subject could be issued without approval of the local diocese; in 1515, Pope Leo X made this prohibition universal throughout the Catholic West.

Scarcely anyone paid heed. Just two years later Martin Luther nailed his Ninety-five Theses to the doors of a Wittenberg church, and in a short time the text had been printed and made available throughout Central Europe in a variety of tongues. "It almost appeared as if the angels themselves had been their messengers and brought them before the eyes of all the people," rejoiced one contemporary chronicler. And Luther himself wrote with some embarrassment to the pope: "It is a mystery to me how my theses . . . were spread to so many places. They were meant exclusively for our academic circle here [and written] in such a language [Latin] that the common people could hardly understand." Printing had changed all that, providing the means by which an obscure theologian could shake St. Peter's throne.

As his rift with the Vatican grew, Luther soon came to embrace the new technology as "God's highest and extremest act of grace" by which the Gospel was "driven forward"; or as John Foxe would later put it in his *Book of Martyrs:* "God hath opened the press to preach, whose voice the pope is unable to stop with all the puissance of his triple crown."

◌

Without benefit of the press, Tyndale would never have achieved the prominence he did. But in the beginning, at least, as a budding reformer, he took Erasmus, not Luther, as his guide. Erasmus had been an early critic of ecclesiastical corruption, and it was sometimes said in fact that Erasmus had "laid the egg" that Luther "hatched." (Erasmus afterward objected: "I laid a hen's egg. Luther hatched a different bird.") In *The Praise of Folly* (1509), Erasmus had ridiculed clerical hypocrisy and elsewhere complained that many churchmen were completely illiterate and could not even read the Bible, whether in Latin, Hebrew, or Greek. He also came down hard on pompous scholastics—"owls and bats," Sir Thomas

More called them—who still governed biblical studies in the schools. "Unsurpassed in the murkiness of their brains," wrote Erasmus, they were also

> incomparable in the stupidity of their natures, the thorniness of their doctrine, and the blackness of their hearts . . . They will explain the precise manner of original sin being derived from our original parents; they will satisfy you in what manner, by what degrees, and in how long a time, our Savior was conceived in the Virgin's womb, demonstrate in the consecrated wafer how accidents may subsist without a subject . . . and a thousand other more sublimated and refined niceties of notions, relations, quantities, formalities, quiddities, haeccities, and such like abstrusities as one would think no one could pry into, except he had such cat's eyes as to see best in the dark.

A strong advocate of Bible translations, Erasmus rejected the idea that "the safety of the Christian religion" lay in ignorance of the text. The evangelists themselves, he pointed out, had translated into Greek what Christ Himself had spoken in Aramaic (or Eastern Syriac)—a point that Wycliffe, of course, had made before. But the scholarly edition of the Greek New Testament which Erasmus prepared in 1516 opened up a general discussion of the faith with consequences far beyond the halls of academe.

☙

The Church had survived many crises since its foundation, including early persecution by the Romans, barbarian invasions, sundry heresies (Arian, Pelagian, Manichaean, and Waldensian, to name just four), the struggle over lay investiture, the split between the Greek Orthodox and Latin Churches East and West, the Babylonian Captivity, and the Great Schism. But the challenge of the Reformation was the most lethal of all. When it was over, "half of Europe was lost to the Roman obedience, and the spiritual unity of Christ's seamless cloak had been shredded by revolt." As a state within a state, the Church had acquired a sickness unto death. All the familiar abuses against which Wycliffe and others had protested, such as clerical immorality and the sale of Church offices, remained. The conciliar reform movement since Constance had languished; the Frenchified popes of Avignon had merely been replaced by Italianized popes in Rome; and by Tyndale's day, the pope, as one writer put it, was hard put to show that he was "not simply a petty Italian potentate motivated by family ambition and political aggrandizement." Reform might have taken a number of paths, had a saintly pontiff assumed direction of the impulse, or a general council enacted the cleansing legislation that almost everyone seemed to recognize was overdue. But a kind of institutional lethargy held the Church in thrall.

∞

While still at Magdalen, Tyndale had been drawn to Protestant ideas and, we are told, had secretly tutored "certain students and fellows" of the college in "some parcel of divinity, instructing them in the knowledge of truth." About 1521, he was ordained to the priesthood, but forsaking an advanced divinity degree became chaplain and domestic tutor to the household of Sir John Walsh in Little Sodbury, at the edge of the Cotswold Hills. There he used to preach "in the common place called Saint Austen's Green" (in front of the church), and his reform ideas stirred up some of the local authorities. From time to time, "divers great-beneficed men" also came to the manor as guests and Tyndale, it seems, could not forbear to engage them in debate. After they had been regularly bested by him in argument—usually by his exact citation of some scriptural texts—they "waxed weary and bore a secret grudge against him in their hearts." Meanwhile, Tyndale had been studying the New Testament edition of Erasmus, where in the Preface he read:

> Let [the student] approach the text . . . with *reverence;* bearing in mind that his first and only aim and object should be that he may catch and be changed into the spirit of what he there learns. It is the food of the soul; and to be of use, must not rest only in the memory or lodge in the stomach, but must permeate the very depths of the heart and mind. . . . A fair knowledge of the three languages, Latin, Greek,

and Hebrew, of course, are the first things. . . . It would be well, too, were the student tolerably versed in other branches of learning . . . and especially in knowledge of the natural objects—animals, trees, precious stones—and of the countries mentioned.

Tyndale took all this to heart, and also translated the *Enchiridion Militis Christiani* (*The Christian Soldier's Handbook*) of Erasmus into English, which insisted on the New Testament as the test of doctrinal truth. The Walshes also read it, became converts to Tyndale's views, and ceased to entertain the local clergy at their home.

The clergy were an ignorant lot. When the Bishop of Gloucester later surveyed 311 deacons, archdeacons, and priests of the diocese, he discovered that 168 were unable to repeat the Ten Commandments, thirty-one didn't know where those Commandments came from, forty could not repeat the Lord's Prayer, and forty couldn't say who the author of the Prayer was! One day Tyndale had an encounter with a priest who was so exasperated by his insistence on scriptural authority that he exclaimed: "We were better without God's law than the Pope's." Tyndale replied, rashly: "I defy the Pope and all his laws, and if God spare my life, ere many years I will cause a boy that driveth the plough shall know more of the Scriptures than thou doest." His outspoken views led to accusations of heresy, and he was brought before the vicar-general of the diocese and sternly rebuked. "He threatened me grievously," Tyndale later recalled, "and reviled me, and rated me as though I had been a dog." But by then he knew what his life's work was going to be. For "I perceived," he wrote, "that it was impossible to establish the lay-people in any truth, except the Scripture were plainly laid before their eyes in their mother tongue, that they might see the process, order, and meaning of the text." To lay it plainly before them is what he meant to do.

With letters of introduction to men of influence in the capital, Tyndale left his country livelihood behind and in London sought out Cuthbert Tunstall, Bishop of London, whose love of learning both More and Erasmus had commended, and whom he hoped to enlist as a patron for his aim. At length with the help of Sir Henry Guilford, the king's Master of the Horse, an appointment was arranged, and as evidence of his linguistic skill Tyndale brought with him an oration of Isocrates, which he had translated from the Greek. But the interview did not go well. Tyndale was evidently tongue-tied and awkward, and Tunstall received him coldly, like "a still Saturn," impatiently heard out his petition, then told him that his "house was full" and suggested he seek elsewhere for support.

He was not likely to find it. The satirical, refined critique of the Church that Erasmus, Sir Thomas More, and even Tunstall himself had indulged in had been superseded by Luther's rhetorical blasts, and the idea of a vernacular version of the Scriptures was now tainted by association with Luther's rebellious ire. In short, Tyndale's timing could not have been worse. It was the fall of 1523, in the reign of Henry VIII, and anything smacking of Lutheran tendencies made official blood boil. Henry himself was still an ardent supporter of the pope, and when the Reformation began he had stood four square behind St. Peter's throne. Even Christian Humanists were divided about the movement, and those in government service like More and Tunstall (Lord Keeper of the Privy Seal as well as a bishop) were bound to reflect the disposition of their king. Henry and Luther had recently exchanged verbal insults, and Henry hated Luther more than any man on earth.

Curiously enough, Henry had actually been marked out by his father for the Church. But after his older brother, Arthur (schooled for the throne) died prematurely, Henry had married his widow (Catherine of Aragon) in an ill-fated match, and instead of an archbishop he became a king. In early manhood, he was accounted the most dashing prince of his time. Tall, handsome, and accomplished in all the arts of peace and war, he seemed to exude both majesty and virtue, and in the beginnning, at least, his ebullient nature seemed tempered by restraint. But a certain aggressive ambition soon made itself known, and just three years after becoming king, Henry invaded France, proved his martial prowess at the "Battle of Spurs," and secured for England a triumphant peace. The Scots thought to take advantage of his absence and invaded England from the north, but were decisively beaten by the king's surrogates at Flodden Field.

Over time, as Henry's manifold appetites increased, he relied ever more on his chief adviser, Thomas Wolsey, who had begun his rise to power in the previous reign. The precocious son of an Ipswich butcher, Wolsey had earned his B.A. from Magdalen College, Oxford, at age fifteen—"a rare thing and seldom seen"—became a fellow of the college, junior then senior bursar, was ordained a priest, and soon attracted noble patrons before entering the service of John Morton, then head of the English Church. Upon Morton's death, he became dean of Lincoln Cathedral and chaplain to the king. Henry soon recognized his energy and abilities and gave them larger scope. After Wolsey organized the expedition that humbled the French, Henry made him successively Bishop of Lincoln, Archbishop of York, and in 1515 Cardinal (by papal appointment) and Lord Chancellor of England. For the next fourteen years he firmly and adroitly held the reins of power in his hands.

If Tunstall was a worldly prelate, Wolsey was a man of the world, and the London of his indulgence was rich in the physical grandeur, commerce, and politics that were his life.

> *Strong be the walls that above thee stand;*
> *Wise be the people that within thee dwells;*
> *Fresh be thy river with his lusty strands;*
> *Blythe be thy churches, well sounding be thy bells;*
> *Rich be thy merchants in substance that excels;*
> *Fair be thy wives, right lovesome, white and small;*
> *Clear be thy virgins, lusty under kellis [gowns];*
> *London, thou art the flower of cities all.*

Wolsey was an immensely covetous prelate, had a mistress or two, and by his own ecclesiastical abuses and inflated pomp contributed to the anticlerical reaction that was a factor in the English Reformation. He acquired one benefice after another, including St. Alban's Abbey, England's oldest and richest religious house, built mansions and palaces (including Hampton Court) on a royal scale, and in general used his vast secular and ecclesiastical power to amass a wealth second only to the king's. Indeed, men talked of him as if he were more powerful than the king himself. "Exceeding wise, fair-spoken, and persuading:/Lofty and sour to them that lov'd him not,/But, to those men that sought him, sweet as summer"—so Shakespeare described him fairly in his drama *Henry VIII.*

In 1522, Wolsey had even stood for Pope. Meanwhile, in the summer of 1520, Luther had written *The Babylonian Captivity of the Church,* which attacked transubstantiation and other doctrines, and rejected four of the seven Sacraments as inauthentic, sanctioning as scripturally based only baptism, penance (or private confession), and the Mass. By penance, Luther meant a confession of sin that one Christian could make to any other, which dispensed with the mediating role of the priest. On June 15, Rome condemned forty-one of Luther's propositions as heretical, and the following April he appeared before the Diet of Worms, where he refused to recant and was pronounced a heretic by the Emperor Charles V.

Henry fully concurred in the verdict, and attacked Luther in a learned and polemical work of his own in which, with numerous quotations from Church fathers, he defended the divine institution of all seven Sacraments, affirmed the authority of Tradition over Scripture, and declared that the Church could not err, since Christ had promised to be with her until the end of time. "I will put myself in the forefront to save her," wrote Henry. "I will receive into my bosom all the poisoned darts of her foe." He called Luther a "limb of the devil," urged "all the servants of Jesus Christ, whatever be their age, sex or rank," to rise up against him as "the common enemy of Christendom," and emphasized the divine authority of the pope so much that even Sir Thomas More ventured to question the wisdom of elaborating such a tender point. Henry, however, remained unmoved. "His Highness," recalled More, "answered me that he would in no wise anything [di]minish of that matter."

Although Henry's polemic may have been animated by pious ardor, there was also something opportunistic in his rush to get it out. He had long sought some special religious title from the pope, comparable to the "Most Christian King" awarded the King of France or a similar honorific granted the King of Spain. Now he was sure his time had come. And he was right. In the fall of 1521, when Henry's ambassador to Rome presented the pope with a handsome copy of Henry's tract, the pope declared that the king's book was filled with the Holy Spirit and promptly conferred upon him the title of "Defender of the Faith." Wolsey was ecstatic, and wrote to Henry at Greenwich: "High and victorious king, it hath pleased our Lord God to indue [endow] your Grace with a multitude of manifold graces, as a king elect in favor of the high Heaven, and so appeareth presently by your noble person, so formed and figured in shape and stature, with force and pulchritude, which signifieth the present pleasure of our Lord God wrought in your noble grace."

Luther, less impressed, responded to Henry's tract with a vitriolic rebuttal in which he denigrated the king's intelligence and called him, among other things, "a swine of hell." Thomas More leapt to defend his monarch and in his *Response Against Luther,* defended the visible Church as the one true Church, upheld the authority of Tradition, and rightly pointed out that Tradition had determined what the scriptural canon was. But then he wrote: "Since he [Luther] has written that he already has a prior right to bespatter and besmirch the royal crown with shit will we not have the posterior right to proclaim the beshitted tongue on this practitioner of posterioristics most fit to lick with his anterior the very posterior of a pissing she-mule." Much similar language sullied the entire tract.

John Fisher, the Bishop of Rochester, also weighed in, but with more restraint. "Take us the little foxes that spoil the vines, says Christ in Solomon's Song; from this we learn that we ought to lay hands upon heretics, before they grow big. Luther is become a large fox, so old, so cunning, so mischievous, that it is very difficult to catch him. What do I say, a fox? He is a mad dog, a ravening wolf, a cruel she-bear; or rather, all these put together, for the monster includes many beasts within himself."

While More and Fisher were busy with their pens, Henry was out for blood. In June 1522, he dispatched a letter to the elector and the dukes of Saxony that called for a crusade. "Luther, the true serpent cast down from heaven," wrote Henry,

> casts out a flood of poison upon the earth. He excites revolt
> in the Church of Jesus Christ, he abolishes its laws, insults
> the authorities, inflames the laity against the priesthood,

both of these against the Pope, the people against kings, and likes nothing better than to see Christians fighting against and destroying one another, and the enemies of our faith enjoying, with a savage grin, the scene of carnage.

What is this doctrine, which he calls evangelical, other than the doctrine of Wycliffe? Now, most honored uncles, I know how your ancestors have labored to destroy it; they pursued it, as a wild beast, in Bohemia, and driving it, till it fell into a pit, they shut it in there, and barricaded it. You will not, I am sure, let it escape through your negligence, lest, making its way into Saxony, it should become master of the whole of Germany, and, with smoking nostrils, vomit forth the fire of hell and spread that conflagration far and wide, which your nation has so often wished to extinguish in its blood.

Therefore it is, most worthy lords, I feel obliged to exhort you, and even to beseech you, by all that is most sacred, promptly to extinguish the cursed sect of Luther. Shed no blood, if it can be avoided; but if this heretical doctrine lasts, shed it without hesitation, in order that this abominable sect may disappear.

Henry's exhortations were quickly publicized but coming as they did from such a mighty monarch, served only to stir up sympathy for the still lowly Luther, as yet but a combative monk. "So renowned a name as Henry mixed up in the dispute," noted Paolo Sarpi, a contemporary theologian, "serves only to give it greater zest, and to conciliate general favor towards Luther, as is usually the case in combats and tournaments, where the spectators tend to lean to the weakest, and like to exaggerate the merits of his actions." The Church had similarly erred when it supposed that its condemnation of Luther at the Diet of Worms would nip the Reformation in the bud. Instead, revolt was breaking out on all sides throughout the Holy Roman Empire. Hamlets, villages, towns, and even large cities joined in the new confession, while monks and nuns in the thousands abandoned their cloisters to propagate the new doctrine in every part of the Western Church.

As yet, the situation in England was under better control. Henry had promised the pope to burn any "untrue translations" (having the Wycliffe Scriptures in mind) and had set his lord chancellor, Cardinal Wolsey, to hunting down heretical books that were then pouring into the kingdom from overseas. On the 12th of May, 1521, Wolsey repaired in solemn procession to St. Paul's Cathedral to see his harvest burned. His garments glittered with gold and silk brocade, and three retainers carried his archepiscopal crozier, silver cross, and cardinal's hat. Others joined the cavalcade, followed by a long line of mules bearing chests full of Lutheran writings. Bishop Fisher preached a fierce sermon before the bonfires were lit—but how much more vehement his words would have been had he known what the future harvest held in store.

∽

As long as the Constitutions of Oxford remained in force, Tyndale could not carry out his purpose anywhere in England, and after he spent a year in London in vain efforts to secure a station favorable to his design, he realized that he would have to abandon it entirely, or seek his fate abroad. But if he lacked the episcopal license he sought, he was not without the moral and material support of those of like mind. For a time he found employment as a preacher at St. Dunstan's-in-the-West, and was given free lodging in the home of Humphrey Monmouth, a man of local prominence, who later recalled: "I took him into my house half a year; and there he lived like a good priest as methought. He studied most part of the day and night at his book; would eat but sodden meat by his good will, and drink nothing but small single beer. I never saw him wear linen [fancy clothes]." The book that engaged Tyndale's whole attention was the Greek New Testament, which he had recently begun to translate into English prose. Although Monmouth later claimed (under interrogation) that he and Tyndale had met by chance, that seems unlikely, on a number of counts.

To begin with, Monmouth belonged to a semisecret society of Merchant Adventurers known as the Christian Brethren, an association of rich cloth merchants (with international Lutheran connections) who traded in forbidden religious literature, subsidized the printing of evangelical books in English abroad, and smuggled them into the country. The Christian Brethren ultimately financed Tyndale's work (among other projects), and were a caste which even the most powerful authorities dared not suppress.

That caste was built on wool. For centuries, English wool, the best in Europe, had supplied Flemish and Italian looms. Eventually, much of it was also worked into cloth in England, and carried to the Continent in English ships. In Wycliffe's day, King Edward's French wars had been fought in part to support the trade, and "during the life-time of Chaucer," Trevelyan tells us, "the production of broadcloth in England trebled, and the export of broadcloth increased ninefold. The enormous advantage that England had over other countries as a feeder of sheep and a producer of the best wool gave her the opportunity gradually to win the command of the world's cloth market, as she had long commanded the European market for raw wool."

Weaving colonies sprang up all over England, in both village and town, till "there was hardly a cottage which did not hum with the spinning wheel, and hardly a street where you might not have counted weavers' shops." Indeed, the whole contemporary controversy over enclosure (to which histories of England devote so much space) arose from the cloth industry's needs. By the early 1500s the manufacture of woolen cloth had become the staple of the English economy, and its many stages of production—which involved sheep farmers, weavers, fullers, tuckers, shearmen, dyers, and so on—dominated town and country alike. English literature and speech were deeply colored by its lingo—"dyed in the wool," "thread of discourse," "spin a yarn," "unravel a mystery," "web of life," "fine-drawn," "homespun," "tease"—while unmarried women were dubbed "spinsters." The growth of the cloth trade, its increasing concentration along the London–Antwerp axis, and the nascent overseas monopoly which the Merchant Adventurers enjoyed, affected almost every aspect of English life.

Tyndale's first patron, Sir John Walsh, had (like Monmouth) made a fortune in the trade, and had built a chapel dedicated to St. Adeline, the patron saint of weavers, behind his house. Monmouth himself had done business with Tyndale's family (Tyndale's brother,

Edward, was said to be the most powerful man in the Vale, where cloth-working "supported half the population"), and despite the survival of the Wycliffite translations, there was a hunger among the Christian Brethren to see the Bible Englished anew. In Tyndale, they put their money on the right man. He was by all accounts perfectly equipped for his task—"so skillful in seven tongues," it was said (Hebrew, Greek, Latin, Italian, Spanish, English, and French) "that whichever he speaks, you would think it his native tongue!"

☙

In May of 1524, Tyndale sailed for Hamburg, never to see his native land again. From Hamburg, he made his way to Wittenberg, where he evidently became acquainted with Luther, conferred with Philipp Melanchthon (who taught Greek at the university there), and surrounded himself with Greek and Hebrew texts. By the following spring, his translation of the Greek New Testament was done, and in April 1525 he settled with his amanuensis, a lapsed friar by the name of William Roye, in Cologne to arrange for its publication. Cologne was something of a haven for reformers, but it was not (like Wittenberg or Worms) a safely Lutheran city, and Catholic zealots flourished in its midst. One of them was Johann Dobneck, known also as John Cochlaeus, who soon did everything he could to frustrate Tyndale's plans.

Dobneck had earned his doctorate in theology at Ferrara and had been dean of St. Mary's at Frankfurt-on-the-Main until driven by reformers from that post. He later held canonries successively in Mainz, Meissen, Erfurt, and Breslau. Cochlaeus was an unwanted nickname (from the Latin *cochlaea,* meaning "snail"), but it stuck and, as he put it, sadly, "I do not like my name but I do not see how I can change it." Some of the other epithets he inspired were worse. William Roye, for one, called him: "A little praty foolish poad/More venomous than any toad," and derision of some sort seemed always to come his way. With peculiar self-importance, he styled himself "the scourge of Luther," and was a vociferous and belligerent pamphleteer. But eventually "his indiscretion aroused distrust" even among Catholics and after his death many of his writings were proscribed.

98

At about the time Tyndale disembarked at Cologne, Dobneck was engaged in editing for publication the works of Rupert of Deutz, a medieval abbot. While he was going over the proofs at the printing house run by Peter Quentel, he heard some of the workers boast confidently over a drink that, "whether the King and Cardinal of England would or no, the whole of England would soon be Lutheran." He managed to wheedle out of them (with the help of a good dinner and some wine) details of the project—the publication of Tyndale's text and its secret shipment to England—and that it was being financed by the English merchant community abroad.

Tyndale had arranged for six thousand copies of his New Testament to be printed—in a small quarto edition with a prologue, references, and marginal notes. Dobneck persuaded the city authorities to interdict it, but Tyndale was tipped off about the raid in advance and with Roye escaped with some of the printed sheets by boat up the Rhine to Worms. There the complete work was reprinted by Peter Schoeffer in both octavo and quarto format, with a short appended "Address to the Reader" and marginal notes. Early in 1526, copies of both, concealed in cases of dry goods, began to make their way in vessels toward the English coast.

Henry VIII and Wolsey were alerted about the contraband shipment and a watch was placed for it at all English ports. Edward Lee, the King's almoner and afterward Archbishop of York, wrote to Henry from Bordeaux in December 1525 that the feared testaments were to be expected in a matter of days. Dobneck also sent word, and the king and Wolsey thanked him, but failed otherwise to reward him in the way he had hoped. Later he complained bitterly that he had been left "like Mordecai at the gate." Henry's lack of generosity, however, bore no relation to the horror with which he regarded the books coming in. Tyndale's translation was associated in the minds of the English authorities with heresy and schism that might well bring anarchy and civil disorder in their wake. For once received authority was questioned, where would it end? That was the anxious question on Henry's mind.

Recent history had sharpened it to a point. In 1524–25, peasants in central and southern Germany, incited by radical evangelists, had risen in revolt against their lords and in a reprise of the great revolt of Wycliffe's time torrents of blood had been shed. By the time the carnage was over, some fifty thousand people had been slain.

Political ferment had long been working in the empire. The peasantry felt itself crushed beneath the weight of taxes and tithes, and had recently found captains for its violent yearnings in disbanded soldiers and bankrupt knights. Wandering radical preachers freighted their sermons with apocalyptic warnings and (in the spirit of John Ball) there was a widespread demand for the abolition of property rights. Central Europe had recently been plagued by a series of uprisings, and since social justice and Church reform were often linked, Luther was justifiably afraid that any bloody turmoil would tend to discredit his cause. During the Diet of Worms, he had preemptively warned: "Rebellion never obtains for us the benefits we seek, and God condemns it. What is rebellion? Is it not to revenge oneself? The devil tries to incite to disobedience those who embrace the Gospel, that it may be covered with reproach." But as the unrest increased, the new religious movement was drawn into its swelling tide. The vehemence of Luther's own writings had doubtless helped to inflame the situation, and a number of moderates who had originally supported reform drew back. In 1523, for example, Erasmus had said: "I seem to myself to teach almost the same things as Luther, only without sedition and violence." By 1525 he was anxious to disclaim any connection whatsoever between them and told Luther bluntly: "Now we are gathering the fruits of what you have taught."

The insurrection began in July 1524 in the Black Forest districts near the headwaters of the Danube and spread to the Rhenish provinces of Franconia, Thuringia, and Saxony. By January 1525 the entire area was in open revolt. The insurgents published a manifesto in twelve articles, studded with biblical quotation, in which they proclaimed an end to servitude, tithes, and inheritance taxes, and concluded with the words, "If we are wrong let Luther set us right." Whether Luther liked it or not, he was now exposed to the coming storm. At first he straddled the fence and accused the Church authorities of having provoked the turmoil by their tithes. At the same time, he urged the peasants to remember that it was "not the Christian way to battle with swords or muskets, but by endurance and the cross."

The people were deaf to his words. At Weinsberg they impaled the Count of Helfenstein "to the sound of pipes" in the presence of his wife and child, then killed his retainers; elsewhere, they broke open granaries, emptied cellars, drew fish ponds, demolished castles, set fire to convents, and swore to make "every man who wore a spur" bite the dust. In the various towns they entered or took, they desecrated Church images and monuments and stripped sanctuaries of their wealth. Swabia, Franconia, Spires, the Palatinate, Alsace, Hesse were engulfed in vandalism and carnage, while Bavaria, Westphalia, the Tyrol, Saxony, and Lorraine were threatened in their turn. Metz, Treves, Frankfurt, and other towns were spared only by acceding to rebel demands. Throughout the empire revolution was in full career. In the wake of reported atrocities, Luther's tone changed and in a strident four-page pamphlet entitled *Against the Murdering Thieving Hordes of Peasants,* he urged princes to draw their swords and "stab, smite, and slay all you can."

Among the insurgents fanatical leaders emerged. Some not only rejected the authority of the Church, but of Scripture too, and began to speak of an inward Word—a special revelation from God. "May God, in His mercy," exclaimed Luther, "preserve me from a Church in which there are only such saints."

The most noted of these enthusiasts was Thomas Munzer, a former Lutheran turned Anabaptist and pastor of the small town of Alstadt in Thuringia, whose exhortations were laced with apocalyptic predictions of divine intervention on the side of the oppressed. Claiming that God spoke directly to him as He had to Abraham, Isaac, and Jacob of old, he exhorted his Saxon army to "exterminate with the sword, like Joshua, the Canaanitish nations," and signed his communiqués "Munzer, God's Servant Against the Ungodly," or "Munzer, Armed with the Sword of Gideon." Stoberg, Schwarzberg, Hesse, and Brunswick were among the districts to answer his call.

For a brief spell the rebels had their way. Then the nobility, recovering from their first shock, struck back with seasoned troops. Under George Truchsess, a proven general, they advanced toward

Lake Constance, defeated a peasant contingent at Belingen, marched on to Weinsberg, and after effecting a junction with the electors of Palatine and Treves at Fürfeld, raced toward the citadel of Würzberg, to which a peasant army was laying siege. As the peasants tried to clamber up its walls, they were met by showers of sulfur and boiling pitch. Hand-to-hand combat continued into the night, before the assailants fell back and turned their frustrated fury on the advancing imperial troops. But their fury was no match for the heavy cavalry arrayed against them, which charged and slashed with impunity through their ranks.

In a second campaign, Phillip, the young Landgrave of Hesse, linked up with the Duke of Brunswick and their combined forces advanced toward Saxony, where Munzer's peasants took up positions on a hill behind a makeshift barricade. In his best pulpit style, Munzer assured his forces, equipped mostly with farm implements and knives, that "the mighty arm of God" would intervene on their behalf—and as he said so a rainbow appeared in the clouds. The fanatic multitude beheld it as a sure omen of divine protection, prompting Munzer to boast: "Never fear, my children. I will receive all their cannonballs in my sleeve." Then he killed an imperial envoy sent to negotiate so that all would know there could be no hope of pardon even if they gave themselves up. For his part, the landgrave told his troops: "I well know that we princes are often to blame for injustice—we are but men; but it is God's will that the powers that be should be respected. The Lord will make us victorious, for hath He not said. 'He that resisteth the power, resisteth the ordinance of God?' "

As Phillip's army moved forward, Munzer's peasants began to sing in slowly swelling, hymnlike strains, "Come, Holy Spirit," fully expecting battling angels to descend from on high. But artillery at once opened a breach in their rude fortress and scattered death and confusion in their midst. In an instant, their resolution gave way to panic, panic to despair. They tried to flee, but there was nowhere to run to; by the end of the day five thousand had been caught and slain. Munzer himself was afterward discovered cowering in the loft of a house in Frankenhau and executed after a brief trial. What remained of the rebellion was quenched in blood.

In England, Sir Thomas More, reflecting on recent events, predicted that if the break-up of the Church continued, only widening circles of disorder could ensue. Princes, he said, would naturally take advantage of the discord and take Church property for their own aggrandizement; then, by example, the people would seek to overthrow their princes and "strip them of whatever they possessed." Finally, individuals would turn on each other and "run each other through."

More's fears were widely shared. Sir Thomas Elyot in *The Governor,* a notable work of political theory published in 1531, wrote: "How far out of reason shall we judge them to be that would exterminate all superiority, extinguish all governance and laws, and under the colors of Holy Scripture, which they do violently wrest to their purpose, endeavor themselves to bring the life of man into confusion, and much worse than beasts?" In fact, in time the struggles of Charles V with a Protestant league of princes would end in a divided Germany, England would be split into two armed camps, and the Thirty Years' War (1618-48) would ultimately lead to the disintegration of the Holy Roman Empire.

∽

But all that was beyond what anyone could know. Nor, if they had known it, would all have cared. For the hunger for an English Bible had grown, and even the prospect of discord was not likely to check that yearning, with such a feast at hand. This was especially so in London and the western counties, where the successors of the old Lollards were strong. They had long treasured manuscript copies of the Wycliffe Scriptures, and so when Tyndale's work reached England in the spring of 1526, they adopted it at once as their own. The truth is, had it not seemed to come before the authorities as part of the Lutheran movement, they, too, might have received it more thoughtfully than they did.

Unfortunately, there was reason enough to suspect it. It was known that Tyndale had consorted with Luther, and it was clear to anyone placing their two translations side by side that they were more than kin. Tyndale, for example, had not only lifted some phrases from Luther's German, but had adopted his format as a whole—including his chapter divisions, order of the books, and most of his ancillary apparatus—"certain prefaces, and other pestilent glosses," as Henry VIII put it, "for the advancement and setting forth of his abominable heresies." The translation, however, was Tyndale's own. In addition to Luther's German, he had before him as he worked the two editions of the New Testament published by Erasmus (in 1516 and 1522); Erasmus's own Latin translation of the Greek text; and the Vulgate. He took something of value (usually what was best) from each, but the Greek remained his ultimate guide. In his own Preface, he swore on his conscience that he had translated the text as "faithfully" as he could, with a "pure intent . . . as far forth as God gave me the gift of knowledge, and understanding," and expressed the hope that "the rudeness of the work" would not offend those learned in the Scriptures, who he hoped would "consider how that I had no man to counterfeit, neither was help with English of any that had interpreted the same, or such like thing in the Scripture before time."

Tyndale did not mean by this (as some have supposed) that he was unfamiliar with the Wycliffe versions or declined to make use of them: moving in the circles that he did, and having been "addicted to the study of Scripture" from an early age, he had to have known them well. What he meant, as one scholar noted, was that he could not "counterfeit" (i.e., follow their general plan, as being a rendering from the Vulgate Latin only) or adopt their language, which had already become archaic and unfamiliar by his day. Even so, rhythms and turns of phrase from the Wycliffe versions found occasional echoes in his text. In his three-page Epilogue, Tyndale also appealed to the reader not to judge his pioneering work too harshly. "Count it as a thing not having his full shape . . . even as a thing begun rather then finished," and he promised greater concision in the future—"to bring to compendiousness that which is now translated at the length." In fact, he would revise his translation three times with impeccable care.

It would be hard to overpraise the literary merits of what he had done. Much of his rendering would later be incorporated into the Authorized or King James Version, and the rhythmical beauty of his prose, skillful use of synonyms for freshness, variety, and point, and "magical simplicity of phrase" imposed itself on all later versions, down to the present day. Ultimately his diction became "the consecrated dialect of English speech."

Here is Tyndale's translation of the Beatitudes (Matthew 5:1–16), familiar to every English ear:

> When he saw the people, he went up into a mountain, and when he was set, his disciples came to him, and he opened his mouth, and taught them saying: Blessed are the poor in spirit: for theirs is the kingdom of heaven. Blessed are they that mourn: for they shall be comforted. Blessed are the meek: for they shall inherit the earth. Blessed are they which hunger and thirst for righteousness: for they shall be filled. Blessed are the merciful: for they shall obtain mercy. Blessed are the pure in heart: for they shall see God. Blessed are the peacemakers: for they shall be called the children of God. Blessed are they which suffer persecution for righteousness' sake: for theirs is the kingdom of heaven. Blessed are ye when men revile you, and persecute you, and shall falsely say all manner of evil sayings against you for my sake. Rejoice, and be glad, for great is your reward in heaven. For so persecuted they the prophets which were before your days.
>
> Ye are the salt of the earth: but and if the salt have lost her saltness, what can be salted therewith? It is thenceforth good for nothing, but to be cast out, and to be trodden under foot of men. Ye are the light of the world. A city that is set on an hill, cannot be hid, neither do men light a candle and put it under a bushel, but on a candlestick, and it lighteth all that are in the house. Let your light so shine before men, that they may see your good works, and glorify your father which is in heaven.

And here is Tyndale's opening to the Gospel of St. John:

> In the beginning was the word, and the word was with God: and the word was God. All things were made by it, and

without it, was made nothing, that was made. In it was life, and the life was the light of men, and the light shineth in the darkness, but the darkness comprehended it not.

The translation was a tour de force. Nothing like it, in fact, had been seen since the Bible had been translated into the elegant, classical Latin of St. Jerome. But the authorities were blind to its virtues. Bishop Tunstall declared that he could find two thousand errors in it, and soon "dreadful and penal" statutes made it a serious crime for anyone to own, sell, or otherwise distribute a copy of the work. Merchant ships were boarded and searched to prevent its importation; the London's German Steelyard was raided and scoured for stock; and not long after the first copies reached London, Wolsey sponsored a second bonfire of all heretical books under the great crucifix known as the Rood of Northen before the gate of St. Paul's.

But the books kept coming, and on the 24th of October 1526, Tunstall issued the following decree:

> By the duty of our pastoral office we are bound dili-
> gently, with all our power, to foresee, provide for, root out,
> and put away, all those things which seem to tend to the
> peril and danger of our subjects, and specially the destruc-
> tion of their souls! Wherefore, we having understanding, by
> the report of divers credible persons, and also by the evi-
> dent appearance of the matter, that many children of iniq-
> uity, maintainers of Luther's sect, blinded through extreme
> wickedness, wandering from the way of truth and the
> Catholic faith, craftily have translated the New Testament
> into our English tongue, intermingling therewith many
> heretical articles and erroneous opinions, pernicious and of-
> fensive, seducing the simple people, attempting by their
> wicked and perverse interpretations to profanate the
> majesty of Scripture, which hitherto hath remained unde-
> filed, and craftily to abuse the most Holy Word of God, and
> the true sense of the same; of the which translation there are
> many books imprinted, some with glosses, and some with-
> out; containing, in the English tongue, that pestiferous and

most pernicious poison, dispersed throughout all our diocese, in great number. . . . Wherefore we. . . . do charge
you, jointly and severally (the Archdeacons), and by virtue of
your obedience. . . . that within thirty days' space . . . they
do bring in, and really deliver unto our Vicar-General, all and
singular such books as contain the translation of the New
Testament in the English Tongue.

A few days later, the Archbishop of Canterbury issued a similar mandate, as more books were gathered up, carted to St. Paul's, and publicly cast into the fire. "No burnt offering," wrote the papal legate,
Lorenzo Campeggio, at the time, "could be better pleasing to God."

The alacrity with which Tyndale's work was disseminated
throughout England, however, was itself cause for alarm, because it
implied the existence of a formidable network of believers willing
to defy the decrees of both Church and state. The underground
book trade was also fed by a number of pirate editions rushed off
the press in Antwerp to meet demand. Between 1525 and 1528 at
least eighteen thousand copies of Tyndale's New Testament, in both
quarto and octavo editions, were printed, concealed in corn ships
and bales of merchandise, and brought into English ports. Many
were confiscated; but a substantial number still found their way
through clandestine cells of sympathetic reformers into more ap-
preciative hands.

Unable to prevent their circulation by force, the government
tried to stop their production overseas. Letters were dispatched to
officials in the Netherlands (including Princess Margaret, aunt of
the Holy Roman Emperor Charles V and regent of Brabant) to enlist
their cooperation; Tunstall, meanwhile, had decided to buy up
copies in large quantities on the Continent so as to destroy them before they were shipped. En route from an embassy with Sir Thomas
More to Cambray, he detoured to Antwerp, where he approached a
cloth merchant by the name of Augustus Packington, who was
thought to know the main sources of supply. Packington said he
could help him, and Tunstall promised to pay him handsomely for
every copy he could get. As it happened, Packington and Tyndale
were friends. So he went to Tyndale and told him, with amusement,

that he knew someone willing to take every unsold copy of his work off his hands. "Who?" said Tyndale. "The bishop of London," said Packington. "Oh, that is because he will burn them." "Yea," said Packington. "Well, I am the gladder," said Tyndale; "for these two benefits shall come thereof: I shall get money of him for these books, to bring myself out of debt, and the whole world shall cry out upon the burning of God's word." And so forward went the bargain—"the bishop had the books, Packington had the thanks, and Tyndale had the money." Tyndale (through Packington) even got Tunstall to buy up the standing type to prevent a reprint, and used the money to prepare a new and improved edition of his work—at Church expense.

About a year later, Sir Thomas More was interrogating one of Tyndale's confederates, George Constantine, and wanted to know where some of the English exiles got their financial support. He was so eager to ascertain this that he promised Constantine a virtual pardon in return for any tip. Constantine asked More if he was sure he wanted to know the truth. "Yea, I pray thee," said More. "Truly, then," said Constantine, "it is the bishop of London that hath holpen us; for he hath bestowed among us a great deal of money in New Testaments to burn them, and that hath been, and yet is, our only succour and comfort." "Now by my troth," exclaimed More, "I think even the same, and I said so much to the bishop, when he went about to buy them."

Even so, it was hard for Tyndale to see his work condemned. "They did none other thing than I looked for," he wrote in 1527, putting as brave a face on the matter as he could. "No more shall they do if they burn me also. If it be God's will it shall so be." In his own estimation, however, he was not a heretic but a reformer, and insisted that he had never written anything, "to stir up false doctrine or opinion in the Church, or to be the author of any sect, or to draw disciples after me, or that I would be esteemed above the least child that is born. But only out of pity and compassion which I had, and yet have, on the darkness of my brethren, and to bring them to the knowledge of Christ."

Of the original octavo edition of Tyndale's New Testament, only three copies remain; and of the quarto edition begun at Cologne and completed at Worms, only one fragment survives, consisting of thirty-one leaves with a prologue, a list of New Testament books, the text of Matthew to 22:12, and a woodcut of an angel holding an ink-stand into which the saint dips his pen.

Tunstall had become obsessed with calling Tyndale to account. Convinced that the spread of Lutheran ideas could not be arrested by official measures, he hoped the tide might be turned by engaging Tyndale in public debate. So he turned to his friend and intellectual idol, a man renowned throughout England and Europe for his wit, scholarship, and literary gift, "the English Demosthenes," Sir Thomas More. In March 1528, he gave More license to read all heretical writings in order to refute them, adding: "You cannot better bestow your leisure hours, if any you have, than in writing an English work, to show to simpleminded people 'the crafty malignity of these impious heretics.' . . . Go forward then to this holy work; succor the church, and win for yourself an immortal name, and eternal glory in heaven."

In some ways, More might have seemed an unlikely choice to stand as "Defender of the Faith." Born in 1478, he had studied classics at Oxford under William Grocyn and John Colet, was an intimate friend of Erasmus, a Humanist with broad sympathy for liberal learning, and had rejected a life in the Church for a public career. That career had been distinguished: as Master of Requests, chancellor of the Duchy of Lancaster, and speaker of the House of Commons—all lofty positions of public trust in which he won esteem for his sagacity and skill. But his authority was not just that of talent and station. His "unspotted domestic virtue, contempt for luxury and show, and his unimpeachable integrity in a time of extravagance and corruption" had given him a reputation for rectitude and candor that no other Englishman possessed. Moreover, as a proponent of Church reform, he had ridiculed scholastic theology and "its addiction to trivia"; had commended the most celebrated of contemporary satires on monastics, *The Praise of Folly,* by Erasmus (which had been written at More's home); had welcomed the publication of Erasmus's edition of the New Testament, which he had publicly defended against an attack by a theologian at the University of Louvain; and had demonstrated support of religious toleration in his own philosophical romance, *Utopia,* completed in 1516. Erasmus has left us a charming portrait of the More household as it was during his stay:

> More has built near London, upon the Thames, a modest yet commodious mansion. There he lives surrounded by his numerous family, including his wife, his son and his son's wife, his three daughters and their husbands, with eleven grandchildren. There is not any man living so affectionate as he, and he loveth his old wife as if she were a girl of fifteen. Such is the excellence of his disposition that, whatsoever happeneth that could not be helped, he is as cheerful and as well pleased as though the best thing possible had been done. In More's house you would say that Plato's Academy was revived again, only, whereas in the Academy discussion turned upon geometry and the power of numbers, the house at Chelsea is a veritable school of Christian religion. In it there is none, man or woman, but readeth or studieth the liberal arts, yet is their chief care of piety. There is never any seen idle, the head of the house governs it, not by a lofty carriage and oft rebukes, but by gentleness and amiable manners. Every member is busy in his place performing his duty with alacrity, nor is sober mirth wanting.

Despite his enraged attack on Luther—which Luther's intemperate attack on King Henry had provoked—nothing but "candor, justice, and enlightened generosity" could therefore be expected from him in the treatment of opponents, if the past was any judge. But during the eleven years that had elapsed since More's *Utopia* saw the light, such great changes had occurred in Europe as threatened to subvert the very foundations of the Christian world. The Peasants' War in Germany was just a part of the larger storm, and the Reformation which had begun to wash across Europe was unlike any cleansing of the Church he could condone. By encouraging a promiscuous freedom of thought, the new doctrines seemed to remove all former restraints. Tumult and insurrection had been the result; and he "would fain unsay the spell and exorcise the unruly elements back into their ancient peace."

More got right to work, labored (by his own account) night and day, and the following summer published his *Dialogue Concerning Heresies* in four books, in which he "treated divers matters, as of the veneration and worship of images and relics, praying to saints and going on pilgrimage, with many other things touching the pestilent sect of Luther and Tyndale, by the one begun in Saxony, and by the other labored to be brought into England." It was an authoritative statement of the position of the Church, and (at 170,000 words) a vast renunciation of the new ideas. In the course of it, he particularly attacked Tyndale's New Testament. Tyndale promptly replied, which brought forth from More in the following year an even larger work.

Both More and Tyndale, as one writer put it, were pious idealists—the one adhering to the authority of the Church, the other of Scripture. But they gave no quarter when they clashed. More had a horror of free speech as we know it, and objected to any interpretation of the Scriptures—even by "scholars of standing"—unless it proceeded under an episcopal license. Nothing appalled him more than the idea that the Bible might soon be available to all, to be disputed in taverns "for every lewd [ignorant] lad to keep a pot-parliament upon." But Erasmus, More's longtime friend, had said:

> I totally dissent from those who are unwilling that the sacred Scriptures, translated into the vulgar tongue, should be read by private individuals, as if Christ had taught such subtle doctrines that they can with difficulty be understood by a very few theologians, or as if the strength of the Christian religion lay in men's ignorance of it. The mysteries of kings it were perhaps better to conceal, but Christ wishes His mysteries to be published as widely as possible. I would wish even all women to read the Gospel and the Epistles of St. Paul. And I wish they were translated into all languages of all people, that they might be read and known, not merely by the Scotch and the Irish, but even by the Turks and the Sara-

cens. I wish that the husbandman may sing parts of them at his plough, that the weaver may warble them at his shuttle, that the traveller may with their narratives beguile the weariness of the way.

Tyndale was entirely of his mind.

More acknowledged that Tyndale had once been "well known for a man of right good living, studious and well learned in Scripture, and in divers places in England was very well liked, and did great good with preaching," but claimed he had "since" become a heretic. And his critique of the New Testament translation was incredibly harsh. He doubted "that any good Christian man having any drop of wit in his head" could complain about its burning, and to his great, perhaps tragic discredit, he claimed that the text was not the New Testament at all, but rather a cunning counterfeit, perverted in the interests of heresy. It was "so corrupted and changed from the good and wholesome doctrine of Christ," he wrote, "that it was a clean contrary thing. . . . To tell all its faults, were in a manner to rehearse all the whole book, wherein there were found and noted wrong above a thousand texts by tale." To search for errors in it was like searching for water in the sea; it was so bad that it could not be mended, "for it is as easy to weave a new web of cloth as it is to sew up every hole in a net."

More knew better, for he knew Greek. When he attempted to specify some of the alleged errors, it turned out that his principal objection had to do with the rendering of certain ecclesiastical terms. Tyndale had translated the word for "priest" as "senior" (later, "elder"); the word for "Church" as "congregation"; the word for "penance" as "repentance"; the word for "confess" as "[ac]knowledge"; the word for "grace" as "favor"; and the word for "charity" as "love." By this means, according to More, Tyndale had attempted (after the fashion of Luther) to persuade people "that such articles of our faith as . . . be well proved by Holy Scripture, were in Holy Scripture nothing spoken of; but that the preachers have, all this fifteen hundred year, misreported the Gospel . . . to lead the people purposely out of the right way."

When it was pointed out that Tyndale was actually following the new Latin version of Erasmus, More replied that the liberties Erasmus had taken had lacked "malicious intent." He also took a swipe at the "great arch-heretic Wycliffe," who, he assures us, was similarly "malicious" and "purposely corrupted the holy text." But "[I] myself have seen, and can shew you," More went on, "Bibles fair and old written in English, which have been known and seen by the bishop of the diocese, and left in laymen's hands, and women's, to such as he knew for good and catholic folk." The Bibles he commended were, in fact, copies of the second Wycliffe version—though he was clearly unaware of that fact.

If we remember that much of the King James Version of the Bible is substantially based on Tyndale's text, More's "book review" is perhaps the most wrongheaded ever penned. Tyndale replied in 1531 to More's attack with a substantial rebuttal (*Answer unto Sir Thomas More*), which brought forth from More in the following year a ponderous and sometimes hysterical work, *Confutation of Tyndale,* in which, among other things, he called his antagonist "a beast," discharging a "filthy foam of blasphemies out of his brutish beastly mouth"; "a shameful, shameless, unreasonable, railing ribald"; a "hellhound" fit for "the hogs of hell to feed upon"; and the son of the devil himself.

More's polemics raise issues of intellectual candor that are uncomfortable to consider in the life of a martyred saint. He was a classical scholar, a learned Humanist, an able lawyer, and in his public career had enjoyed a meteoric rise—from master of requests to Lord Chancellor of England, succeeding Cardinal Wolsey in 1529. Without doubt, he was a substantial man—some have even said "a man for all seasons"—but not more of a martyr than Tyndale, and perhaps not more of a saint.

"We may well rub our eyes," writes one scholar. "Now, Tyndale's New Testament lies before us, and Erasmus's Greek Testament of which it is a translation, and we can only be surprised that a scholar like More should go to such lengths in denouncing so good an achievement. True, there were things in it which were capable of improvement, as Tyndale himself acknowledged, but it was a pioneer work; the New Testament had never been turned from Greek directly into English before." Tyndale himself not unjustly complained that if his printer so much as failed to dot an "i," "it was solemnly noted down by his opponents and reckoned a heresy." His complaint rather exactly recalls that of St. Jerome, whose Latin version was also at first so critically judged.

More himself had become so habituated to the Vulgate that he could not properly consider the context in which the disputed terms were used. When Tyndale challenged him to prove "that I gave not the right English unto the Greek word," More was hard put to hold his ground. In Greek, the word *ekklesia* signified "a properly constituted assembly," for which Tyndale's choice of "congregation" was apt. This was how it had been used in the Septuagint, and *congregatio* in the Latin translation by Erasmus conveyed the same sense. The Church, however, had come to apply the word to an "organized body of the clergy" (as well as to a place of worship) even though the Greek word for church (*kuriakon*) that conveyed either is not found in the New Testament and did not come into use until the third century A.D.

Again, More found fault with Tyndale's choice of "senior" (later "elder") for *presbyter*, which he thought should be "priest." And he noted Tyndale's use of "priest" for rabbi, as if he were giving more dignity to the sacred office of the Jews. But in both instances Tyndale's rendering was literally correct. *Presbyter* did mean "senior" or "elder"; and the word he chose to render as "priest" was *hiereus*, which meant "sacrificer," a member of the priestly tribe of Levi, from whom all Jewish "priests" or rabbis (according to the Bible) derive. But More was unquestionably correct when he charged that "Tyndale [would] make us to believe that we need no priest to offer up daily the same sacrifice that our Savior offered once. . . . And that a priest is nothing else but a man chosen among the people to preach." For that is what the Reformers believed.

Again, the verb to "[ac]knowledge" had long been used in the sense of to "admit"—Wycliffe, for example, had so used it in his translation of John 1:20. Even so, in perfectly orthodox fashion, Tyndale had generally opted for "confess." As for the Greek word *charis* (Latin *gratia*), the meaning at their core was "favor" or "kindness," freely and gladly bestowed. Tyndale understood that "grace" was often the better word in context, so that More's charge that he "commonly" changed "grace" to "favor" was a kind of willful slander, without grounds.

When it came to "penance" as against "repentance" (Greek *metanoia*, Latin *penitentiam ago*) a great deal was at stake. By 1529, many scholars and theologians (Erasmus among them) knew that "penance" as a translation for the Greek word and its cognates was not right. Luther in the first of his Ninety-five Theses of 1517 had remarked: "When our Lord and Master Jesus Christ said, 'Poenitentiam agite,' he willed the entire life of believers to be one of repentance," not devoted to acts of contrition. "Penance" was a Sacrament; "repentance" or "penitence" offered a new beginning by breaking with the past. But through the sale of indulgences and other penitential commerce, "penance" had proved a lucrative source of Church income. Protestants were convinced that the clergy were determined to keep the word "because that word kept them."

Finally, in the Greek New Testament there were three words for the noun "love" (*agape, eros,* and *philia*), of which the equivalents in the Latin Vulgate and English are: Latin *caritas,* English "charity," "compassion," or "lovingkindness"; Latin *dilectio,* English "physical love" or "desire,"; Latin *amicitia,* English "friendship" or "affection." In the Greek Septuagint and New Testament *agape* and its cognates occur more often than the other two and tend to mean something broadly equivalent to the English word "love." In the writings of Paul and John, the word was often used in the sense of "benevolence," or "the love of God"; and in the 13th chapter of 1 Corinthians, verse 7, it occurs eighteen times. Tyndale pointed out that the translator who chose "love" over "charity" had the advantage of being able to use the word both as a noun and as a verb.

Nevertheless, More remained convinced that Tyndale was trying to undermine the authority of Tradition—which, in a sense, was true, because he placed his whole trust in Scripture; Tyndale, on the other hand, was sure that More was trying to maintain Church prerogative by clinging to the ecclesiastical bias of the terms.

Both were right. Like Wycliffe, Luther, and others, Tyndale believed that the invisible Church of the faithful was the only true Church, and that, as C. S. Lewis observed, "the mighty theocracy with its cardinals, abbeys, pardons, inquisition, and treasury of grace" connoted by the word "Church" was "in its very essence not only distinct from, but antagonistic to, the thing that St. Paul had in mind whenever he used the Greek word *ekklesia*. More, on the other hand, believed with equal sincerity that the 'Church' of his own day was in essence the very same mystical body which St. Paul addressed."

∽

More's historical argument went something like this: The sacred writers may have adopted words of everyday use, but they had invested them with inspired meanings that expressed Christian ideas. The Greek word *presbyter* may have originally meant nothing more than "senior" or "elder," but when it was used to designate an office in the Church, to which certain mystical functions and prerogatives were attached, its meaning changed, and the better expression was "priest." "Senior" or "elder" therefore failed to convey the sense. So with *ekklesia*, which originally meant a "congregation" or "assembly," but was now properly represented in English by "Church." Erasmus, More explained, had settled for the word *congregatio* simply because there was no other Latin word for the concept. But there was such a word in English; and it should be used.

More's argument had considerable merit; but Tyndale's did, too. The latter insisted that in apostolic times there had been "no society like the later 'Church,' no person like the later 'priest,' no institution like 'confession.' Long usage had given a prescriptive sanctity to the words More cherished, but who was to settle the issue? More's ready answer was: the Holy Catholic Church, which cannot err. In this way, he provided for all those doctrines and usages in the Church—established by Tradition—which were not ordained by Scripture.

"By these traditions have we the praying to saints, and the knowledge that they pray for us," he wrote. "By these have we the hallowing of chalices, vestments, paschal taper, and holy water, with divers other things. By these hath the Church also the knowledge how to consecrate, how to say Mass, and what thing to pray for and to desire therein. By this have we also the knowledge to do reverence to the images of holy saints, and of our Savior, and to creep to his cross, and to do divine honor unto the blessed sacrament." More was so concerned to present Church practice as incontestable that he defended praying to St. Loy (a blacksmith) for sick horses, to St. Appoline (whose teeth had been torn from her gums by pagans) for toothaches, and to St. Sythe for lost keys. He thought discontented wives were not amiss to offer pecks of oats to St. Wilgefort, to rid them of their husbands, and accepted the fact that the bones of some saints (like the head of John the Baptist) could be enshrined in more than one place. As for the comparative authority of Scripture and Tradition, More pointed out that the biblical canon had been established by the Church.

Between the two men, there was scant hope of a meeting of minds. Tyndale had also been stung by More's charge that he had consciously twisted the Scriptures to his own ends. "I call God to record," he exclaimed, "against the day we shall appear before the Lord Jesus, to give reckoning of our doings, that I never altered one syllable of God's word against my conscience, nor would this day if all that is in the earth, whether it be pleasure, honor, or riches, might be given me." Meanwhile, relentlessly adhering to his purpose, he had begun to translate the Old Testament into English, beginning with the first five books of Moses—Genesis, Exodus, Leviticus, Numbers, and Deuteronomy—known as the Pentateuch. In so doing, he had no doubt that the text could be Englished well. For just as it was easier to translate Greek into English than Latin, so Hebrew syntax had an affinity with English form. "The manner of speaking is both one; so that in a thousand places thou needest not but to translate it into the English, word for word." In addition to a number of editions of the Hebrew Scriptures, Tyndale had access, of course, to the Septuagint, the Vulgate, Luther's German translation (published in 1526), and the literal word-for-word translation "with a strong Hebrew emphasis" made by Sanctus Pagninus into Latin and published in 1528.

Early in 1529, with manuscript in hand, Tyndale set sail from Antwerp for Hamburg, where printing arrangements had been made in advance. Off the coast of Holland, however, his ship was caught in a storm, driven off course, and smashed to pieces on the rocks. With other passengers and crew he managed to struggle ashore, but his entire manuscript along with reference books and other materials was lost. Some weeks later, he reached Hamburg by another ship, and put up in the house of "a worshipful widow, Mistress Margaret van Emmerson," who belonged to the city's Protestant community. A number of English expatriates were also there, including one Miles Coverdale, who had been awaiting Tyndale's arrival and was soon engaged in helping him reconstruct his text. For six months they holed up together and, working night and day (with Coverdale acting as Tyndale's amanuensis), produced a fresh translation by the end of the year.

On January 17, 1530, Tyndale returned to Antwerp, where his work was now printed by John Hoochstraten under the pseudonym of "Han's Lufft in the land of Hesse." By summer, copies had been smuggled into England, and the "pestilent glosses" that had so offended King Henry in Tyndale's New Testament were multiplied in the margin of the Pentateuch. For Numbers 23:8, for example, which read, "How shall I curse whom God curseth not," Tyndale had the note: "The pope can tell how"; and for Deuteronomy 23:18, which read, "Neither bring the hire of an whore nor the price of a dog in to the house of the Lord thy God," he had: "The pope will take tribute of them yet and bishops, and abbots desire no better tenants."

Each book or section had its own prologue and title page, so that they could be bought or sold separately, as people wished. In his General Introduction, Tyndale humbly invited anyone to improve upon what he had done: "I submit this work, and all other that I have either made or translated, or shall in time to come (if it be God's will that I further labor in that harvest), unto all them that submit themselves unto the word of God, to be corrected by them; yea, and moreover, to be disallowed and also burnt, if it seem worthy, so that they first put forth of their own translating another that is more correct."

That was unlikely. All the virtues of his New Testament translation were in evidence, even as he proved faithful to the force of Hebrew idiom, matching its common constructions to the forms of English speech. The syntactical rapport between the two tongues was clear: in word order (which was virtually the same, except that in Hebrew the verb normally precedes its subject, and the adjective follows the noun); and a propensity for the parallel phrase. The latter was especially true of Anglo-Saxon, enabling Tyndale to draw on traditions of native expression to give the Hebrew an English feel. His fidelity to the original also gave rise to the quintessential "noun + of + noun" construction of English biblical prose. Instead of "Moses' book," we have "the book of Moses"; instead of "a strong man," "a man of strength." This extended to the way superlatives were expressed: instead of "the holiest place" or "the best song," Hebrew had "the holy of holies" and "the song of songs." This imparted to English a certain rhythmic sonority it had not formerly possessed. Indeed, there was something in the pattern that completely captivated the English ear, and directed the language to a form of eloquence that became its paradigm.

Tyndale also boldly adopted a number of Hebrew words and compounds, such as "scapegoat," "passover," and "mercy seat," which English has kept, as well as various Hebraic turns of phrase—among them, "to die the death," "the Lord's anointed," "the gate of heaven," "a man after his own heart," "the living God," "sick unto death," "flowing with milk and honey," "to fall by the sword," "as the Lord liveth," "a stranger in a strange land," "to bring the head down to the grave," and "apple of his eye." It is said that he also introduced into English the adjective "beautiful," and was the first to use the name "Jehovah" for the Lord.

Here is Tyndale's translation of Genesis (1–10):

In the beginning God created heaven and earth. The earth was void and empty, and darkness was upon the deep, and the spirit of God moved upon the water.

Then God said: let there be light. And God saw the light that it was good: and divided the light from the darkness, and called the light day, and the darkness night: and so of the evening and morning was made the first day.

And God said: let there be a firmament between the waters, and let it divide the waters asunder. Then God made the firmament and parted the waters which were under the firmament, from the waters that were above the firmament:

And it was so. And God called the firmament heaven. And so of the evening and morning was made the second day.

And God said, let the waters that are under heaven gather themselves unto one place, that the dry land may appear: And it came so to pass. And God called the dry land the earth and the gathering together of waters called he the sea. And God saw that it was good.

In the following year (1531), Tyndale published his translation of the book of Jonah (emulating Luther, who had also done a separate translation of this book), and in 1534 a revised New Testament. For the latter, Tyndale supplied more commentary but toned down some of his earlier marginal notes. He also appended to the volume the "Sarum" epistles (mostly Old Testament extracts used in services of the Church on certain days of the year), and his rendering of some of them was charming, as this from the Song of Songs: "Now is winter gone and rain departed and past. The flowers appear in our country and the time is come to cut the vines. The voice of the turtle dove is heard in our land. The fig tree hath brought forth her figs, and the vine blossoms give a savor. Up, hast my love, my dove, in the holes of the rock and the secret places of the walls. Show me thy face and let me hear thy voice, for thy voice is sweet and thy fashion beautiful."

Although the short book of Jonah might almost be quoted entire, chapter two may stand for the whole:

But the Lord prepared a great fish, to swallow up Jonas. And so was Jonas in the bowels of the fish three days and three nights. And Jonas prayed unto the Lord his God out of the bowels of the fish.

And he said: in mine tribulation I called unto the Lord, and he answered me: out of the belly of hell I cried, and thou heardest my voice. For thou hadst cast me down deep in the midst of the sea: and the flood compassed me about: all thy waves and rolls of water went over me: and I thought that I had been cast away out of thy sight. But I will yet again look toward thy holy temple. The water compassed me even

unto the very soul of me: the deep lay about me: and the
weeds were wrapped about mine head. And I went down
unto the bottom of the hills, and was barred in with earth on
every side for ever. And yet thou Lord my God broughtest up
my life again out of corruption. When my soul faintest in me,
I thought on the Lord: and my prayer came in unto thee,
even into thy holy temple. They that observe vain vanities,
have forsaken him that was merciful unto them. But I will
sacrifice unto thee with the voice of thanksgiving, and will
pay that that I have vowed, that saving cometh of the Lord.

And the Lord spake unto the fish: and it cast out Jonas
again upon the dry land.

No one worked with more painstaking care than Tyndale at his
craft. But to his dismay, pirate editions of his work—some containing unauthorized changes—were becoming common, and the chief
culprit in this regard was a former assistant, George Joye, a miscre-
ant scholar and linguist. In the Prologue to his revised New Testament of 1534, Tyndale gave him a sharp rebuke: "I beseech George
Joye, yea and all other too, for to translate the Scripture for themselves, whether out of Greek, Latin or Hebrew. . . . Let them put
their own names [to it], and not play bo-peep. . . . But I neither can
nor will suffer of any man, that he shall go take my translation and
correct it without name, and make such changing as I myself durst
not do."

∞

Immediately after publishing his *Dialogue Concerning Heresies* in
the spring of 1529, More had left England for Cambray, where with
Tunstall he helped negotiate a treaty between King Henry and the
emperor, which (among its other provisions) entailed a mutual
pledge to prohibit the printing and circulation of heretical books.
Of these Tyndale's New Testament stood first on the list. Meanwhile, Tyndale had published two more polemical works: *The Parable of the Wicked Mammon* and *The Obedience of a Christian
Man*, both in 1528, which set forth the two great principles of the
English Reformation: the authority of Scripture in the Church and

the supremacy of the king in the state. The latter was an unflinching exposition of the divine right of kings. "He that judgeth the King," wrote Tyndale, "judgeth God and damneth God's law and ordinance . . . the King is, in this world, without law; and may at his lust [pleasure] do right or wrong, and shall give account to God alone."

In both works, Tyndale detailed various abuses of the priesthood, how (as he saw it) they had corrupted Christian doctrine, and the "feigned ordinances" by which they had sometimes usurped civil authority, acquired their worldly goods, and ruled over the consciences of men. In their insatiable arrogance and greed, he said, they had taken the people for all they were worth: "The parson sheareth, the vicar shaveth, the parish priest polleth, the friar scrapeth, and the pardoner pareth; we lack but a butcher to pull off the skin." He staunchly defended vernacular translations of the Bible and noted that Moses had given his people the law in Hebrew, that Christ and his apostles had preached in the language of their hearers (mainly Aramaic and Syriac), and that St. Jerome had translated the Bible into his own (Latin) tongue. "Why then," he asked, "should we, who walk in the broad day, not see as well as they that walked in the night, or . . . as well at noon as they did in the twilight? Came Christ to make the world more blind?" And he reminded his readers that just as the God of the Old Testament required his people to know the law, so Christ in the New had commanded them to search the Scriptures, that they might discriminate between prophets false and true.

As for the power of prayer, "as good the prayer of a cobbler," he wrote "as of a cardinal; of a butcher, as of a bishop; and the blessing of a baker that knoweth the truth is as good as the blessing of the pope."

☙

As the debate between More and Tyndale raged, More grew increasingly narrow in his views. In principle, he had once favored vernacular translations, and in the sixteenth chapter of his *Dialogue Concerning Heresies* confessed that he had "never yet heard any reason laid why it were not convenient to have the Bible in English." To argue against it, he said, was to disparage "the holy writers that wrote the Scriptures in Hebrew, the blessed evangelists that wrote them in Greek, and also those that had translated it out of those tongues into Latin." He had even experimented with Bible translation himself, and some of his occasional renderings in the *Four Last Things* (published in 1522), as well as longer passages in the devotional treatises he later wrote in the Tower (all made from the Vulgate) were marked by a homely vigor akin to Tyndale's style: "For as Scripture saith, wheresoever the stone falleth there shall it abide" (Ecclesiastes II); "Yet death shall shortly take away all this royalty, and his glory shall never walk with him into his grave" (Psalm 4:8); "It were as hard for a rich man to come into heaven, as a great cable or a camel to go through a needle's eye" (Matthew 19); "Where thy treasure is, there is thine heart" (Matthew 6).

More had also scoffed at the idea that because some might abuse the privilege of reading Scripture (by debating matters they didn't understand), it should be withheld from all—as if "a surgeon should cut off the leg by the knee, to keep the toe from the gout." Even so, he thought the Bible should be carefully parceled out to parishioners at the discretion of their local bishop. One man, for example, might be allowed to read the Gospels according to Matthew, Mark, or Luke (but not necessarily John); another, the Acts of the Apostles, but not Revelation. But how any given bishop could justly determine the fitness of each and every individual for a particular text More does not say.

He was not above taunting. After recounting the trial of one heretic (to whose constancy Tyndale had alluded in one of his books) he exclaimed, "And this lo! is Sir Thomas Hytton, the devil's stinking martyr, of whose burning Tyndale maketh boast." He then refers to another named John Tewkesbury, a leather merchant who had been guilty of owning contraband books. For this More is sure that Tewkesbury "lieth now in hell and crieth out on [Tyndale]; and Tyndale, if he do not amend in time, he is like to find him, when they come together, a hot firebrand burning at his back that all the water in the world will not be able to quench."

As C. S. Lewis once remarked, More was "monotonously anxious to conquer . . . to show that every heretical book was wrong about everything." As a result, "he loses himself in a wilderness of opprobrious adjectives," and his grandiloquent rebukes always seemed to fail.

☙

Even as Church and state worked to discredit Protestant doctrine, other reformers of note, variously affiliated with Tyndale, were targets of official wrath. One was Robert Barnes, prior of the monastery of Austin Friars at Cambridge, who belonged to a society of students and scholars known as the German Club that met regularly at the White Horse Tavern to discuss theological issues raised by Luther's revolt. On Christmas Eve, 1525, Barnes had preached a Lutheran sermon against special feast days in which he also mocked Wolsey's extravagant trappings and garb. Hauled before the cardinal, he was subjected to bitter taunts. "What! Master Doctor," asked Wolsey, "had you not scope enough in the Scriptures from which to teach? . . . We were jollily that day laughed to scorn. Verily, it was a sermon more fit to be preached on a stage." At length, Barnes was told, "Abjure or burn." He yielded, and the following Sunday was forced to publicly expiate his offense before a large crowd at St. Paul's. The triumphant cardinal, attired in purple and surrounded by thirty-six mitered abbots, priors, and bishops, in damask and satin, sat enthroned in all his pomp as Barnes and five others (indicted for related transgressions) stood before him in a penitential row. Barnes knelt, begged for forgiveness, and declared that he had been "more charitably handled than his horrible heresies deserved." Great baskets piled with contraband literature, including Tyndale's New Testament, were also on display, and after an anti-Lutheran sermon delivered by Bishop John Fisher, a bonfire was lit and the books cast into the blaze.

Some time afterward, however, Barnes returned to his dissident ways, and in the spring of 1528 Tunstall set out to catch and burn him at the stake. To escape, Barnes "faked his own suicide." When Tunstall's agents entered his home, they found a note on a table that directed them to a pile of clothing with another note on the banks of the Thames. The second note "urged the mayor to drag for his body, and promised that the corpse would have yet a third note on it, sealed in wax." While the authorities were trying to drag him up,

Barnes embarked for Antwerp. But death kept his fiery appointment in the end. A decade later Barnes returned to England and under Queen Mary met a martyr's fate.

Another thorn in the side of the Church was Simon Fish, a lawyer and playwright of Gray's Inn, London, who had fled to the Continent after ridiculing Wolsey in a play. While in exile he had written *The Supplication of Beggars,* an anticlerical tract addressed to the king, in which he claimed that clerical lust and avarice had beggared the nation and turned 100,000 women into whores. The clergy had fathered so many bastards, he said, by taking advantage of women in confession, that no man knew whether his children were his own. Scripture, he noted, did not condone such behavior, and "this is the great scab why the Church refuses to not let the New Testament go abroad in our mother-tongue."

On Candlemas Day, February 2, 1528, someone took advantage of a royal procession to Westminster to scatter copies of Fish's tract in the streets. On the very next day, Wolsey launched a "secret search" for prohibited books throughout London, and ransacked the rooms of reform-minded students and their sympathizers at all the university schools. One of his chief targets was Thomas Garrett, an Oxford bookseller and London curate prominent in the black-market trade.

Garrett had long sold books throughout the Thames valley, mostly to priests and academics with a special interest in the biblical tongues. The prior of Reading Abbey had bought sixty books from him in 1527, and Erasmus had been a good customer, too. But nobody's favor could save him now. He sought refuge in the rooms of Anthony Dalaber, a younger Oxford associate, where he hastily "cast off his hood and his gown" and asked Dalaber for "a coat with sleeves and another kind of cap . . . but," recalled Dalaber, "I had none but priestlike, such as his own was." They prayed together for his escape,

> lifting up our hearts and hands to God. . . . And then we embraced, and kissed the one the other, the tears so abundantly flowing out from both our eyes, that we all bewet both our faces, and scarcely for sorrow could we speak. . . . When he

was gone down the stairs from my chamber, I straightways did shut my chamber-door, and went into my study, shutting the door unto me, and took the New Testament of Erasmus translation into my hands, kneeled down on my knees, and with many a deep sigh and salt tear, I did with much deliberation read over the tenth chapter of St. Matthew's Gospel; and when I had so done, with fervent prayer I did commit unto God . . . our dearly beloved brother.

Garrett's immediate pursuer (one of the bishop's trustees) was desperate to catch him and had recourse to an astrologer to try to figure out where he was. The astrologer cast a chart for the occasion and told him Garrett had fled "in a tawny coat south-eastward, and is in the middle of London and will shortly be by the sea." Not long afterward, he was captured in the village of Hinksey, on his way to take a ship abroad. Imprisoned at Osnet Isle, he was eventually tried and executed. Ten members of Wolsey's own Cardinal College (later Christ Church) were also arrested and immured in a deep cellar used as a repository of salt fish. There in its putrid hollows four eventually died.

~

Both More and Tyndale had dueled as if their lives depended on it, but their ends would not be determined by their skill in debate. Both were captives to a supranational contest for power, indifferent to their merit and far beyond their own control. The situation in England was rapidly changing. After 1527, Henry was preoccupied with legitimizing his divorce from Catherine of Aragon, who had failed to provide a male heir; and he had apparently convinced himself that his marriage violated divine law, as enunciated in Leviticus 18:16. That verse contained a biblical injunction against marrying a brother's widow, which implied to Henry that he was living in mortal sin. He appealed to Rome for an annulment, but the pope (Clement VII), who would otherwise have obliged him, was politically captive to Emperor Charles V, the nephew of Henry's wife. Meanwhile, Henry's growing aversion to Catherine was intensified by his infatuation with Anne Boleyn, a twenty-year-old lady-in-waiting at court. From the beginning, Anne's vivacity, raven hair, and almond-shaped eyes had held the king in thrall. "I would you were in mine arms or I in yours, for I think it is a long time since we kissed," the king wrote to her in 1527, well into his courtship. In February 1528 he assured her (too optimistically, it proved) that "shortly you and I shall have our desired end."

But there was much more to it all than lust. England had recently recovered from the Wars of the Roses and an uncertain succession could easily dissolve the Tudor peace. Catherine had borne the king several children, but all had died except for one daughter, Mary; and Henry was unwilling for a woman to inherit the throne. Under the last queen regent of England (Matilda, in the twelfth century) the country had been torn apart by civil war.

In exchange for his cooperation, Charles V wanted Henry to accept his control of Italy, which Henry was prepared to do. But Wolsey could not countenance a solution that meant abandoning to imperial control an institution from which he derived so much of his power. To Wolsey, as to Charles, the real struggle was for control of the papacy, and it had to be fought to the end. Before it played out, Rome would be sacked by the emperor's army, a new pope enthroned, England allied to France (her historical enemy) against Charles, and France would invade Italy. The fortunes of war thereby undid all of Wolsey's machinations, and Henry found that he had gained nothing by them in the end.

In the meantime, a papal legate, Cardinal Lorenzo Campeggio, arrived in England to adjudicate the king's divorce. In May 1529 a Church court convened at Blackfriars, and on June 21, Henry and Catherine both appeared before it, with the two cardinals (Campeggio and Wolsey) in the judges' chairs. Henry, seated under a canopy of cloth-of-gold, spoke about the state of his own conscience. Catherine swore she had never consummated her first marriage (to Henry's brother, Arthur), and turning to Henry said, "When ye had me at the first I take God to be my judge, I was a true maid without taint of man." Then she threw herself at her husband's feet, calling on him to remember her honor and that of their daughter, Mary, who would be no better than a bastard if she were deemed his mistress or whore. But on that very day, a thousand miles away in an Italian field, the last French army, supported by the English, was crushed by imperial troops at Landriano, and Italy fell to the control of Charles V. Within days, the pope had come to terms with him, and at the behest of Charles, the Church court in England was adjourned.

Henry's hopes for a swift divorce were dashed. On October 9, he indicted Wolsey for alleged misdeeds, and after forty-four articles of impeachment were drawn up against Wolsey by the Commons, he was stripped of his offices and rank.

More was appointed in his place. He accepted the post with some reluctance, in part because he did not approve of the king's intended divorce. On the other hand, he hoped to use his expanded powers to combat heresy more effectively. And so he brought to the post a certain mordant zeal.

Previously, the government had not been directly engaged in persecution, but under More's administration, it took the lead. On the 24th of December, 1529, just two months after his appointment, More issued a proclamation in the name of the king that bound all civil authorities to assist the Church with their "whole power and diligence" in the extirpation of heresy. The measure made a special target of proscribed books. One hundred eighteen of them were named, and once again Tyndale's New Testament stood at the head of the list.

One proclamation followed another, but all of More's efforts failed to still dissent. He was driven even to defend torture and the use by the clergy of the ex officio law, by which persons could be arrested on secret information and without being confronted by their accusers condemned in a secret trial. One such martyr was James Bainham, a lawyer of the Middle Temple married to the widow of Simon Fish. At the end of 1531, he was arrested, taken to More's garden at Chelsea, and whipped at the Tree of Troth. More afterward sent him to the Tower to be racked. At length, Bainham admitted to owning five of Tyndale's works, abjured, and went through a public ritual of penance at Paul's Cross. But his conscience gave him no rest.

A month later he went to a warehouse in Bow Lane, where a reformed congregation was accustomed to meet, and apologized for his weakness. He then made a more public profession of his Protestant faith in the great nave of the London priory of the Austin Friars. The following day, he was arrested, and on the last day of April 1532 he was taken out to Smithfield and burned at the stake. Before his death, he declared to the crowd: "I came hither, good people, accused and condemned for an heretic, Sir Thomas More being my accuser and my judge. And these be the articles that I die for. First, I say it is lawful for every man and woman to have God's book in their mother tongue. Second, that the Bishop of Rome is Antichrist [all Protestants thought so then], and that I know of no other keys of heaven's gates but only the preaching of the Law and the Gospel; third, that there is no other purgatory but the purgatory of Christ's blood." His last words were: "The Lord forgive Sir Thomas More."

Another to suffer was Thomas Bilney, a priest and fellow of Trinity Hall, Cambridge, who rejected purgatory and the intercessory power of saints, subscribed to the Lutheran doctrine of justification by faith, but remained orthodox on the supremacy of the pope, the authority of the Church, and transubstantiation and confession. In November 1527 he was declared a heretic, spent a year in the Tower, recanted and was freed. Like Bainham, however, he was tormented by pangs of conscience, and eventually announced to friends that he was going "up to Jerusalem," meaning to a martyr's fate. With copies of Tyndale's New Testament and *The Obedience of a Christian Man* in hand, he set out on his last pilgrimage, preaching as he went, until at last he came to Norwich, where the authorities picked him up. As a doubly lapsed heretic he was condemned without delay, and a writ for burning was procured with alacrity from More. More is said to have remarked that "in so flagrant a case they should have burnt him first and asked for a writ afterwards." Scant time in any case was lost. On the morning of August 19, 1528, he was led out of the city, and across Bishops Bridge to an open space carved out of the hillside, known to this day as Lollards Pit. There he "sealed up his faith in the flames." His Bible, still preserved at Corpus Christi College, Cambridge, has a mark in the margin at the verse which reads, "Fear not, I have redeemed thee. . . . I will be with thee . . . when thou walkest through the fire."

A third notable victim of More's wrath was John Frith, a junior canon of Cardinal College, Oxford, who had once been incarcerated as an undergraduate by Wolsey for owning forbidden works. In exile, he had collaborated with Tyndale on several polemical tracts, and had written a book on the doctrine of purgatory in which he claimed that neither transubstantiation nor purgatory were necessary articles of faith. Frith remained abroad until 1532, when he returned to England, was arrested, tried, convicted, and burned at Smithfield on July 4, 1533. Before his death, Tyndale wrote two letters to him—one urging him not to be too dogmatic on Eucharistic doctrine; the second, to give him heart: "If there were in me any gift that could help at hand, and aid you if need required," he wrote, "I promise you I would not be far off, and commit the end to God. My soul is not faint, though my body be weary. But God hath made me evil-favored in this world, and without grace in the sight of men, speechless and rude, dull and slow-witted: your part shall be to supply what lacketh in me; remembering that as lowliness of heart shall make you high with God, even so meekness of words shall make you sink into the hearts of men.

Where did Henry stand in all of this? More had persuaded him to declare that "divulging [the whole of Scripture] at this time in English to the people, should rather be to their farther confusion and destruction, than to the edification of their souls." But that was more the voice of Sir Thomas than his king. Henry had begun to look at the matter differently, and about this time Anne Boleyn read Tyndale's *The Obedience of a Christian Man*. She urged Henry to read it, and he did, paying particular attention to a number of passages she had marked for him with her nail. When he had finished, he reportedly remarked: "This is a book for me, and for all kings." Meanwhile, in 1530 he had sent to Oxford for a copy of Wycliffe's Articles (condemned at the Council of Constance), which he thought strengthened his position in his quarrel with the pope.

Henry also now moved to divest the Church in England of its independent power. Beginning in 1532, each successive session of Parliament saw an increase in measures directed against clerical abuses, all intended to do three things: to unite the anticlerical party behind the king, to overawe the clergy, and to frighten the pope into granting the divorce. An Annates Statute, for example, empowered

Henry to abolish payment to Rome of the first year's income of all newly installed bishops; the Act of Restraint of Appeals boldly decreed that "this realm of England is an empire," with one head.

The rupture with Rome widened, and before the end of 1532 Anne Boleyn was also with child. For the child to be legitimate (and able to inherit the throne), it had to be born in wedlock. In January 1533 Henry and Anne were secretly married in Westminster Abbey; in March, Thomas Cranmer, now one of Henry's principal advisers, was elevated to the Canterbury see, and in May Cranmer nullified Henry's marriage to Catherine "from the beginning" and declared Anne to be Henry's lawful wedded wife. On June 1, she was crowned Queen of England, and three months later gave birth to a daughter, Elizabeth (the future queen). Cranmer and Henry were both excommunicated, and that winter Henry severed the Church of England from Rome. At the end of 1534, Parliament passed the Act of Supremacy, making the king "supreme head" of the English Church. Thereafter the English Church became effectively a spiritual department of the state under the rule of the king as God's deputy on earth.

☙

More once told his wife, who was impressed by the king's apparent affection for her husband, that if Henry thought he could gain a single castle by it, he wouldn't hesitate to cut off More's head. Yet over the years More had managed to make his way nimbly along "the slippery precipice of royal favor," though he would soon begin to slide. Tyndale's circumstances were likewise never free from risk. Imperial Catholic agents were always on the lookout for him, and during this tumultuous period attempts were made both to co-opt him as a propagandist for Henry and to lure him back to England to a martyr's fate. The government's agent in these matters was Stephen Vaughan, whom More and Tunstall had previously engaged to report on heresy among the English merchants in the Netherlands.

Vaughan tried to locate Tyndale, and in January of 1530 sent copies of a letter (with the promise of a safe-conduct from the king) to Frankfurt, Hamburg, and Marburg. At length, Tyndale replied through an intermediary, and Vaughan was conducted to a field outside Antwerp where he found Tyndale waiting, muffled in a cloak. Tyndale insisted that he had always shown "the heart of a true subject," and that for sixteen years he had suffered poverty, hunger, want, loneliness, and danger for his country's sake. But the safe-conduct did not take him in. Remembering the fate of Jan Hus, who had attended the Council of Constance under such a pass, he predicted that it would be revoked once he was in England and slipped off into the night.

A second meeting was arranged, and Vaughan told Tyndale that the King was prepared to pardon him if he would only modify his views. This had some effect—for "I perceived the man to be exceedingly altered," wrote Vaughan, "and to take it very near unto his heart, in such wise that water stood in his eyes; and he answered, 'What gracious words are these!' " Indeed, Tyndale promised to return to England, even at the peril of his life, if only Henry would allow an English translation of the Bible—done "by whomsoever his Majesty please"—to be published for all to read. Otherwise, said Tyndale, "I will abide the asperity of all chances, whatsoever shall come, and endure my life in as much pains as it is able to suffer and bear."

For years, Tyndale led a hunted life on the Continent, moving from town to town. Toward the end, he found permanent refuge in Antwerp, then a free and independent city, but still surrounded by territory under the control of Charles V. In Antwerp, he had taken lodgings at the English House, an English merchants' club run by Thomas Poyntz, a member of the Grocers Company and a relative of John and Lady Walsh, with whom Tyndale had once stayed. The English merchants provided him with a stipend (how much is not known) and in the security and comfort of his new abode he hoped to proceed unmolested with his work. It is said that almost everyone who came into contact with him was left with an impression of his exalted moral worth. In Antwerp, he devoted much of his time to charitable work, and every Saturday apparently roamed the streets looking for people to help—the poor, the old, the weak, the disabled, and the sick. "He was a man," wrote John Foxe, "without any spot or blemish of rancor or malice, full of mercy and compassion,

so that no man living was able to reprove him of any sin or crime."
Sir Thomas Elyot, King Henry's ambassador to Brussels, noted with
chagrin that Tyndale was "venerated almost as an apostle" by many
members of the English community.

But hired assassins of a sort had him in their sights. One of them
was "a needy and profligate adventurer" named Henry Phillips, who
masqueraded as a knightly gentleman of reform views; the other, a
monk of England's Stratford Abbey by the name of Gabriel Donne,
who pretended to be Phillips's servant, though he was possibly "the
real director of the enterprise." Little, in fact, is known of Donne; but
Phillips was an Oxford graduate and the sometime holder of two
benefices in the see of Exeter who had gambled himself into debt,
stolen money from his father (high sheriff of the county where he
lived), and fled abroad. In Europe, he let it be known that he was prepared to do anything for cash. It is thought that John Stokesley, Tunstall's successor as Bishop of London, may have bought his services,
though Phillips also sold himself to imperial agents in Brussels who
hoped to take Tyndale before Henry (as they feared) could co-opt
him into serving as a propagandist for his regime.

One day Tyndale was introduced to Phillips at a dinner party,
found him engaging, welcomed him to the English House as his occasional guest, and eventually secured rooms for him there next to
his own. In this way Phillips became completely familiar with
Tyndale's routine. On May 21, 1535, soon after Poyntz went off to
the great annual cloth fair at Barrow (Bergen-op-Zoom), Phillips invited Tyndale to dinner. He already knew Tyndale had another engagement and would insist instead that Phillips come along. Thus
the trap was laid. In the early evening, they left the English House together and proceeded down a narrow lane. On either side of the entrance, imperial officers were waiting to grab him. Phillips, walking
behind, "pointed with his finger over Tyndale's head down to him,
that the officers might see who to take." They seized him without a
fight (indeed, they "pitied to see his simplicity") and whisked him
out of Antwerp to Vilvorde Castle, an impregnable fortress north of
Brussels modeled on the Bastille. There in spite of great efforts by
English merchants and others to free him, he remained in a dungeon
until October of the following year.

Sometime that winter he wrote the governor of the prison a letter that has often been compared to the last letter St. Paul wrote from his own confinement in a Roman jail. In that letter, Paul asked his friend Timothy to bring him before winter set in "the cloak that I left at Troas with Carpus, and the books, but especially the parchments." (2 Timothy 4:13) In a similar vein, Tyndale asked that he might have from among his belongings "a warmer cap, for I suffer greatly from the cold, and have a cough . . . a warmer coat also, for what I have is very thin; a piece of cloth, too, with which to patch my leggings; and a woollen shirt . . . for my clothes are all worn out. . . . And I ask to be allowed to have a lamp in the evening, for it is wearisome to sit alone in the dark. But most of all I beg and beseech your clemency that the commissary will kindly permit me to have my Hebrew bible, grammar, and dictionary, that I may continue with my work. In return I pray every good may come to you, consistent with the salvation of your soul."

Some part of his request must have been granted, for while incarcerated he evidently completed his English translation of the Old Testament books of Joshua through 2 Chronicles before he was arraigned.

His trial was presided over by the procurer general, Pierre Dufief, who "had an awful reputation for cruelty among Lutherans of the Netherlands," and he was prosecuted by Jacques Latomus and Ruwart Tapper, two theologians from the University of Louvain. Tapper, who was afterward to become inquisitor general of the Low Countries, once remarked: "It doesn't matter whether those we execute are really guilty or not. What matters is that the people are terrified by our trials." Tyndale declined the help of an advocate, saying he would answer for himself; but his was already a hopeless case. Under the Decree of Augsburg (1530), death was to be imposed on anyone subscribing to justification by faith. In the Preface to his 1534 edition of the New Testament, Tyndale had clearly stated his belief in this doctrine (one of the many heretical ideas with which he was charged): "The New Testament is an everlasting covenant made unto the children of God through faith in Christ, upon the deservings of Christ. Where eternal life is promised to all that believe, and death to all that are unbelieving." That alone would have been enough to condemn him. His *Parable of the Wicked Mammon* was also culled for such passages as: "The fruit that grows on a tree does not make a tree good or bad, it only makes known whether the tree is a good or a bad tree; and works do not make a man good or bad, they only make it plain to other men whether the man who performs them is good or bad. There is an inward justification of a man before God which is by faith alone; works serve only to make his justification known before men." Again: "It is the grace of God that does everything; without Him we can do nothing; it is God that works; we are but the instruments, we deserve no reward for what God does by us, and can claim no merit for it."

In August 1536, Tyndale was found guilty of heresy, degraded from his priestly office, and handed over for punishment to the secular powers. On October 6, he was brought forth to the place of execution, tied to a stake, strangled first by the hangman, then "with fire consumed." Before he lost consciousness, he cried "with a fervent zeal and a loud voice: 'Lord, open the King of England's eyes.' "

Phillips is said to have relished the prospect of Tyndale's execution, but his own fate was a fit one for his kind. Disowned by his parents, judged a traitor at home, and ostracized by the English community abroad, he would drift around Europe for years, looking for a patron, while trying to pass himself off as a true zealot for the Church. All his letters home pleading for help were intercepted—including one last desperate appeal concealed in a loaf of bread; and even the party "for whose sake he had marred his life ultimately shunned him and he was fated to go down in history as the author of one perfidious deed."

As for Gabriel Donne, he somehow escaped the stigma of complicity and returned to England where he obtained the abbey of Buckfastleigh in Devon worth a thousand marks a year.

Meanwhile, More himself had also been martyred. Obliged to take sides in Henry's quarrel with the pope, he had resigned the chancellorship in May 1532 and retired to private life, where he hoped to live out his days. But after he refused to attend the coronation of Anne Boleyn, Henry's anger was aroused against him, and he was pursued vindictively to the end. After escaping various attempts to tarnish him with bribery and other crime's, More was

Miles Coverdale

As all nations, in the diversity of speeches, may know one God in the unity of faith, and be one in love, even so may diverse translations understand one another . . . though they use sundry words.

—Thomas Cranmer, Preface to the Great Bible, 1540

CHAPTER THREE

Protestant, Catholic, Bishop, Queen

ing Henry had many faults. But a zeal for religious persecution was not one of them. With the end of More's regime, a measure of calm returned to the realm, and some who had championed a vernacular Bible were appointed to positions of rank. Even Reformed literature began to make its way among the folk. One of the reasons for this change was the countenance given to the dissemination of the English Scriptures by Anne Boleyn. A gilded copy of Tyndale's revised New Testament of 1534, bound in vellum, was presented to her with her coat of arms emblazoned on the title page and *Anna Regina Angliae* stamped in large red ornamental letters on the spine.

Henry's two most prominent officials were now Thomas Cranmer and Thomas Cromwell, the one head of the Church, the other of the state.

☙

Born in 1489, the son of a squire, Cranmer had studied at Jesus College, Cambridge, where he earned his doctorate in divinity and was one of the young men of talent selected by Wolsey to adorn his new "Cardinal" College at Oxford. He declined the honor, became divinity lecturer at Magdalen College, and from about 1520 belonged to the German Club, the reform-minded coterie of scholars. His ambitions for reform might have remained academic had it not been for the political events into which he was soon drawn. About 1529, he was introduced to two of the king's chief advisers, Stephen Gardiner and Edward Fox, who sounded him out about the king's intended divorce. Cranmer pondered the matter in a lawyerly way, and suggested the king appeal to university experts in canon law as to whether the marriage to Catherine had been valid in the first place. When the king was told of Cranmer's proposal, he reportedly exclaimed, "By God!" That man has the right sow by the ear!" Entering the royal service, Cranmer wrote a treatise on behalf of the king's position (quoting Scripture, the Church fathers, and decrees of Church councils) which influenced scholarly opinion; became archdeacon of Taunton and one of the king's chaplains; and in 1530 accompanied the Earl of Wiltshire to Rome as part of a high-level delegation sent by Henry to plead his cause before the pope. Upon his return to England, he was made chaplain to Anne Boleyn. In the meantime, More had announced to Parliament that the consensus among university experts favored the king. Two years later, on an embassy to Emperor Charles V, Cranmer quietly married a niece of the prominent Lutheran divine Andreas Osiander, but this idyll was shattered when Henry called him to the Canterbury see. Cranmer was not enthusiastic about the appointment, and over the next few months "moved slowly across Europe in the hope that his nomination would be withdrawn."

His new prominence, moreover, created an awkward situation for him, for although he rejected clerical celibacy, the Church did not. As archbishop he therefore did his best to conceal the existence of his wife, and (legend has it) even carried her about with him from place to place in a steamer trunk pierced with holes. It may be that the incongruity of his own situation helped lend urgency to the reforms he promoted; but throughout Henry's reign, he enjoyed a unique place in the trust and affections of the king. "You were born in a happy hour," Cromwell once told him, "for do or say what you will, the King will always take it at your hand."

That might have been said of Cromwell, too, at least for a time. Like Cranmer, he stood for ecclesiastical reform, but he was a protégé of Wolsey and upon the Cardinal's fall, his prospects had seemed dim. However, he boldly repaired them at a single stroke. Two days before Parliament was to meet (stripping Wolsey of power), he set out for court, remarking to a member of his household: "I shall make or mar ere I come again!" The very next day he arranged to see the king, and laid out to him the daring program that in time replenished the king's coffers by the reduction of the monasteries, and made Henry "Supreme Head of the English Church."

Born about 1485, Cromwell had been a soldier of fortune in Italy in 1503, then a merchant in the Netherlands until 1512, before returning to England to practice as a solicitor in London. By 1515, he had become a busy and influential member of the House of Commons, entered Wolsey's service about 1528, and supervised the building of the colleges the cardinal founded in Ipswich and Oxford. After Wolsey's fall in 1529, he rose in the service of the king, became a member of Parliament and in 1530 a privy councillor. When it was clear that Pope Clement VII would not grant Henry's divorce, Cromwell recommended that Henry arrange for Parliament to declare him ecclesiastically supreme. With this "sword of Supremacy," he might then proceed himself "to cut the knot which the captive pope was afraid to help him untie." Before long, a new honorific— "Protector and Supreme Head of the English Church"—was included in the litany of Henry's royal titles in a petition from Convocation to the King.

Cromwell had a winning way, and on one occasion (so the story goes) persuaded the banker Francesco Frescobaldi to give him access to unlimited funds; on another, he reportedly induced Pope Julius II, who had a craving for "strange delicacies and dainty dishes" to rubber-stamp some pardons for a client in return for the recipe for a type of English jam.

But he also established a kind of terror machine. He played upon Henry's fears for his own safety, and cultivated a vast network of spies to help secure his purpose, which was "to raise the king to absolute authority on the ruins of every rival power within the realm."

Cranmer would later tell Henry (when Cromwell's life hung suspended in the balance) that he thought Cromwell had loved him "no less than God."

⌾

Henry now owed a lot to Scripture (as opposed to Church prerogative or Tradition), for his open repudiation of papal supremacy left him "inferentially pledged" to the Bible's paramount authority. After all, he had argued his divorce on the basis of a biblical injunction in Leviticus which canon lawyers had assured him carried more weight than the opinion of the pope. Under the circumstances, he began to intimate that he was not unwilling that under certain conditions the people might have the Bible in their own tongue.

Pressure for this had gradually been building from above and below. In June 1530, during his developing dispute with the pope, Henry had published a royal proclamation as a bill or direction for provincial pulpits in which he acknowledged that many of his subjects wanted him to allow an English Bible to circulate without constraint. At the time, he had declared that it was not yet "expedient" to do so, but implied that at a more stable time he would have the New Testament done into English "more faithfully and purely than heretofore" by "learned men."

That time had come. For several years, copies of Tyndale's New Testament had been pouring into England "by the whole vats-full at once" (as More had complained in 1532) with as many as fifty-thousand copies about in the land. In a sense, the state could only hope to co-opt the rising demand. Cranmer now opportunely approached the king on the subject, and he had the power of the court on his side—including Hugh Latimer, Bishop of Worcester and the king's chaplain; Thomas Cromwell, the new viceregent; and Anne Boleyn, the new queen. In December 1534, the English bishops in Convocation asked the king to authorize a new English translation for the people's instruction, and Cromwell at once took the matter up. It now became his purpose that an English Bible be placed by authority in every church in England, to be read as a part of the service, and that free access to it be allowed to all who might desire to read it for themselves. John Foxe tells us that about this time

Cromwell memorized the whole of the Latin New Testament of Erasmus on a trip between England and Rome, not only to improve his Latin, but to prepare himself as a knowledgeable patron of the new translations he meant to take in hand.

He then cast about for the right man to see them through. That man was Miles Coverdale, who had studied philosophy and theology at Cambridge under Robert Barnes (where he had been a member of the German Club), and "drank in good learning with a burning thirst." In 1506, he had become an Augustinian friar, then in 1514 a priest. When the Reformation in England began, "he was one of the first," we are told, "to make a pure confession of Christ. Other men gave themselves in part, he gave himself wholly to the propagating of Christ's Gospel." In 1525, when Robert Barnes had been summoned to London to answer charges of heresy, Coverdale had stood faithfully by him and helped prepare his defense. When he returned to Cambridge, he attracted Cromwell's attention, became tutor to a relative of Sir Thomas More, and evidently met with Cromwell at More's house "upon Easter eve" in 1527 to discuss an orthodox translation from the Vulgate. Soon thereafter, "with ardent soul ablaze, scarcely able to wait before embarking on his new studies," he wrote to Cromwell: "Now I begin to taste of Holy Scriptures . . . [and] the Godly savor of holy and ancient doctors, unto whose knowledge I cannot attain without diversity of books. . . . Nothing in the world I desire but books; they once had, I do not doubt but Almighty God shall perform that in me which He, of His most plentiful favor and grace, hath begun." Meanwhile, he began to make a name for himself as an evangelical preacher in Suffolk, where he inveighed against compulsory confession, the worship of images, and the Catholic doctrine of the Mass. Perhaps the fact that he was a protégé of Cromwell, himself a protégé of Wolsey (then still in power), gave him some cover, but in 1528 he was obliged to flee England, and (as we have seen) joined Tyndale at Hamburg, where he worked with him on the Pentateuch.

Coverdale's exile was to last six years. For much of it, he toiled as a translator and proofreader for Flemish printers, while pushing ahead with his own more ambitious task. By the fall of 1535, Convocation had spoken, Henry's mood had changed, Cromwell could openly sponsor the translation he had helped to initiate eight years earlier, and Coverdale could take his manuscript (completed on October 4) to the press. The first printed sheets were run off either at Zurich or Antwerp, and shipped to England, where they were bound up and republished as a small folio by James Nicolson of Southwark, with an amended title page and a handsome dedication to the king.

The latter addressed Henry as "Defender of the Faith, and under God the chief and Supreme Head of the Church of England," and profusely invoked scriptural blessings upon him, including the "plenteous abundance of wisdom that God gave unto Solomon," and the "multiplication of seed, which God gave unto Abraham and Sarah his wife."

It was the first complete Bible ever to be printed in English. The order of the Old Testament books followed the Vulgate rather than the Hebrew; the order of the New, Luther's German rather than Erasmus's edition of the Greek. Baruch was placed among the prophets "next unto Jeremiah, because he was his scribe, and in his time"; Samuel 1 and 2 were called Kings 1 and 2; Nehemiah was called the second book of Esdras; and Hebrews and James were placed between 3 John and Jude. The text was therefore clearly divided into six parts: the Pentateuch; the Historical Books (Joshua to Esther); the Poetical Books (Job to the Song of Solomon); the Prophets (Isaiah to Malachi); the Apocrypha; and the New Testament. Chapter summaries replaced the terse chapter headings found in copies of the Vulgate, and some of the cherished ecclesiastical terms (such as "penance") ousted by Tyndale had been prudently restored. The margins were also free of contentious notes. "I have neither wrested nor altered so much as one word for the maintenance of any manner of sect," Coverdale wrote, "having only the manifest truth of the Scripture before mine eyes."

Since Coverdale was a Latinist and knew little Hebrew and Greek, his Bible was largely based on other translations, especially the work of Tyndale, the Vulgate of St. Jerome, a new Latin rendering from the original languages by the learned Dominican Sanctus Pagninus, published in 1528 "with the sanction of two popes"; and two German translations—one by Luther, the other a collaborative effort by Ulrich Zwingli and Leo Juda known as the Zurich Bible, published in 1529. Such a pastiche may not seem a promising way to proceed, but Coverdale had a remarkable editorial gift, and an exquisitely melodic ear. With an almost unerring eye, he managed to blend and modify the best of his materials into a splendid whole. In his Prologue he freely confessed his own inadequacies as a translator, paid indirect tribute to Tyndale as one whose "ripe" knowledge had been of the right kind, and said he had taken the work in hand himself "for the sake of the English nation" only by default. "Though I could not do so well as I would," he wrote, "I thought it yet my duty to do my best and that with a good will." He was also careful not to undermine his work by antagonizing the authorities. "I am but a private man," he once remarked, "and obedient unto the higher powers." Although his original title page had read "translated out of Dutch [Deutsche] and Latin into English," it now more discreetly had, "faithfully translated into English," to free it of any German (i.e., Lutheran) taint. In the end, quite a bit of the translation—the Poetical Books, the Prophets, and the Apocrypha—was also Coverdale's own.

The English Bible was enriched thereby. A number of his fine phrases endure: "the pride of life" (1 John 2:16); "the world passeth away" (1 John 2:17); "cast me not away from thy presence, and take not thy Holy Spirit from me" (Psalms 51:11); "Enter thou into the joy of the lord" (Matthew 25:21,23); "And forgive us our debts, as we forgive our debtors" (Matthew 6:12). (The more familiar "And forgive us our trespasses, as we forgive them that trespass against us" is Tyndale's.) It is to Coverdale that we also owe "tender mercies," "respect of persons," "lovingkindness," and the phrase "the valley of the shadow of death" in the Twenty-third Psalm. Some things later discarded might have endured. For Proverbs 15:17, Coverdale had "Better is a mess of potage with love, than a fat ox with evil will," which is surely preferable to the oddly obscure "Better is a dinner of herbs where love is, than a stalled ox, and hatred therewith," which is the Authorized Version of the text. Occasionally, his renderings were quaintly anachronistic—as "the beer shall be bitter to them that drink it" (for Isaiah 24:9), and "Thou shalt not need to be afraid for any bugs by night" (for Psalm 91:5). That passage caught everybody's eye, and the translation became known, colloquially, as the "Bugs Bible" soon after it appeared.

Cromwell presented Coverdale's Bible to King Henry, who directed his bishops to review it. They took a long time to do so, out of reluctance for their task. At length the king demanded their opinion. They then told him it had many faults. "But," asked Henry, "are there any heresies maintained thereby?" No, none, they confessed, so far as they could tell. "If there be no heresies," cried Henry, "then in God's name let it go abroad among our people." It was immediately put into limited circulation, and Anne Boleyn laid a copy of it open on a desk at court for all to read.

Cromwell was now the king's vicar-general in all things ecclesiastical (as well as his viceregent in all secular affairs), and had near royal powers at his disposal and precedence over prelates and peers. When the bishops met in Convocation in 1537, it was Cromwell (not Archbishop Cranmer) who presided, and as he entered, the prelates stood and acknowledged him and directed him to the highest place. The English Bible came up for discussion. Stephen Gardiner, the staunchly Catholic Bishop of Winchester, said that "all the heresies and extravagant opinions now in Germany and thence coming over to England, spring from the free use of the Scriptures. . . . And to offer the Bible in the English tongue to the whole nation during these distractions would prove the greatest snare that could be." Bishop John Stokesley of London (Tunstall's successor) complained that fundamental Church doctrine, the service of the Mass, the worship of saints, auricular confession, penance, absolution, purgatory, and so on were everywhere being questioned and that it was "commonly preached, taught, and spoken" that all Church ceremonies not indicated in Scripture should be abolished as "the inventions of men." Cromwell calmly replied that it was the king's will that any decisions the gathering might make be based on Scripture alone. Then Edward Fox, the Bishop of Hereford, got up and stunned the assembly with a speech none of them had ever expected to hear from one of their own:

Think ye not that we can, by any sophistical subtleties, steal out of the world again the light which every man doth see. Christ hath so lightened the world at this time that the light of the Gospel hath put to flight all misty darkness; and it will shortly have the higher hand of all clouds, though we resist in vain never so much. The lay people do now know the Holy Scripture better than many of us. And the Germans have made the text of the Bible so plain and easy, by the Hebrew and Greek tongue, that now many things may be better understood, without any glosses at all, than by all the commentaries of the doctors. . . . Wherefore, ye must consider earnestly what ye will determine of these controversies, that ye make not yourselves to be mocked and laughed to scorn of all the world.

He went on to urge them not to deceive themselves by the hope that there was nothing which the power and authority of the pope could not quench, but rather to see that there was no truth "so feeble and weak . . . but it shall find place, and be able to stand against all falsehood. Truth is the daughter of Time and Time is the mother of Truth; and whatsoever is besieged of Truth cannot long continue; and upon whose side Truth doth stand, that ought not to be thought transitory or that it will ever fall." Others rose to express their agreement, until at last Stokesley cried out: "Yet are ye far deceived if ye think that there is none other word of God but that which every souter and cobbler doth read in his mother tongue!" He meant, of course, the higher Word of Tradition. But in the end a majority of his colleagues stood with Fox. At the conclusion of their deliberations, the assembly as a whole appealed to the king to "permit the use of the Scriptures to the laity." But the fact that "every souter and cobbler" was reading them meant that the bishops were consenting to what had already taken place.

In 1537, two revised editions of Coverdale's Bible appeared, "set forth with the king's most gracious license," and in the following year Coverdale published a diglot edition of the New Testament (as a study aid for the clergy) with the Latin and English side by side.

Meanwhile, yet another whole Bible translation (also sponsored by the state) was being readied for the press. This was the work of John Rogers, an Oxford scholar who had been chaplain to the English House in Antwerp, and to whom Tyndale had entrusted the prison manuscript of his translation of the Old Testament from the Book of Joshua to 2 Chronicles, which had yet to see the light. Rogers now brought the whole of Tyndale's contribution under one roof, together with Coverdale's version of the rest of the Old Testament and the Apocrypha, to make his Bible complete.

Rogers was a careful editor. He preserved Tyndale's prologue to Romans, added the Prayer of Manasses to the Apocrypha (which Coverdale, following the Zurich Bible, had omitted), corrected the numbering of the Psalms to agree with the original Hebrew, and took over the concordance explaining Hebrew tropes and sayings included in the French Bible of Pierre-Robert Olivetan, published in 1535. The whole was also furnished with two hundred illustrations—including two full-page woodcuts by Lucas Cranach borrowed from Luther's German Bible of 1533—introductions, chapter summaries, and marginal notes. The initials W. T. (for William Tyndale) were inserted in conspicuous ornamental letters at the end of the Old Testament, but Tyndale's name, for political reasons, was deliberately omitted from the title page, and the name of "Thomas Matthew" (a pseudonym for John Rogers) appeared in its stead.

Printed at Antwerp by two London publishers—Richard Grafton and Edward Whitchurch, both belonging to the ever-present company of Merchant Adventurers—the Matthew's Bible reached England toward the end of July 1537, and Cranmer was clearly expecting it. He at once wrote to Cromwell, on August 4:

> You shall receive by the bringer hereof a Bible in English, both of a new translation and a new print . . . which, in mine opinion, is very well done; and therefore I pray your Lordship to read the same. And as for the translation, so far as I have read thereof, I like it better than any other translation heretofore made. . . . I pray you, my Lord, that you will exhibit the book unto the King's Highness, and to obtain of his Grace, if you can, a license that the same may be sold and

read of every person, without danger of any act, proclamation, or ordinance, heretofore granted to the contrary, until such time that we, the Bishops, shall set forth a better translation, which I think will not be till a day after doomsday!

Within a week Cromwell replied that he had shown the Bible to the king, who had also looked it over and authorized its publication. Obviously its path had been well paved in advance. And so, "within twelve months of Tyndale's martyrdom," as one historian notes, "his translation, which had been denounced, proscribed, and repeatedly burned at St. Paul's Cross, had now, under an assumed name, been formally approved by the king, and published under the shelter of a royal license and proclamation."

There were now two English Bibles—Coverdale's and Matthew's—authorized by royal decree. The first had been compiled from various sources, not translated from the original tongues; the second was a compilation of translations of varying value, with somewhat controversial notes. The abrasive Protestant tone of those notes did not commend Matthew's Bible to a majority of the clergy, and it was therefore decided—apparently by Cromwell—that a revision free of them (that is, a third authorized version) should be undertaken so that "the reader might swim for once without a cork." Again Cromwell turned to Coverdale, his ever-willing servant in such matters, to make it right. According to Cromwell's instructions, he was to base his text on Matthew's Bible, but consult the Vulgate, Sebastian Munster's Latin translation of the Old Testament, and Erasmus's Latin translation of the New. Though that would make it merely the revision of a compilation, the new Bible was cast as an authoritative text. And the state had large ambitions for it. In the spring of 1538, Cromwell sent Coverdale to Paris with a royal typographer to meet with the great French printer François Regnault, who, at that time, surpassed all English printers in the development of his craft. Regnault agreed to produce the new English Bible on an opulent scale, and the king of France gave him license to proceed. But independent of that license—or rather indifferent to its face—the Inquisition decided to intervene. It soon was breathing down the printer's neck.

Just before Christmas, when the work was far advanced, Coverdale entrusted some of the finished sheets as a precautionary measure to the English ambassador for safekeeping—and scarcely had he done so when the remaining sheets were seized. But a handsome bribe apparently prevented their destruction, and instead they were neatly placed in "four great dry vats" and sold by pre-arrangement as waste paper to a haberdasher "to lap in caps." The haberdasher resold them to Cromwell's agents, who conveyed them out of France. Then Cromwell did what only state authority can do—he not only bought up the standing type, but the printing presses Regnault had been using, together with Regnault's entire staff of compositors, and had them shipped across the Channel to England. And so it was that in April 1539, in London, the first edition of the Great Bible (so called from its lavish size and adornment) rolled off the press.

It was in every respect a magnificent tribute to the art of book design. A large folio, printed in black letter type, it featured (among its other comely aspects) an elaborate frontispiece by Hans Holbein of King Henry enthroned, shown handing the Bible down to Cranmer (as head to the clergy) and to Cromwell (as head of the laity). These two lieutenants of his will in turn distributed it to the people amid shouts of "Vivat Rex!" and "God save the King!" From above, borne upon the clouds, God benignly surveyed the scene. Two bannerlike scrolls fluttered from his mouth. One proclaimed: "The word that goeth forth out of my mouth shall not return to me void, but shall accomplish that which I please" (Isaiah 55:11); the other: "I have found a man after my own heart, who shall perform all my desire" (Acts 13:22).

Henry was that man. In the eyes of those around him (and doubtless in his own eyes, too) he embodied the Reformation in England—and there was some sense in which this presumption was correct. Although the Wycliffe and Tyndale translations had "laid the foundation for Protestant thinking in England," and their survival under ban proof enough that the new Church was based in part upon a revolution from below, that revolution had been legitimized from above by Henry's acts. England was still predominantly Catholic, and so "the change was royal before it was completely popular," and political before most of the tenets of Protestant doctrine took root.

It was not the purpose of the new Bible to hammer those tenets home. Pursuant to his mandate, Coverdale refrained from glossing the text with any "private or contentious opinions," though he had still hoped to indicate alternative readings and occasional interpretations in the notes. But everything he did that way was cut. However, in an eerie memorial to their absence, the marginal icons designed to mark them (such as pointing hands) remained in the printed text.

By and large, that text improved upon its models, and was a tribute to Coverdale's elegaic gift. One striking example may serve. In Matthew's Bible, Isaiah 21:4 had read, "Mine heart panted, I trembled for fear. The darkness made me fearful in my mind." In the Great Bible, this became: "My heart panted, fearfulness came upon me. The night of my voluptuousness hath he turned against me into fear."

With the Great Bible the Scriptures in English finally achieved that official status Tyndale had envisioned for them when he died. By royal injunction, the Lord's Prayer and the Ten Commandments in English were to be taught sentence by sentence on Sundays and holy days throughout the year; at least one sermon on the Gospel was to be preached every quarter "with exhortations to Scriptural works of mercy rather than to such things as pilgrimages, relics, or the saying over of beads"; and every parish church in England was to "set up in some convenient place" a copy of the English Bible accessible to all as "the very lively Word of God." Throughout the kingdom, copies for public use and edification were soon chained to lecterns in the vestibules of churches—six of them in St. Paul's Church alone.

There were some constraints. The people, for example, were admonished "to avoid all contention and altercation" in their discussion of biblical passages and "refer the explication of obscure places to men of higher judgment." But they ignored such injunctions and yielded completely to their new, blissful sense of spiritual awakening and release. "It was wonderful to see with what joy the book of God was received," wrote an early biographer of Cranmer, "not only among the learneder sort and those that were noted for lovers of the reformation, but generally all England over among all the vulgar and common people; with what greediness God's word was read, and what resort to places where the reading of it was. Everybody that could bought the book and busily read it; or got others to read it to them, if they could not themselves; and divers among the elderly learned to read on purpose. And even little boys flocked among the rest to hear portions of the Holy Scriptures read." Indeed, crowds sometimes assembled in the church vestibules during Sunday service and eventually the king found it necessary to issue a proclamation (in April 1539) forbidding the reading of the Bible aloud at such times.

The first edition of the Great Bible was soon bought up and a second followed in April 1540 with a Preface by Cranmer that commended it to all: "Here may . . . men, women; young, old; learned, unlearned; rich, poor; priests, laymen; lords, ladies; officers, tenants, and mean [lowly] men; virgins, wives; widows, lawyers, merchants, artificers, husband men, and all manner of persons of what estate or condition soever they be . . . learn all things, what they ought to believe, what they ought to do, and what they should not do, as well concerning Almighty God as them selves and all other." Between 1539 and 1541, the Great Bible went through seven editions (formidable for a book designed only for liturgical use) and was preeminent thereafter for almost thirty years. Down to 1662, it supplied the Church of England through its Prayer Book with the lessons to be read in all its acts of divine service, and to this day part of the Great Bible (both in the Psalter, and the words repeated in the office of Communion) lives in the Prayer Book still.

About the time the Great Bible was published, not incidentally, another revision of Matthew's Bible was also done, in this case by Richard Taverner, a former student at Cardinal College, Oxford. At Oxford, Taverner had studied Greek, sung in the choir, and was briefly imprisoned by Wolsey for concealing contraband literature under the floorboards of his room. Wolsey eventually released him out of consideration for his musical ability, and because he "thought it a pity to spoil so fine a voice by the dungeon's damp air." In after years, Taverner had devoted himself to the law, practiced at the

Inner Temple, and in 1535 became clerk of the king's signet in Cromwell's employ. Although his Bible was licensed by the king, of all English versions it proved the least worthy of note, and was eclipsed by the Great Bible even before it appeared.

∽

As Henry's principal adviser from 1532 to 1540, Cromwell was responsible for establishing the Reformation in England in the king's name. That meant not only "flooding" the kingdom with English Bibles, which freed Scripture from Church control, but secularizing Church property, a principal source of papal power and prestige. With the decline of monastic fervor, the government began to make a lurid (if not unwarranted) case against cloisters, chantries, and other endowed institutions as dens of iniquity and vice. Cromwell was a practiced hand at such litigation, and had been Wolsey's chief agent in the unpopular work of suppressing a number of small monasteries in 1525 in order to fund the cardinal's two new colleges at Ipswich and Oxford. So there was precedent enough for what transpired. But as the king's vicar-general with powers to visit and reform all such institutions, Cromwell now proceeded against them on a grand scale and became known as "the hammer of the monks." In 1535 there were two great inquests—one into monastic habits and morals, the other into Church revenues—which supplied the pretext for the state's assault. Parliament decided that most of the cloisters were "sinks of carnal and abominable living" and that, at the same time, their income was not substantial enough for the services they claimed to perform.

Early in 1536, Cromwell began to coax and coerce some of the lesser foundations into surrendering their property and wealth, and by the end of the year had dissolved 345 of them by statute in the name of fiscal reform. Even conservative bishops like Stokesley fell into line. "The lesser houses are as thorns soon plucked up," he said, "but the remaining great Abbeys are like petrified oaks, yet must follow." Those Abbeys fell apace—Westminster, St. Edmondsbury, Canterbury, Glastonbury, York, Cirencester, Malmesbury, and Battle—by December of 1539, fifty-seven in all, yielding the government diverse holdings worth over £2 million. Parliament set up a Court of Augmentations to receive the treasure, with priority given to jewelry and plate, which went straight to the coffers of the king. Lead was also stripped from the roofs, other movable property and valuables taken, and many of the ancient buildings locally pillaged for their stone. Beginning in 1540, the appropriated land was put up for sale. The Church bought back some of it; some went to officials and peers; most by far found its way into the hands of the gentry. The Commons thereby grew in strength (which was all to the good) but at some cost to the realm: by the sudden eviction of monastics, the random destruction of their priceless libraries (which even a little care might have spared), and the demolition of church buildings to which many "bare ruined choirs" would later attest.

It was one thing to be rid of a foreign overlord, like the pope; another to allow the old religious life, which the country folk still loved and cherished, to be subjected to a wholesale assault. Images of the Virgin were publicly burned, the miraculous rood of Boxley paraded through the streets, and the bones of St. Thomas of Canterbury pilfered from their shrine. Even the most sacred words of the Mass—"Hoc est corpus"—were held up to ridicule, and slurred into "Hocus-pocus," as slang for a cheap magic trick.

Cromwell and his cohorts overreached, and in October 1536 (while the dissolution of the monasteries was still in progress) there were rebellions in Lincolnshire and Yorkshire—known as the Pilgrimage of Grace—that threatened the country with the horrors of civil war. The initial rising was quickly checked, but before it was over a more serious revolt had begun in the north, led by Robert Aske, a country gentleman and lawyer. Taxation, rising prices, and agrarian discontent (due to enclosure) were contributing factors, but when the thirty thousand rebels advanced with Aske at their head they carried banners decorated with crosses, chalices, and the "Five Wounds of Christ." They were met at York by royal troops under Thomas Howard, the third Duke of Norfolk, who stalled for time, made promises, conveyed pardons, and otherwise extended the negotiations with Aske through the fall until, with the onset of winter, the rebels quietly dispersed. The king's revenge then "followed them homewards with rope and sword."

Coincident with the rising, Henry's private world had been shaken by its own discord. Though he had married Anne Boleyn, at least in part, for love, he had also expected her to produce a male heir. But she had not lived up to his expectations, and after her second child came forth stillborn, she was sent to the block. Henry turned for solace to Jane Seymour, Anne's lady-in-waiting, and married her on May 30, 1536. Jane died in October of the following year after giving birth to a son. Even in his mourning the king was merry, for at last he had the heir for which he had longed.

Meanwhile, Rome had lost almost all hope of reclaiming England to its fold. On the Continent, the Lutheran revolt had spread and in Germany could have been suppressed only by force of arms. At the Diet of Speyer in 1529, princes favorable to the Reformation delivered a "Protest" against the proceedings of the emperor and their Catholic peers—and thereafter, all such dissidents were known as "Protestants." Meanwhile, the Augsburg Confession of 1530, which repudiated the Mass as an expiatory sacrifice, compulsory confession, enforced priestly celibacy, and Communion under one kind, had been adopted by a number of Protestant dominions, linked in a political confederation called the Schmalkaldic League. This league had grown, and by 1540 included Brandenburg, Prussia, Saxony, Hesse, Mansfeld, Brunswick, and Anhalt, as well as twenty cities of the empire. Under the circumstances, the lines between religious, political, and military interests blurred. "It was not always clear," writes one historian, "whether the league was defending Protestants against Catholics or the rights of princes against the emperor; or whether the emperor was defending Catholics or imperial supremacy." At times, the Holy Roman Emperor Charles V was at war with Catholic France, and, at times, with Pope Clement VII himself. At times, German Protestants received covert aid from France.

In the reformed states and cities, the Lutheran Church took shape. A German Bible was placed in every pulpit; monks were released from their vows; priests allowed to marry; and churches rang out with "Ein feste Burg ist unser Gott" and other German hymns. Cromwell made skillful use of the changing balance of power, but he also involved himself in projects of a Lutheran alliance distasteful to the king. In 1539, in furtherance of the latter, he persuaded Henry to marry the Lutheran princess Anne of Cleves, whom Henry detested from the start.

Nevertheless, there was good strategic reason for the match. England was just then facing a possible coalition of powers promoted by Charles V, who had begun to raise forces in his Italian and Burgundian states for an English campaign. Anne happened to be the sister of William, Duke of Cleves, whose territories commanded the vital route down the Rhine that split those states in two. But Henry had already begun to lust after Catherine Howard, a promiscuous twenty-year-old lady-in-waiting at court. En route to his own wedding, he told Cromwell through clenched teeth that but for sake of his realm "I would not do that I must do this day for none earthly thing." So repelled was he by his bride that over the next several months he was unable to consummate the marriage—and while he tossed and turned in his joyless bed, the dreaded Continental alliance failed to cohere. This gave tremendous impetus to an anti-Cromwell faction at court, and Henry decided to make Cromwell the scapegoat for his own anticlerical policy, while holding on to its material reward. So far as Henry was concerned, the English Reformation had gone far enough. On June 10, 1540, Cromwell was arrested as a heretic and traitor, condemned without a hearing, and on the morning of July 28, beheaded on Tower Hill. As he was led out to his fate, he reportedly met another man who was also scheduled to die. The man was "very cast down about it," but Cromwell with a cheerful demeanor urged him to pluck up heart, saying: "Though breakfast be sharp, trusting to the mercy of the Lord, we shall have a joyful dinner."

This story (perhaps apocryphal) has a martyr's ring, and its meaning merits pause. Under a capricious and bloodthirsty king, Cromwell had fostered a revolution in the kingdom from which the nation emerged transformed and altered in every aspect of its life. With singular tenacity he had pursued his vision of the sovereign national state, rooted in the supremacy and omnipotence of statute, or (as it came to be called) the legislative supremacy of the king-in-Parliament. The integrity of such a system, insofar as it exalted the king's power, depended on the acquiescence of Parliament to the will of the Crown. But that acquiescence was not destined to last. As a legal construct, therefore, Cromwell's measures marked the beginnings of an idea of monarchy truly limited by dependence on consent. As a parliamentary statesman, Cromwell also managed to replace administration of the state by the royal household with a national administration divorced from the person of the king. Though his vision cost him his life, the foundations he laid endured. Indeed, the novel standing Parliament had achieved under his aegis was dramatically demonstrated in 1542 when a member of the Commons was arrested on his way to the chamber in a private suit for debt. The Commons, claiming parliamentary privilege against such action, sent its own sergeant-at-arms to release him, and when the London sheriff balked at the order of the House, he was imprisoned in his turn and forced to apologize. It was thereby acknowledged (if not quite yet established) that the prerogative of Parliament overrode the acts and processes of all other courts. Shortly thereafter, the standing of Parliament was affirmed by Henry himself. "We at no time stand so highly in our estate royal," he told its members, "as in the time of Parliament, wherein we as head and you as members are conjoined and knit together as one body politic." Although from time to time, as one historian points out, the king packed Parliament, bullied Convocation, and made judges and juries accomplices in his unrighteous deeds, "he neither ignored nor suppressed any one of these bodies, and by thus draping his despotic powers in the old constitutional forms, he unconsciously safeguarded, until the coming of more settled days, the liberties of the land."

After Cromwell's death, his heraldic arms were removed from the title page of the Great Bible, and in new editions (issued in 1540 and 1541) the words appeared, "Overseen and perused at the commandment of the King's Highness, by the right reverend fathers in God Cuthbert Bishop of Durham, and Nicolas Bishop of Rochester." Times had indeed changed. This Cuthbert, Bishop of Durham, it seems, was none other than Cuthbert Tunstall, formerly Bishop of London, "who had refused the hospitality of his palace to Tyndale, and who had subsequently burned the book on which, in its revised version, he now pronounced his official benediction and assent."

The twilight years of Henry's reign were years of reaction. Those who had been in opposition before, led by Stephen Gardiner, Bishop of Winchester, gained in power. Although Gardiner had supported Henry's antipapal policies, he rejected Protestant doctrine and lacked enthusiasm for other changes in the kingdom Cromwell had brought about. The king (noting his ambivalence) had bypassed him in favor of Cranmer to fill the Canterbury see, but he had since recovered favor, and in 1539 (on the eve of Cromwell's fall) he led the conservative effort in Parliament on behalf of the Act of Six Articles—also known by its opponents as the "Whip with Six Strings"—which insisted on transubstantiation, clerical celibacy, vows of chastity, the private Mass, and auricular confession. Essentially, the act made the Church of England Catholic in doctrine, while rejecting obedience to Rome.

With Henry's acquiescence, Gardiner also pushed through Parliament the remarkably titled Act to Abolish Diversity of Opinion, which facilitated persecution of dissent. Within fourteen days bishops charged with carrying the statutes into effect had indicted five hundred persons in London alone; and it was clear that the number of offenders would soon exceed the capacity of the city jails. Appalled at such inquisitorial zeal, Henry quashed the indictments with a royal pardon, so that of all the accused only a few were brought to trial. Even so, over the next several months a number of dissenting Protestants were tried as heretics and burned at the stake.

There was also some attempt to remove the English Bible from circulation and restore the Vulgate to its former place. Henry was unwilling to go that far, but in 1542 he suggested the bishops revise the best of the English translations (presumably as given in the Great Bible) according to their own mind. Cranmer was called upon to parcel out the text. Five strident meetings were held to discuss the project, without any progress being made. At the sixth, Gardiner brought in a list of ninety-nine Latin words, "which for their genuine and native meaning, and for the majesty of the matter in them contained," he thought should not be translated at all, but only Anglicized. The list included: *poenitentia* (penitence or penance);

caritas (love or charity); *gratia* (favor or grace); *ecclesia* (congregation or church); *sacramentum* (mystery or sacrament); *simulacrum* (image); *idolum* (idol); *spiritus sanctus* (holy ghost); *benedictio* (blessing); *adorare* (to worship); and *elementa* (rudiments). He also proposed an occasional macaronic mix of Latin and English that gave an untenable result. For example, for Matthew 3:17 ("This is my beloved Son, in whom I am well pleased," in the later, Authorized Version), he had, "This is my dilect son in whom complacui."

The opposing bishops returned each other's sullen stares.

Gardiner argued his case. He claimed that an inadequate or imperfect translation of certain esoteric terms could only debase their meaning, especially if their meaning was imperfectly known. Otherwise, a translator was bound to render such terms according to his own, mere understanding, which (however well intentioned) might not be right. The text might read intelligibly; but it also might not be what the Bible said. Protestants naturally suspected Gardiner's motives, and thought he was simply trying to prevent translation itself. "Wanting the power to keep the light of the Word from shining," one of them wrote, "[Gardiner] sought, out of policy, to put the light of the Word in a dark lantern . . . to teach the laity their distance; who, though admitted into the outer court of common matter, were yet debarred entrance into the holy of holies of these mysterious expressions, reserved only for the understanding of the high priest." Yet it must be said that Gardiner had tradition on his side. According to many church fathers, certain passages had been made obscure in order to turn the mind from the literal to the symbolic meaning of the words. Cranmer raised the general issue with the king, who decided to table the whole project. Instead, he promised in the future to turn it over to leading university scholars to sift. But nothing that way would be done for a long time.

Meanwhile, on the day Cromwell perished, Henry had married Catherine Howard, having divorced Anne of Cleves two weeks before. This, his fifth marriage, lasted just eighteen months. Catherine's numerous premarital affairs came to light, as well as a possible postmarital fling, and the incensed and incredulous Henry arranged for

Parliament to pass a bill declaring it treason for an unchaste woman to marry the king. Two days later she was beheaded in the Tower. Henry's last spouse was Catherine Parr, whom he married on July 12, 1543, and who was as much a nursemaid as a wife.

Henry was tired of turmoil. Supreme head of his Church and master of its wealth, he had everything he wanted. And he wanted it all to remain just as it was. But it was a living, not a dead thing that he had created, and "he could not lull back into spiritual and intellectual torpor a nation he had so violently aroused." In vain did he persuade Parliament in the spring of 1539 to frame the Act of Six Articles against heresies Cromwell and others had fostered; or ban "the crafty, false, and untrue translation" of Tyndale; or make it a crime for any unlicensed person to read or expound the Bible "in any church or open assembly." In his famous last speech to Parliament the king complained, with tears in his eyes, that the Bible was being "disputed, rhymed, sung and jangled in every ale-house and tavern." Once again large quantities of the vernacular translations were pried from their owners and burned; but this, too, proved in vain. One Anne Askew, the last of Henry's martyrs, declared on July 16, 1546, as she perished with three companions at the stake: "I believe all those Scriptures to be true which [Christ] hath confirmed with his most precious blood. Yea, and as St. Paul saith, those Scriptures are sufficient for our learning and salvation, that Christ hath left here with us."

☙

Henry died on January 28, 1547, "his hand in Cranmer's and his speech gone." He was succeeded by his son, Edward VI. Edward's birth, on October 12, 1537, in the twenty-eighth year of Henry's reign, had seemed next to a miracle. "We had all hungered after a prince so long," recalled one bishop, "that there was as much rejoicing as at the birth of John the Baptist." His mother (Jane Seymour) never recovered from the ordeal of childbirth, and elaborate precautions were naturally taken to safeguard the prince's health. But he turned out to be congenitally frail. His upbringing was thoroughly Protestant, guided by tutors imbued with the New Learning, and from a very young age, he became familiar with the English Bible and New Testament Greek. His instruction also had a very moral cast. He soon learned, we are told, "to fear God's commandments, respect his elders, beware of strange and wanton women, and be thankful to him that telleth him his faults." By the age of nine (when his father died) he reportedly gave "such wonderful proofs of his piety that the whole kingdom and all godly persons entertained the greatest hopes of him." But that piety had a fanatic tinge, and none can say what his reign might have come to had it lasted longer than it did.

Henry had made careful arrangements for the government during his son's minority, but the new king's uncle, Edward Seymour, Earl of Hertford (afterward Duke of Somerset), seized control of the Council of Regents and made himself lord protector and sole guardian of the king. Under Somerset, a convinced reformer, England was unequivocally established as a Protestant state. Henry's Act of Six Articles was repealed, priests allowed to marry, images removed from churches by royal injunction, and the chantries—the last of the great endowed Church institutions—seized, making the expropriation of Church property complete. In 1547, Cranmer published the Book of Homilies designed to encourage preaching, and in 1549 (with help from Continental theologians such as Martin Bucer) composed the Book of Common Prayer and Administration of the Sacraments, which amounted to a reform of the liturgy along Protestant lines. A much revised edition was issued in 1552. In the following year, Cranmer drafted the Forty-two Articles, which gave the Church of England its first creed. Henceforth, the Epistles and the Gospel in the Communion service were to be heard in English, the entire Psalter read through each month, and all services conducted in the vernacular. Gone were the veneration of saints and the remembrance of the departed; and here and there in spasms of iconoclastic zeal church wall paintings were whitewashed, stained glass windows smashed, and monuments defaced.

The English Bible was reenthroned. It had been carried before Edward in the procession at his coronation, and the government at once renewed the royal injunction that a copy of the Great Bible be set up in the vestibule of every church. All restrictions were also removed from other versions then in print. Between 1547 and 1553 the Great Bible went through seven editions, Matthew's Bible through three, Coverdale's through two, and Tyndale's New Testament through thirty-five. Tyndale's name, once proscribed, even appeared in full at last on the title page of at least fifteen editions of his work. At the same time, all medieval manuals, missals, processionals, primers, and other flowers of the Catholic faith and its heritage were shamefully "abolished, extinguished, and forbidden for ever" by parliamentary act.

Opponents of such policies had a hard time. Stephen Gardiner, Bishop Edmund Bonner, and other high churchmen were imprisoned, and Gardiner even denied writing implements and books. More radical reformers (such as the Anabaptists, who scorned the Forty-two Articles as not radical enough) also suffered from the attempt to enforce a single standard of worship in the realm.

Dislike of the Regency Council grew. Made up (by and large) of greedy nobles, conspicuously eager to fill their own pockets at Church expense, its plundering proclivities provoked two serious risings—in the West Country and in Norfolk—which threatened the regime. Somerset was toppled by John Dudley, Earl of Warwick, who assumed control of the council and made himself Duke of Northumberland in October 1551. If anything, Northumberland's policies proved more predatory still. In addition to episcopal lands, he set out to despoil English bishops on a more personal scale. But it was a dangerous game. Although England was now officially Protestant, constrained to uniformity of a revolutionary kind, it was served by a Church whose basic structure remained unaltered from earlier days. Nor had the Reformation yet been established securely in the people's hearts.

Time would shortly show how conflicted those hearts were.

Edward never grew out of his minority. His health failed, and on July 6, 1553, he died of tuberculosis at the age of fifteen. His elder sister, Mary, the child of Catherine of Aragon, stood next in line to the throne, but Northumberland "had climbed to the top by treading her down," and in order to prevent her accession (which he knew would cost him his life) he tried to alter the legal course by marrying his son to Lady Jane Grey, the great-granddaughter of Henry VII. Jane had no dynastic aspirations of her own and fainted in horror when first told that Northumberland planned to make her queen. But he held the reins of power, and the dying Edward (in order to preserve Protestant rule in England) had formally disinherited his two sisters and given his blessing to the coup. Four days after he expired, Jane's accession was proclaimed; but hers was to prove the briefest of reigns. Mary, forewarned, had withdrawn to Framlingham in Suffolk, where she gathered her forces about her, as the country rallied to her cause. It had been more than fifty years since England had seen an armed contest for the throne, but Northumberland's force was no match for the thousands who flocked to Mary's camp. He fell back to Cambridge, and there received word that the capital had declared against him, which meant that all was lost. One August 3, nine days after Jane's pretended coronation, Mary entered London, Jane was arrested, and eventually, with Northumberland, went to the block.

Mary's swift triumph owed nothing to religion and everything to the legalities of Tudor rule. She was incontestably the legitimate sovereign; and no one wanted civil war. But that did not mean the people wanted to change their faith—or to have any faith imposed against their will. Northumberland had given them enough of that. But Mary in her folly would answer him in kind.

A stern adherent of the Church of Rome, Mary had begun her life with the most brilliant prospects, but it had since become a vale of tears. Rejected by a number of princely suitors in her youth, she had seen the marriage from which she had sprung declared incestuous; her mother supplanted; and herself degraded by her own father and declared a bastard. Mortification and sorrow had thereafter consumed and embittered her life; but mingled with her sense of personal wrong was a true indignation at the repudiation of the faith to which she subscribed. Even so, she had been obliged to acknowledge her father as head of the English Church in order to secure her place in the line of succession, as confirmed in Henry's will. Only the greatest kind of soul could have emerged intact out of such testing; but "the fearful tempest of her life had withered and chilled her," and when she came to the throne at the age of thirty-six, she was "a bigoted and blighted soul."

At first she proceeded with some caution, reinstated "her three most Catholic bishops," as she called them—Stephen Gardiner, Cuthbert Tunstall, and Edmund Bonner—and sent a number of prominent reformers to the Tower. But the matter of restoring the pope's supremacy was deferred. The prospect of her marriage, as determining the succession, was, on the other hand, of urgent concern to all. Over the advice of the Commons, who urged her to marry an Englishman of royal blood, she obstinately set her heart on the future King Philip II of Spain. Parliament resented her refusal to respect its counsel, and in 1554, when it became clear that her marriage to Philip would go forward, a Protestant insurrection broke out under Sir Thomas Wyatt, son of the poet and diplomat, who raised a large army at Rochester and advanced on London. A force sent to meet him under the Duke of Norfolk largely defected to his side, and on February 3, 1554, he entered Southwark on the city's outskirts, only to find London Bridge blocked by those loyal to the queen. On the night of the 17th, he carried out a flanking movement which carried him over the Thames at Kingston, and from there made his way toward London from the west. He pushed through Fleet Street to the city wall at Ludgate, but there found himself hemmed in on all sides. London (which had yet to taste the bitter wine of Mary's rule) stood firm, and "the cup of victory was snatched from his lips." After a brief engagement, he surrendered, and later went to the block. In July of that year, Mary married Philip, restored the Catholic creed, revived the laws against heresy, and attempted to enforce the wholesale conversion of the realm.

One of her chief instruments in this regard was Reginald Pole, a cardinal and papal legate of royal English blood. Pole's father had been a cousin of Henry VII, and his mother a niece of Edward IV: that made him the cousin of Henry VIII. Henry, in fact, had paid for his education at both Oxford and the University of Padua, but with seeming ingratitude Pole had denounced Henry's attempts to obtain an annulment of his marriage and returned to Padua under the protection of the Church. In 1536, he wrote a long treatise, *In De-*

fense of Ecclesiastical Unity, attacking Henry's claim of royal supremacy, and in December a gratified pope made him a cardinal and sent him to the Low Countries to confer with English malcontents. Henry retaliated by beheading his mother and other members of his family. Pole, however, refused to modify his views. He rose in the Church, was the presiding legate at the Council of Trent in 1545 and upon the death of Pope Paul III in November 1549 was nearly elected pope "by adoration" with the backing of the Emperor Charles V.

Upon the accession of Mary, the new pope, Julius III, appointed Pole legate for England, and on November 20, 1554, he landed at Dover and made a triumphal entry into London. Ten days later he formally received the country back into the Catholic fold. Before Parliament at Whitehall, he praised Mary as "a virgin, helpless, naked, and unarmed" who had "prevailed in victory over tyrants"; explained that he had been given the power to formally reunite England with the Church of Rome in a spirit of welcome and forgiveness; and indicated that once England submitted, no attempt would be made to take back the lands that had belonged to the Church. "Touching all matters that be past," he said, "they shall be as things cast into the sea of forgetfulness. . . . I come not to compel, but call again." Parliament, by prearrangement, then petitioned the queen and her consort as "persons undefiled in the offense of this body" to intercede for the papal pardon, and as Pole pronounced the general absolution the Lords and Commons fell on their knees. The following Sunday a huge crowd of fifteen thousand gathered in St. Paul's churchyard and heard Gardiner deliver a two-hour sermon on the text, "It is time to awake out of sleep." He concluded by announcing that he had been given the authority to absolve all present, and as the entire crowd knelt for his blessing, "the silence was such that not a cough was heard." Meanwhile, an Inhibition had been proclaimed against the printing of vernacular Bibles and the reading of Scripture in church.

It remained for Parliament to enact the legal instruments that would restore the ancient faith. That was done in December, when the Reformation acts of Henry VIII and Edward VI were repealed. But in so doing, the Parliament (and Mary) paid effective homage to the political legacy Henry and Cromwell had wrought. Although Mary had regarded the royal supremacy as an offense against God, she was obliged to accept that until that title (which had automatically become part of her own title as queen) was repealed by Parliament, it remained in place. Moreover, before the Reformation acts were repealed, they were subjected to prolonged political debate. "If the Mass was now legally restored," one historian observed, "it was because parliament had restored it; and if Mary was now accounted legitimate, it was because parliament had declared her to be so. What a statute had taken away, only a statute could restore; and what one statute had restored, another could rescind. In grounding his Reformation upon parliamentary authority Henry VIII had invested that body with a competence in matters spiritual that not even the most Catholic of his successors could take away."

In an attempt to right a grievous wrong, Parliament also reaffirmed Henry's marriage to Catherine of Aragon, making Mary legitimate; but in the same breath it managed to wrong a right, and charged Cranmer with high treason, seeing fit to blame him as the sole instigator of Henry's divorce. In truth, nobody's hands were clean. Gardiner had supported the divorce well before Cranmer became involved in it; Bonner had tried to persuade the pope to approve it; and Tunstall had subscribed to it by taking the oath of allegiance Henry required. On the other hand (though he had plenty to answer for), Cranmer had done what he could to save those (including More) who fell into disfavor, and had even once interceded with Henry to save Mary herself from the Tower. He had also openly opposed (until the very end, yielding only to King Edward's dying entreaties) Mary's exclusion from the throne.

But Gardiner, whom Mary had appointed chancellor, had emerged from prison thirsting for revenge. An Inquisition was launched, and "the alacrity with which the commissioned prelates discharged their bloody office shows with what impatience they had awaited the appointed hour." Many reformers were condemned and executed; books and authors proscribed; the whole country placed under surveillance; and justices of the peace in every county exhorted to extirpate heresy from the land. The queen urged on these proceedings, and a hysterical pregnancy soon added ferocity to her intent.

From February 1555 to November 1558, roughly four hundred persons perished, some by torture, but most (two hundred eighty-eight) at the stake. John Rogers, the compiler of Matthew's Bible, was the first to die (and did so bravely); thereafter many were fated to suffer in groups. At Colchester, for example, it is said that five men and five women were burned in one day, six in the morning, and four in the afternoon; at Lewis, in Kent, six men and four women perished together; at Bow, near London, on June 27, 1556, thirteen together, two women and eleven men. The southeast supplied most of the victims—one hundred twelve in Bonner's diocese of London alone.

The government also sought to disband informal Protestant congregations, which had proliferated during Edward's reign. The pastor of one of them was handed over to Bonner for trial, and when, under interrogation, he inveighed against the Catholic Mass as an "abomination," Bonner "flew upon him like a wild beast and tore out part of his beard!" A Protestant deacon received even less consideration—if more grudging respect. "Ye see this man what a personable man he is," said Bonner to his colleagues. "And furthermore, concerning his patience, I never saw his like; for I tell you he hath been thrice racked in one day in the Tower. Also in my house he hath felt some sorrow; yet I never saw him break." But Bonner's respect remained untainted by compassion, and the deacon was carted off with two others to Smithfield and burned at the stake.

Most of those singled out for destruction were simple folk bewildered by years of "shifting orthodoxy," by conflicting doctrine, and ever-changing pronouncements from the throne. "Young people who had grown to maturity hearing only evil of the pope," writes one historian, "were now punished for reviling him; villagers who had heard their own priests denounce the Mass and the Catholic sacraments were now ordered to the stake for holding imprecise opinions on the nature of the Eucharist." Apart from several Protestant bishops, in fact, there were few gentlemen among the victims, "and only one gentlewoman." The rest were artisans, day laborers, and their wives.

By Continental standards the number of English martyrs was

small (about one hundred sixty people had been executed as heretics since Wycliffe's day) but the concentration of burnings under Mary was unlike anything England had seen. And it seared itself into the mind. "The spectacle of a man dying in the flames, singing a psalm until his lips were burnt away, was a haunting image, as was the sight of a sixty-year-old widow bound to the stake, or a young blind woman, a ropemaker's daughter, sentenced to burn by a bishop she could not see." Some of the executions were also grotesquely bungled, because the wood for the fire was green, or the rushes too damp to burn quickly, or the bags of gunpowder, tied to the victim's throat to expedite his annihilation, maimed without killing—prolonging his agony and cries.

The martyrs became enshrined in legend. John Rogers, burned at Smithfield in February 1555 in the presence of his wife, a baby at her breast, reportedly went to his death promising to pray for his executioner, and "as one feeling no smart, washed his hands in the flames." Two prominent bishops, Hugh Latimer and Nicholas Ridley (of London and Worcester, respectively, under Edward), were bound together to the same stake with an iron chain. As the pyre was lit, Latimer said to Ridley, "Be of good comfort, and play the man. We shall this day light such a candle, by God's Grace, in England, as I trust shall never be put out." Still another victim went "with a merry courage" toward his fate, barefoot and dressed in an old gown and shirt, and when he came to the stake took it in his arms and kissed it, saying "Welcome the cross of Christ! welcome everlasting life!" And as his body burned, he "seemed to sleep sweetly" in the fire.

Cranmer was tried in September 1555, and on February 14, 1556, in a ceremony full of carefully designed humiliation, degraded from his episcopal office and handed over to the state. The previous October he had witnessed the martyrdom of Latimer and Ridley, and he was now repeatedly pressed by his captors to abjure. Eventually, he wrote several humble recantations in which he repudiated almost the whole of his life's work, and in a desperate appeal to the queen's mercy, ascribed most of the damage done to the Catholic faith in England to his own heretical pronouncements and acts. This did not save him, and on March 21, 1556, he was led forth to be burned at the stake. Both Pole and the queen had expected him to make his abjuration public, but with great dignity and self-possession he shocked them by disavowing it completely before a large crowd, and when the fires were lit, thrust his right hand—which had signed it—into the heart of the flames. There he held it, crying, "This hath offended! Oh this unworthy hand!" until it shriveled up like dried grass.

The queen's inquisition proved a catastrophe for her reign. The executions created nothing but resentment, and showed the whole world that there were English Protestants of such courage and conviction that they would die for their faith. Many English Catholics were also appalled at the methods adopted in their name. Bishop Tunstall, while not averse to burning books, was one of those who recoiled in horror at the carnage, and it stands to his credit that not a single Protestant of his diocese is known to have perished at this time. Once when pressed by Gardiner about an accused man in his charge, he replied: "I pray you bring not this poor man's blood upon my head."

Cranmer's martyrdom alone probably did more to further the cause of the Reformation in England than all the queen's violent effort to reverse its course. Chesterton once remarked with regret that Mary was "a bad queen; bad for many things, but especially bad for her own most beloved cause. . . . She set herself to burn out 'No Popery' and managed to burn it in. The concentration of her fanaticism into cruelty . . . did remain like something red-hot in the public memory." Even still.

Meanwhile, in an unpopular war with France (in which Spain was allied to England and France to the pope), Mary lost Calais, England's last foothold on the Continent, and the pope canceled Reginald Pole's legatine authority and even denounced him as a heretic. The entire Catholic community in England was utterly demoralized, and the queen herself, grief-stricken, sick, and exhausted by a series of false pregnancies, died on November 17, 1558. Within a few hours of her passing, Pole himself expired in despair.

☙

Mary was succeeded by her half-sister, Elizabeth, the child of Anne Boleyn. When first told of her accession, the future queen expressed her surprise by quoting from an English version of the Psalms: "This is the Lord's doing; it is marvellous in our eyes." In a proclamation issued at York, she was saluted as a sovereign "of no mingled blood . . . but born mere English here among us," and in London, where there was universal rejoicing, tables were brought out into the streets for revellers to eat and drink off in honor of her name. En route to the capital, she was cheered by adoring crowds, and outside London was received by the lord mayor, who presented the local dignitaries to her, one by one. As each approached, she smiled and extended her hand to be kissed; but when Edmund Bonner approached and knelt before her, her face changed and she turned away.

On January 15, 1559 (a day chosen as auspicious by her astrologer, John Dee), Elizabeth was crowned and after attending a Mass celebrated in both Latin and English in Westminster Abbey, proceeded to Whitehall for her coronation feast. Earlier that day, as the royal procession had made its way along Cheapside, a venerable old man representing Time, with Truth standing beside him as his child, had emerged from an artificially constructed cave to present the new queen with a copy of the Bible in English. Thousands watched as she stopped and reverently kissed it and pledged herself "diligently to read therein." Reginald Pole had once compared Queen Mary to Truth leading her people out of the Cave of Protestant Night into the Light of Rome. Elizabeth's coronation tableau was clearly designed as a rebuttal, and in a re-creation of the scene by the poet Thomas Heywood, she was made to declare:

This is the jewel that we still love best,
This was our solace when we were distressed.
This book that hath so long concealed itself,
So long shut up, so long hid; but now Lords, see!
We here unclasp, forever it is free!

As monarch, she would reaffirm her position as head of the English Church, and in that sacred capacity, her rule was reasoned and (all things considered) relatively mild. Although the pope would eventually pronounce her excommunicate and deposed, and absolve her subjects of their allegiance, she repudiated persecution on religious grounds and assured all who obeyed the law of her "favor, lenity, and grace in all causes requisite, without any molestation to them by any person by way of examination or inquisition of their secret opinions in their consciences, for matters of faith."

Though raised as a Protestant, Elizabeth was partial to Catholic ritual; but she disliked fanatics of any kind. "There is only one Jesus Christ," she told a French ambassador. "The rest is a dispute over trifles." And she tellingly compared scholastic disputes over points of doctrine to "ropes of sand or sea-slime leading to the Moon." "I see many overbold with God Almighty, making too many subtle scannings of His blessed will," she remarked on one occasion, "as lawyers do with human testaments."

It is hard to say exactly what her convictions were. Although she reportedly believed in the real presence of God in the Sacrament, she also referred to Catholicism as "the darkness and filth of popery," while the Elizabethan "Homily Against Willful Rebellion" (an official admonition to her subjects) referred to the "Babylonical Beast of Rome." Her deliberately ambiguous views on transubstantiation are aptly expressed by an equivocal quatrain she is said to have composed soon after she came to the throne:

Christ was the Word that spake it,
He took the bread and brake it,
And what the Word doth make it,
That I believe and take it.

In the end, most Protestants thought they knew where she stood. In his *Book of Martyrs*, John Foxe wrote that it was thanks to Elizabeth's "true, natural and imperial crown" that "the brightness of God's word was set up again to confound the dark and false-vizored kingdom of Antichrist." Few doubted, in any case, that her faith was real. She trusted that Providence would safeguard her kingdom, and though she built up her navy and made other military preparations to meet the threat from Spain, she told the French ambassador not long before the Spanish Armada sailed, "I think that, at the worst, God has not yet decided that England shall cease to stand where she does, or at least that God has not given the power to overthrow her to those men who would like to undertake it."

She liked sermons to be brief and to the point, and the less controversial the better, for she didn't care to see contention stirred up. The Puritan zeal for preaching alarmed her, and Puritan strictness in some things struck her as absurd. She rejected a bill in Parliament that would have banned all sports and entertainments on Sundays, defended the public theater against prudish attacks, and dismissed attempts to make heresy, adultery, and blasphemy crimes under the law. On the other hand, although she banned incense in church and insisted that the service be conducted in English, she also believed in clerical celibacy and insisted that traditional vestments be worn.

Not many were executed during her rule. Queen Mary had burned over three hundred Protestants in three years; Elizabeth, in the course of her long, difficult reign, sent only four people, all Anabaptists (advocates of adult baptism), to the stake. Sir Francis Bacon once remarked that she had no "liking to make windows into men's hearts and secret thoughts," and indeed all she asked for was "loyalty to herself and the state and outward conformity to her laws." That she managed as she did surpassed the hope and expectation of even her most fervent admirers, for no one could have predicted she would have a long and distinguished reign.

In religion, her difficulties were apparent from the start. The Church hierarchy under Mary had been packed with Catholics, and the new queen had trouble even finding a bishop to celebrate Communion at Christmas according to her taste. The see of Canterbury was vacant, and other prelates (such as Nicolas Heath, Archbishop of York) were openly hostile to her. She therefore asked Owen Oglethorpe, Bishop of Carlisle, to do the honors in her chapel at Whitehall, but sent word to him in advance not to elevate the Host. After the Gospel had been read, however, Oglethorpe slowly began to raise the bread and wine. The queen ordered him to stop, but he proceeded anyway, whereupon she abruptly stood and withdrew.

Even so, she seldom allowed personal animus to express itself in immoderate political acts, and her first official measure was a temporary ban on evangelical preaching, until Parliament could convene. This was followed in April 1559 by two great statutes, the Act of Supremacy and the Act of Uniformity, which together with a series of injunctions established the Anglican Church. The first act recognized Elizabeth as supreme governor of the Church of England; the second made uniformity in religion the law of the land. The liturgy in English once more replaced the Latin Mass; Anglican communicants were exhorted to "feed on [Jesus Christ] in their hearts, with faith"; and all beneficed clergy were compelled to take the Oath of Supremacy and renounce the jurisdiction of every foreign prince or prelate, on pain of forfeiting their posts. Beyond that, "the use of Church ornaments and vestments was subject to the queen's discretion, and every subject over sixteen was required to attend church." Catholics, however, could excuse themselves on payment of a moderate fine. Her relatively balanced approach was noted by the Austrian envoy, who wrote: "She seems both to protect the Catholic religion and at the same time not entirely to condemn or outwardly reject the new Reformation."

Her religious compromise became known as the Elizabethan Settlement, which essentially embraced Protestant doctrine with respect to the Eucharist but otherwise gave the Church, in its ritual and organization, a Catholic form. The Anglican creed, known as the Thirty-nine Articles (composed by a commission of bishops, and based on the Forty-two Articles Cranmer had crafted in 1553), soon followed as an official statement of belief. Most of the lesser clergy acceded, but the hierarchy opposed her legislation tooth and nail. In time, fourteen bishops, twelve deans, fifteen heads of colleges, and between two hundred and three hundred clergy from the previous reign resigned their offices or were dismissed.

Throughout her long reign, Elizabeth demonstrated prudence and political acumen, an almost unerring eye for superb talent in her choice of officials, and an extraordinary ability to inspire loyalty and devoted service. After the sorrows of Mary's rule, her accession inevitably produced a degree of optimism and hopeful expectation, but it was one of her great achievements, as one writer noted, that she was able "to convert this ephemeral goodwill into a constant loyalty and awe." Wiser and more careful than her father, she had an independent and skeptical mind that enabled her to steer a sensible and moderate course. But "the essence of her policy was to do her utmost to avoid war, and in the meantime to build up a strong and united England in the shadow of peace." In so doing, she was prepared to be tolerant of anything that fell short of political faction. "The *via media* which is the spirit of Anglicanism," T. S. Eliot once remarked, "was the spirit of Elizabeth in all things."

Her purpose was put to a number of difficult tests. When she ascended the throne, the Treasury was empty; the king of France (through his daughter-in-law, Mary Queen of Scots) had one foot in Scotland; and the country was torn by religious strife. Many in England also had doubts about the legitimacy of her own title to the throne. The struggle between competing interests was played out in a number of arenas and, as ever, was reflected in the form the English Bible took.

Every party had its chosen text. During Mary's brief reign, hundreds of Protestant scholars had sought refuge on the Continent in Reformed strongholds such as Basel, Zurich, Frankfurt, and Geneva, where they plotted the return of Protestant rule to England and quarreled over points of doctrine and the authority of the *Book of Common Prayer.* The more moderate party was led by Richard Cox, ex-tutor to King Edward and afterward Bishop of Ely; the radicals by John Knox, a former royal chaplain and future "apostle to the Scots." Cranmer's Prayer Book was too High Church for him, and he rejected it as tainted by "popery and superstition on every page." At length, in 1555, the Knox faction established itself in Calvinist Geneva, "the holy city of the Alps."

Under Calvin's administration, Geneva had become a second Wittenberg, with a famous academy that attracted students and refugees from all over Europe, and where the "new model church" of Reformed Christianity had been organized as an experiment in theocratic rule. It was also a city humming with biblical scholarship—"the store of heavenly learning and judgment," as one Puritan put it, "where God hath appointed us to dwell." The English exiles compiled a service or prayer book of their own (based on Calvin's French liturgy), and prepared new Bible translations. In 1557, William Whittingham, a sometime fellow of All Souls College, Oxford, and afterward dean of Durham, published a fresh English version of the New Testament, and three years later, in collaboration with Anthony Gilbey (a Hebrew scholar), Thomas Sampson, William Cole, and Christopher Goodman (good classicists all), produced a new English Bible. Based in part on the Great Bible for the Old Testament, and on Whittingham's own revision of Tyndale for the New, the Geneva Bible, as it was called, paid meticulous attention to the Greek and Hebrew originals, and made use of the best of the most recent translations into Latin and French.

It was unquestionably the most scholarly, well-annotated, and accurate English Bible yet to appear. Its readability, portable size (in quarto format), and simple roman type stood in bold contrast to earlier black letter versions, some of which (like the Great Bible) were suitable only for liturgical use. As in many Bibles today, words not in the original but inserted to complete the sense were printed in italic, and for ease of reference the text was divided (for the first time, in English) into chapter and verse. There were also maps, woodcuts, elaborate tables, an appendix of metrical psalms, and a running commentary of explanatory notes. Some two thousand alternate readings and 725 literal renderings were packed into the margins of the New Testament alone.

In their Address to the readers, the translators stressed how conscientious their labors had been: "God knoweth with what fear and trembling we have been now for the space of two years and more, day and night, occupied herein. . . . And this we may with good conscience protest, that we have in every point and word, according to the measure of that knowledge which it pleased Almighty God to give us, faithfully rendered the text, and in all hard places most sincerely expounded the same." Their work won broad acceptance, soon became and long remained the household Bible of English-speaking Protestants, and was the Bible on which Shakespeare and other great Elizabethan poets and dramatists were reared. Within England its recognized superiority to all other versions, and its wide distribution and use, made it a powerful instrument of religious reform. Over the course of the next eighty-five years (between 1560 and 1644), it went through 140 editions, sixty during the reign of Queen Elizabeth alone.

Some of its happiest turns of phrase remain familiar, as "smite them hip and thigh," "vanity of vanities," "except a man be born again," "Remember now thy Creator in the days of thy youth," "Solomon in all his glory," "My beloved Son in whom I am well-pleased," "a cloud of witnesses," and "a little leaven leaveneth the whole lump." These and other phrases were often on the lips of children growing up, and gave an oracular quality to the pronouncements of their parents on all matters viewed through a biblical lens. Indeed, its many virtues "cast the Great Bible completely into the shade." On the other hand, it could not hope for ecumenical appeal. Its margins bristled with annotations galling to all Church authorities, in England as well as Rome. Although some of the notes merely expanded upon traditional readings, others seemed designed to provoke ecclesiastical wrath. The locusts of the Apocalypse, for example, were declared to represent "worldly subtle Prelates"; the religious observances of Easter, Whitsuntide, the Feast of Tabernacles, and other holy days were repudiated as servile; and almost anything involving elaborate ritual dismissed as "superstition" worthy of the pope. Rome itself, of course, was identified as a type of Sodom and Gomorrah where "falsehood and ungodliness" reigned.

As her first Archbishop of Canterbury, Elizabeth chose Matthew Parker, sometime chaplain to her mother, Anne Boleyn. An early, but moderate, reformer, Parker possessed good sense, learning, and tact, and both Henry VIII and Edward VI had bestowed honors upon him. But Mary had ordered him defrocked because he had taken a wife. Elizabeth (who also disapproved of his marriage) restored him to favor as one on whom she could rely, but he was not an ambitious cleric and she had to overcome his extreme reluctance to take the Canterbury post. When first informed of his promotion, he declared: "I would rather go to prison than accept," and it was only after William Cecil, Elizabeth's state secretary, intervened with partriotic exhortations that he agreed.

It was Parker's task to carry out the religious settlement. He supervised the formulation of the Thirty-nine Articles that, with the Book of Common Prayer, presented the liturgy and doctrine of the English Church, but after the ouster of so many Catholics from their livings, he had to rely more than he would have liked on Protestants in the divided realm. Some of them were zealots. Mary's inquisitions had infected the body politic with an anti-Catholic bias that would long sicken at its heart, while a number of the returning exiles (afterward known as Puritans) also brought with them the radical doctrines and practices of Calvin and a desire to "purify" the Anglican Church. The Book of Common Prayer was a particular object of their ire. Although it called an altar a "table" and considered the Lord's Supper a commemorative rite, it still retained much they thought unwarranted by Scripture, such as vestments, the sign of the Cross, kneeling at Communion, and formal prayer. Many also wished to replace episcopal Church government with a more Presbyterian form, and in general their congregationalist (and semidemocratic) tendencies ran counter to the organization of the Tudor state.

Although from first to last Elizabeth was a popular sovereign, her government was autocratic, and (despite the increasing powers of Parliament) not a parliamentary system in the modern sense. Generally speaking, as Trevelyan observed, Parliaments were summoned to do three things: to vote taxes, to pass legislation submitted to them, and to give advice when asked. Each session was called primarily for gaining the cooperation of the country for some great matter at hand, and once the object was achieved, the assembly was dismissed. The queen refused to allow debate on matters to which she was averse—forbidding all discussion of the succession, for example, and (after 1559) of religion, which she claimed as a matter for her determination alone. She recognized that the state Church was the foundation of her supremacy, and that under a government which united in one person the highest ecclesiastical and civil rank, habits of obedience to authority in matters of conscience assured acquiescence to her will.

In the day-to-day exercise of her powers, she made use of several prerogative courts through which her legal immunities and discretionary authority were exercised. Of these, the most important were the Star Chamber, which dealt with offenses against public order; and the High Commission, which was set up to enforce the religious settlement of 1559.

The Court of the Star Chamber had grown out of the king's Privy Council and claimed a jurisdiction beyond that of the common-law courts. Nor were its procedures constrained by any of the safeguards the latter embraced. It dispensed with juries; could act upon clandestine information or the petition of an individual complaint; and had the power of life and death. Its decisions were as binding as the acts of Parliament. The Court of High Commission, on the other hand, was an ecclesiastical body empowered to inquire into all offenses against the Acts of Supremacy and Uniformity, such as "heretical opinions, seditious books, contempts, conspiracies, false rumors or talks, slanderous words and sayings, etc., contrary to the aforesaid laws, or any others ordained for the maintenance of religion in this realm, together with their abettors, counsellors, and coadjutors." It could also "examine, alter, review, and amend" the statutes of all colleges, cathedrals, grammar schools, and other public foundations. Made up mainly of canon lawyers, bishops, and prominent laymen (some of whom were also members of the Star Chamber), it sanctioned self-recrimination (based on the administration of the so-called ex officio oath) and could turn anyone over to the Court of the Star Chamber for criminal trial. Although its sweeping powers remained in abeyance until 1565, thereafter in the face of growing opposition to the Church from both Catholics and Protestant nonconformists alike, it was transformed into a standing court.

Elizabeth's government also kept a tight rein on the press. In 1557, Queen Mary had chartered the Stationers' Company, which obliged anyone printing anything for sale in the kingdom to obtain a special privilege or patent first. Elizabeth enforced that constraint, and enacted various rules and ordinances that also required printers to keep the government up to date on the type and variety of their equipment and made it illegal for anyone to print, bind, stitch, or sell a book without permission on penalty of six months' imprisonment and disbarment from his trade.

The Puritans in England enjoyed a numerical preponderance among the lower clergy, had standing in Parliament, and allies in the high councils of the realm. For the most part the queen shared their foreign policy concerns, and often heeded their prompting, if she did not follow their lead. Without her assistance, neither the Huguenots in France nor the Protestant Dutch (under Catholic rule) could have stood their ground. She also helped the Scots against their Catholic queen regent, Mary, and the Protestant princes of Germany against Charles V.

But on the home front, the Puritans and Elizabeth were often at odds. In the beginning, the Act of Uniformity was not strictly enforced, and ministers who declined to subscribe still often managed to secure places (however lowly) in the Church. But over time a developing chaos in liturgical practice created confusion, and in January 1564 Elizabeth directed Archbishop Parker and the High Commission to ensure that "all diversities and varieties among the clergy and laity, as breeding nothing but contention . . . [be] brought to one manner of uniformity throughout the kingdom." William Cecil then sat down to enumerate the "diversities" in a list:

VARIETIES IN THE SERVICE AND ADMINISTRATION USED.

Service and Prayer. Some say the Service and Prayers in the chancel others in the body of the Church. Some say the same in a seat made in the church; some in the pulpit with their faces to the people. Some say it with a surplice, others without a surplice. *Table.* The table standeth in the body of the church in some places; in others it standeth in the chancel. In some places the table standeth altar-wise, distant from the wall yard. In some places in the middle of the chancel, north and south. In some places the table is joined; in others, it standeth upon tressels. In some it standeth upon a carpet; in others it hath none.

Administration of the Communion. Some with surplice and cap; some with surplice alone; others with none. Some with chalice; some with a communion cup; others with a common cup. Some with unleavened bread; some with leavened.

Receiving. Some receive kneeling, others standing, others sitting. *Baptising.* Some baptize in a font; some in a basin. Some sign with the sign of the cross; others sign not. Some minister in a surplice; others without. *Apparel.* Some with a square cap; some with a round cap; some with a button cap; some with a hat. Some in scholars' clothes; some in others.

To curb this spirit of innovation, the High Commission devised Articles for the regulation of divine service, and the queen issued a proclamation requiring uniformity in clerical garb. On March 24, ninety-eight Nonconforming clergymen were brought before the commissioners to explain their dissent. Prior to their examination, a model minister (one Robert Coles of London) was paraded out, arrayed like a manikin in the prescribed vestments—square cap, tippet, and surplice, all according to statute—and offered as an example of how to dress. The dissenters were then told to "inviolably observe" the queen's injunctions and conform. "Ye that will subscribe, write Volo; ye that will not subscribe, write Nolo. Be brief. Make your words." When some attempted to argue the matter, they were immediately silenced *sub poena contemptus* and the roll was called. Sixty-one subscribed; thirty-seven refused. The latter were at once suspended from office and warned they would be deprived of it altogether if they did not yield within three months.

Miles Coverdale was among them. In 1559, he had taken part in Parker's consecration as archbishop, but could not reconcile himself to aspects of the settlement and chose instead the life of a wandering priest. At length Edmund Grindal, the Bishop of London, procured the little parish of St. Magnus, London, for him but even this was afterward taken, and he died in poverty on May 26, 1569, at the age of eighty-one. Two days later he was buried in the Church of St. Bartholomew, behind the Royal Exchange, where to the astonishment of the authorities a multitude turned up for his funeral to "reverence his memory and bewail his loss."

There was also a misguided attempt to make an example of John Foxe, another Nonconformist, whose *Book of Martyrs* had done more than any other work except the Bible to establish the Reformation in the people's hearts. When required to subscribe, he had drawn a copy of the Greek New Testament from his pocket, and said: "I will subscribe to this!" Threatened with the loss of his livelihood, he rejoined: "I have nothing in the Church but a prebendary in Salisbury, and much good may it do you if you take it." In the end, they did not dare.

The Protestant host of England "now parted into two hostile camps, never to reunite." One was High Church, linked indissolubly with the state; the other, Nonconforming or Puritan, holding to various degrees of dissent. The Puritans were later accused of having brought the schism about by their insistence on matters having nothing to do with important points of faith; but to this they replied that unimportant things became important in principle when "imposed as necessary by a self-constituted power." For them the question became whether the Bible was the authority for the Church in all things. Elizabeth and her archbishop (both being "Catholic" in this) held that it was not—that the apostolic Churches had been congregational in form because of the circumstances of their founding, and that "it belonged to the government of each country to settle the organization, rites, and observances of the Church" within its own realm.

Nothing was resolved. A decade later the dean of York could write: "At the beginning, it was but a cap and surplice, and a tippet; but now it is grown to [opposition to] Bishops, Archbishops, and Cathedral churches, and the overthrow of order established, and (to speak plain) of the Queen's Majesty's authority in causes ecclesiastical . . . I warrant you, she must draw her sword."

In this context, an attempt was made to come up with an English Bible of more Anglican character, since neither the Great Bible nor the Geneva Bible would do. The Geneva Bible was reckoned a better translation, and its marked superiority to the Great Bible called uncomfortable attention to the latter's faults. But the Puritan bias of its notes made it plainly impossible for Convocation (or the queen) to give it their official stamp. Accordingly, Archbishop Parker revived Cranmer's idea of an authorized translation to be done by the bishops, and in 1564 he "sorted out the whole Bible into parcels" which he distributed to fifteen learned prelates "to peruse, collate, and correct." In general, they were to follow the text of the Great Bible except where it differed from the original tongues; to compare their reading of any given passage with the Latin translations of Pagninus and Munster; to mark "genealogies" and other "unedifying" passages so that readers could skip them if they wished; to amend "with more convenient terms and phrases" any passage thought to give offense through "lightness or obscenity" (the bishops disliked phrases like "a pissing she-mule"); and not to mar their margins with "bitter notes."

The known translators (or revisers) in addition to Parker were: Edwin Sandys, Bishop of Worcester; Andrew Pierson, prebendary of Canterbury Cathedral; John Parkhurst, Bishop of Norwich; Richard Davies, Bishop of St. David's, Wales; Robert Horne, Bishop of Winchester; William Barlow, Bishop of Chichester; Thomas Bentham, Bishop of Coventry and Lichfield; Edmund Scambler, Bishop of Peterborough; Edmund Grindal, Bishop of London; Nicholas Bullingham, Bishop of Lincoln; Richard Cox, Bishop of Ely; William Alley, Bishop of Exeter; Gabriel Goodman, dean of Westminster; and Andrew Perne, dean of Ely. A sixteenth collaborator (responsible for translating the Psalms) remains unknown.

Some were men of prominence then, and of some interest still. One was Sandys, a fellow of St. John's College, Cambridge, Bishop of Worcester, later Archbishop of York, and a forebear of George Washington. (His son, Sir Edwin Sandys, was also involved in the early fortunes of Virginia and with the Pilgrims of Plymouth Rock.) Assigned the four books of Kings and Chronicles, Sandys closely adhered to the Great Bible readings but put alternative renderings from the Geneva Bible in the notes. Some of his notes were rather anxiously chaste. At 1 Kings 1:2, where old King David is nursed by a lovely maid, he explained: "David took this virgin, not for lust but for the health of his body, by the advice of his Council; which seemeth to be done by a special dispensation of God, and therefore not to be followed as an example." At 1 Kings 11:1, he felt obliged to justify Solomon's polygamy: "God tolerated in his people the Israelites plurality of wives, as well for the increase of his people, as also for their mystery [mystical meaning], for Abraham's wives and Jacob's wives were figures of the Synagogue and the true Church. But Christ hath called us to the first institution, 'There shall be two in one flesh.' " Ironically enough, after Sandys became Archbishop of York, one of his tenants tried to blackmail him by hiding a woman in his bed. He came home, drew open the curtains, and there she was! And just at that moment her husband rushed in! With blushing embarrassment, Sandys immediately reported the incident to the queen.

The Bishops' Bible, as it was called, was published in October 1568 as a stately and imposing volume, similar to the Great Bible in design, with a portrait of Queen Elizabeth on its title page, a portrait of the Earl of Leicester before the Book of Joshua, and a portrait of William Cecil, Lord Burghley before the Psalms. The text (as in the Geneva Bible) was divided into chapter and verse, and considerable space was given to calendars, almanacs, woodcuts, tables, and maps. Cranmer's Preface to the Great Bible was reprinted, together with another by Parker, which argued for the priority of Scripture as the ground of faith. In defense of a diversity of translations, Cranmer quoted St. Augustine: "By God's providence it is brought about, that the holy Scriptures, which be the salves for every man's sore, though at the first they came from one language, now by diversity of many languages . . . are spread to all nations."

But the whole project failed in its intent. Although the bishops had corresponded with Parker as the work went forward, there seems to have been no regular conference between them or comparison of their work. And as general editor, Parker failed to make a coherent whole of what his colleagues had done. Tyndale once caustically remarked: "When a thing speedeth not well, we borrow speech and say, 'The Bishop hath blessed it; because nothing speedeth well that they meddle withal. If the porridge be burned too, or the meat over-roasted, we say, The bishop hath put his foot in the pot, or, The bishop played the cook.' " In this case, the bishops spoiled the stew. Some of the renderings—"the voice of one crying in the wilderness" (Matthew 3:3); "persecuted for righteousness' sake" (Matthew 5:10); and "overcome evil with good" (Romans 12:21)—were worthy, and have come down to us intact; but patently superior readings from the Geneva Bible were often ignored. Instead of "Cast thy bread upon the waters," the bishops, for example, had "Lay thy bread upon wet faces," which was not only grotesque but wrong; and they unaccountably preferred "Backbite not one another" to "Speak not evil of one another," which was more proper, to say the least.

Parker presented a copy of the new Bible to the queen and

asked that "it might have her gracious favor, license, and protection," but she took no public notice of it, nor ever offered to give it her sanction. The bishops, however, stood stubbornly by their work. In 1571 they decreed in Convocation that every church was to have a copy, displayed in a convenient place, and every bishop a copy in his house accessible to servants and guests. Over the course of forty years, it went through twenty-two editions—six in quarto, one in octavo, and fifteen in folio (the last in 1606). But its official status failed to win it acclaim. Altogether it was a prohibitively expensive and unwieldy tome, yet negligently done, and some of the illustrations (including an erotic woodcut of Leda and the Swan from the *Metamorphoses* of Ovid, placed at the beginning of the Epistle to the Hebrews) seemed of doubtful taste. As a result, though it superseded the Great Bible in liturgical use, "its circulation was practically limited to the Churches supplied with it," and it failed to supplant the Geneva Bible in the affections of the land.

It might have enjoyed a better fate. Here and there the bishops had done something of interest, as in the following passages from two of the Apocryphal books. The first is from Judith, chapter 13: "As for Holofernes he lay upon the bed all drunken, and of very drunkenness, fell asleep. And she went to the bedstead and loosed the sword that hanged upon it and drew it out. Then she took hold of the hairy locks of his head and gave him two strokes upon the neck and smote off his head." The other is from the Additions to Esther, chapter 15: "She was ruddy through the perfection of her beauty, but her heart was in anguish through fear. The king, clothed with all his robes of majesty glittering with gold and precious stones, was very dreadful. The Queen fell down very pale and fainted. God changed the spirit of the King, who leaped from the throne and took her in his arms." These passages, and perhaps some others, are arguably better than the versions we now know.

∽

If the Puritans gave Elizabeth and her bishops little peace, there was much to be feared also from Catholic unrest. The center of Catholic resistance was the north, where the monastic movement had been especially strong, and where, under Henry VIII and Edward VI, risings had previously occurred. Under Elizabeth, it once again began to churn. But it was Mary Stuart's captivity in England that sparked the unrest into revolt.

Better known to history as Mary Queen of Scots, Mary Stuart was the only child of James V of Scotland and his French wife, Mary of Guise. Mary had Tudor blood in her (her grandmother was a sister of Henry VII), and had become queen of the Scots as an infant, in December 1542. But for seventeen years, while she was raised at the French court of Henry II, a regency had ruled. In the interim, she grew into an accomplished woman of remarkable beauty, with amber-colored eyes and reddish gold hair. The charm of her soft, sweet voice was said to be irresistible and wonderfully tuned to song. She could also play the harp, the virginal, and the lute with skill; spoke three or four languages; and wrote poetry in Italian and French. At age sixteen, she was married to Francis, the French king's eldest son and heir, and upon the accession of Elizabeth also became, by virtue of her Tudor blood, next in line to the English throne. Those who thought Henry's marriage to Anne Boleyn unlawful regarded Mary in fact as the rightful queen. This was Mary's own view, too, and she never ceased to hope for circumstances that would place the crown of England on her head. In the following year, Francis succeeded his father as King of France; but then he died; and power fell to Catherine de Medici as regent for Charles IX.

In August 1561, Mary returned to Scotland at last to reign. A policy of religious toleration was indispensable to her governance, and she managed well enough at first, until in July 1565 she married her cousin, Henry Stuart, Lord Darnley, which started the complex train of events that was to lead to her demise. Darnley was detested by much of the Scottish nobility and (as Mary soon discovered) was vicious and cruel. She allowed him the title of king, but he wanted it for life and demanded that it also descend to his heirs. Her secretary advised her against complying and Darnley had him butchered before her eyes. Three months later she gave birth to the prince who would become king of both Scotland and England; but all affection for her husband had died. Not long afterward, she took up with James Hepburn, the Earl of Bothwell, and together they plotted Darnley's death. On the night of February 9, 1567, they blew up his house, and then caught and killed him as he fled through a nearby field.

Mary's own conduct thereafter was fatally unwise. Three months after Darnley's death, she and Bothwell were wed, but he was just as unappealing as Darnley to most of the Scottish lords. They rose up, deposed and imprisoned her on the tiny island of Loch Leven, and crowned her one-year-old son, James, in her place. But on May 2, 1568, she escaped from her island-prison and tried to reclaim power at the head of a rebel force. Near Glasgow on May 13, she met defeat, and three days later crossed into England, where she sought Elizabeth's protection, only to find herself a prisoner for life. Mary's former pretensions to the throne had incurred Elizabeth's hostility, but as a captive she proved even more of a threat to the queen. Plot followed plot, as many English Catholics placed their hopes in a dynastic coup, and Mary herself eventually became involved in three major conspiracies against Elizabeth's rule. A northern rising in November 1569 under two Catholic earls heightened the tension, which was immeasureably increased by a rash action of the pope. In February 1570, Pope Pius V issued a bull that formally excommunicated Elizabeth as "the Pretended Queen of England, the serpent of wickedness," and declared her deposed, absolving her subjects from their allegiance to her. The result was to make all English Catholics incipient traitors in their countrymen's eyes. The penal laws against them increased, especially after 1574, when militant priests of English stock began arriving from overseas.

At about this time, Philip II of Spain also began drafting plans for an attack on England. Then, in December of 1580, the pope was asked by two English Catholic nobles if it would be lawful before God to kill the queen. Yes, replied the pope, since only good could come of putting an end to "that guilty woman who is the cause of so much intriguing to the Catholic faith and the loss of so many million souls. There is no doubt that whoever sends her out of the world with the pious intention of doing God service, not only does not sin but gains merit."

This amazing pronouncement did not remain secret for long.

On March 18, 1581, legislation was passed which sharply increased the fine for nonattendance at church, imposed a year in prison on anyone caught celebrating Mass, and branded anyone who converted to Catholicism as a traitor to the state. It also became a grave crime to defame the queen. For a first offense, the culprit faced a heavy fine, time in the stocks, and the loss of both his ears; for a second, death. Finally, "it was declared illegal for anyone to cast the queen's horoscope or to prophesy how long she might live or who her successor would be. Even so, there was no widespread persecution, and over the course of the next twenty years, no more than 250 Catholics in all England perished in prison" as a result of these laws.

The Catholic challenge, however, remained a stern one, and was also pressed on the biblical front. Just as a number of Protestant scholars had fled to the Continent under Mary, so, upon the accession of Elizabeth, their Catholic confreres had sought refuge in a Continental stronghold of their own. That stronghold was Douai in Flanders, where in 1568 (the year the Bishops' Bible was published) they established an English college under the direction of William Allen, an Oxford scholar and former canon of York, whom the pope would eventually reward with a cardinal's hat. Allen's college, founded for the maintenance of the Catholic cause, was affiliated with the University of Douai, which had been established a few years before by Philip II of Spain.

In 1578, a new English translation of the Bible was begun at the college to counter "the corruptions whereby the heretics have so long lamentably deluded almost the whole of our countrymen"— though this represented a break from the past position of the Church. That position had been succinctly stated after the Spanish conquest of Granada in 1492 by Cardinal Ximenes, the great biblical scholar and compiler of the Complutensian Polyglot, who discouraged a fellow bishop from translating the Scriptures into Arabic for the instruction of the Moors. "It would be throwing pearls before swine," he said. "For the word of God should be wrapped in discreet mystery from the vulgar, who feel little reverence for what is plain and obvious. It was for this reason that our Savior himself clothed his doctrines in parables, when he addressed the people. The Scriptures should be confined to the three ancient languages [Latin, Hebrew, and Greek], which God, with mystic import, permitted to be inscribed over the head of his crucified Son." More recently, in 1546, the Council of Trent had prohibited the official use of any other text but the Vulgate in lectures, disputations, or sermons, and had heaped scorn upon vernacular translations as unholy and impure. But in the competition for the hearts and minds of the English people, the Church reconsidered, and ultimately tried to compete on that unhallowed ground.

The way had already been prepared by the vernacular preaching Allen and his colleagues had adopted among the Catholic exiles. As Allen explained in a letter to a friend in September 1578:

> On every Sunday and Festival English sermons are preached by the more advanced students on the Gospel, Epistle or subject proper for the day. These discourses are calculated to inflame the hearts of all with piety towards God and zeal for bringing back England from schism to the path of salvation.
>
> We preach in English in order to acquire greater power and grace in the use of the vulgar tongue, a thing on which the heretics plume themselves exceedingly, by which they do great injury to simple folk. In this respect, the heretics, however ignorant they may be in other points, have the advantage over many of our more learned Catholics, who do not commonly have at command the text of Scripture, to quote it, except in Latin. Hence, when they are preaching to the unlearned and are obliged on the spur of the moment to translate some passage into the vulgar tongue, they often do it inaccurately, and with unpleasant hesitation, because either there is no English version of the words or it does not there and then occur to them.
>
> Our adversaries, on the other hand, have at their fingers' ends all those passages of Scripture which seem to make for them, and by a certain deceptive alteration of the sacred words, produce the effect of appearing to say nothing but what comes from the Bible. This evil might be remedied if we too had some Catholic version of the Bible, for all the English versions are most corrupt. I do not know what kind

you have in Belgium. But we on our part, if His Holiness shall think proper, will undertake to produce a faithful, pure and genuine version of the Bible. For we already have men most fitted for the work. Perhaps it would have been more desirable that the Scriptures had never been translated into the barbarous tongues. Nevertheless, at the present day there is often such a need to confute our opponents that it is better that there be a faithful and a Catholic translation.

Allen won approval for it and entrusted the task to an Oxford colleague, Gregory Martin, sometime fellow of St. John's College, and lecturer in Hebrew and Holy Scripture at the University of Douai at Rheims. Fortified by up-to-date scholarship, Martin proceeded at a uniform (and heroically steadfast) rate of two chapters a day over the course of three and a half years. Each day his labor was carefully reviewed and sometimes revised by Allen and another colleague, Richard Bristow, Allen's prefect of studies, and by March 1582, the work was done. The New Testament portion was published that year at Rheims; the Old Testament (for reasons still unclear) was not issued until 1609–10, and then at Douai. The whole thereafter was known as the Douai Bible.

The Rheims New Testament was furnished with a long, controversial, and highly polemical Preface that explained the work's character and intent. In it, the translators claimed to have based their version entirely on the Vulgate, "because we wish this to be a sincere Catholic translation. We are very precise and religious in following the old approved Latin (not Greek) text, that was used in the Church 1,300 years, corrected by Saint Jerome, commended and allowed by Saint Augustine, and which the Holy Council of Trent [1545–65] defined as the only one to be authentical. . . . We [follow it] not only in sense, which we hope we always do, but sometimes in the very words also and phrases. . . . Moreover we presume not in hard places to mollify the speeches or phrases, but religiously keep them word for word, and point for point for fear of missing, or restraining the sense of the Holy Ghost to our fantasy."

The Council of Trent had declared the Vulgate "not only better than all other Latin translations, but better than the Greek text itself in those places where they disagree." This allowed the translators to claim in the Epistle to the Reader prefixed to the whole Bible published in 1610, that the ancient Hebrew and Greek texts "which Protestants prefer" were impure, as having long since been "foully corrupted by Jews and Heretics," since the time of St. Jerome. In other words, the Vulgate was based on texts no longer extant which had been captured in its authentic Latin for all time. That, however, would have been hard to prove. The Vulgate itself had been marred by error (not always traceable to scribes), and over the years various editors and scholars had seen fit to revise the text. At length, in the thirteenth century the University of Paris produced an edition intended to provide an agreed standard for theological teaching and debate. The earliest printed Vulgate Bibles were all based on that Paris edition. Although the Council of Trent pronounced the text (so received) the "only authentical Latin," it had also called for an emended edition of it, and over the next forty years a papal commission undertook to collate the oldest and most reliable manuscripts. In 1590 Pope Sixtus V published the result (edited by himself), with the following proclamation attached: "By the fulness of Apostolic power, we decree and declare that this edition . . . approved by the authority delivered to us by the Lord, is to be received and held as true, lawful, authentic and unquestioned, in all public and private discussion, reading, preaching and explanation." But his version was almost immediately repudiated by the papal commission in charge of the project, and after the pope's sudden death on August 27, 1590, the College of Cardinals canceled its publication and destroyed every copy it could find. Two years later, in 1592, a new authentic edition (differing substantially from the first) was issued under Pope Clement VIII. This Clementine Vulgate of 1592 became the standard edition of the Roman Catholic Church. This means that in 1582, when the Rheims New Testament was published, the "only authentical" text of the Vulgate in fact did not yet exist.

The new translation was nevertheless remarkable—an eminently learned, often excellent English version of the text studded with Latinate terms and phrases in which words were either transliterated or retained in their original form. Some had staying power—including "acquisition," "adulterate," "advent," "benignity," "allegory," "verity," "calumniate," "character," "cooperate," "evangelize," "prescience," "resuscitate," and "victim"—and ultimately entered into and enriched the English tongue. Others—including "inquination," "potestates," "longanimity," and "correption," for example—remained to all but a Latinist obscure. As a result, a number of passages were virtually impenetrable: "supersubstantial bread" (Matthew 6:1); "odible to God" (Romans 1:30); "ebrieties, commessations" (Galatians 5:2); "concorporat and comparticipant" (Ephesians 3:6); "coinquination and spottes, flowing in delicacies" (2 Peter 2:13); "shall be consummate, as he hath evangelized" (Revelation 10:7); and so on.

At times the combination produced a frankly droll effect: "Purge the old leaven that you may be a new paste, as you are azymes" (1 Corinthians 5:7); "He exinanited himself" (Phillipians 2:7); "if thou be a prevaricator of the law, thy circumcision is become prepuce" (Romans 2:25); "Thou hast fatted my head with oil, and my chalice inebriating how goodie it is" (Psalm 23:5). In the parable of the Good Samaritan in Luke (10:35), the Samaritan tells the innkeeper, "Whatsoever thou shalt supererogate, I at my return will repay thee." And Ephesians 3:8–10 reads: "To me the least of all saints is given this grace among the Gentiles to evangelize the unsearchable riches of Christ, and to illuminate all men, what is the dispensation of the sacrament hidden from worlds in God, who created all things: that the manifold wisdom of God may be notified to the Princes and Potestats in the celestials by the Church, according to the prefinition of worlds, which he made in Christ Jesus our Lord."

It may be remembered that Stephen Gardiner in 1542 had insisted that at least ninety-nine Latin words be either retained in their original form "for their genuine meaning and mystery," or "fitly Englished with the least alteration." But the Douay Bible went beyond anything he had conceived. And as before, Protestants charged that the language of the Bible had been deliberately "darkened" to keep the text "from being understood."

If that was not quite true, it was not quite false, either; for the translators frankly confessed that the text was not meant to be read by all. "We must not imagine that in the primitive Church," they wrote, everyone was free to "read, reason, dispute, turn and toss the Scriptures; or that our forefathers suffered every schoolmaster, scholar, or grammarian that had a little Greek or Latin, straight to take in hand the holy Testament: or that the translated Bibles were in the hands of every husbandman, artificer, prentice, boy, girl, mistress, maid, man: that they were sung, played, alleged, of every tinker, taverner, rimer, minstrel: that they were for table-talk, for ale-benches, for boats and barges, and for every profane person and company." On the contrary, in those bygone days, "the poor ploughman could then, in laboring the ground, sing the hymns and psalms either in known or unknown languages, as they heard them in the holy Church, though they could neither read nor know the sense meaning and mysteries of the same." The plowman of Erasmus and Tyndale, in other words, had gained nothing by reading the Bible for himself.

To Protestants that seemed preposterous. But when the Old Testament version of the text at length appeared, it too conspicuously featured many words taken more or less directly from the Vulgate. "Conculcation" was used for "treading down" (Isaiah 22:5); "dominator" for "sovereign" (Isaiah 3:1); "excelse" for "high place" (1 Samuel 9:25); "exprobating" for "reproaching" (Job 16:11); "holocaust" for "burnt-offering" (Isaiah 1:11); "hyacinth" for "blue" (Exodus 28:5); "immolated" for "offered" (1 Samuel 2:13); "libaments" for "drink-offerings" (Numbers 6:17); "peregrination" for "sojourn" (Ruth 1:22); "rationale" for "breast-plate" (Exodus 25:7); and "recordation" for "memorial" (Numbers 5:18). There were also some Latinized Hebrew words, such as "gith" for "fitches" (Isaiah 28:27); "mamzer" for "bastard" (Deuteronomy 23:2); "musach" for "canopy" (2 Kings 16:18); and "sculptils" for "graven images" (Isaiah 21:9).

Such neologisms betrayed the diversity of texts the translators had actually used. For they had not been quite candid in claiming the Vulgate as their only guide. To their credit, in fact, they had closely consulted both the Hebrew and the Greek, and had sometimes depended on the "heretical" English translations they condemned. From the Geneva Bible they adopted: "This wicked generation" (Matthew 12:45); "a great multitude" (Matthew 14:14);

"whited tombs" (Matthew 23:27); "salted with salt" (Mark 9:49); "the things that are Caesar's" (Mark 12:17); "a desert place" (Luke 11:12); "salvation is of the Jews" (John 4:22); "Centurions" (Acts 21:32); "Knowledge puffeth up" (1 Corinthians 8:9); "in the shambles" (1 Corinthians 10:25); "Pentecost" (1 Corinthians 16:8); "the word of reconciliation" (2 Corinthians 5:19); "before God in Christ" (2 Corinthians 12-19); and "according to the flesh" (Ephesians 6:5); among other words and phrases.

With many of these the King James Version would later concur.

Here is the Rheims rendering of the first two verses of 1 Corinthians 13: "If I speak with the tongues of men and of angels, and have not charity, I am become as sounding brass, or a tinkling cymbal. And if I should have prophecy, and know all mysteries, and all knowledge, and if I should have all faith so that I could remove mountains, and have not charity, I am nothing." Except for the word "charity," where the Geneva used "love," that is the Geneva Bible all the way. The Parable of the Ten Virgins in Matthew (to take another example, at random) is extremely close to the Geneva (and Tyndale), too:

> Then shall the kingdom of heaven be like to ten virgins, who taking their lamps went out to meet the bridegroom and the bride.
> And five of them were foolish, and five wise.
> But the five foolish, having taken their lamps, did not take oil with them:
> But the wise took oil in their vessels with the lamps.
> And the bridegroom tarrying, they all slumbered and slept.
> And at midnight there was a cry made: Behold the bridegroom cometh, go ye forth to meet him.
> Then all those virgins arose and trimmed their lamps. (Matthew, 25:1-7)

Another important source for the Catholic scholars was the diglot or bilingual Latin-English edition of the New Testament that Miles

Coverdale had prepared in 1538 in response to Cranmer's advice to the clergy to "confer the Latin and English together" in their own study of the text.

∞

By 1582, when the Rheims New Testament was published, twelve years had passed since the Vatican had pronounced Elizabeth excommunicate and deposed, and in England, Scotland, and Ireland Jesuit agents sought to foment sedition and rebellion against her. The government as well as the queen herself were felt to be at risk, and this general peril had a moderating effect on even the most radical Puritans, who understood that the fortunes of their cause were more dependent on her survival than on the triumph of their sectarian demands. "From every side," it is said, "the feeling was borne in upon the nation at large" that England was nearing the hour of her destiny; and this united her people and made Protestants and patriots one.

Then in 1584, William the Silent, who had organized Dutch resistance to the Spanish in the Netherlands, was assassinated. In the following year Elizabeth dispatched a small force under the Earl of Leicester to aid the Dutch, and two years later, a devastating raid by Sir Francis Drake on Spanish shipping and stores at Cádiz and Lisbon "singed the king of Spain's beard." Meanwhile, copies of letters reputedly written by Mary Stuart approving the assassination of Elizabeth had fallen into the government's hands. Under the Act for the Preservation of the Queen's Safety, Mary was tried by an English court, condemned, and executed in 1587 in the great hall at Fotheringhay Castle, near Peterborough, at the age of forty-four. On the night before her execution, she swore a last solemn oath of innocence on a copy of the Rheims New Testament. The Protestant Earl of Kent, who was present, unkindly upbraided her for it, saying she had sworn "a valueless oath on a false book"; but she replied with quiet strength, "Does your lordship think that my oath would be any better if I swore on a translation in which I do not believe?"

The Spanish Armada was launched against England the following July, but gales worked havoc on the Spanish galleons, which were driven into the North Sea. Superior English seamanship did the rest. In the face of the invasion, most Catholics in England in the

end remained loyal to their queen. Many, indeed, had willingly en-
rolled in the defense force she hastily assembled, and some heard
and cheered the stirring speech she gave to the troops drawn up at
Tilbury to resist the expected assault. "I have but the body of a weak
and feeble woman but I have the heart and stomach of a king, and a
king of England, too, and think foul scorn that any Prince in Europe
should dare to invade the borders of my realm." It was afterward reported (by one of Walsingham's agents) that nothing so much dis-
pleased the king of Spain as the loyalty of the Catholics to their
queen during that hour of national trial.

∽

On May 17, 1575, Matthew Parker, Elizabeth's first and most tolerant
Archbishop of Canterbury, died. Lord Burghley recommended Edmund Grindal, Archbishop of York, as his replacement, but this
turned out to be a mistake. Grindal was a dogmatic Puritan with
whom the queen could not get along. He had encouraged evangelical preaching as well as "prophesyings," or private meetings of the
clergy for scriptural study (which Elizabeth abhorred), and as
Bishop of London (1558–70) had given Parker no help in his efforts
to enforce the wearing of clerical garb. On the other hand, as Archbishop of York, he had staunchly opposed the Puritan Presbyterian
party that sought to abolish the Prayer Book as well as episcopal
rank. A learned, if prudish, man, Grindal had revised the Minor
Prophets for the Bishops' Bible, and was so devoted to study that it
was said that "his book was his bride." Even so, his promotion to
Archbishop of Canterbury (in the hope that he might drive a wedge
between the Puritan factions) was something of a surprise. In the
fall of the following year, his mettle was put to the test.

The queen thought the time had come to suppress all Puritan
forms of worship. To her consternation, Grindal refused to help. She
asked him again; and again he refused; and she banished him from
court. In May of 1577, she firmly suggested he reconsider his position but he obtusely reminded her that "she too was mortal and
would have to answer for her actions at God's judgement seat." With
that, he was suspended from all official duties and placed under
house arrest.

At length, in July 1583, he died and was succeeded by John Whitgift, formerly Bishop of Worcester, regius professor of divinity at Cambridge, and chaplain to the Queen. Although a committed Protestant, Whitgift supported the Elizabethan Settlement, and as Archbishop of Canterbury dealt harshly with those who refused to conform. He was also an able administrator, and it was largely due to his management of Church affairs that the Puritan movement for a time was not only checked but held at bay. His punitive Eight Articles banned preaching or catechizing in households; preaching without ordination; enforced the use of clerical vestments; and obliged all to subscribe to the queen's supremacy, the Prayer Book, the Thirty-nine Articles, and the Book of Common Prayer. Hundreds of dissident ministers were suspended for noncompliance and Whitgift persuaded Elizabeth to set up a new Court of High Commission with expanded powers.

Resentment among the Puritans grew, but their movement lost ground. After the execution of Mary Queen of Scots, the defeat of the Armada, and the emancipation of Holland from Spain, the Catholic threat receded, and the Crown had less reason to rely on Puritan support. In 1595, Richard Bancroft, the new Bishop of London, transferred the prosecution of Puritans to the secular courts, which effectively stigmatized church officials of whatever rank (charged for their dissent) as felons; and in the summer of 1598, Whitgift went so far as to try to bar any apparent Noncomformist from election to Parliament.

But the force and direction of English history lay far beyond their ken. The Puritans were destined in time to resurrect themselves with a vengeance, while Elizabethan visionaries like Richard Hakluyt, preacher, propagandist, and geographer, foresaw (with a mix of imperial hubris and evangelical pride) that England would one day, as he put it, spread "the incomparable treasure of the truth of the Gospel" along with English freedom and commerce to the farthest corners of the globe. "A thousand kingdoms we shall seek from far," wrote the poet Michael Drayton,

> *And those unchristened countries call our own,*
> *Where scarce the name of England hath been known.*

JAMES I

Translation it is that openeth the window, to let in the light; that breaketh the shell, that we may eat the kernel; that putteth aside the curtain, that we may looke into the most Holy place; that remooveth the cover of the well, that wee may come by the water, even as Jacob rolled away the stone from the mouth of the well.

—Miles Smith, "The Translators to the Reader"

CHAPTER FOUR

King

 lizabeth's health declined. "Lonely as she had always been," one historian tells us, "her loneliness deepened as she drew toward the grave. The statesmen and warriors of her earlier days had dropped one by one from her Council-board; and their successors were watching her last moments, and intriguing for favor in the coming reign. . . . Her face became haggard, and her frame shrank almost to a skeleton. At last her taste for finery disappeared, and she refused to change her dresses for a week. A strange melancholy settled down upon her. . . . Gradually her mind gave way. . . . Food and rest became alike distasteful. She sat day and night propped up with pillows on a stool, her finger on her lip, her eyes fixed on the floor without a word." The Privy Council was summoned, and on March 22, 1603, its members gathered at her bedside. With a kind of dread (knowing her temper) the problem of the succession was raised. A relative, Lord Beauchamp, was mentioned. She started up: "I will have no rogue's son in my seat," she cried, "but a king." They urged her to be clear. Who did she mean (though more than one of them must have known)? "Who but our cousin of Scotland," she answered hotly. "I pray you trouble me no more." But the following afternoon they returned to confirm her will. By then, however, she had lost the power of speech. The king of Scotland was brought up again as they asked her for some ratifying sign. Slowly she raised her frail arms above her head and brought the fingers together to form a crown.

The next morning, she died—"mildly like a lamb, easily like a ripe apple from the tree. . . . The doctor told me that he was present, and sent his prayers before her soul; and I doubt not but she is amongst the royal saints in Heaven in eternal joys." So her passing was recorded in the diary of one of the many anxious and grieving courtiers who had hovered about the scene. Her reign of forty-five years, for all its difficulties, would be remembered as a kind of Golden Age, to which her own name would be attached; and her manner of governance, for all its autocratic assumptions, would be judged by posterity a paradigm of enlightened monarchical rule. Toward the end, the coronation ring, which symbolized her marriage to England in faith and truth, had to be filed from her finger—so deeply had it worked its way into her flesh from such long wear. Upon her death, her body was embalmed and wrapped in lead and brought at once to Whitehall, and from there, on April 28, carried to Westminster, where a mourning crowd of sixteen hundred dignitaries had gathered to attend her burial in the ornate chapel of her grandfather King Henry VII.

Meanwhile, on the morning of her passing, the Privy Council had proclaimed James VI of Scotland King of England, France, and Ireland as James I. This was not only in accord with Elizabeth's wishes, but in keeping with arrangements made in secret code by an exchange of letters with James by Sir Robert Cecil, First Earl of Salisbury, son of Lord Burghley, and Elizabeth's last secretary of state. Flanked by five trumpeters and several heralds, Cecil had read the proclamation first at the gates of Whitehall, then at Cheapside, as Sir Robert Carey took horse up the Great North Road to Edinburgh to bear the tidings to James. Hard at his heels rode the dean of Canterbury, driven on by the trembling anxiety of his aged master, Archbishop Whitgift, for the fate of his Church.

In London bonfires blazed in the streets, amid popular rejoicing over the peaceful change of crowns.

James, however, already knew he was king before Carey arrived.

For at the very moment the great queen expired, a Scottish biblical scholar, astrologer, and confidential adviser, Robert Pont, had come to his chamber to salute him as the new English sovereign. James had rebuked him then, saying: "I told you you would go daft with all your learning; and now I see you are so!" "Oh, no," replied Pont, "the thing is certain. Elizabeth is dead."

When Carey and the dean of Canterbury arrived—almost together, in a sweat—"be-bloodied with great falls and bruises"—James quickly reassured them that he would respect the established forms of Church and state. Soon thereafter, he set out on a triumphal progress to London, riding south through a land he found more bountiful than any he had known. Somewhat to his surprise, the people welcomed him with open arms. "It shall never be blotted out of my mind," he said later, "how, at my first entry into this kingdom, the people of all sorts rode and ran, nay, rather flew to meet me—their eyes flaming nothing but sparkles of affection—their mouths and tongues uttering nothing but sounds of joy—their hands, feet, and all the rest of their members discovering in their gestures a passionate longing and earnestness to meet and embrace their new king." Immense throngs lined the route to applaud him, and gathered to cheer him in every marketplace and square. Masques of welcome were staged at country mansions; church bells rang; mayors gave him the keys to their cities; and an ever increasing number of courtiers attached themselves to his train. There were stag-hunting forays in parks, banquets, and other entertainments, and in fulsome gratitude he scattered knighthoods and other high honors with a liberal hand.

On April 6, 1603, the caravan reached Berwick, where the city fathers gathered on the outskirts to present James with a number of precious gifts, including (most precious to him) a purse of gold, as the cannons of the city roared. From Berwick he proceeded to Northumberland, then Newcastle and Durham. At Newark-upon-Trent he demonstrated royal justice and mercy together when he had a cutpurse caught in the crowd hanged at once, but in a general amnesty also freed almost all the prisoners the local castle held.

When he came to the palace home of Sir Robert Cecil, called Theobalds, he lingered for several days, captivated by the splendor of its grounds. Its elaborate hedgerow gardens were interspersed with sculpted fountains; gilded weather vanes surmounted its high turrets of rosy brick. Along the long walls of a loggia, the entire history of England was depicted in brilliantly colored murals; in another building, he was conducted down a "great green hall," lined with artificial trees, complete with bark and numerous bird's nests nestled in their boughs. When asked to cast his eyes aloft, James beheld a ceiling adorned by an artificial sun moved by a concealed device, and constellations of stars that shone and twinkled in the dark.

It was indeed a good time to have come into the Crown. Although English society had a hierarchical cast, with the royal family at the top and the nobility still savoring most of its hereditary privileges of "degree, priority, and place," a general prosperity as a result of economic growth had also begun to blur some class distinctions, as merchants, artisans, and members of the landed gentry surged upward through the ranks. This social mobility gave a real vigor and freedom to English life, if still mostly in the economic sphere, and an imperial confidence to the nation as a whole as it united at last with Scotland in the person of the king. James would soon attempt to make the union formal, and fulfill a dream to which England had long clung. Toward the bottom of the social ladder, of course, were the indentured servants and the working poor; but Elizabeth's Poor Laws had done much to relieve the plight of the destitute, indigent, and disabled by obliging localities to take responsibility for the suffering in their midst. The general opening up, and out, of English life, enlightened to some degree by social conscience, was wonderfully symbolized by the new and abundant use of glass, which adorned so many of the houses of the time. Every manor seemed to have its own windowed hall and oriel, flooding the rooms with light—as one lord gently complained, "You cannot always tell where to come out of the sun."

In other areas, James had much to be thankful for. The rebels in Ireland had recently been crushed; the mighty power of Spain was now in the timid hands of Philip III; and the King of France was preoccupied with domestic affairs. But all things good or bad are also strapped to Fortune's Wheel. There were issues enough in England liable to turn, and the king was introduced to some of them in the course of his triumphal progress when (according to custom) he was approached by various persons and parties with petitions and requests. Most notably, while pausing at an estate near Huntingdon, he was met by a deputation of divines who presented him with the Millenary Petition, so called because it was subscribed by almost a thousand Puritan ministers (a tenth of the English clergy) from twenty-five counties, which enumerated a number of grievances against the Church of England they hoped he might address.

☙

The religious situation in England remained unsettled. Although a constitutional revolution had replaced papal power with royal authority by the creation of a national Church, that Church was still trying to define itself, and in the process had alienated not only Catholics but many of the Protestant devout. Although the Act of Uniformity embraced Protestant doctrine with respect to the Eucharist, in its ritual and organization the Church had otherwise assumed a more or less Catholic form. From the beginning there had been disaffection with the splendor of High Church practice, and with the language of the Sacraments in the Book of Common Prayer. The Church of England alone among the Protestant Churches of Europe claimed to have an episcopate derived in apostolic succession from St. Peter, and its hierarchical structure was modeled on that of Rome. Moreover, the official Anglican Creed as set forth in its Thirty-nine Articles (composed by a commission of bishops) had never been embraced by the majority of Protestants as a definitive statement of their beliefs. By her own extraordinary ecclesiastical statesmanship, Elizabeth had managed for a time to impose a measure of religious peaceful coexistence on her realm, but toward the end of her life there had been growing friction between the Puritan and Anglican wings of the Church.

Generally speaking, the Puritans wished to "purify" the Church of residual "popish" practices which (in their view) the Elizabethan Settlement retained. They hoped to eliminate such things as the use of the cross in baptism, the ring in marriage, bowing at the name of Jesus, liturgical vestments such as the cap and surplice, certain despotic procedures in the ecclesiastical courts, and in general to

203

replace the emphasis on ceremony with one on preaching and prayer.

But if the Puritans had a tenth of the clergy behind them, they soon found their path to "a due and godly reformation" of the Church blocked by all the power of Church and state. Neither John Whitgift, the Archbishop of Canterbury, nor Richard Bancroft, the Bishop of London—who together in the 1580s had tried to destroy Puritanism as a politically organized sect—had any patience for their complaints. Indeed, they regarded the petition as a revolutionary document with seditious intent. The universities of Oxford and Cambridge, anxious to prove themselves "responsible," also denounced the petition. Cambridge even decreed that whosoever set himself against the doctrine and discipline of the established Church would be stripped of his university degrees. Not to be outdone, Oxford accused the petition's signers of tending to foment rebellion, at which the divines of Cambridge, in an open letter of thanks to their Oxford brethren, asked to be numbered in their camp, so that if "Saul hath his thousands, David may have his ten thousands."

But the petition had caught the king's eye. He decided he had to make an adequate response to it, and in October proclaimed a three-day conference for mid-January to discuss the issues it had raised.

The different factions did not at first know what to expect of him. Although his mother, Mary Queen of Scots, had been a Catholic, James had been raised as a Presbyterian Calvinist, and many Puritans not unreasonably hoped he might be sympathetic to their demands. A Scottish edition of the Geneva Bible, published in 1579, had been dedicated to him; and he had publicly subscribed with his own hand and seal to the Solemn League and Covenant of Scotland, which guaranteed Presbyterian forms of worship forever in the land. On several occasions thereafter he had affirmed his attachment to Presbyterian principles—most notably at the General Assembly of the Church at Edinburgh in 1590 when, "standing with his bonnet off and his hands lifted up to heaven, he praised God that he had been born in the time of the light of the Gospel, and in such a place as to be king of such a Kirk [Church], the sincerest [purest] kirk in the world."

He had also favorably compared Presbyterian practice to other forms of observance. "The Church of Geneva," he said, "keep Pasche [Easter] and Yule [Christmas]; what have they for them? They have no institution. As for our neighbor kirk of England, their service is an evil-said Mass in English [faulting the Mass, not the English]; they want nothing of the Mass but the liftings. I charge you, my good ministers, doctors, elders, nobles, gentlemen, and barons, to stand by your purity, and to exhort the people to do the same; and I, forsooth, as long as I brook my life, shall maintain the same." Upon leaving Scotland to take possession of the English throne, the last thing he had done was to thank the Scottish Church and proclaim that he did not intend to alter it (or the kingdom of Scotland) in any way.

But Anglican doctrine was more congenial to his royal heart. In Scotland the king had in religion been little more than the first among equals, and the head of the Presbyterian Church had once pulled him by the sleeve to remind him that he was nothing but "God's silly vassal." In England, on the other hand, he gratefully inhaled "the sweet-smelling incense of episcopal adulation," and regarded all his subjects as nothing but vassals of the Crown. His own idea of kingship was based on the divine right of kings, and if he was uncomfortable with the constitutional limits on his authority, he was positively repelled by the newfangled Puritan ideas of self-government based on their congregational form of worship. Yet he was a canny enough statesman to realize that the Puritans were a force in his new kingdom; and he must hear them out.

Theological disputation was also to his taste. The king's early life and training had made him a student of the Bible (in almost all its languages), and he once complained that he had been forced to learn Latin before he knew Scots. By the age of eight, he was able extempore to translate any chapter of the Bible (selected at random) from Latin into French, then from French into English, "as well as few men could"; paraphrased the Book of Revelation; and in his teens made metrical translations of a number of the Psalms. He also wrote religious sonnets and translated two narrative poems by the

French Huguenot Salust du Bartas into Scots. He later published a collection of his own compositions which he quaintly styled "His Majesty's poetical exercises at vacant Hours." At a Kirk assembly in 1601, he had discussed aspects of the Bible and Bible translation in such learned detail that he seemed, wrote one Church historian, "no less conversant in the Scripture than they whose profession it was."

He was a true bibliophile. He built up a considerable private library in the classics; owned a host of theological works (including those by Calvin, which he read in Latin); was especially well read in the French poets, such as Ronsard, Du Bellay, and Marot; and of course had many writings in English and Scots. Upon receiving an honorary degree from Oxford after he had become King of England, he was given a tour of the Bodleian Library and noted the chains that bound the books to the shelves. "I could wish, if ever it be my lot to be carried captive," he remarked on that occasion, "to be shut up in this prison, to be bound with these chains, and to spend my life with these fellow captives which stand here chained."

It was a felt turn of expression for one who had once been kidnapped, and twice held captive by his own subjects, and whose life had often been at risk. Born three months after his mother's court favorite had been butchered before her eyes, James had endured a pitiable childhood under four different regents, and had been closely confined for his own safety in Stirling Castle while his adherents and those loyal to his mother fought for power. He had never known his father, Henry Stuart, Lord Darnley, and his tutors had taught him to despise his mother as an adulteress who had colluded in his father's death. He later spurned any attempt she made to become close to him, and when he first heard the news of her arrest in England, observed merely that she would have to "drink the ale she had brewed." In 1587, he did nothing aside from a few formal protests to delay her execution, and thereafter placed all the hope of his own future in Elizabeth's goodwill.

All this left its mark. He had large, prominent, staring eyes; walked with a "tottering gait" (due in part to childhood rickets); and at times "waddled like a duck in the quilted doublet and stuffed and stiff Dutch breeches he wore for fear of an assassin's dagger thrust." His breeches were also fitted with an enormous codpiece, suggesting either prodigious sexual endowment or an unnatural anxiety about the safety of his private parts. A "neurotic terror of naked weapons," in fact, haunted him all his life. He also had a kind of speech impediment (perhaps an inherited stutter, which showed up later and more clearly in his son, Charles I), though at the time it was said that his tongue was too large for his mouth.

His belief in the power and enmity of the devil was uncommonly fierce and he sometimes blamed evil spirits for the misfortunes of his life. He was convinced, for example, after his ship was nearly wrecked in the North Sea, that some witches had cast black cats into it in order to create the storm. On another occasion, he credited reports that the devil had supplied some witch with a little wax image of himself to be tormented like a voodoo doll. James rounded the witches up, questioned them himself at a sensational trial held in Edinburgh, and had them burned at the stake. In 1597, he published a slender volume in three books, *Daemonologie,* in which he set forth his own rational understanding of the parameters of the devil's power. "To the most curious sort," he wrote, the devil will sometimes enter into a corpse "and thereout to give such answers, of the event of battles, of matters concerning the estate of commonwealths, and such like other great questions: yea, to some he will be a continual attender, in the form of a Page." Elsewhere, he condemned witchcraft above murder as a crime.

But if his learning and superstition were oddly entwined, he was also a man of his age; and whatever the Privy Council might have thought of some of his opinions, they also recognized in James a monarch of experience, intelligence, and skill. By the time he was called to England, in fact, he had worn the crown of Scotland for thirty-seven years. In that capacity, he had shown an aptitude for choosing able advisers, had dealt tactfully with the Presbyterian party in the Scottish Church, showed care in implementing liturgical reform, and in 1592 had given parliamentary sanction to the system of Presbyterian courts. The league he had established with England in 1586 had withstood a number of strains, including the execution of his mother, and his wise acceptance of Elizabeth's regal rights had helped secure his own claim to the English throne. In 1599, he had publicly praised the queen as "lawful . . . who hath

so long with so great wisdom and felicity governed her kingdom as
. . . the like hath not been read or heard of, either in our time, or
since the days of the Roman Emperor Augustus; it could [therefore]
no ways become me, far inferior to her in knowledge and experience, to be a busy-body in other princes matters, and to fish in other
folks waters, as the proverb is." He fished a little all the same, but
made a balanced appeal to the main English religious factions, and
as king of Scotland avoided the enmity of Catholic rulers on the
Continent while keeping his own nobles in check at home. If he
was not a heroic king (like his forebear James IV), he was certainly a
shrewd and discerning ruler, and a far cry from "the pedantic and
cowardly buffoon" depicted by Sir Walter Scott in one of his later
tales. And so it was with every high hope and expectation that on
the 25th of July, 1603, "being the Blessed Feast of St. James," he was
crowned at Westminster Abbey in time-honored ceremonies performed with all the magnificence and ancient rites of the English
kings.

∽

Soon after the coronation, London had to contend (as it did periodi-
cally) with a bout of the plague, and for safety's sake the king removed to Hampton Court, a huge brick palace of a thousand rooms,
with stone gargoyles, mullioned windows, and cloistered walks, that
Cardinal Wolsey had built for his own aggrandizement some twelve
miles up the Thames. There James and Anne, his still young queen
(who adored masques, balls, and other entertainments), found the
setting ideal for their Christmas holiday revels, which included banquets of staggering opulence, nights of dancing, gambling, and
amorous intrigue, a performance of Shakespeare's *Measure for
Measure,* and a masque called the *Twelve Goddesses* staged by
Inigo Jones in which Queen Anne and eleven maids of honor appeared with "their hair down" and in "gauze costumes scandalously
sheer."

Once the Twelfth Night revels were past, the king gathered himself together and prepared to demonstrate his fitness to be head of
the English Church.

On Saturday, January 14, 1604, the Hampton Court Conference

convened. The king's Privy Council and a mighty array of bishops and deans assembled to represent the power of the establishment; only four Puritans, handpicked as moderates by the king and his advisers, stood for the other side; and these were pointedly excluded from the opening session, which got underway in the king's Privy Chamber, a large reception hall of the palace on the east side of the Clock Court.

The king welcomed the bishops and deans into his presence, and removing his high black beaver hat, said how glad he was to be in the "Promised Land" at last among learned, grave, and reverend men, and not as formerly in Presbyterian Scotland "without honor, without order, where beardless boys would brave us to our face." He seemed eager to put the prelates at ease. "It is no novel device," he declared, by way of explaining the conference,

> but according to the example of all Christian princes, for Kings to take the first course for the establishing of the Church both in doctrine and policy. . . . Particularly in this land, King Henry VIII towards the end of his reign altered much, King Edward VI more, Queen Mary reversed all, and lastly Queen Elizabeth (of famous memory) settled religion as it now standeth. Herein I am happier than they, because they were fain to alter all things they found established, whereas I see yet no such cause to change as confirm what I find settled already. . . . I assure you we have not called this assembly for any innovation. . . . Yet because nothing can be so absolutely ordered, but something may be added thereunto, and corruption in any state (as in the body of man) will insensibly grow . . . our purpose therefore is, like a good physician, to examine and try the complaints, and fully to remove the occasions thereof, if scandalous; cure them, if dangerous; and take knowledge of them, if but frivolous, thereby to cast a sop into Cerberus's mouth that he bark no more.

Then he roundly criticized the corruptions of the Church of England for five solid hours. Lancelot Andrewes, dean of Westminster, later noted that "the king did wonderfully play the Puritan that day!" and in particular came down hard on three theological "errors" he claimed to find in English worship pertaining to "Baptism," "Confirmation," and "Absolution," which smacked to him of popish belief.

It was an astonishing performance. While it lasted, the High Churchmen might have supposed, despite the bias implied in their numerical superiority, that the king was a Puritan at heart. But Andrewes (and doubtless others) knew better; for having seemed to incorporate Puritan dissent into his own person, he proceeded on the second day of the conference (January 16), when the Puritans were ushered into his presence, to deny all their specific requests.

The four Puritans—John Reynolds, president of Corpus Christi College, Oxford; Laurence Chaderton, master of Emmanuel College, Cambridge; Thomas Sparke, lecturer in divinity at Oxford; and John Knewstubs of St. John's College, Cambridge—sat across from the prelates and council with the king enthroned in between. Young Prince Henry, ten years old at the time, sat near his father on a stool; behind them the nobles and privy councillors of the realm were all solemnly arrayed waiting to hear "things pretended to be amiss in the Church." The fullest account to survive of what followed is by William Barlow, dean of Chester, who afterward recorded his recollections in a little tract entitled, *The Sum and Substance of the Conference, Which It Pleased His Excellent Majesty to Have with the Lords, Bishops, and Other of His Clergy at Hampton Court.*

The king began with an hour-long oration on the theme, "Religion is the soul of a kingdom, and Unity the life of religion," in which he denounced those clergy who, by refusing to conform, had bred dissension "now amounting almost to a schism, a point most perilous to the common weal as to the Church." When at length Reynolds was invited to speak, he explained that Puritans only wanted some modest reforms in Church government; minor changes in the rites of the Church (having to do with the sign of the cross in baptism, and the use of the ring in marriage); sermons to be given before Communion; an end to absentee pastorates; a better-educated clergy; and some corrections made in the Book of Common Prayer, that it might "be suited to more increase of piety."

When the topic of wedding rings came up, James said, "I was married with a ring and think others scarcely well married without it." Reynolds (a lifelong bachelor) then questioned the phrase "with my body I thee worship," which formed part of the marriage sacrament. "Many a man speaks of Robin Hood," replied the king with a laugh, "who never shot his bow; if you had a good wife yourself, you would think that all the honor and worship you could do her were well bestowed."

Reynold said that the sign of the cross had been abused. "Inasmuch as the Cross was abused to superstition in time of popery," replied James, "it doth plainly imply it was well-used before. I detest their courses who peremptorily disallow of all things which have been abused in popery, and know not how to answer the objections of papists, when they charge us with novelties, but by telling them we retain the primitive use of things, and only forsake their novel corruptions."

Reynolds then objected to the repressive Church policies then in place, and began to discuss some changes in the articles of the Church and the rite of confirmation. He had not gotten far before Bancroft suddenly fell down on his knees before the king and beseeched him to prevent Reynolds from saying anything further, "for it was an ancient canon that schismatics must not be heard against their bishops." The king replied calmly, "My Lord, you ought not to interrupt the Doctor. Either let him proceed or answer his objections." Bancroft thereupon attacked various points of Nonconformist doctrine, especially predestination as a "desperate conceit" that encouraged debauchery and license. He also disparaged the "millenary plaintiffs," as he called them, as "schismatic scholars, breakers of your laws; you may know them by their Turkey grograins," suggesting that their rough woolen gowns made them look like Turks. After this implied slander—comparing the Puritans to infidels—Reynolds spoke up and asked that the king not allow the charge of schismatic to stand against himself and his brethren; but James brushed his request aside.

After a break in the proceedings, John Knewstubs asked whether the Church was competent to add anything to what Christ Himself had commanded, as given in Scripture, and, if so, how far

Church authority was binding on matters of that sort. James heatedly replied: "I will not argue that point with you, but answer as kings in parliament, *Le roi s'avisera.* This is like Mr. John Black, a beardless boy, who told me at the last Conference in Scotland that he would hold conformity with his Majesty in matters of doctrine, but everything having to do with ceremonies was to be left to his own discretion. I will have none of that. I will have one doctrine and one discipline, one religion in substance and in ceremony. Therefore I charge you never speak more on how far you are to submit!"

Reynolds next tried to explain his objections to the procedures of the ecclesiastical court, and suggested as a final court of appeal in each diocese "the episcopal synod where the bishop with his presbytery" should determine all points in dispute. This seemed reasonable enough (and not directed at an usurpation of episcopal powers), but at the word "synod" the king was reminded of his youthful humiliations under the Scottish Kirk and "lost his composure." "If you aim at a Scots Presbytery," he declared, "it agreeth as well with monarchy as God and the devil! Then Jack, and Tom, and Will, and Dick, shall meet and at their pleasure censure me and my council and all our proceedings. How they used the poor lady, my mother, is not unknown; and how they dealt with me in my minority. Therefore, I say again, *Le roi s'avisera.*"

James asked Reynolds whether he knew of anyone who objected to the king's supremacy? Reynolds answered no. But the king smiled and reminded him that Scots reformers had also once "cried up the supremacy of the monarch till the Popish bishops were put down," and then, "being illuminated with more light," began in turn to reduce the powers of the Crown. He turned toward the bishops. "My Lords, . . . if once you were out and they in place, I know what would become of my supremacy. No Bishop, no King!" He paused to let these words sink in. Then he gestured to the Puritans: "If this be all they have to say," he declared in a loud voice, "I will make them conform themselves, or harry them out of the land."

With that, the second day of the conference came to a close.

On the third day, the king called the bishops and deans (but not the Puritans) back in, together with many nobles and doctors of law, to discuss the Court of High Commission and the ex officio oath whereby accused persons were compelled to give evidence against themselves. One of the lords present acknowledged some merit in the Puritan complaints, and a letter that Lord Burghley had once written was read comparing the court's proceedings to those of the Spanish Inquisition—"where men were urged to subscribe more than the law requireth; and by oath forced to accuse themselves." Whitgift vehemently denied the parallel, and the lord chancellor noted that the same oath was used in the Star Chamber and "in divers Courts." The king himself next defended the practice in a long speech. After that, he proceeded to a consideration of the complaints against the Book of Common Prayer, and indicated that he would allow a few verbal changes in the titles of certain portions, but "not," he pointedly remarked, "in the body of the sense, and by way rather of some explanation than of any alteration at all." In closing, he assured the bishops that although he had once lived among Puritans, "and was kept for the most part as a ward under them," yet from the age of ten he "ever disliked their opinions. As the Savior of the world said, 'Though he lived among them, he was not of them.' "

The High Churchmen were in ecstasies. Whitgift fell on his knees and exclaimed: "Undoubtedly your Majesty speaks by the special power of God's Spirit!" And Bancroft went down for the second time and said, "I protest my heart melteth into joy that Almighty God, of his singular mercy, hath given us such a king, as since Christ's time the like hath not been." (Later, he would take vindictive advantage of the king's anti-Puritan sentiment to deprive more than three hundred Puritan clergymen of their livings.) The Puritans were then readmitted and told what had been decided. This was so far from what they had hoped for that two of them, Laurence Chaderton and John Knewstubs, now went down on their knees in turn to plead against renewed persecution by the Church. As things now stood, it seemed likely that even those Puritan ministers known to be devout would be hounded if they did not conform completely, and so Chaderton and Knewstubs asked that there be some discrimination in the charge. Letters for certain ministers might be drafted by the Archbishop of Canterbury, they suggested.

But Bancroft would have none of it. If such letters were granted, he said, copies of them would "fly all over England"; and then all Nonconformists would beg the same protection for their dissent. The king concurred: "I will have none of this arguing. That is the Scots way. Let them [the Puritans] conform, and that quickly too, or they shall hear of it. I will have them enforced to conformity!" Then: "And surely if these be the greatest matters you [the Puritans] be grieved with, I need not have been troubled with such importunities and complaints as have been made unto me. Some other more private course might have been taken for your satisfaction." And with that, he turned again to the bishops, and smiled and shook his head.

The assembly was dismissed.

James was so enraptured by his own performance that on the following day he wrote to a friend in Scotland with coarsened pride: "We have kept such a revel with the Puritans here as was never heard the like; I have peppered them as soundly as ye have done the *papists* there," and claimed that the Puritans had presented their views so poorly that if it had been a college debate, their teachers would have thrashed their behinds. But to Sir John Harington, Elizabeth's godson and a witness to the proceedings, the king had seemed merely crude: "James talked much Latin and bid the petitioners away with snivelling. The Bishops seemed much pleased and said his Majesty spoke by power of inspiration! I wist [know] not what they meant, but the Spirit was rather foul-mouthed."

Though the Puritans had seemed to gain nothing by the conference, James had made one notable concession—not so much to them as to a perceived national need. On the second day, Reynolds had asked the king, in connection with Puritan complaints about the Prayer Book, to consider a new translation of the Bible, "because those that were allowed in the reigns of Henry the Eighth and Edward the Sixth were corrupt and not answerable to the truth of the Original." Most of the "corruptions" had to do with the intrusion of unwanted passages from the Apocrypha (accepted as Scripture by the Bishops' Bible, following the Great) into the Anglican service. But Bancroft, seeking to stifle any attempt to topple the Bishops' Bible from its throne, had leapt to his feet to object that "if every man's humor was followed there would be no end of translating." The king disagreed. Reynolds's proposal appealed to him at once, and he embraced it with a fervor that caught the prelates off guard.

There was reason enough to attempt a new translation at this time. In the last thirty or forty years substantial progress had been made in Greek and Hebrew studies, and most of the major European universities, including Oxford and Cambridge, had endowed chairs to foster the study of both. At least 150 Hebrew grammars were now available, the Hebrew Scriptures in a number of editions, as well as selections from the Mishna, Talmud, and other sacred commentaries and texts. In England and elsewhere there was also a growing knowledge of the cognate languages of Aramaic and Syriac.

Yet nothing of note had been done in the way of English Bible translation since the Bishops' Bible of 1568. Moreover, it was the Geneva Bible that almost everybody read. At least eighty-six editions of it—in octavo, quarto, and folio format—were printed between 1568 and 1611, compared to thirty of the Bishops', and though Whitgift and Bancroft had done everything in their power to make the latter popular, the Geneva enjoyed de facto official status, and some of its bindings in folio even had "Queen Elizabeth Bible" stamped on their spines. To make matters worse, the Bishops' Bible had been singled out by the editors of the Rheims New Testament of 1582 for special scorn. In short, even though the Anglican Church had at its disposal a variety of Protestant versions of the Scriptures, these differed among themselves in some important respects (as Catholics loved to point out) and none was sufficient to match the Act of Uniformity in force and effect.

Toward the end of Elizabeth's reign, agitation for a new translation had increased behind the scenes. An act of Parliament was secretly drafted "for the reducing of diversities of Bibles now extant in the English tongue to one settled" version, to be done by scholars from Oxford and Cambridge and subsidized by the Church; and Elizabeth, in giving it her backing, had discussed it in 1597 with Sir Francis Walsingham and Bishop John Aylmer, then Bishop of London, who was "most earnest to take it in hand."

Meanwhile, in Scotland King James himself had independently been turning the same matter over in his mind. In the Kirk Assembly at Burntisland in May 1601, he had suggested that the Geneva Bible might be revised "both for the profit of it and the glory of it," and specifically discussed metrical and other errors in the Psalms. The assembly endorsed his proposal and recommended that scholars "most skill'd in the different languages" take it up.

But now James was on the throne of England, and the notion of directing in his own royal person a great national enterprise such as the translation would be was both flattering to his vanity and in accord with his desires. It also gave him a chance to show off his biblical learning; make a real contribution to the religious debate; and appear to heed some of the Puritans' concerns. And so no sooner did Reynolds voice his proposal than the king made it his own. He said he had "never yet seen a Bible well translated into English"—including, by inference, the Bishops'; yearned "for one uniform translation," which all denominations could accept; and thought this could best be done by outstanding scholars "in both the Universities, after them to be reviewed by the Bishops and the chief learned of the Church." The new translation would then be presented to the Privy Council, and lastly ratified by royal authority. "And so this whole Church to be bound unto it and none other."

Bancroft warned against allowing the text to be skewed by contentious notes, and the king agreed. He condemned the notes in the Geneva Bible in particular as "partial, untrue, seditious, and savoring of traitorous conceits," and gave as examples the gloss on Exodus 4:19, "where the margin alloweth disobedience to kings"; and that on 2 Chronicles 15:20, where "King Asa is taxed on the note for only deposing his mother for idolatry, and not killing her." James added: "Let errors in matters of faith be amended, and indifferent things be interpreted, and a gloss added unto them."

The project was apparently organized rather quickly, on a most ambitious scale. An attempt was made to identify and enlist all outstanding biblical scholars in the kingdom, and in June 1604, James wrote to Bancroft, now acting Archbishop of Canterbury following Whitgift's death, and pressed him to spur the project on. By then, Bancroft had opportunistically allied himself to the king's enthusiasm and in turn wrote to a colleague: "I . . . move you in his majesty's name that, agreeably to the charge and trust committed unto you, time may be overstepped by you for the better furtherance of this holy work. . . . You will scarcely conceive how earnest his majesty is to have this work begun." Before the end of July, the king had approved a list of fifty-four translators arranged into six companies, two to meet at Westminster under its dean, and two each at the universities of Oxford and Cambridge under the direction of their royal Hebrew professors. Both universities were also directed to enlist any other biblical scholars of proven capacity, and prelates to secure the advice of any known to them who "in their private studies" had taken pains to correct mistakes in former English versions or clear up "obscurities," and who were especially skilled in Hebrew and Greek. All such information and advice was to be passed on to the three directors of the enterprise—Edward Lively, regius professor of Hebrew at Cambridge; John Harding, regius professor of Hebrew at Oxford; and Lancelot Andrewes, dean of Westminster—"so that," in the king's words, "our said intended translation may have the help and furtherance of all our principal learned men."

Money, however, was needed to cover the working expenses of the effort, and for the remuneration of those called to serve. To pay for their time and labor, the king suggested to the bishops that they reserve ecclesiastical preferment for those in need of it, and in the end seven were made bishops, and ten more received prebends, benefices, and other emoluments and rewards. The universities were also directed to supply room and board for those centered at their facilities.

The selection of the two universities and Westminster, not incidentally, made good political sense: by tradition, Oxford was associated for the most part with High Church and royalist sentiments; Cambridge with dissidents—reformers, martyrs, and exiles. Both were also, strictly speaking, secular institutions. Westminster, on the other hand, represented the clerical and legal aspects of the venture, for all the officials of the abbey were appointed by the sovereign, making it a sort of Cathedral of the Crown.

∽

Most of the translators, or revisers, were middle-aged men (on average, about fifty years old); some were married; all but one (Sir Henry Savile) ordained. Without exception, all were academically distinguished, belonged to the established Church—though quite a few (about a fourth) had Puritan leanings—expert in ancient or modern languages or both, and (depending on their other specialties) deeply conversant with biblical scholarship, theology, and other fields. Although they deliberately cultivated anonymity as a group, we know something about a number of them, though in a certain sense we cannot know enough. What we don't know (beyond an occasional plausible surmise) is the individual contribution each made to the final version of the King James text.

The Old Testament was entrusted to three panels, the New Testament to two, the Apocrypha to one. The First Westminster Company was assigned Genesis through 2 Kings; the Second, Romans through Jude; the First Oxford Company, Isaiah through Malachi; the Second, the Gospels, Acts, and Revelation; the First Cambridge Company, 1 Chronicles through The Song of Solomon; the Second, the Apocrypha.

The Westminster group was headed by Dean Lancelot Andrewes, an immensely learned man who, it was said, "might have been interpreter general at Babel . . . the world wanted [lacked] learning to know how learned he was." The son of a master mariner, Andrewes had studied at the Merchant Taylors' School under Richard Mulcaster, a classical and Hebrew scholar of note, and as "a great long lad of 16," went up to Pembroke College, Cambridge, on scholarship, where one of his companions was Edmund Spenser, the poet and author of *The Faerie Queene.* From a very tender age, Andrewes was "addicted to the study of good letters," avoided "games of ordinary recreation" such as cards, dice, chess, or croquet, and preferred long solitary walks or the company of earnest students like himself. He became a fellow of his college in 1576, took orders in 1580, and was successively vicar of St. Giles's, Cripplegate, prebendary of St. Paul's, and dean of Westminster, as well as serving as one of twelve chaplains to the queen.

A remarkable linguist, he eventually mastered fifteen languages, including Latin, Greek, Hebrew, Syriac, and Chaldee; had an encyclopedic memory—"he not only calls to mind any matter," noted one colleague, "but the very time, place, persons, and all other circumstances"; and was sought after by fellow scholars from all over the world. Hugo Grotius, the great Dutch legal authority and historian, counted a meeting with Andrewes "one of the special attractions of a visit to England."

He was also a preacher of great power—"an angel in the pulpit," whose sermons were studded with classical quotations and marked by word play and metaphysical conceits. T. S. Eliot commended his memorable gift of expression and his way of "taking a word and deriving the world from it"—such meaning as "we should never have supposed any word to possess." This was not to every listener's taste. One visiting Scotsman complained that Andrewes played with his text, "as a Jack-an-apes does, who takes up a thing, tosses and plays with it, then takes up another, and plays a little with that, too."

But there was also a homely vigor to his style that was alive with the speaking voice. Here is Andrewes in a sermon preached on Christmas Day before the king at Whitehall, on Luke 2:10–11: "Men may talk what they will, but sure there is no joy in the world to the joy of a man saved; no joy so great, no news so welcome, as to one ready to perish, in case of a lost man, to hear of one that will save him. In danger of perishing by sickness, to hear of one will make him well again; by sentence of the law, of one with a pardon to save his life; by enemies, of one that will rescue and set him in safety. Tell any of these, assure them but of a Savior, it is the best news he ever heard in his life." And here is Andrewes on the Three Wise Men from the East in his Christmas sermon of 1622: "It was no summer progress. A cold coming they had of it at this time of the year, just the worst time of the year to take a journey, and specially a long journey in. The ways deep, the weather sharp, the days short, the sun farthest off, *in solstitio brumali*, 'the very dead of winter.' " Anyone familiar with T. S. Eliot's *The Journey of the Magi* will recognize its debt to these lines.

But for Andrewes, eloquence was not the point. "The only true praise of a Sermon," he once wrote, "is some evil left [abandoned], or some good done, upon the hearing of it," and he had little patience with pulpit rhetoric of an ostentatious kind. As rector of St. Giles's, Cripplegate, his congregation contained noblemen and paupers, actors and minstrels; and at St. Paul's Cathedral it included Thomas Nashe, the playwright, and John Lyly, whose elegant balanced prose was the very model of the euphuistic style.

As a King James translator, his linguistic skill and vast learning equipped him for the task of deciding between proposed versions and on what manner of expression was best. And he bears the final—and glorious—responsibility, it may be, for the form of such celebrated passages as the Creation and Fall; Abraham and Isaac; the Exodus; David's laments for Saul, Jonathan, and Absalom; and Elijah's encounter with the "still small voice."

In his youth, Andrewes had shown Puritan leanings, under the influence of his patron, Sir Francis Walsingham, and had been a champion of Puritan reform; but over time he became more critical of Calvinist dogma, shed his former affiliations, and became quite High Church. His richly furnished private chapel—with its silver candlesticks, cushion for the service book, and elaborate Communion plate ("a silver gilt canister for the wafers like a wicker basket lined with cambric lace, the flagon on a cradle, and the chalice covered with a napkin on a credence," as scornfully described in a Puritan tract) was controversial; but no one doubted the piety of the man himself. He reportedly spent up to five hours a day in prayer, and a posthumously published little book of his own private devotions, written in Hebrew, Latin, and Greek, became an Anglican classic and an inspiration to the poet George Herbert, who had been one of his pupils as a boy. At the same time, he wisely steered clear of sectarian disputes, and some trace of his Puritan past also remained. He occasionally quoted Calvin "with praise and affection," and under the Puritan Commonwealth a selection of his sermons entitled *Orphan Lectures* would be esteemed "a rich contribution to theological literature" and not incompatible with Puritan belief.

Like Richard Mulcaster, his beloved tutor, whose portrait he kept above his study door, Andrewes was also a dedicated teacher, and after Elizabeth made him dean of Westminster in 1601 he often took charge of Westminster School. There the younger students were his special care. "What pains Dr. Andrewes did take [with us] both day and night," one of them later remembered. "He never walked to Chiswick for his recreation without a brace of young fry, and in that wayfaring leisure had a singular dexterity to fill those narrow vessels with a funnel." Several times a week he also held tutorials in his rooms from eight to eleven at night for the more advanced pupils, unfolding to them his knowledge of Hebrew and Greek. All this he did, "without compulsion or correction," being a most mild-mannered master to those in his charge. "Nay, I never heard him," wrote one, "utter so much as a word of austerity among us."

Both Queen Elizabeth and King James esteemed Andrewes "beyond all other divines." He had delivered the farewell sermon at the queen's funeral at Westminster, and four months later played a prominent part in the coronation of King James. He opened the royal robes for the anointing, helped James on with the Supertunica, and handed him the royal scepter before Archbishop Whitgift placed the crown upon his head.

It is said that James sometimes slept with notes of Andrewes's sermons under his pillow, but was uncomfortably awed by "his gravity of manner" and refrained in his presence from a certain uncouth "mirth" that was his wont. But over the years he showered Andrewes with offices, responsibilities, and honors; deployed him in theological debate with Catholics opposed to the Anglican Church; prized his erudition; and cherished his support of the doctrine of divine right.

Andrewes providentially also saved the king's life. On November 3, 1605, his consecration as Bishop of Chichester delayed the convocation of Parliament by a day, and thereby helped foil the Gunpowder Plot, in which an attempt was made by Catholics to blow up the king and Parliament in one great blast. Soon thereafter the king imposed the controversial Oath of Allegiance on all his subjects, which some found harsh; but Andrewes saw fit to defend it, although he was never in any sense a flattering minion of his king. It is said that one day the king asked Andrewes and a fellow bishop (Richard Neile of Durham), "Cannot I take my subjects' money when I want it without all this formality in Parliament?" The two bishops were standing behind his chair at dinner. Neile, who was even more of a royalist than Andrewes, said, "You should; you are the breath of our nostrils." Andrewes said he was not qualified to offer an opinion, but added, "I think you could take my brother Neile's money, because he offers it."

Under Andrewes, the First Westminster Company met in the famous Jerusalem Chamber, which was part of the original Abbey

House. After Andrewes became Bishop of Chichester, they customarily met in the abbey library, where most of their reference works had already been gathered for their use.

Other notable scholars in the company included Hadrian a Saravia, John Layfield, William Bedwell, and John Overall. And something may be said of each.

Saravia, the oldest of the translators at seventy-three, had been a professor of divinity at the University of Leyden before settling in England in 1587, when he became rector of Tattenhill in Staffordshire. Four years later, in 1591, he wrote a defense of episcopacy as the God-given form of church government, for which the Church establishment rewarded him with a doctorate in divinity from Oxford and a prebend at Gloucester Cathedral. William Cecil, Elizabeth's secretary of state, took him under his wing, and other preferments followed, under both Elizabeth and James.

Though "a terrible high churchman"—and extremely close to Richard Hooker, whose five-volume work, *Of the Laws of Ecclesiastical Polity,* was the definitive defense of Anglican doctrine—he was also known as a reconciler, and (according to Isaac Casaubon, the great textual scholar) one who earnestly sought "for peace and concord in the Church."

Saravia was expert in Hebrew. His colleague, John Layfield, fluent in Greek. A former fellow and lecturer at Trinity College, Cambridge, and rector of St. Clement Danes in the Strand, Layfield also had an unusual knowledge of ancient architecture and "was much relied on" for passages having to do with the tabernacle and the temple as described in Exodus and 1 Kings. He had traveled widely, and was the only one of the translators who had been to the New World. In 1597, he had served as chaplain to an expedition to the West Indies and had sailed as far as Puerto Rico, where, he tells us, in an account published in *Purchas, His Pilgrims,* he marveled at the physical strength and beauty of the natives, and was beguiled by the succulent fruits and hanging vines. The taste of the "woody pine apple" which "groweth upon a bush like an artichoke," he wrote, was "like unto ripe strawberries and cream."

A more famous scholar was William Bedwell, a fellow of Trinity College, Cambridge, and "the father of Arabic studies in England."

Fluent in languages of the Near and Middle East, he had compiled a Persian dictionary, an Arabic lexicon, had written two pioneering works on philology (one of which argued that a knowledge of Arabic was indispensable for an understanding of ancient Hebrew texts), and was universally regarded as one of the great linguists of the day. As a translator, he also brought a specialist's knowledge of astronomy, mathematics, and geography to the task. As rector of St. Ethelburga's in Bishopsgate, London, not incidentally, he also administered the sacraments to Henry Hudson, the famed navigator, and some of his "rough sea dogs" before they set sail on their voyage of discovery to the New World.

Almost as prominent was John Overall, regius professor of divinity at Cambridge, and the dean of St. Paul's. The great courtier poet Fulke Greville had helped him secure the latter appointment, and part of his task as dean was to clean up "Paul's Walk"—a sort of bowery strip (mentioned by Ben Jonson, Shakespeare, and others) which had made the nave a notorious haunt for illicit traffic and low life. "Whilst devotion kneels at her prayers," wrote Thomas Dekker, "doth prophanation walk under her nose."

Overall knew Greek but was primarily known as a Latinist and was so fluent in that language that he once admitted it was sometimes difficult for him to speak English at any length. This can only have been to his advantage in some aspects of the work, since much of the biblical scholarship was in Latin, and most of the discussion in committee was in Latin, too. His own English tended to have a theological savor, yet he could also be plain and direct. "I was requested to come visit some of my parish that were sick," he wrote on one occasion, "and coming I found them sicker in mind than body. The thing that troubled their minds was this. They could not be persuaded that Christ had died for their sins." Christ, he explained, had "died for all men sufficiently," but only for the believer "effectually—as the sun shineth sufficiently to give light to all, though it doth it effectually only to them that open their eyes; as water is sufficient to quench all the thirsty, but doth it only to them that drink it; as physic is sufficient to cure all maladies, but doth it effectually only where it is applied."

One malady in his own life was beyond the power of physic to cure. About the time he joined the Westminster group, he married a young woman reputed to be "the greatest English Beauty of her time." But it was not a happy match. She was said to be "wondrous wanton, and so tender-hearted that (truly) she could scarce deny any one." One contemporary sung her charms:

> *Face she had of Filberd hue*
> *and bosom'd like a Swan.*
> *Back she had of bended Ewe*
> *and waisted by a span.*
> *Haire she had as black as Crowe*
> *from her head unto the toe.*
> *Downe downe all over her,*
> *hye nonny, nonny noe.*
>
> *To sport it on the merry downe*
> *to daunce the Lively Haye;*
> *To wrastle for a green gowne*
> *in heate of all the day*
> *Never would she saye me no*
> *yet I thought me had tho*
> *Never enough of her*
> *hye nonny nonny noe.*

Overall "loved her infinitely" and put up for a time with her infidelities, until she ran off with Sir John Selbye, a local squire. Then he went after her and (according to a popular song), before long he "found her/Even upon John Selbye's bed,/as flatte as any Flounder."

Yet they seem to have reconciled. Once asked by the pleasure-loving Earl of Essex whether a man might lawfully enjoy recreation on the Sabbath after evening prayer, Overall wearily replied that, yes, he might, since "both body and mind should have it," then added, "A man may be so tedious and worn out in the service of God that he may not be fit to serve." And as he said it, "there was something divided in his eyes."

Although Overall stood with the church hierarchy, he was to the "left" of Andrewes in some of his views (particularly on kingship), and argued in a book on Church-state relations (1606) "that a new government established after a lawful revolution can claim the obedience of the people as a duty to God." This ran directly counter to the king's own views (as expressed in a treatise entitled *The True Law of Free Monarchies,* 1598), which insisted that kings, chosen by God, enjoy a rule that is absolute. And at the king's order, Overall's book was suppressed.

Overall was not the only panelist touched by scandal. His colleague Richard Thomson, a Hebrew scholar and the rector of Upwell in Norfolk, was an urbane, worldly, and cosmopolitan man who "seldom went to bed sober" and was notoriously partial to racy epigrams.

Little is known about the four remaining members of the panel—Robert Tighe, Geoffrey King, Francis Burleigh, and Richard Clarke—aside from their academic and ecclesiastical rank. Tighe had been educated at both Oxford and Cambridge, and was vicar of All Hallows, Barking, and archdeacon of Middlesex; King was a fellow of Kings College, Cambridge, vicar of Horsham in Surrey, and afterward regius professor of Hebrew (1606); Burleigh, a fellow of Chelsea College, Cambridge, and rector of Thorley; and Clarke, a fellow of Christ's College, Cambridge, and vicar of Munster on the Isle of Thanet.

Altogether the First Westminster Company was rich in talent, sensibility, and experience—well fit (as one writer put it) to "sit down in a cold stone room by the fire and discuss in capable fashion" the legendary, historical, and biographical narratives, short stories, and lyric poetry in the books of Genesis through 2 Kings entrusted to their care.

The First Cambridge Company (in charge of 1 Chronicles through the Song of Solomon) was led by Edward Lively, who as the university's long-standing regius professor of Hebrew had trained dozens of younger scholars, and was more responsible for the growth of Hebrew studies in England than any other man. But a secure life of scholarly retirement was not to be his lot.

Born into poverty, he never quite got out of it, and was harried by creditors to the end of his days. On one occasion, he returned home from a lecture attended by the queen to find all his goods impounded against payment of debts. He did some hack writing on the side, contributed anonymously to *Purchas, His Pilgrims* (a survey of the peoples and religions of the world), and wrote a little book called the *True Chronology of the Times of the Persian Monarchy,* which (among other curiosities) contained speculation about the nature of the locusts eaten by John the Baptist. But as the father of thirteen children, he could never get ahead of his bills. Ultimately, he had to sell his large library "for a pittance" to a covetous bishop, and from time to time found himself obliged to pawn other goods. "My life," he once said in a despondent mood, "is nothing but a continual Flood of waters." After his wife died, he was completely overwhelmed. In 1602, his situation was briefly eased by the award of a prebend at Peterborough, and in September 1604, in keeping with the king's scheme for helping translators in need, Bishop Bancroft procured the living at Purleigh in Essex for him. But the strain of it all was too much for him, and only months afterward he died of "an ague and a squinsey," leaving his children destitute.

Other members of the company did their best to make up for his loss. One was John Richardson, regius professor of divinity at Trinity College, and later master of Peterhouse and vice-chancellor of Cambridge University; another, Laurence Chaderton, born in 1536 (the year of Tyndale's martyrdom), and one of the four Puritans to attend the conference at Hampton Court. While a student at Cambridge, Chaderton (of Catholic stock) had become a Calvinist, much to the horror of his father, who in a memorable letter threatened to cut off his funds. "If you do not renounce the new sect which you have joined," he warned, you will have nothing to fall back on. I will care for you as a father only if you heed my advice. Otherwise, "I enclose a shilling to buy a wallet. Go and beg." Chaderton bought a wallet, won a full university scholarship, and developed into an outstanding linguist, proficient in Hebrew, Latin, Greek, Spanish, and French. The "writings of the Rabbis" (as contained in the Mishna and Talmud) were also said to be his familiar terrain. He enjoyed a number of distinguished appointments, as dean of Christ's College, master of Emmanuel College (a Puritan institution, founded to "train up godly ministers"), and prebendary of

Lincoln Cathedral. But—on principle—he never held more than one parish living at a time.

One of the great preachers of his day, he had a "clear and pleasing" voice "of wonderful flexibility, accompanied by a great dignity of manner." His listeners seemed unable to get enough of it. On one occasion, having preached for two hours straight, he broke off so as not to try their patience, but the entire congregation reportedly cried out, "For God's sake, go on! go on! We beg you!"—and, for another hour, he did.

Though Chaderton was a moderate who accepted the discipline of the established Church, he often spoke against the "swarms of idle ignorant and ungodly curates" who lacked "soundness of doctrine and integrity of life." His own life was marked by charity, with "a living affection for the poor." As master of Emmanuel College (a post he held for thirty-eight years), Chaderton also attracted legions of devout scholars and in time "scores of zealous Puritan ministers" (later to figure prominently in the Commonwealth) came forth from its hallowed halls.

Vigorous to the end, Chaderton proved the longest-lived of the translators, surviving through the reigns of four Tudors and two Stuarts into the English Civil War. In extreme old age, he kept to his studies, devoted himself to botany and gardening, and at the age of 105 (when he died) was apparently still able to read "without spectacles" a copy of the Greek New Testament "with very small type."

One of Chaderton's fellow panelists (and, it happened, his first biographer) was Francis Dillingham, a fellow of Christ's College, Cambridge, vicar of Wilden, and "an excellent linguist and subtle disputant." In the course of his life, he wrote eight books, including three antipapal tracts, as well as a treatise entitled *Household Government and the Duties of Husbands and Wives.* Although unmarried himself, he expounded at great length on the Old Testament theme that the "golden key" to marital happiness was an obliging and submissive wife.

Other colleagues were Thomas Harrison, a fellow of Trinity College, Cambridge, and noted for his "exquisite skill in Hebrew and Greek idioms"; Roger Andrewes, the younger brother of Lancelot and master of Jesus College, Cambridge; Robert Spalding, a prominent Hebraist and a fellow of St. John's; and Andrew Bing, a fellow of Peterhouse and vicar of Everton.

Lively's counterpart as regius professor of Hebrew at Oxford was John Harding, a canon of Lincoln Cathedral, a fellow of Magdalen College, and chairman of the First Oxford Company. Harding had the right credentials to lead, but was completely overshadowed in committee by John Reynolds, the president and longtime Greek reader of Corpus Christi College, and the man whose whole idea the translation project had been. Aside from Andrewes, in fact, none of the other translators cast quite the shadow he did. Admirers described him as a "living library," "a third university," "a university unto himself"; and his "memory and diversity of reading" were said to be "near unto a miracle" and "an ever springing and never failing well."

Born in 1549, Reynolds had studied at Christ Church, Oxford—with Sir Walter Ralegh and Sir Philip Sidney, two illustrious compatriots—was ordained in 1572, and soon emerged as an eloquent spokesman for the Puritan camp. When Sir Francis Walsingham founded an Oxford lectureship in 1586 for the refutation of papal doctrines, he saw to it that Reynolds was appointed to the chair. The lectures were popular, but from time to time Queen Elizabeth (who had a good opinion of him) sought to temper his zeal. In 1592, she scolded him for "his obstinate preciseness" and advised him "to follow her laws, and not run before them." Reynolds paid heed, became dean of Lincoln in 1593 and president of Corpus Christi in 1599. Under his regime, the college thrived. As a centrist Puritan, he was not averse to some aspects of High Church practice, such as kneeling to receive the Sacraments, which Nonconformists abhorred; and he accepted the Anglo-Catholic dogma of the apostolic succession, which held that English bishops were in direct descent in authority from the apostles of the early Church. Even so, he had received rough handling from Bancroft at the Hampton Court Conference; and an irate Jesuit once reputedly tried to assassinate him as he took his daily constitutional through London's Finsbury Fields.

Moderate in most things, he could be extreme in some, and never quite forgave himself for consenting to play the part of a girl in a college comedy staged in honor of the queen. Years later, quoting Deuteronomy 22:5 ("Neither shall a man put on a woman's garment, for all that do so are an abomination to the Lord"), he raked himself over for it in a treatise against stage plays, which he condemned as corrupting to youth. Generally speaking, he regarded acting as immoral and the theater itself as a den of iniquity, where tender youths were inflamed with love, enticed to "dalliance, whoredom, and incest," and corrupted by "dissolute railings" and "brainsick, drunken conceits." As president of Corpus Christi, he worried about students drinking in taverns, dancing, gambling, or even playing croquet with girls. Yet in practice he ruled the college with "a gentle discretion," and was so happy in the post that he declined a bishopric from the queen.

Corpus Christi had been the first Oxford college to encourage the study of Greek, and Reynolds was one of the foremost Greek scholars it ever possessed. As Greek reader, he lectured on Aristotle's *Rhetoric* among other texts, and the Bodleian Library has preserved his own annotated copy, with a handwritten introduction, synopsis, index, and notes.

The First Oxford Company generally met once a week in Reynolds's lodgings, where he was often laid up with consumption and gout. Over the course of the two and a half years they toiled over their portion of the Old Testament text (Isaiah through Malachi), he seemed to waste away—his decline apparently accelerated by the hard translation work. By the time he died, on May 21, 1607, he looked "a very skeleton."

Not all the members of Reynolds's own family, incidentally, were Protestants. His father was a Catholic, and two of his brothers, Edmund and William, reconverted to Catholicism after briefly embracing Puritan thought. William came under the influence of William Allen (of Douai Bible fame), whom he joined at the Jesuit College of Douai before going on to the English College at Rheims. There he lectured on Paul's Epistles, held the chair of divinity and Hebrew, and evidently helped Gregory Martin produce the Rheims New Testament of 1582.

Reynolds himself bore no personal ill will toward Catholics, and in fact was not a bigot of any stripe. He closed his will with the words: "Give of none offense, neither to the Jews nor to the Grecians [Gentiles] by the Church of God."

Less accepting that way was his colleague Thomas Holland, whose learning was "mighty in Scripture" but whose habitual benediction in parting was: "I commend you to the love of God and to the hatred of Popery and superstition." But he was also a man to be reckoned with on several counts. A fellow of Balliol College, he had served as chaplain to the Earl of Leicester on his expedition against the Spaniards in the Netherlands in 1585, and four years later became regius professor of divinity at Oxford. All of the revisers may have been learned, but Holland more than most, for he was "drowned in books, so familiarly acquainted with the Fathers as if he had been one of them, so versed in the Schoolmen as if he were the 'Seraphic Doctor,' and so celebrated for his preaching, reading, disputing, and moderating, with other excellent qualifications, that all who knew him commended him," according to one who did.

Richard Kilbye, a fourth member of the company, was a fellow and rector of Lincoln College, Oxford, and a prebendary of Lincoln Cathedral. Said to have been "wild in his youth," he preached like "a brand plucked from the burning" in an evangelical style, and in one sermon, "The Burden of a Loaden Conscience," he lamented his own sinful strayings and "reprobate heart." "Young and old, take heed by me," he warned. "Have no more Gods but one." A substantial Hebrew scholar, Kilbye produced two Latin commentaries on parts of Genesis and Exodus, and eventually succeeded to John Harding's university chair. Upon his death in 1620, he left his entire estate to his parishioners, and in the college chapel at All Saints, Oxford, the plaque over his tomb reads:

> *Lo! Richard Kilbye lieth here,*
> *Which lately was our minister.*
> *To the poor he ever was a friend,*
> *And gave them all he had at his end.*

A fifth member of the company was Miles Smith, who not only contributed his portion, but would be one of the two men chosen to help edit the complete Bible text. He also wrote the great Preface for it—in its own right, a famous piece of prose.

His lofty mind belied a humble birth. The son of a butcher, Smith had studied classics and Semitic languages at both Corpus Christi and Brasenose College, Oxford, and was said to be so expert in Syriac, Arabic, Hebrew, and Chaldee that he had them "at his fingers' ends." Throughout his life he claimed that he desired nothing but books, but many preferments came his way—as chaplain of Christ Church, vicar of Bosbury, prebendary of Hereford Cathedral, prebendary of Exeter Cathedral, and rector of Hartlebury. In 1612, in reward for his work on the Bible translation, he was appointed Bishop of Gloucester. In his Preface, he spoke for the modesty (or deliberate anonymity) of the translators as a whole: "There were many chosen, that were greater in other men's eyes than in their own, and that sought the truth rather than their own praise." Despite his own eminence, he was unpretentious himself, and once broke off a conference with a fellow bishop to make way for a lowly cleric, saying, "He must not wait, lest we should seem to take state upon ourselves."

A sixth member of the company was Richard Brett, a fellow of Lincoln College, Oxford, and rector of Quainton, Buckinghamshire, who wrote a number of Latin tracts on Church doctrine, and was "famous in his time for learning as well as piety, skill'd in debate, and well-versed to a criticism" in the languages of the Near and Middle East.

Of Richard Fairclough and William Thorne, little is known. Richard Fairclough was a fellow of New College, Oxford, and rector of Bucknell, Oxfordshire; William Thorne, rector of Tallard Royal in Wiltshire, dean of Chichester, and (later) a regius professor of Hebrew. After receiving several handsome preferments, he gratefully wrote *A Kenning Glass for a Christian King*, a portrait of the perfect monarch quite flattering to James.

These three companies had the Old Testament in their hands. The New Testament and Apocrypha were given, respectively, to the Second Oxford and Westminster companies, and the Second Cambridge Company, as described. The last was led by John Duport, master of Jesus College and the son-in-law of Bishop Richard Cox of Ely, who had worked on two of the New Testament books for the Bishops' Bible of 1568. One of his notable colleagues was Samuel Ward, at age twenty seven the youngest of all the translators and a chaplain to the king. As master of Sidney Sussex College, a Puritan institution, Ward later welcomed Oliver Cromwell to the student body on April 23, 1616 (the day Shakespeare died).

Ward was quite a bibliophile and assisted James Ussher, the antiquarian scholar, chancellor of St. Patrick's Cathedral, Dublin, and later Bishop of Armagh, in collecting rare books for the Bodleian Library and ancient Irish manuscripts for King James. Yet despite his many accomplishments, he was an introspective and uncertain soul, stuttered badly, and "was a Moses not only for slowness of speech, but otherwise for meekness of nature." Extremely self-critical, he upbraided himself in a diary kept from the age of eighteen for everything from pride to eating too many raisins and plums.

But Puritans came to regard him as not one of their own. Although he once condemned himself for an excessive "desire of preferment," he accepted a number of livings—as prebendary and canon residentiary of Wells Cathedral, archdeacon of Taunton, prebendary of York, rector of Great Munden, Hertfordshire, and of Terrington, Norfolk—and eventually won appointment as Lady Margaret Professor of Divinity at Cambridge. In time, his fellow clergy "gasped at his pluralism," and when the English Civil War came, he was expelled by the Puritans from Cambridge and imprisoned with a number of Anglican dons.

Though Ward was an able scholar, the most important members of the Apocrypha panel were probably Andrew Downes and John Bois. Downes was a fellow of St. John's College and (for forty years) regius professor of Greek at Cambridge; but he is chiefly remembered now from his connection with Bois.

Bois was a prodigy. By the age of six he could read the Old Testament in Hebrew, and by thirteen he was competent in New Testament and classical Greek. At fourteen, he entered St. John's College, studied hard, often from four in the morning until eight at night, and in one week advanced from the first to the second level in Greek (a course of study that normally took a year). In the next month, he advanced from the second level to the third, which normally took two years. Downes, who was chief lecturer in Greek at the time, understandably took a "singular delight in him" and not only went over his daily lessons with care, but tutored him in "twelve of the hardest, and, for dialect and phrase, both in verse and prose, most difficult Greek authors" he could find. In time, Bois was elected a fellow of St. John's, and although he came down with smallpox on the eve of his senior exams, took them anyway in a fever wrapped up in blankets, excelled all his classmates, and was appointed lecturer in Greek.

But a strictly academic career was not his choice. In 1591, he succeeded his father as rector at West Stow, and was soon promised a better living by the rector of Boxworth near Cambridge, on condition he marry his daughter. Bois went to look her over and, "they liking each of the other," he agreed. As rector of Boxworth, Bois ceased to be a member of the university community. But he could hardly bear to be away. He audited lectures whenever he could, and at his parish home kept a young scholar as tutor to his children, while others sought him as tutor to their own. "Many knights and gentlemen of quality," his biographer tells us, "did importune him to take their children in." But when Bois was invited to join the Second Cambridge Company, some scholars remarked that "they needed no help from the country," meaning, from a man without academic rank. But he soon outshone all his detractors, completed his own portion of the Apocrypha ahead of schedule, helped another translator in another group, and later served on the select General Committee of Review.

Of Bois it was said that he was "Respectful of superiors, loving of equals, and familiar with inferiors, though humility made him think not many below himself. He gave and forgave, being hospitable to strangers, real to friends, refrained from meddling in other men's matters," and was a just keeper of the promises he made. He was also singularly conscientious, devoting the whole of the week at Cambridge to his assignments, before returning on the weekends to his parish cares.

Like Chaderton, Bois was mindful of his health and lived to a ripe old age. He ate lightly, fasted often, and seldom drank, and after each meal "was careful almost to a curiosity in picking and rubbing his teeth, esteeming that a special preservative to health." To the end, his countenance was fresh, his eyes clear, his hearing sharp, and he had "almost an Hebrew alphabet of teeth" when he died.

In his will, he left careful instructions for the dispersal of his books and papers, for "books and papers," he poignantly wrote, "may easily catch Harm."

Three other scholars—Jeremiah Radcliffe, Robert Ward, and William Branthwaite—served to round the panel out. Radcliffe had studied at Trinity College, "acquired a string of livings," and was the brother of the king's physician; Ward (unrelated to Samuel) studied at Kings College, Cambridge, and held a prebendary at Chichester Cathedral; Branthwaite, a Greek scholar and fellow of Emmanuel College, was known as a wit.

At the head of the Second Oxford Company stood Thomas Ravis, dean of Christ's Church, prebendary of Westminster Abbey, Bishop of Gloucester (1605), and afterward Bishop of London (1607). One of the many deans who attended the Hampton Court Conference, he had belittled the Puritans, and in its aftermath "adopted Bancroft's uncompromising tone: 'By the help of Jesus I will not leave one preacher in my diocese who doth not subscribe and conform.'" Such a "harsh and haughty dean," as one writer remarked, "was an odd choice to direct the translation of material [the Gospels, Acts, and Revelation] that contains the heart of Christian teaching."

But the strong man on the panel was really Sir Henry Savile, warden of Merton College, provost of Eton, and one of the foremost classical scholars of his age. In his early prime he had served as Latin secretary to Queen Elizabeth and had tutored her in mathematics and Greek. His own translation into English of the *Histories* of Tacitus, published in 1591, was a remarkable achievement and cherished by knowledgeable Latinists, including Ben Jonson, the poet and friend of Shakespeare. Subsequently, Savile put together an eight-volume folio edition of the complete works of St. John Chrysostom (the "golden-mouthed patriarch" of Constantinople and father of the Eastern Church), which became the largest publication venture of its day. Over the course of twenty years, he collated all known manuscript editions of Chrysostom's work, from libraries at home and abroad, and gathered round him at Eton several fine scholars, including Andrew Downes and John Bois, to help him with his task. Their labors, in fact, overlapped with those of the Bible translation, and it wasn't until 1610 that the edition went to press. Then the printing itself took three years. Savile's wife, Lady Margaret, reportedly felt utterly neglected during this period and once exclaimed, "I would I were a book too." Hearing her outburst, a bystander retorted, "Madam, you must then be an almanac that he might change every year."

The only translator not ordained, Savile was "an extraordinarily handsome and beautiful man—no lady had a finer complexion." His generosity, courtliness, and hospitality were sometimes likened to those of an Italian prince, and he was a great patron of learning, founding professorships in geometry and astronomy at Oxford.

Another notable member of the panel was George Abbot, master of University College, chaplain to the chancellor of Oxford, and in 1604 on the cusp of an illustrious career. Though a Puritan, he "always advocated reasonable obedience to duly constituted authority," and as proof of his commitment to Church discipline once briefly imprisoned one hundred forty undergraduates for sitting with their hats on in his presence in St. Mary's Church. As a result, he was favored by the powers that be. Eventually, he was made Bishop of Lichfield and Coventry, then, upon the death of Thomas Ravis, Bishop of London. Upon the death of Bancroft, the king would call him to the Canterbury See.

Abbot was a close reader of texts, and in 1600 wrote a six-hundred-page study of Jonah, one of the shortest of the Old Testament books. In 1605, he also published a geographical work entitled *A Brief Description of the Whole World*. The king liked to engage him in epistolary debate, usually on some theological topic, and some of the letters they exchanged ran to several thousand words. For the most part, their tone was affectionately polemical, but from time to time the king became irked if his own views did not prevail. On one occasion, he tactfully suggested that Abbot "have a kind of faith implicit in my judgment, as well as in respect of some skill I have in divinity."

Though Abbot became a trusted adviser of the king, the bottom fell out of his world when he accidentally killed a gamekeeper with his bow while hunting in a park. After a prolonged inquiry, he was cleared by a special commission and also received a royal pardon from James. But not all could clear him in their hearts. Some prelates refused to be consecrated by his hands, and one bishop wrote: "For the King to leave . . . a man of blood as primate and patriarch of all his churches is a thing that sounds very harsh in the old courts and canons of the Church." Many commoners could not forgive him either, and ten years later Abbot "one day found his coach blocked in a London street. When he implored the crowd to let him pass, a woman screamed, 'Ye had best shoot an arrow at us, too!' "

Other members of the company included the Calvinist John Harmer, a fellow of New College, Oxford, regius professor of Greek, and a canon of Winchester Cathedral; John Perin, a fellow of St. John's College, Oxford, regius professor of Greek, and a canon of Christ Church; Giles Thomson, dean of Windsor and a former chaplain to the queen; Richard Edes, a former playwright, dean of Worcester and chaplain to the king; John Aglionby, principal of St. Edmund Hall; James Montague, Bishop of Bath and Wells; Ralph Ravens, a fellow of St. John's College, Oxford; and Leonard Hutten, a canon of Christ Church.

The Second Westminster Company (in charge of Romans through Jude) was chaired by William Barlow, dean of Chester, Bishop of Rochester (afterward of Lincoln), and a supporter of all things royal. Also on the panel was John Spencer, who succeeded John Reynolds as president of Corpus Christi College. Spencer saw the first five books of Richard Hooker's great work, *The Laws of Ecclesiastical Polity,* safely through the press; and subsequently endeavored to render the remaining books fit for posthumous publication. One of Spencer's friends later claimed for him some credit for the work itself. "This of mine own knowledge I dare affirm," wrote Hamlett Marshall, "that such was his humility and modesty that when he had taken extraordinary pains . . . about compiling a learned and profitable work [the *Laws*] now extant, yet would he not put his hand to it, though he had a hand in it. Therefore it fell out that another took his honors." Spencer's own surviving work, however, cannot compare to Hooker's in distinction, but he was a popular preacher, with a style given to "intricate figures of speech."

Others members of the company were: Roger Fenton, a fellow of Pembroke College, vicar of Chigwell, and the author of a three-volume treatise on usury; Thomas Sanderson, a London rector and later a canon of St. Paul's; Michael Rabbett, a vicar; Ralph Hutchinson, president of St. John's College, Oxford, and a prebendary of St. Paul's; and William Dakins, a professor of divinity at Gresham College, London. Hutchinson (or "Hutch," as he was known to his friends), was perhaps the most important of the five, for though he died just two years into the project, he left behind notes on the New Testament Epistles that his colleagues apparently prized.

∞

These, then, were the translators of the King James Bible. Such an array of knowledge, temperament, and ability had to be carefully harnessed to certain rules of procedure, and these were drawn up by Bishop Bancroft in consultation with both the king and Robert Cecil, his principal secretary of state. On the whole, their mandate was conservative, as Samuel Ward afterward explained in November 1618 to the Synod of Dort: "Caution was given that an entirely new version was not to be furnished, but an old version, long received by the Church, to be purged from all blemishes and faults." Specifically, the rules ordained that the new version be based on the Bishops' Bible, as the official Bible of the Church, which was to be "as little altered as the truth of the original will permit"; that other translations could be consulted, but that the time-honored rendering of certain ecclesiastical terms (such as "Church" and "charity") should be kept; and that marginal notes were only to be used for the citation of parallel passages, or to give alternate readings of difficult words. The chapters were to have new headings, but existing chapter and verse divisions were to stand, and the spelling of names standardized and given in their most familiar form. Words not in the original but necessary to complete the sense were to be printed in distinctive type.

Once the fourteen rules had been drawn up, a fifteenth was added requiring any intractable dispute to be referred to a board of "overseers" selected in consultation with the company chairmen and composed of "three or four of the most ancient and grave divines."

By November 1604 the work had certainly gotten underway, for we have a record that month of Lancelot Andrewes excusing himself from a meeting of the Society of Antiquaries by saying: "This afternoon is our translation time . . . [or] I would have seen you," though it is possible the companies had already begun to meet early that fall.

The great lines which were to be followed had long since been marked out by Wycliffe, Tyndale, Coverdale, Rogers, Whittingham, and others; and although the text immediately before them was the Bishops' Bible, that Bible was itself a revision of the Great Bible, which in turn was substantially the product of Tyndale's and Coverdale's work. In the evolution of the text, one version had borrowed from another, so that, as one scholar put it, "each one had entered into the making of the one that came after it and was improved with it, thus transmitting its own influence down the whole line of descent."

In working over their material, the translators consulted every known text, commentary, and translation, ancient or modern, and as Miles Smith tells us in the Preface, repeatedly "[brought] back to the anvil that which we had hammered" and did not "disdain to revise that which we had done." They pored over all previous English versions; consulted the Complutensian Polyglot of 1517; the Antwerp Polyglot of 1572 (which included a fresh interlinear Latin translation of the Hebrew by Arias Montanus); the Tremellius-Junius Bible of 1579 (which contained a Latin translation of the Old Testament from the Hebrew and the New Testament from Syriac); Sebastian Munster's Latin translation of the Old Testament; Theodore Beza's Latin translation of the New; Latin translations of the whole Bible by Sanctus Pagninus, Leo Juda, and Castalio; the Zurich Bible; Luther's Bible; the French translations of Lefevre (1534) and Olivetan (1535); the Spanish translations of Cassiodoro de Reyna and Cypriano de Valera (1602); and Giovanni Diodati's Italian Bible (1607)—not to mention numerous commentaries by the early Church fathers, rabbinical scholars, and contemporary scholars of renown. Years later, when translator Richard Kilbye overheard a young parson suggest that a certain passage be reworded, he took him aside and told him that not only had his panel discussed at length the proposed reading, "but thirteen others. Only then did we decide on the phrasing as it appeared."

This is not to be doubted. For we have a pretty good idea as to how carefully the translators worked. To begin with, Robert Barker, the King's printer, supplied forty folio-sized "Church" or Bishops' Bibles for the six panels to use, and delivered them unbound in quires, or signatures, "so they could pass easily from hand to hand." Each scholar went over some portion of the text, emending it verse by verse as he saw fit; then he compared his work with that of his colleagues, who afterward conferred together as to what should or should not stand. Once a book of the Bible was completed in this way, it was sent to all the other groups for suggestion and review. Eventually, every word passed through the hands of the whole body of revisers.

When the collective work was done, an annotated and emended copy of the Bishops' Bible was sent to London by each of the three translation heads, where the General Committee of Review, with members drawn from each company, met to "extract one [copy] out of all three, to be committed to the press."

The makeup of the committee has been the subject of some debate. Some say it consisted of six translators, one from each company (as indicated by a passage in a contemporary life of John Bois); others, of twelve, each company contributing two (as indicated by a statement made by Samuel Ward to the Synod of Dort in 1618). However, it may also be that six were chosen by the translators from their own number—one from each company, or two from each center—and six by the king from learned ecclesiastics as overseers.

Altogether the work of translation took about six years. When it was done, it surpassed all others in the majesty and music of its words. If Tyndale had managed to render the original Hebrew and Greek into the sound and sense of living English, those who followed him could do no better than amplify his strain. The King James translators were the last of that line, but some of their adjustments had the Midas touch. Sometimes they changed only a word or two, or merely the order of the words for rhythmic or dramatic effect; sometimes whole chapters were markedly transformed.

Some excellent examples are given by Olga S. Opfell, in her book on the translators, and by H. W. Robinson, in his general history of the Bible. I can do no better than allude to a few of them here. In Tyndale, the first two verses of Genesis read: "In the beginning God created heaven and earth. The earth was void and empty, and darkness was upon the deep, and the spirit of God moved upon the water." This is substantially the version that we know. Yet it lacks the rhythmic grandeur of what it became: "In the beginning God created the heaven and the earth. And the earth was without form, and void; and darkness was upon the face of the deep. And the spirit of God moved upon the face of the waters." Tyndale's rendering of a slightly later passage—"Then said the serpent unto the woman, Tush, ye shall not die" (Genesis 3:4)—was considered too colloquial, and was emended to, "And the serpent said unto the woman, Ye shall not surely die." This was more stately, though Tyndale's "Tush" had wit to it, in keeping with the wiles of the serpent, who might well pretend nonchalance about a matter so grave. In the last line of David's poignant lament for Saul and Jonathan, he had, "How were the mighty overthrown." This was changed to, "How are the mighty fallen," (2 Samuel 1:27) which has become proverbial in English speech.

In their rendering of Isaiah 1:18, one can see how the revisers took a word from one version, another from another, as they carefully picked their way through the options until they settled on the right text. In Coverdale and Matthew, the passage read, a bit strangely: "Though your sins be as red as scarlet shall they not be whiter than snow. And though they were like purple shall they not be like white wool." The Bishops' Bible improved this to: "Though your sins be as red as scarlet, they shall be as white as snow: and though they were like purple, they shall be as white as wool." The Geneva Bible followed a similar path "Though your sins were as crimson, they shall be made white as snow: though they were red like scarlet, they shall be as wool." The Authorized Version blended the best of these to read: "Though your sins be as scarlet, they shall be as white as snow; though they be red like crimson, they shall be as wool."

In translating the Psalms, the revisers were on especially controversial ground. The English prose Psalter had been adapted from Coverdale's Bible of 1535 into the Great Bible and the Book of Common Prayer. Puritans had condemned some passages as "most corrupted" and erroneous. Psalm 1:1-2 in Coverdale's version read: "Blessed is the man that goeth not in the counsel of the ungodly; that abideth not in the way of sinners, and sitteth not in the seat of the scornful. But delighteth in the law of the Lord, and exerciseth himself in his law both day and night." In the King James Version this became: "Blessed is the man that walketh not in the counsel of the ungodly, nor standeth in the way of sinners, nor sitteth in the seat of the scornful. But his delight is in the law of the Lord; and in his law doth he meditate day and night." In the Bishops' Bible, the Twenty-third Psalm began: "God is my shepherd, therefore I can lose nothing; he will cause me to repose myself in pastures full of grass, and he will lead me unto calm waters." In the hands of the King James men, this became: "The Lord is my shepherd; I shall not want. He maketh me to lie down in green pastures: he leadeth me beside the still waters." They also improved upon the last verse, as given in the Geneva Bible, which came close to what the translators chose: "Doubtless kindness and mercy shall follow me all the days of my life, And I shall remain a long season in the house of the Lord." This was revised to read: "Surely goodness and mercy shall follow me all the days of my life: and I will dwell in the house of the Lord for ever."

The unforgettable seventh verse of the thirty-eighth chapter of Job had already gone through a remarkably subtle evolution. In Coverdale it read: "When the morning stars gave me praise, and when all the angels of God rejoiced." Matthew's Bible (and after it, the Bishops' Bible) had: "When the morning stars praised me together, all the children of God rejoiced triumphantly." In the Geneva Bible, the language was heightened: "When the stars of the morning praised me together, and all the children of God rejoiced." But the rapturous phrasing of the King James Version surpassed them all. "When the morning stars sang together, and all the sons of God shouted for joy?"

The Bishops' Bible managed to get a now famous passage (12:6) of Ecclesiastes just about right: "Or ever the silver cord be taken away, or the golden well be broken; or the pot be broken at the well, and the wheel broken upon the cistern." This was perfected to: "Or ever the silver cord be loosed, or the golden bowl be broken, or the pitcher be broken at the fountain, or the wheel broken at the cistern."

In their rendering of the first two verses of Psalm 17, they avoided a metaphorical temptation in favor of the literal Hebrew sense. The Geneva Bible had:

> *Hear the right, O Lord, consider my cry: hearken unto my prayer of lips unstained.*
> *Let my sentence come forth from the presence, and let thine eyes behold equity.*

This became:

> *Hear the right, O Lord, attend unto my cry, give ear unto my prayer, that goeth not out of feigned lips.*
> *Let my sentence come forth from the presence, and let thine eyes behold the things that are equal.*

"Unstained lips" had suggested a voice purified of drink. That was imaginative, but limited the Hebrew meaning, which referred to deceitful speech. At the same time, "things that are equal" made the intention of "equity" clear.

In the hands of the revisers, the fourth verse of Isaiah, chapter 2, familiar to all who know even a little Scripture, also found its immortal form. In Coverdale's version, it read:

> they shall break their swords and spears to make scythes, sickles, and saws thereof. From that time forth shall not one people lift up weapon against another, neither shall they learn to fight from thenceforth.

The Geneva had reworked this to read:

> they shall break their swords also into mattocks, and their spears into scythes; nation shall not lift up a sword against nation, neither shall they learn to fight any more.

But the finely tuned ear of the King James men found the just and enduring phrase:

> they shall beat their swords into plowshares, and their spears into pruninghooks: nation shall not lift up sword against nation, neither shall they learn war any more.

In Isaiah 41:24-25, the stirring voice of prophecy falters a bit in the Geneva version, which reads:

> Behold, ye are of no value, and your making is of nought: man hath chosen an abomination by them.
> I have raised up from the North, and he shall come: from the East sun shall he call upon my name, and shall come upon princes as upon clay, as the potter treadeth mire under the foot.

But not when the King James men tuned it to their ears:

> Behold, ye are of nothing, and your work is of nought: an abomination is he that chooseth you.
> I have raised up one from the north, and he shall come: from the rising of the sun shall he call upon my name: and he shall come upon princes as upon mortar, and as the potter treadeth clay.

(The Douai version, however, is even stronger: instead of "your work is of nought" it was: "of that which hath no being," as from an empty source; and instead of "shall come upon princes as upon mortar" had "shall make princes to be of dirt.")

With respect to the Apocrypha, some things done poorly in the Bishops' Bible were strangely retained. Again, with examples from Opfell. Chapter 7, verse 29 of the Wisdom of Solomon had been given as: "For she is more beautiful than the sun, and above all the order of stars; being compared with the light, she is found before it." This was confusing. Coverdale's version was superior by far: "For she is more beautiful than the sun, and giveth more light than the stars, and the day is not to be compared unto her." But in their version of Ecclesiasticus (24:19–20 and 43:17, for example) the revisers surpassed what had gone before:

> Come unto me, all ye that be desirous of me, and fill your-selves with my fruits.
> For my memorial is sweeter than honey, and mine inher-itance than the honeycomb. (24:19–20)

> as birds flying he scattereth the snow, and the falling down thereof is as the lighting of grasshoppers: (43:17)

Until about 1825, their rendering of the Apocrypha was included in all English Bibles. Then it fell by the wayside, a casualty of a doctrinaire Protestant repudiation of all things savoring of Rome. It is a shame it is so hard to come by today.

In their version of the New Testament, the translators followed Tyndale quite closely, as in the Lord's Prayer (Matthew, Chapter 6). But where Tyndale had: "And forgive us our trespasses, even as we forgive our trespassers" (verse 12) they adopted from Coverdale "debts" and "debtors" instead. Again, Tyndale's "Come unto me all ye that labor and are laden and I will ease you" (Matthew 11:28) was improved to "Come unto me, all ye that labor and are heavy laden, and I will give you rest." And his "Greater love than this hath no man, than that a man bestow his life for his friends" (John 15:13) became "Greater love hath no man than this, that a man lay down his life for his friends."

From the Rheims New Testament, the translators saw fit to borrow a number of Latinate words: "Whom God hath set forth to be a propitiation (Romans 3:25); "wrought in me all manner of concupiscence" (Romans 7:8); "If by any means I may provoke to emulation" (Romans 11:14)—all to the enrichment of the English tongue. At the same time, in numerous passages throughout, they rather closely followed the Geneva Bible, showing a wise deference to what they could not excel. The translators, in fact, were ecumenical in that respect: all previous versions (including a phrase or two from the Second Wycliffe) resonate somewhere in their text.

By the end of 1608, the six companies could rest from their labors, and all the manuscript copies were called in for revision by the General Committee of Review. In January 1609, that committee met at London's Stationers' Hall, and over the next nine months carefully went over what their colleagues had done. The names of only three of the members are definitely known—John Bois, Andrew Downes, and John Harmer—though surviving notes of the proceedings contain some scattered initials, including AL, which may refer to Arthur Lake, a fellow of New College, Oxford, and (some think) one of the independent scholar/translators enlisted to help. At thirty shillings a week "duly paid them," the committee members weren't recompensed much for their pains, and Andrew Downes, for one, didn't feel he was paid enough. Apparently, he "would not go 'till he was either fetcht or threatned with a pursivant [constable]." He complained to the King's Privy Council that although he had been regius professor of Greek for many years, had worked harder (he said) on the translation than most, and was now called upon to do still more ("the hardest part") he had not received any consideration for it, and had even seen "inferiors" preferred before him. And so he needed a stipend of some sort to go on. On May 17, 1609, the king responded with prudent generosity and sent him fifty pounds.

The committee's work might have remained inscrutable to posterity had not thirty-nine pages of notes of the proceedings made by John Bois suddenly turned up in a manuscript copy in the Bodleian Library in 1958. These long-lost notes (sought in vain by historians for three hundred fifty years) cover the committee's deliberations on Romans through Revelation, and give us more than a glimpse into the revisions it made. On the whole, they were cautious, free of doctrinal dispute, and chiefly concerned with details of language and style.

A remarkable number of options were discussed. Bois and Downes in particular offered numerous alternative readings, and it is intriguing to see what might have been.

Bois first. For Romans 3:9, he offered, "What then? Are we safe, and out of danger? are we preferred? are we God's darlings?" The final version has, "What then? are we better than they?" For 1 Corinthians 9:18, "that I strain not . . . or that I rack not, or stretch not," etc.; the final reading has, "that I abuse not my power in the gospel." For the eleventh verse of 1 Corinthians 13, "I understood, I cared as a child, I had a child's mind, I imagined as a child, I was affected as a child"; the final version has, "When I was a child, I spake as a child, I understood as a child, I thought as a child." For Philippians 1:19, "the bounty of the Spirit"; the final reading has, "the supply of the Spirit." For Philippians 1:21, "life unto me is Christ, and death an advantage"; the final version has: "For me to live is Christ, and to die is gain." For Philippians 3:14, "I follow directly to the prize of the high calling"; here AL (probably Arthur Lake) proposed, "I follow toward the mark for the prize"; the final reading has, "I press toward the mark for the prize of the high calling." For Hebrews 11:1, "Faith is a most sure warrant of things, is a being of things hoped for, a discovery, a demonstration of things that are not seen"; the final version has, "Now faith is the substance of things hoped for, the evidence of things not seen." For Hebrews 11:26, "He looked at the reward to be rendered"; the final reading has, "he had respect unto the recompence of the reward." For Hebrews 13:21, "disposing of you, or working with you as it pleaseth him"; the final version has, "working in you that which is well-pleasing in his sight." And so on.

Next, Andrew Downes. Whatever his reluctance to participate in the committee's assignment, he showed himself in its deliberations "a most subtle weigher of words." For 1 Corinthians 10:20, he offered, "and I would not have you partakers with the devil"; the final reading has, "and I would not that ye should have fellowship with devils." For 1 Thessalonians 5:23, "that your spirit may be kept perfect"; the final version has, "your whole spirit . . . be preserved blameless." For Hebrews 4:15, "such an one as had experience of all things"; the final reading has, "in all points tempted like as we are." For Hebrews 13:8, he suggested that "if the words be arranged in this manner—'yesterday, and today the same, and for ever'—the statement will seem more majestic." His colleagues did not agree. The final reading has, "Jesus Christ the same yesterday, and to day, and for ever." A heated exchange took place over 1 Corinthians 10:11, when Downes "sharply and vehemently exerted himself beyond measure for the interpretation of Augustine that 'examples' were always understood as concerning the types and figures of the people of old." The Geneva Bible had opted for "examples" but the Rheims New Testament had "figure," which agreed with the reading shared by Augustine and Downes. In a compromise, "types" was adopted as a marginal note.

John Harmer appears in the discussions twice. For 1 Peter 2:24, he suggested "carried up our sins to the tree"; the committee decided on "bare our sins in his own body on the tree," but Harmer's reading was more accurate, and found vindication in the marginal note. For Revelation 13:5, where the final text reads, "And power was given unto him to continue forty and two months," Harmer argued that the word "continue" actually meant "to make war." This, too, was allowed in the note.

One by one the critical choices were made. For Luke 1:57, "full time" prevailed over "time"; for 1 Corinthians 15:33, "evil communications corrupt good manners" prevailed over "good natures" and "good dispositions"; for Galatians 3:24, "the law was our schoolmaster" prevailed over "leader" and "pettymaster"; for Ephesians 4:19, "past feeling" prevailed over "senseless" and "past shame"; for 1 Timothy 3:13, "a good degree" prevailed over "dignity"; for 1 Timothy 4:14, "neglect" prevailed over "dispise"; for 1 Timothy 6:9, "hurtful" prevailed over "noisome"; for Hebrews 1:3, "glory" prevailed over "forthshining"; for Hebrews 10:27 "fiery indignation" prevailed over "vehement wrath"; for 2 Peter 2:2, "pernicious ways" prevailed over "lascivious ways," "impure ways," "flagitious facts," "an outrage," and "a sin worthy of lashes." In retrospect, almost all the choices seem unerringly right.

And so at length, when "all things had been maturely weighed and examined," as Samuel Ward put it in his recollections, Miles Smith of the Second Oxford Company, "a distinguished man, who had been deeply occupied in the whole work from the beginning," and Thomas Bilson, Bishop of Winchester and an "overseer"—the one a moderate Puritan, the other High Church—"put the finishing touches to the whole." Though not one of the original translators, Bilson had long been a towering presence in ecclesiastical circles, "as reverent and learned a Prelate as England ever afforded, a deep and profound scholar, and . . . a principal sustainer" of the Anglican Church. Queen Elizabeth had once called upon him to rebut the Rheims New Testament; and the king obviously deemed him a safe man to entrust part of the final revision to. It was said that he "carried prelature in his very aspect," and though some of his writings were said to give "strange liberty especially concerning religion, for subjects to cast off their obedience" (and would later be used by Puritans against Charles I), in 1610 he was certainly the king's man, and "with frowning concentration and spluttering pen" underlined, crossed out, accepted, or rejected, the final choices offered to him by the committee at Stationers' Hall.

The editorial hand of Miles Smith may have been even more substantial, and it is fairly certain that he was also responsible for the various page and chapter headings, and the profusion of commas which punctuate the text. (Legend had it that these were inserted "on horseback"—in accord with the cantering rhythms of his frequent rides between Hereford and London.) But just as Bilson and Smith thought they were finally done, "in came my Lord of Canterbury [Richard Bancroft] to Stationers Hall," claiming for himself the ultimate say. This had not been expected, and Smith afterward complained that Bancroft made fourteen changes on his own account. One of them was to insist on that "glorious word Bishopric" for the titular authority of Judas in Acts 1:20, where the Geneva Bible had "charge" and the Bishops' Bible "office": "His Bishoprick let another take." Smith evidently objected, but Bancroft "is so potent," he wrote, "there is no contradicting him."

No one knows what the other thirteen changes were.

While the text was made ready for the press, Bilson wrote the brief but florid dedicatory Epistle to the King, and Smith the long and learned Preface ("The Translators to the Reader"). Bilson praised the king as the "principal Mover and Author of the work," and boldly dismissed any criticism of it in advance. "Since things of this quality have ever been subject to the censures of illmeaning and discontented persons . . . your allowance and acceptance of our labors shall more honor and encourage us than all the calumniations . . . of other men." Weighed against royal grace and favor, the slanders of "Popish persons at home or abroad" would not count for much, he said, nor the carping, on the other hand, "by selfconceited Brethren [i.e., dogmatic Puritans], who run their own ways, and give liking unto nothing, but what is framed by themselves, and hammered on their anvil."

Yet there was always the possibility criticism would be just, and Bilson seems to have given the translators some cover by alluding to the pace at which the work was done at the king's behest: "Your Majesty did never desist to urge and excite those to whom it was commended, that the work might be hastened, and that the business might be expedited in so decent a manner, as a matter of such importance might justly require."

The more substantial Preface by Smith thoroughly reviewed and justified the working methods the revisers had adopted for their task. He defended the project with numerous quotations from Clement of Alexandria, Jerome, Cicero, Augustine, Chrysostom, Sophocles, Horace, Plutarch, Josephus, and Virgil, among others; paid tribute to the earlier translators "that travailed before us, either in this land or beyond sea . . . [who] deserve to be had in everlasting remembrance"; and acknowledged that the King James Version stood on the shoulders of their work: "We never thought to make a new translation, nor yet of a bad one to make a good one, but to make a good one better, or out of many good ones, one principal good one" true. In so doing, he said, the translators had not shirked their task. "If you ask what they had before them, truly it was the Hebrew text of the Old Testament, the Greek of the New. These are the two golden pipes, or rather conduits, wherethrough the olive branches empty themselves into the gold." They had also consulted all other commentaries and translations—whether Latin, Greek, Chaldeen, Arabic, Gothic, Anglo-Saxon, French, Syriac, or "Dutch"

[Deutsch]—and had refused to proceed (Bilson's comments notwithstanding) with "that posting haste that the [makers of the] Septuagint did, if that be true which is reported of them, that they finished it in seventy-two days . . . but . . . fearing no reproach for slowness, nor coveting praise for expedition, we have at the length, through the good hand of the Lord upon us, brought the work to that pass that you see."

Smith chided Pope Sixtus V for completely excluding variant readings from the margin of the Vulgate, and stoutly defended the alternate readings the King James margins gave: "They that are wise had rather have their judgments at liberty in differences of readings, than to be captivated to one, when it might be the other." In the spirit of Tyndale, they had embraced the use of synonyms, "not tied ourselves to an uniformity of phrasing, or to identical words," and saw no reason not to use "purpose" for "intent," "journeying" for "travelling," "think" for "suppose," "pain" for "ache," "joy" for "gladness." As for their rendering of most of "the old ecclesiastical words," the translators had been careful, he said, to avoid both "the scrupulosity of the Puritans" and "the obscurity [i.e., Latinate terminology] of the Papists . . . whereof their late translation is full." He also repudiated Catholic charges that earlier Protestant translations were perverted and corrupt, and defended the manner in which the Bible had evolved: "For to whom ever was it imputed for a fault (by such as were wise) to go over that which he had done, and to amend it where he saw cause?" This led to an eloquent defense of biblical translation itself:

But now what piety without truth? what truth (what saving truth) without the word of God? What word of God (whereof we may be sure) without the Scripture? The Scriptures we are commanded to search. . . . If we be ignorant, they will instruct us; if out of the way, they will bring us home; if out of order, they will reform us; if in heaviness, comfort us; if dull, quicken us; if cold, inflame us. *Tolle, lege, Tolle, lege,* Take up and read. . . . But how shall men meditate in that which they cannot understand? How shall they understand that which is kept close in an unknown tongue?

. . . Translation it is that openeth the window, to let in the light; that breaketh the shell, that we may eat the kernel; that putteth aside the curtain, that we may look into the most Holy place; that removeth the cover of the well, that we may come by the water, even as Jacob rolled away the stone from the mouth of the well, by which means the flocks of Laban were watered. Indeed without translation into the vulgar tongue, the unlearned are but like children at Jacobs well (which was deep) without a bucket or some thing to draw with.

Smith closed with an appeal that their labors be gratefully received:

Ye are brought unto fountains of living water which ye digged not; do not cast earth into them. . . . If light be come into the world, love not darkness more than light; if food, if clothing be offered, goe not naked, starve not your selves. . . . It is a fearful thing to fall into the hands of the living God: but a blessed thing it is, and will bring us to everlasting blessedness in the end, when God speaketh unto us, to hearken; when he setteth his word before us, to read it; when he stretcheth out his hand and calleth, to answer, Here am I.

Either a manuscript representing the finished work of all, or a fully annotated copy of the Bishops' Bible, was given to the royal printer, Robert Barker, at his establishment at Northumberland House in Aldersgate Street. Barker helped underwrite the printing costs with £3,500 of his own money as an investment (which was huge), and obtained a new cast type and boldface for the Gothic text. But he soon began to worry about losses, and one day as he went over some proofs reportedly exclaimed: "I do groan under the burden of this book." He would soon have reason to sympathize with Richard Grafton, publisher of the Great Bible, who had once told Thomas Cromwell in 1538, "Look, however so many sentences there are in the Bible—even so many faults and errors shall be made." For all Barker's exertions, it turned out that in the King James Version there was a typographical error for every ten pages of text. And the first folio took its nickname from one of them, becoming known as the "He" Bible from a confusion of pronouns in Ruth 3:15 which read, "and he went into the city," when it should have been "she."

Yet as it rolled off the press, the new Bible was—to all who had eyes to see—a many-splendored thing. Its title page featured a handsome engraving by Cornelius Boel, an Antwerp artist who had recently done official portraits of the king's family, in which the Twelve Apostles were depicted with the Lamb of God (Agnus Dei) in their midst. Crowning the ensemble was the tetragrammaton or sacred name of God in Hebrew, and the Holy Spirit in the form of a dove. To the right and left sat two of the evangelists—Mark, accompanied by a lion; Matthew, by an angel. These were grouped on an entablature or architrave adorned with medallion-like emblems or shields of the Twelve Patriarchs in their tents, according to Jacob's prophetic last speech to his sons in Genesis 49: "And Jacob called unto his sons, and said, Gather yourselves together, that I may tell you that which shall befall you in the last days." Below, to the right and left, were two columns with niches: in the left stood Moses holding the Tablets of the Law; in the right, his brother Aaron, the high priest. At the foot of the page, to complete the frame, the other two evangelists found their place—Luke, accompanied by a bull, and John, by an eagle, beside a pelican (symbol of Christ) shown feeding her young with blood from her own breast.

In the center of the engraving stood the title, which described the text as "Newly Translated out of the Originall tongues: & with the former Translations diligently compared and reuised by his Maiesties speciall commandement." The reader was also provided with an almanac, a table of holy days, a guide to the order of the Psalms and Lessons to be read at morning and evening prayer, and a calendrical guide to calculating the date of Easter "for ever." The New Testament had its own title page, which featured an allegorical woodcut with some of the same figures as the Old, including emblems of the Four Evangelists, the tents of the Twelve Tribes of Israel, the Twelve Apostles, and the tetragrammaton, but at the bottom was an image of the Lamb of God "slain." Some of the copies included a map of the Holy Land and a long, thirty-eight-page genealogy that contained an illustrated family tree from Adam to Christ.

The text itself, printed Gothic type and folio format (sixteen inches by ten and a half inches), was laid out in double columns enclosed within rules. Ornamental capitals adorned the beginnings of chapters, but the chapter summaries, headings, and marginal notes were set in roman type. Also in roman were those words not in the original but inserted to make the meaning clear. The spelling followed the conventions of the day—"i" for "j," "y" (at times) for "th," "u" and "v" interchangeably (depending on the position of these letters in a word); some doubling of consonants; occasional final "e" 's. The verses were numbered, notes and cross references appeared in the margins. In keeping with the idea that the new version was but a revision of the old, there were emblems of continuity; for example, some of the general ornamentation of the title page had been borrowed from the Geneva Bible, while the Bishops' Bible supplied a figure or two as well.

Although the King James Version got off to a respectable commercial start, Barker, the king's printer, did not prosper as well as he might. In the course of production, he had taken on partners, but the relationship soured. Just about the time sales began to soar, litigation overwhelmed him. In 1631, he was fined £300 and rebuked by the Crown for an edition that became known as the "Wicked Bible" because it omitted the word "not" from the seventh commandment, which therefore read, "Thou shalt commit adultery." All the copies were recalled. That was the beginning of the end for him, and eventually he was remanded to the King's Bench debtors' prison, where he died in 1643.

The ultimate success of the new Bible would owe much to the enthusiasm of James. Published by royal authority, it "swept forward with a majestic stream of editions"—in folio, quarto, and octavo—which eventually left all its rivals behind.

But it took time to win its way. The Puritans at first were not partial to it, for it "smacked too much of the king, the bishops, and the Church establishment," while in their own beloved Geneva Bible they had a version with which they were content. Legions of readers had also come to depend on the Geneva notes, professing that without "such spectacles" they could not understand the text. Between 1642 and 1715 several attempts, in fact, were made to adapt them to the King James Version, but the grafting did not take. Meanwhile, some of the translators themselves—including Lancelot Andrewes and Miles Smith—continued to quote from the Geneva version as the one familiar to the congregations they addressed. Andrewes, in fact, quoted from it on one occasion when he preached in Whitehall before the king; and Smith, in his preface, had taken all fourteen of his biblical quotations from it—a clue, perhaps, to the Puritan leanings he possessed. But over time the King James Version, by its own merits and intrinsic excellence, won its way into the hearts of the folk. In the end "its victory was so complete," wrote one historian, "that its text acquired a sanctity properly ascribable only to the unmediated voice of God; to multitudes of English-speaking Christians it has seemed little less than blasphemy to tamper with its words." In the English-speaking world, it would become the Vulgate of the Protestant faith.

And that is what George Bernard Shaw must have meant when he wrote: "To this day the common Britisher or citizen of the United States of North America accepts and worships it as a single book by a single author, the book being the Book of Books and the author being God."

To a remarkable degree, the translators had proved faithful to the Hebrew, to the Greek, even (in a sense) to the Vulgate, "for the rhythm of the English Bible, as it finally emerged," Sir Herbert Grierson noted, "owes not a little to the Latin of St. Jerome." At the same time, nine tenths of the words were of Saxon derivation, and the entire translation had a vocabulary of only eight thousand words. It fused Anglo-Saxon and Latin elements—the Latin, as one scholar notes, imparting stateliness and sonority to its diction; the Anglo-Saxon conforming to the Hebrew in homely vigor, concreteness, and directness of style. In Anglo-Saxon, the translators captured the form of Hebrew superlatives, such as "Holy of Holies," "Song of Songs," "King of Kings," and "Vanity of Vanities"; and the inverted phrase—"throne of ivory" "altar of stone," "helmet of brass," "man of war," "children of wickedness," "man of truth," "prisoners of hope," "rock of ages," "man of sorrows," and "Son of Man." The learned and literary John Selden (an eminent seventeenth-century lawyer, scholar, and orientalist, with expertise in rabbinical law) once complained that the Bible had been "rather translated into English words than into English phrases. The Hebraisms are kept and the phrase of that language is kept." But that was precisely what gave it special dignity and strength. "It so happens," wrote Joseph Addison with more understanding in the *Spectator* of 1712,

> that Hebrew idioms run into the English tongue with a particular grace and beauty. Our language has received innumerable elegancies and improvements [thereby] . . . out of the poetical passages in Holy Writ. They give a force and energy to our expressions, warm and animate our language, and convey our thoughts in more ardent and intense phrases, than any that are to be met with in our own tongue. There is something so pathetick [moving] in this kind of diction, that it often sets the mind in a flame, and makes our hearts burn within us. How cold and dead does a prayer appear . . . when it is not heightned by that solemnity of phrase, which may be drawn from the Sacred Writings.

The King James men also proved faithful to the English biblical tradition from which they drank. Their conservative mandate—not to make a new translation but to revise the old—restrained them to some degree from modernizing the English of it, even up to the usage of their own time. Some of the expressions they adopted were already a bit archaic in 1611—such as *verily* and *it came to pass*—but these were kept because they had become familiar and because they also seemed to endow the text with a certain "antique rightness" for which it has always been prized.

There were critics, of course, besides Selden, and they are not to to denied. The first and foremost was Hugh Broughton, a Hebrew scholar and Puritan divine whose irascible disposition had kept him from being chosen to serve on any of the translation teams. By 1604, he had an almost unparalleled record of conflict with other scholars and the Church authorities. "I will suffer no scholar in the world to cross me in Hebrew and Greek," he once remarked, "when I am sure of the truth," and he was often absolutely sure of what the truth was. He had quarreled with both John Reynolds and Edward Lively over Scripture chronology; with Andrewes over the meaning of the word "sheol" and "Hades"; had denounced Bishop Bancroft in a letter to the House of Lords as "a deadly enemy to both Testaments, unallowable as a teacher, or to rule in learning"; had accused Whitgift and Bilson of intervening with the queen to prevent his advancement; and had ridiculed the Bishops' Bible as more "pestered with lies than the Koran. . . . The cockles of the seashores, the leaves of the forest, and the grains of the poppy may as well be numbered as the gross errors of this Bible, disgracing the ground of our hope." In 1593, in a letter to Lord Burghley, he had offered with five others to revise the bishops' work. Four years later, in an "Epistle to the Learned Nobility of England Touching the Translation of the Bible," he also suggested how he thought biblical translation should be done. "The holy text must be honored, as sound, holy, pure"; heed taken to render everything with literal exactness; and ambiguous passages "stayed safety of ancient warrant," i.e., understood according to time-honored interpretations of the text. He also thought (as the King James men did not) that the same word should always be translated in the same way.

For some thirty years, in fact, Broughton had been preparing his own translation, and in 1595 he had published a version of part of the Old Testament, with short explanatory notes. He sent a copy to Lord Burghley, with a letter stating his plan and appealing for support. But the Church hierarchy opposed the project, in part because they disliked him, and in part out of fear "that hereby an occasion might be given to the enemies of our religion, the Papists, of discrediting our common English Bible and the doctrines that were founded on it, and weaken the reputation of that former translation [the Bishops' Bible] then used in the churches."

Later, when King James appealed for advice from independent scholars, Broughton had sent his in. At the time, he had endorsed the idea of a committee effort; urged that it be done in "a good English style and true sense"; and sensibly recommended that technical specialists be consulted about certain passages, "as embroiderers for Aaron's ephod; geometricians, carpenters and masons for the Temple of Solomon; and gardeners for all the boughs and branches of Ezekiel's trees." He also quaintly suggested that there be seventy-two translators in all, in emulation of the seventy-two Jewish elders who had supposedly prepared the Septuagint in seventy-two days. And while the new version was in progress, he had expressed high hopes for it—"All true-hearted subjects will be ready for forbearance," he had said; but when he saw it, his verdict was incredibly harsh: "The late Bible sent to me to censure [critique], bred in me a sadness that will grieve me while I breathe, it is so ill done. Tell his Majesty I had rather be rent in pieces by wild horses than that any such translation by my consent should be urged upon poor churches. It crosseth me and I require it to be burnt!" One can only be thankful he did not have that power! Aside from hundreds of mistranslated words he alleged to find in it, the marginal notes (7,402 in all) were a particular object of his ire. "Who bade them put the error in the text and [the] right [reading] in the margin?" he asked, and implied the translators might be damned on the Day of Judgment for their work.

Yet so impartial had the translators been, that even something of Broughton himself was in the text. The genealogies contributed by John Speed had been prepared at his urging (perhaps even with his help), and a striking metaphor, from his own translation of Job 39:19, had been used. In the Geneva Bible it had read: "Hast thou given the horse strength? or covered his neck with neighing?" Following Broughton, it became: "Hast thou given the horse strength? hast thou clothed his neck with thunder?"

In truth, though his temperament had deprived him of a place to which his scholarship had otherwise entitled him, his energetic, if crusty, eloquence suggests that if he had found a seat on one of the panels, he might have contributed something of value to the task.

∽

Although the King James Version (as it is called in the United States) became known as the Authorized Version in England, no known act of Parliament or Convocation, royal proclamation or Privy Council decree ever officially authorized or sanctioned its use. Officially, it was "authorized" only in the sense that it was "appointed to be read in churches" and assumed the privileges the Bishops' Bible had enjoyed. But in the end its true imprimatur came by a kind of general acclaim.

In a cumulative way, all the virtues of the various translations which preceded it were gathered up. Tyndale had coined words and phrases like "peace maker," "passover," "long-suffering," "scapegoat," "the Lord's Anointed," "flowing with milk and honey," "filthy lucre," "the salt of the earth," and "the spirit is willing, but the flesh is weak." Coverdale, "tender mercies," "respect of persons," "lovingkindness," "a perfect Babel," "the eleventh hour," "to cast pearls before swine"; the Geneva Bible, "Vanity of vanities," "except a man be born again," and other unforgettable turns of phrase. The Second Wycliffe version, Matthew's Bible, and the Bishops' Bible had likewise been sifted for their own grains of gold.

From Coverdale's diglot, via the Rheims New Testament, the Authorized Version received such renderings as "The Son of Man hath not where to lay his head" (Matthew 8:20); "I see men as trees, walking" (Mark 8:24); and "given to idolatry" (Acts 17:16). From the Bishops' Bible came: "the voice of one crying in the wilderness," "less than the least of all the saints," "Sufficient unto the day, is the evil thereof," and "Rend your hearts and not your garments." And from the Second Wycliffe version came "gave up the ghost," "well-stricken in age," "held his peace," "three score and ten," "to know" in the sense of carnal knowledge; "Strait is the gate and narrow the way," and "a well of water springing up into everlasting life." In a number of places, the King James Version also adopted Rheims or Douai readings, for example in the Song of Solomon 6:8, Mark 10:52, 2 Corinthians 6:16, and Hebrews 13:14.

At least one instance of Taverner's orginal phrasing survived almost intact: "Which of you (by taking thought) can put one cubit unto his stature" (Matthew 6:27); and the familiar phrase, to "go a whoring after strange gods" (Deuteronomy 31:16) was borrowed from Luther's German by Tyndale, who also introduced the word "Jehovah" into English, and (perhaps) the word "beautiful," as well.

Over time, the diction had undergone "a slow, almost impersonal evolution, more or less free from the eccentricities of individual translators," as one writer put it, and from that, perhaps, its "transcendent merits" derive. Few of the translators themselves possessed outstanding literary gifts, but their "private interpretations and communal blendings" somehow surpassed what they otherwise could have done. Individual genius was not, perhaps, what was called for. And its presence would only have seemed a vanity of art. Milton, for example, could scarcely improve on the first verse of Psalm 1 when he wrote:

> *Blest is the man who hath not walked astray*
> *In counsel of the wicked, and in the way*
> *Of sinners hath not stood, and in the seat*
> *Of scorners hath not sat,*

which in the King James Version reads: "Blessed is the man that walketh not in the counsel of the ungodly, nor standeth in the way of sinners, nor sitteth in the seat of the scornful." The lesser poet James Thomson did no better (or worse) with his rendering of Matthew 6:28–29:

> *Observe the rising lily's snowy grace,*
> *Observe the various vegetable race;*
> *They neither toil nor spin, but careless grow;*
> *Yet see how warm they blush! how bright they glow!*
> *What regal vestments can with them compare,*
> *What king so shining, and what queen so fair?*

We have only to set this beside: "And why take ye thought for raiment? Consider the lilies of the field, how they grow; they toil not, neither do they spin:

"And yet I say unto you, That even Solomon in all his glory was not arrayed like one of these."

In the end, the King James Version was such a book, wrote Macaulay (in his essay on Dryden), that "if everything else in our language should perish it would alone suffice to show the whole extent of its beauty and power." Its subsequent impact on English (and American) literature might be traced in a thousand ways—in the work of religious writers like Milton and Bunyan, or their more secular brethren like D. H. Lawrence, Walt Whitman, and Defoe. Without the King James Version, it has been said, "there would be no *Paradise Lost*, no *Pilgrim's Progress*, no Negro Spirituals, no Gettysburg Address.

Whitman's Preface to *Leaves of Grass* proclaimed a New Testament creed ("This is what you shall do: Love the earth and sun and the animals, despise riches, give alms to everyone that asks, . . ."), and in such poems as "Song of the Answerer," Biblical cadences are used to make manifest the signs by which the poet-messiah will make himself known:

> *Now list to my morning's romanza, I tell the signs of the Answerer,*
> *To the cities and farms I sing as they spread in the sunshine Before me.*
>
> *A young man comes to me bearing a message from his brother,*
> *How shall the young man know the whether and when of his brother?*
> *Tell him to send me the signs.*
>
> *And I stand before the young man face to face, and take his right hand in my left hand and his left hand in my right hand,*
> *And I answer for his brother and for men, and I answer for him that answers for all, and send these signs.*
>
> *Him all wait for, him all yield up to, his word is decisive and final*
> *Him they accept, in him lave, in him perceive themselves as amid light,*
> *Him they immerse and he immerses them.*

John Bunyan's whole schooling was the Bible, and his *Pilgrim's Progress* and *Grace Abounding* are pure biblical prose. "As to the situation of this town," he writes in one description, "it lieth just between the two worlds, and the first founder, and builder of it, so far as by the best, and most authentic records I can gather, was one Shaddai; and he built it for his own delight. He made it the mirror, and glory of all that he made, even the Top-piece beyond anything else that he did in that country; yea, so goodly a town was Mansoul, when first built, that it is said by some, the Gods at the setting up thereof, came down to see it, and sang for joy." And here (in an oft-cited passage) is D.H. Lawrence in the opening chapter of *The Rainbow*, where, according to his own erotic fashion, he describes the rhythm of country life:

So the Brangwens came and went without fear of necessity, working hard because of the life that was in them, not for want of the money. Neither were they thriftless. They were aware of the last halfpenny, and instinct made them not waste the peeling of their apple, for it would help to feed the cattle. But heaven and earth was teeming around them, and how should this cease? They felt the rush of the sap in spring, they knew the wave which cannot halt, but every year throws forward the seed to begetting, and, falling back, leaves a young-born on the earth. They knew the intercourse between heaven and earth, sunshine drawn into the breast and the bowels, the rain sucked up in the daytime, nakedness that comes under the wind in autumn, showing the birds' nests no longer worth hiding. Their life and inter-relations were such; feeling the pulse and body of the soil, that opened to their furrow for the grain, and became smooth and supple after their ploughing, and clung to their feet with a weight that pulled like desire, lying hard and un-responsive when the crops were to be shorn away. The young corn waved and was silken, and the lustre slid along the limbs of the men who saw it. They took the udder of the cows, the cows yielded milk and pulse against the hands of the men, the pulse of the blood of the teats of the cows beat into the pulse of the hands of the men. They mounted their horses, and held life between the grip of their knees, they

harnessed their horses at the wagon, and, with hand on the
bridle-rings, drew the heaving of the horses after their will.

The King James Version held undisputed sway in the English-
speaking world for more than two centuries, but it was not without
its flaws. Although the translators had worked from as good a text of
the Old and New Testaments as they could find, both contained ac-
cumulated errors from long centuries of copying, and in the nineteenth century scholars began to discuss the need for revision
based on the discovery of older and more accurate manuscripts,
particularly in the Greek. In the Old Testament, the Messianic implications of "until Shiloh come" (Genesis 49:10), "a virgin shall conceive" (Isaiah 7:14), or "I know that my redeemer liveth" (Job
19:25), to give a few familiar examples, were also unwarranted in-
terpolations that viewed the Hebrew through a Christian lens. At
length, a number of new editions—the Revised Version of 1885, the
American Standard Version of 1901, and the Revised Standard Version of 1952, among others—all committee efforts—were published, which corrected some errors, reconceived the chapter and
verse divisions, printed some of the poetical sections of the Old Testament in separate lines, and modernized the prose. But the results
were often disappointing.

And intractable disputes arose. When the Revised Standard Version appeared, fundamentalist conservatives denounced it as too
"liberal," and pointed to Isaiah 7:14, which in the King James Version read: "Behold, a virgin shall conceive, and bear a son, and shall
call his name Immanuel." The new version replaced "virgin" with
"young woman," which was viewed as an attack on the Virgin Birth.
But "young woman" is what the Hebrew word *almah* means. The
Hebrew word for "virgin" is *bethulah*. However, in the Christian tradition, more than philological correctness was at stake. In the New
Testament, Matthew (1:23) quoted Isaiah's prophecy not from the
Hebrew but the Septuagint Greek. In that version, the word used is
parthenos, for which "virgin" is apt. Who then should decide?
"Many attempts have been made to purge [the King James Version]
of its errors and obscurities," wrote H. L. Mencken, "and many
learned but misguided men have sought to produce translations

that should be mathematically accurate, and in the plain speech of everyday. But the Authorized Version has never yielded to any of them, for it is palpably and overwhelmingly better than they are."

It was the poetry of the Psalms that King James himself loved most. Even after he became King of England, "he made the revising of the Psalms his own labor," we are told, "and at such hours as he might spare from the public cares, went through a number of them," in an effort to improve upon the metrical versions of his youth. The Bishop of Lincoln alluded to this in his funeral oration for the king at Westminster in May 1625 when he said that God had called James home at last "to sing psalms with the angels." Six years later, Charles I arranged to have his father's translations printed at Oxford, and approved the handsome title page which showed King James and King David together receiving the Psalms from the hand of God. That might have seemed a presumptuous pairing, by any standard; but thanks in part to James, the angels seem to sing the Psalms in English still.

JOHN BUNYAN

In the Bible there is enough clarity to enlighten the Elect, and enough obscurity to humble them.

—Blaise Pascal

CHAPTER FIVE

The Common Wealth

*hough James* was a devoted student of the Bible, and a sometimes eloquent man, he was a deeply flawed king. Macaulay said of him (with tendentious harshness) that he "was made up of two men—a witty, well-read scholar, who wrote, disputed, and harangued, and a nervous, drivelling idiot, who acted." In all fairness, he did a number of sensible and commendable things (the Bible translation and the prompt peace he made with Spain being two of them); but he surrounded himself with corrupt, ill-chosen favorites, and at the heart of his troubled reign was a constitutional crisis of his own destructive making that would eventually dissolve the nation into civil war.

Queen Elizabeth, through her domestic diplomacy and tact, had never "allowed the Reformation to get out of hand." Although Protestant refugees from all over Europe found asylum in her kingdom and brought with them every variety of Reformed belief, she had made the established Church broad enough to accommodate all but those of extreme views. Her flexibility, in turn, had nurtured a spirit and expectation of tolerance among her subjects that her successors could not repress. By the end of her reign, the English public was the most literate in Europe—indeed, it had become "the people of a book," and that book was the English Bible. Its legends, histories, war songs, and Psalms; its sacred biographies of the Hebrew fathers, who loomed as large in the imagined past as classical gods; the stern words of its mighty prophets; the infinitely illuminating parables of Christ; the life of Christ itself; apocalyptic visions— all were absorbed by the popular mind "unoccupied for the most part by any rival learning." However much the ruling powers might wish to direct the understanding of their subjects, no state or Church authority could any longer hope to force it in a mold. "Pandora's box was open," as one historian put it, "and no power could put back the thoughts on religion that took hold of the minds of men."

The growth of independent thought in the interpretation of the Bible was symptomatic of a larger spirit of questioning and inquiry which marked the age. Traditional explanations of the physical universe were rapidly yielding to the revelations of astronomy and the New Science, even as continued exploration of the globe "stimulated imaginations in every walk of life." In politics, people began to insist on their right to a government that ruled with equity and justice, and in religion, on their right to worship as they pleased. "The mother of modern democracy," it has been said, "was the Reformation, with its evolving principles of free inquiry and the priesthood and equality of all believers."

It was in Protestant England that democratic theory was first put to the test. And in time the results of that experiment rippled outward to the margins of the globe.

∽

Daniel Webster once remarked that the tavern was the headquarters of the American Revolution—meaning, in part, that ideas of self-determination could only emerge in a setting where free discussion naturally took place. That discussion was free because the English Reformation had established the ground and right to it, by virtue of the place the English Bible had in people's lives. Already in 1546, we may remember, Henry VIII had complained to Parliament that the Bible was being "disputed, rhymed, sung and jangled in every ale house and tavern," and there is a kind of poetic rightness to the notion that it was the tavern where the Reformation was also born.

Before the advent of the vernacular Bible, which was made available to the general public by printing, most people did not know what the Bible actually said. Thereafter, they could read it for themselves and decide, for themselves, what it meant. Their free discussions about the authority of Church and state fostered concepts of constitutional government in England, which in turn were the indispensable prerequisites for the American colonial revolt. Without the vernacular Bible—and the English Bible in particular, through its impact on the reformation of English politics—there could not have been democracy as we know it, or even what today we call the "Free World."

In short, the English Bible, with all that followed in its train, had sanctioned the right and capacity of the people to think for themselves.

But from the supremacy of the individual conscience to egalitarian democracy was a hard and winding road. The right to think for oneself did not always mean an absolute right of individual action, and much blood would be shed in learning that bitter lesson as the forms of constitutional government and democracy evolved. In English political history, the lines were drawn for a historic struggle between royal prerogative and parliamentary privilege, a struggle which was to culminate (at the end of its first great phase) in the beheading of a king.

Already in Wycliffe's day, Parliaments had established the principle that no legislation was binding unless it was concurred in by both houses. The representatives of towns and counties were empowered to commit their constituents to the payment of taxes, as well as to present grievances and petitions on their behalf; but it was customary, even in matters of religion, to follow the sovereign's lead. Thomas Cromwell had strengthened parliamentary precedent in the guise of strengthening his king. His system of king-in-Parliament had helped make Henry supreme in Church as well as state, but had legally tied his supremacy to parliamentary acts. The reign of Elizabeth had seen the advent of a more assertive House of Commons, which embodied the growing strength of the landed gentry and other members of the new middle class. Although Elizabeth tampered with juries in political trials, imprisoned at will, and claimed for her own royal proclamations the force of law, she generally used her power with caution (in implicit recognition of its limits) and left the ordinary course of justice intact. If the House, under Elizabeth, remained an ally of the Crown, she in turn proved wise enough to respect its privileges, for she understood that her strength lay not in "right divine" but in the loyalty of her subjects. Not long before she died, she summoned the members of the Commons to Whitehall and in a kind of poignant farewell told them: "Though God hath raised me high, yet this I count the glory of my crown, that I have reigned with your loves."

The practical political wisdom of Elizabeth appeared to die with her. England entered a period marked by a fierce struggle over the relative rights of king and Parliament, and especially over the extent of the royal prerogative—as James sought to claim his powers from a source higher than custom and law. That source was "divine right." Although the idea had its roots in Roman imperial concepts—and was destined to be embraced for two centuries by Continental despots—it was novel to the English, and ran counter to the whole current of English thought.

James had expounded his theory of kingship in 1598 in his treatise *The True Law of Free Monarchies,* which pictured the monarch as "the absolute master of the lives and possessions of his subjects; his acts are not open to inquiry or dispute, and no misdeeds can ever justify resistance." Whatever responsibilities he may have toward his subjects, he is beyond (or above) their chastisement and reproof. "The state of Monarchy," James wrote, "is the supreme thing on Earth. Kings are called Gods by God Himself because they sit upon God's earthly throne, and have the count of their administration to give unto Him." A king was therefore "God's lieutenant," and though he might, if he was a good king, "frame his actions according to law, yet he was not bound thereto," but "above all restraints except his own inspired will." These notions were softened a bit in a little book of advice he wrote for Prince Henry the following year, which imagined the monarch as a Christian prince and benevolent despot, whose Parliament was but "the king's head

Court," as he was "the father and shepherd of his people." But neither version appealed much to the enterprising lawyers, country gentlemen, and commercial entrepreneurs the House of Commons had come to represent.

One such member of the House had long ago seen the conflict brewing, and that man was Thomas More. In his *Utopia* he had sternly criticized the tyrannical maxim that "the king can do no wrong, however much he may wish to do it; that not only the property, but the persons of his subjects are his own."

The question ultimately became whether or not the king was above the law. Early Protestants, of course, had relied on the monarchy to break the might of the Church, and under such circumstances had given it all the power it cared to claim. Tyndale, for instance, had written in *The Obedience of a Christian Man* that "the king is in this world without law, and may at his lust do right or wrong and shall give accounts but to God only." Henry VIII naturally thought Tyndale's book (if not his Bible translation) a book "for all kings" to read. But Henry also paid attention to what his subjects thought and felt. Elizabeth in turn had traveled throughout her kingdom and managed to rule as an autocrat without becoming a tyrant; James cut himself off from all but his own court. Despite the wild welcome he had received upon his accession, he hated crowds, and it is said that almost the only working people he came in contact with were his huntsmen and outdoor servants. Yet "in my own person," he would grandly inform his first Parliament, "God has bestowed his blessings on all of you." Although James was too shrewd, or realistic, to let his theories entirely govern his conduct, he continued to have an exalted view of his place reminiscent of that of Shakespeare's Pericles:

> *Kings are earth's gods; in vice their law's their will,*
> *And if Jove stray, who dares say, Jove doth ill?*

That was the opinion of Archbishop Bancroft, too, and from the first the religious and constitutional issues were fatefully entwined.

Before his accession, James had listened sympathetically to English Catholics, who hoped he might relax the standing laws against them. When he failed to do so, Catholics began to agitate against his rule. Already by March 1604, it was widely rumored among them that they were to be stripped of their property and fortune and expelled from the realm. "From this it is to be gathered," said one underground pamphlet, "what is to be expected from this king." On November 4, 1605, one day before the second Parliament under James was to meet, a Catholic zealot named Guy Fawkes was discovered in a cellar beneath the House of Lords with thirty-six barrels of gunpowder and a fuse.

In the aftermath of the Gunpowder Plot, as it was called, Parliament had stiffened anti-Catholic legislation with acts "for the better discovery and repressing of Popish recusants." These laws excluded Catholics from various professions, such as medicine and law; barred them from serving as the executors of an estate; and even prohibited them from traveling more than five miles from their homes. James also required submission to a new Oath of Allegiance (the one Lancelot Andrewes defended), which obliged English Catholics to deny the pope's claimed power to depose rulers not sanctioned by Rome.

But the king's punitive impulse now assumed a widening arc, and the Puritans ultimately bore the brunt of it. After 1605, the established Church fought all divergences, Catholic or Puritan, as heresy, and when Thomas Ravis became Bishop of London in 1607, he at once began to harass those who would not fully submit. With haughty sureness, he announced: "By the help of Jesus, I will not leave one preacher in my diocese who doth not subscribe and conform." This, in fact, was but the king's will. "If ministers are intractable," James told his Privy Council, "they must be compelled. . . . They must either conform or dispose of themselves in other ways, as . . . proceedings will be taken against them." What did he mean? The Church in Convocation had already enacted canons that threatened to excommunicate those who failed to conform strictly to the rubrics of the Prayer Book or dissented from the Anglican Creed, and in one year alone (1607) three hundred dissenting ministers were not only deprived of their livings, but in some cases fined, imprisoned, or otherwise "disposed of" by the law. That "law" consisted of the arbitrary edicts of the Ecclesiastical Court of High Commission, which held its prerogative from the Crown.

In theory, there was no appeal from its rulings, but a number of the punished ministers petitioned the common law courts for redress; and some of the judges lent a sympathetic ear to their pleas. In certain cases, the judges issued "prohibitions" against High Commission rulings, which made the king irate. At one meeting of his Privy Council in 1608, he "most bitterly inveighed against the Puritans," and blamed all the troubles in England and Scotland alike on their legal appeal. He said that the "revolt in the Low Countries, which had lasted ever since he was born and whereof he never expected to see an end," had begun with such a petition; that he had been haunted from his cradle by a Puritan "devil" which "he feared would not leave him till his grave"; and that he was determined to "suppress such malicious spirits" even at the hazard of his Crown. Meanwhile, Bancroft had formally asked the Star Chamber—the legal tribunal of the Privy Council and another prerogative court—whether the High Commission had the power it thought it had, not only to interrogate and banish dissenters but suppress petitions (including legal motions) at will. He was told that it did.

Much of the judiciary thought otherwise.

In February 1609, Sir Edward Coke, chief justice of the Court of Common Pleas, was called to Whitehall to confer about the matter with the king, his Privy Council, and the ecclesiastical authorities. The archbishop spoke about the king and his powers. All judges, he said, were merely representatives of the king, and could therefore be overruled since their judgments were but extensions of his. Coke replied that the Magna Carta had established the legal basis of the common law courts, and that these courts had jurisdiction over both high and low. The king leapt to his feet and shouted that he was qualified to sit as a judge himself because he possessed the faculty of reason. Coke answered that, in fact, since the king was not a member of the bar, he could not sit as a judge in the usual sense, or "in his own person adjudge a case." The conference broke up without agreement, but in its wake Coke scrutinized with an extremely legalistic eye the Act of Supremacy, by which the High Commission had been established in the first place. He noted that the commission had originally been empowered to try only extraordinary cases—namely, those involving heresy, schism, and other "enormities"—and that most of its recent rulings were therefore invalid, as falling beyond the scope of its writ.

Coke was all the more formidable as an adversary because he had long been allied to the Crown. Called to the bar in 1578, he had quickly made a name for himself in property and libel cases involving members of the court, and under the patronage of William Cecil, Lord Burghley, had risen to prominence in the public eye. He entered Parliament in 1589, became solicitor general and recorder of London in 1592; and in 1593 was elected speaker of the House of Commons, where he skillfully cooperated with the queen in curbing religious debate. One year later, he won appointment as attorney general, and was ever the champion in that post of the Crown and its prerogative powers. Then in 1606 he became chief justice of the Court of Common Pleas. The changed venue opened a new window to his mind. And he soon began to view his responsibilities in a different light. Eventually, he emerged as the champion of the reasoned judgment that judges and not the king must decide which laws are valid and which not. Although Sir Francis Bacon (Coke's successor as attorney general) declared that judges were but "lions under the throne," and therefore (by implication) obliged to implement the pleasure of his will, Coke viewed them in a more dignified and independent light, as custodians of the tried and true but still evolving tenets of the law. Not long after his appointment, he stated in one of his opinions: "When an act of Parliament is against common right and reason, or repugnant, or impossible to be performed, the common law will control it, and judge such an act to be void." This became one of the fundamental precedents for the later American doctrine of judicial review. In 1610, Parliament challenged the power of the king to make or break laws by the force of his proclamations—even though Queen Elizabeth, for example, had occasionally done just that. The Court of Common Pleas considered the matter, and concluded that the king enjoyed only those prerogatives allowed to him by law. Specifically, Coke stated that the king could not change any part of the common law nor create any offense by proclamation that was not an offense before. In yet another ruling, he disputed the authority of the High Commission to imprison anyone for private behavior (such as adultery) which it did not condone.

In 1611, an exasperated James tried to put Coke himself on the commission in order to muzzle his dissent. Coke declined the offer, but in August 1613 accepted the king's invitation to become a privy councillor and chief justice of the King's Bench. As such, he was the first to be called Lord Chief Justice of England. But honors and elevation did not alter his mind. He continued to maintain the supremacy of the common law over all persons and institutions except Parliament, and even (in a blow to the political use of Church wealth) challenged the king's right to grant anyone permission to hold several benefices at the same time. In 1616, he stood alone, among all the judges, for the independence of the judiciary by refusing to countenance the king's interference in a suit to which the king was a party himself. Dismissed by the king, Coke later joined the opposition in Parliament and continued his historic career under Charles I.

Meanwhile, the first Parliament James called had asserted a number of parliamentary privileges for its members, including freedom from arrest and complete freedom of speech. These were propounded in the form of an apology drafted but not voted on by members of the Commons, which declared such privileges to be the "right and due inheritance" of its members, and not arbitrary luxuries which the Crown, by its sufferance, allowed. In addition, the king was boldly informed that in all matters pertaining to the law he could not act "otherwise than by Parliament's consent," and that far from having absolute power in himself, "the voice of the people, in the things of their knowledge," was declared to be "as the voice of God." In subsequent sessions, Parliament declared the king's decision to impose unauthorized custom duties illegal; demanded that the High Commission be regulated by statute; and criticized the king's foreign policy (part of his traditional prerogative). James ordered the Commons to desist from "such deep matters of State."

In reply, the House issued a "Protestation" that gathered all the issues under contention into two succinct paragraphs of plain rhetorical force. The king dissolved the Parliament and in a rage ripped the "Protestation" out of the journal of the House.

When James died in 1625, he left all the constitutional conflicts of his reign unresolved. Parliament went its own way; the prerogative courts went theirs. The presumed powers of the king remained unfettered by statute or law. The practicalities of governing made this stalemate untenable on its face, even as tension increased throughout the realm.

Charles I did nothing to set things right. He had imbibed his father's doctrine of divine right only too well, and his rule had scarcely begun before he clashed with Parliament over their respective powers. Although his personal dignity and reserve seemed to contrast favorably with "the gabble and indecorum" of his father, he had an obstinate streak which showed itself early and caused alarm. One prescient courtier, observing the prince before he took power, prayed God that "he might be in the right way when he set; for if he was in the wrong he would prove the most willful of any king that ever reigned."

Charles's immediate problem was to get the Commons to pay for a new war with Spain. The war was judged ill advised, and Parliament refused to grant him tonnage and poundage (import and export) duties for life; so he dissolved it in a fit of pique. The king's favorite, George Villiers, the first Duke of Buckingham, helped finance an expedition against Cádiz, but the venture proved a disaster and Charles had to turn again to Parliament for funds. The second Parliament at once demanded Buckingham's impeachment, and the Commons linked its willingness to grant the king a subsidy "to that time when we shall have presented our grievances, and received his Majesty's answer thereto." Charles summoned the members to Whitehall and demanded that their condition be withdrawn. "I will grant you liberty of counsel, but not of control," he told them, and reminded them that he could call and dissolve Parliament at will. The Commons stood firm and presented Buckingham's impeachment to the Lords.

Buckingham took his seat as a peer to hear the charge. He was dressed in extravagant silk and lace, and literally dripped with jewels. The insolence of his apparel was quickly turned against him. Sir John Eliot, chosen to prosecute the case, at once proceeded to upbraid him for his profligate waste of the kingdom's wealth. "He has broken the nerves and sinews of our land, the stores and treasures of the King," began Eliot. "There needs no search for it. It is visible. His profuse expenses, his superfluous feasts, his magnificent buildings, his riots, his excesses, what are they but the visible evidences of an express exhausting of the State, a chronicle of the immensity of his waste of the reserves of the Crown?" He recounted the duke's greed, corruption, and ambition; compared him to Sejanus, captain of the guard under the Emperor Tiberius; and urged the Lords to strip him of his titles and rank. The king hurried to the House, and had Eliot and another member plucked from their seats and committed to the Tower. But the members of Commons refused to proceed with the public business until their colleagues were released. Ten days later they were freed, but when the House presented Charles with a remonstrance, he dissolved the body and flung the text into the flames.

Meanwhile, war had also erupted with France. Even more haughty than James, Charles proceeded to adopt policies that eventually led to unparliamentary taxation, billeting, arbitrary imprisonment, and martial law. The House of Commons stood against these measures and pronounced them illegal in the immortal Petition of Right of 1628, largely shaped by Coke, which molded ancient precedents, including the Magna Carta, into a charter of parliamentary and civil liberties. At length, with bitter reluctance, Charles was forced to accept the petition in return for the subsidies he needed, but he later reversed himself and attempted to dispense with Parliament outright.

Once again, politics and religion were joined. In 1633, the king appointed William Laud, a High Church zealot, Archbishop of Canterbury and gave him leave to reconstitute the Church of England as a reformed branch of the Church of Rome. Laud moved quickly to sever the English church from Reformed churches on the Continent, emphasized the ritual side of worship, reintroduced the doctrine of the real presence in Communion, banned evangelical practice and preaching, disparaged the sanctity of the Sabbath, and

was even more vigorous in hounding Puritans and other Nonconformists than Ravis had been. As parishes fell vacant, they were filled
with neo-Catholic clergy, while the power of the bishops' courts,
which had fallen into decay, was revived. Once again it was the
warning voice of Eliot in Parliament that rang out from the floor:
"The Gospel is that Truth in which this kingdom has been happy.
. . . Let us lay for a foundation of our building, that we will maintain
that Truth, not with words, but with actions! . . . There is a ceremony in the Eastern Churches of standing at the repetition of the
Creed, to testify their purpose to maintain it, not only with their
bodies upright, but with their swords drawn. Give me leave to call
that a custom very commendable!"

The king sent word for the House to adjourn. But before the
speaker could rise to carry out the king's order, he was rushed and
held down in his chair. By successive resolutions, the Commons declared that anyone who attempted innovations in religion, or urged
the king to proceed with unparliamentary levies, or cooperated
with such acts, was "a capital enemy to the kingdom" and "a be-
trayer of the liberty of England."

Neither Charles nor Laud paid heed. Illegal levies and religious
persecution both increased, and to many it seemed that the general
danger "had enlarge[d] itself in so great a measure," as one put it,
"that nothing but Heaven shrouds us from despair." Laud's hand in
Scotland was even more severe. Despite the most vociferous
protests, he increased the power of the bishops—instituted by
James—and imposed a more conservative prayer book on the Kirk.
He even inserted Catholic prints of the life of the Virgin into Scottish editions of the King James Version of the New Testament, and
burned every copy of the Geneva Bible he could find. The Scots re-
belled, abolished episcopal rule, and swore to uphold a National
Covenant based upon their Presbyterian faith. Many signed their
names to it in blood.

Charles raised an army to enforce his will, but the First Bishops'
War, as it was called, failed even before it started and he was obliged
to summon a new Parliament to finance a second campaign. Parliament opened with a long recitation of its grievances against the
Crown, and Charles, with impatient folly, dissolved it after only a few

weeks. A second Scots campaign, organized by Thomas Wentworth, Earl of Strafford, met defeat, and in a humiliating blow to his regal pride, Charles even had to pay the costs of the covenanter army encamped on English soil.

Meanwhile, Buckingham had been assassinated, Coke had died of old age, and Eliot had perished in the Tower.

Turmoil among the population increased. From the first, Charles had refused to accept any instructions from Parliament, and had thrice summoned and thrice dismissed that body when it refused to bend to his will. From 1629 for eleven years he had governed by personal rule. In the interim, he had filled his exchequer by the sale of monopolies and by other unpopular measures, such as "ship money," a kind of tax subsidy demanded first from seaports and later from inland towns. Parliament demanded an end to it, and as the political battle lines were drawn, the High Church faction and scions of the old aristocracy allied themselves with the king, while Puritans and other Nonconformists cast their lot with Parliament, as the kingdom split into two military camps.

Charles and his new archbishop were convinced that unrestricted Bible reading had fueled the popular discontent. Access to the Scriptures had certainly helped to develop the habit of reading—indeed, it was often by reading biblical passages that children learned their ABCs—while more than two thirds of the books printed in the kingdom from 1480 to 1640 were of a religious character. Over a million Bibles and New Testaments had also been published in England by the time the confrontation between Charles and the Parliament came to a head; and by that time, as a result, men and women had grown accustomed to regarding Scripture as the source of wisdom on all matters, including their worldly estate.

This was perilous for the established powers. "Few sources," as one historian notes, "are as rich as the Old Testament in undesireable kings who come to exemplary bad ends," while the New Testament is "full of libertarian ideas." The Protestant doctrine of the priesthood of all believers, of the supremacy of the individual conscience, encouraged many to read their destiny into such verses as: "Where the spirit of the Lord is, there is liberty." Through prayer and meditation, they learned to approach God without assistance, and in reading the Word of God to themselves heard it, as it were, not from a priest on high and at a distance, but from deep within their own immortal souls. They turned out tracts proclaiming themselves "free-born," and by the time Laud and his prelates attempted to inculcate passive obedience as a virtue of the faith, scriptural notions of their obligation to righteous disobedience had taken hold.

From the beginning, as we have seen, "popular Bible reading had alarmed conservatives." Many, like Sir Thomas More, had regarded "faith in plain Scripture," that is, without the mediation of Church authority, as a "pestilential heresy" and feared that free interpretation would lead to sedition. One English bishop declared: "Either we must root out printing, or printing will root out us." Others predicted that lay preachers would set man against wife, master against servant, or "move [the people] to rise against their princes, and to make all common, and to make havoc of other men's goods."

Protestants, on the other hand, looked forward to a general overturning as correcting man's estate. The development of the vernacular marked the origin of a culture belonging to the masses, which increasingly reached toward popular and democratic institutions that expressed the popular will. With a popular will went a popular press. That press had begun to develop in England and elsewhere in the form of newspapers and magazines. The earliest English "newsbook," as it was called, or news-pamphlet (which recounted a contemporary battle) had been printed in London in September 1513. Between 1590 and 1610 at least 450 English news-books were issued, and after the middle of the seventeenth century they were superseded by the newspaper or news-sheet. "The art of Printing," one reformer prophesied in 1641, "will so spread knowledge that the common people, knowing their own rights and liberties, will no longer be governed by way of oppression but will rule their own lives."

George Abbot, Laud's Puritan predecessor as archbishop, had once told King James that "Scripture doth directly or by consequence contain in it sufficient matter to decide all controversies." The king found that absurd, but for Puritans it was axiomatic, and the introduction to one edition of the Geneva Bible (1603) typically insisted that Scripture was not only a guide to "the common life of all men, as riches, poverty, nobility, favor, labour, and idleness," but to "commonwealths and governments . . . magistrates (good and evil), peace and war." The King James Version had inherited the scope (if not the commentary) of this claim, and throughout the ensuing years the Bible was used "to justify" in the list of Christopher Hill, "both resistance to and defense of the king, democracy, communism, regicide, the rule of the saints, the overthrow of international Catholicism, even free love. It called into question all established institutions and practices. The ideas which divided the two parties in the impending civil war . . . were all found in the Bible." And it was by recourse or reference to the Bible that all these matters were thrashed out.

In England at least, reading of the Scriptures had tended at first to enhance rather than undermine the sovereign's power. In the Old Testament one read much concerning good as well as evil kings, while the New Testament tended to render up to Caesar the things that were his due. The Old Testament also provided the precedent for a national church under a divinely ordained national monarch, as in King David, "the Lord's Anointed" a "type" of Henry VIII. The Elizabethan *Homily Against Disobedience and Wilfull Rebellion* had likewise insisted that all kings, queens, and other governors were God's anointed, and—citing David as an example—warned "that neither exceptional virtue, high rank nor the favor of God could justify rebellion even against the manifestly wicked King Saul." "Let every soul be subject unto the higher powers," read Romans 13:1. "The powers that be are ordained of God." Among royalists, that was the most cherished of the New Testament texts, just as David's refusal to kill Saul as God's anointed was their favorite Old Testament tale.

The Geneva Bible adopted a different view, as James had glumly noted at the conference at Hampton Court. The statement in Acts 5:29, "We ought rather to obey God than men," was said to mean "We ought to obey no man, but so far forth as obeying him we may obey God." And Calvin boldly interpreted the story of Daniel and the lion's den to mean that "Earthly princes deprive themselves of all authority when they rise up against God, yea, they are unworthy to be counted amongst the company of men. We ought rather to spit in their faces than to obey them."

It is in this biblical light that much of the language of the constitutional struggle must be viewed. Speeches were drenched in it. No sooner had King James levied a tax not cleared by Parliament (in 1614) than one member got up and declared it a sin which God would avenge. For such sins the Spaniards had been punished by the loss of the Low Countries, he declared, and Henry IV of France "had died like a calf under the butcher's knife." He quoted Daniel 11:20 (from the Geneva text): "Then shall stand up in his place in the glory of the kingdom one that shall raise taxes, but after a few days he shall be destroyed." Again, just as Henry VIII had justified his revolt against the pope by casting himself as "the Lord's Anointed," so Puritan preachers excused rebellion against the king by linking themselves to the Old Testament prophets who had rebuked their sovereigns in the Lord's name. They had likened Edward VI to good king Josiah, who destroyed idols, but compared Charles to Pharaoh, Saul, Ahab, Herod, and other wicked kings who suffered a lamentable fate. England under Charles was compared to Egypt and Babylon; Laud's ecclesiastical rule to an "Egyptian tyranny"; Buckingham to Goliath, felled by a youth. All these were meant as examples in the biblical sense, not mere figures of speech.

Even on those rare occasions when a Puritan had commended James, the language of Scripture supplied most of the analogies. "All must acknowledge him to be zealous as David," wrote Archbishop Abbot in fulsome praise, "learned and wise, the Solomon of our age, religious as Josiah, careful of spreading Christ's faith as Constantine the great, just as Moses, undefiled in all his ways as Jehoshaphat, or Hezekiah, full of clemency as another Theodosius."

Sermons on the occasion of the Gunpowder Plot—by William Barlow at Paul's Cross and Lancelot Andrewes at Whitehall—likewise had an Old Testament ring. Barlow took Psalm 18:50 as his text: "Great deliverance giveth He to His king, and sheweth mercy to His anointed, to David, and to his seed for evermore. . . . This whirling blast would have been unto our sacred king . . . as the whirlwind and fiery chariot of Elias, to have carried up his soul to heaven." Andrewes took flight from Psalm 118:23–24: "This is the Lord's doing; it is marvellous in our eyes. This is the day which the Lord hath made; we will rejoice and be glad in it. . . . We have therefore well done . . . by law to provide that this day should not die, nor the memorial thereof perish, from ourselves or from our seed."

Through this body of ideas was woven another strand, the notion that England occupied a special providential place in history. "O Lord God, save thy chosen people of England," Edward VI exclaimed in 1553, while both the Geneva Bible and John Foxe's *Book of Martyrs*—the two most popular books in Elizabethan England—provided a view of the nation as elect. Milton, in turn, wrote: "God revealed things, as his manner is, first to his Englishmen," and (strange to say) in some sense he was right, for it was also their lot to be the first to test the new doctrines of their age. Social upheaval had accompanied free discussion. It remained to discover whether it would all lead finally to anarchy and bloodshed (as Sir Thomas More had predicted) or to some new and agreed upon social order and truth, out of the free and open contest of ideas. "Truth is compared in Scripture (Proverbs 18:4) to a streaming fountain," wrote Milton in *Areopagitica,* the greatest tract against press censorship ever penned. "If the waters flow not in perpetual progression, they sicken into a muddy pool of conformity and tradition. . . . Let [Truth] and Falsehood grapple," for, in a fair encounter, "who ever knew Truth put to the worse?"

∽

When Parliament finally reconvened again in 1640, it impeached the Earl of Strafford for treason, and not only compelled the king to sign a bill of attainder authorizing his execution, but to agree that the new Parliament could not be dissolved without its consent. Laud was imprisoned in the Tower, the Triennial Act passed to guarantee Parliament's own existence against future periods of "personal rule," ship money and other arbitrary levies annulled, and the prerogative courts quashed. Thus did the reign of the Long Parliament begin. This was too much for the king. On January 4, 1642, he entered Parliament flanked by soldiers and tried to arrest four members of the House, including the leader of the opposition, John

Pym. But Pym and the others, forewarned, had slipped out before the king arrived. When Charles demanded where they were, the speaker of the House replied: "I have neither eyes to see nor tongue to speak . . . but as this House is pleased to direct me."

Pym and his allies regarded the king's refusal to work with Parliament as tantamount to his abdication, which vested the executive power in the two houses until new arrangements could be made. Civil War followed. Charles gathered an army and raised his standard at Nottingham, "like the feudal barons of old," and four hard years of war began. Both sides sought Scots help, which was soon accorded to Parliament, which promised to help preserve Presbyterian Church government in Scotland in return for military aid. The king controlled most of the north and west of England, including Wales, and had the advantage of a well-trained cavalry led by his nephew, Prince Rupert of the Palatinate. Parliament effectively controlled London, Hull, Bristol, Plymouth, and other principal ports containing most of the country's population and wealth. Although the king's army proved valiant, and the outcome of the war was by no means certain for some time, by 1644 the New Model Army, organized by Thomas Fairfax and Oliver Cromwell, had gained the upper hand. On June 14, 1645, Cromwell's "invincible Ironsides"— with copies of *The Soldiers Pocket Bible* in their boots—met and annihilated the Royalist troops at the battle of Naseby, which foreshadowed the end of the war. A year later, the king surrendered himself to the Scots, who handed him over to his parliamentary foes.

On January 20, 1649, he was arraigned before a specially constituted tribunal of 135 judges, denounced by the prosecutor as the very image of "Nimrod, the first tyrant," and charged with treason, murder, and "other high crimes against the realm of England." Although he stoutly refused to recognize the legality of the proceedings, since "a king cannot be tried by any superior jurisdiction on earth," that did not save him; and by the margin of a single vote he was condemned to death and beheaded at Whitehall on January 30 before a shocked and silent crowd.

Cromwell emerged at the head of the new government. Over the next several months, he subdued the remaining pockets of Royalist resistance, assumed the title of Lord General of the Commonwealth, then Lord Protector. The latter effectively gave him dictatorial powers, though the nation in theory was ruled by a Council of State. Meanwhile, the victorious Puritans had seized the opportunity to urge the nation to renew its covenant with God. Many of the faithful regarded Cromwell almost as "a second Moses . . . that great deliverer of his people out of the house of Egypt"; but to Royalists (no less steeped in the English Bible) he seemed more like a wicked tyrant, "a second Jeroboam" because "he did authorize and encourage all the scum and refuse of the people to preach" (1 Kings 13:33–34).

Under his rule, the monarchy was abolished, together with the House of Lords, the Commons purged of moderates, and England proclaimed a "Free State" with a republican form of government. That government was not intolerant of other religious groups, but it favored the Puritans, just as the Anglicans had been favored under the king. But it was a cheerless reign. The Puritan temper was stern. Self-restraint and sobriety ruled the outer life, but humor was often repressed as profane levity, while the inner world of the believer tended to be "overborne by the terrible reality of 'invisible things.' " The old relationship between Church and state was also reversed. At least from the time of Henry VIII, explains one historian,

> the Church had been looked upon primarily as an instrument for securing, by moral and religious influences, the social and political ends of the State. Under the Commonwealth, the State, in its turn, was regarded primarily as an instrument for securing through its political and social influences the moral and religious ends of the Church. The aim of the Puritan had been to set up a visible kingdom of God upon earth. In the Puritan theory, Englishmen were "the Lord's people"; a people dedicated to Him by a solemn Covenant, and whose end as a nation was to carry out his will. For such an end it was needful that rulers as well as people should be "godly men." Godliness became necessarily the chief qualification for public employment. The new modelling of the army filled its ranks with "saints." Parliament resolved to employ no man "but such as the House

shall be satisfied of his real godliness." The Covenant which bound the nation to God bound it to enforce God's laws even more earnestly than its own. The Bible lay on the table of the House of Commons; and its prohibition of swearing, of drunkenness, of fornication became part of the law of the land.

The government, in short, was organized as a Church government, in a covenanted community, and as such enfranchised only the "elect." In a sense, as G. K. Chesterton remarked, that really made it a kind of aristocracy, but of the most "awful kind: for it was based "not on a right of birth but a right before birth, and alone of all nobilities was not laid level in the dust."

After a Royalist uprising in 1655, Cromwell divided the country into eleven military districts, imposed martial law, and made his dictatorship complete. In effect, one form of authoritarian rule had been replaced by another. "If Power without Law may make Laws," as the king had said truly enough before he went to the block, "I do not know what subject he is in England, that can be sure of his life or any thing that he calls his own." The nation remained deeply divided, and though Cromwell's rule was often capable and shrewd, he failed utterly to find a path to domestic peace. "I am as much for government by consent as any man," he once said, "but where will you find that consent?" When he died on September 3, 1658, few expected the commonwealth to last. His son, Richard, succeeded to his title, but he lacked the talent of command. Early in 1659, he called and dissolved his only Parliament, then resigned. The army sought some legitimate replacement, but Royalists and Presbyterians alike had made their own arrangement that cleared the way for the Restoration in the person of Charles II.

The return of the monarchy was welcomed by most of the nation, which ardently wished a return to constitutional rule. Between the defeat of Charles I and the coronation of his son, England had lacked any clearly legitimate government, since Parliament had also managed to all but destroy itself. Not since the dethronement of Richard II in 1399 (at which Parliament had also connived) had the nation learned what the fall of fixed authority could mean. The

Crown had then become a mere object of ambition. "That which one could snatch another could snatch from him. The spell of an undethronable thing seated out of reach was broken, and for three unhappy generations adventurers strove and stumbled on a stairway slippery with blood." No one wanted to see England go down that path again. The authority of king and Parliament were once more regarded as inextricably linked, but the kind of absolutism James and Charles I had both espoused was discredited by the havoc it had caused. The great prerogative courts, with their rival system of jurisprudence, were allowed to lapse and expire; and when Charles formally restored episcopal church government, the bishops were told to act in accord with the synods they ruled.

At the same time, republicanism as an alternative to monarchy had become unpalatable to most, while ideas of the right and obligation of the individual to act as the spirit moved him were scanned more closely than before. Divines (and not just the Anglicans among them) counseled against blindly following that elusive "inner light." "Let a man but persuade himself," one told his congregation, "that the *Spirit* dwells *personally* in him, and speaks upon all occasions to him; how easily and readily may he plead that the *Spirit* tells him he may kill his enemy, plunder his neighbor, cast off all obedience to his governors. . . . Thus the late rebel army having conquer'd and imprison'd their conscience as well as their prince, *completed* all by bringing *the Spirit* to their lure." In *Religio Laici*, John Dryden was a bit more blunt:

> *The Book thus put in every vulgar hand,*
> *Which each presumed he best could understand,*
> *The common rule was made the common prey*
> *And at the mercy of the rabble lay.*
> *The tender page with horny fists was galled,*
> *And he was gifted most that loudest bawled.*
> *The spirit gave the doctoral degree,*
> *And every member of a Company*
> *Was of his trade and of the Bible free.*
> *Plain truths enough for needful use they found,*
> *But men would still be itching to expound;*

Each was ambitious of the obscurest place,
No measure ta'en from knowledge, all from grace.

More secular (and semidemocratic) theorists like John Locke concurred. In his *Essay Concerning Human Understanding* (1690),
Locke emphasized "the labor of strict reasoning," and scoffed at
those who supposed that "whatever groundless Opinion comes to
settle itself strongly upon their Fancies, is an Illumination from the
Spirit of God, and presently of divine Authority," or that "whatsoever
odd Action they find in themselves a strong Inclination to do, that
Impulse is concluded to be a Call or Direction from Heaven, and
must be obeyed."

Thomas Hobbes gave revelation even less scope, and in effect
dismissed it as a psychological phenomenon. "To say that God hath
spoken to man in a dream," he wrote, "is no more than to say man
dreamed that God hath spoken to him." And, "To say one hath seen a
vision or heard a voice, is to say he hath dreamed between sleeping
and waking."

Pride goeth before a fall: in a sense Protestants had become
more Catholic than they knew. For they had exchanged one authority for another: "in the place of the medieval Church," as one scholar
put it, they had Scripture; in the place of an infallible institution, an
infallible text; in the place of Tradition, a printed book. "The Puritan
iconoclast had himself become a bibliolater," who supposed himself
subscribed to a "self-interpreting" text. But the Bible was not doctrine; it was a narrative; and though portions of it contained laws
and strictures, it could, it seems, be all things to all men. Anyone with
any position could find a supporting text—even "the devil," as
Shakespeare's Antonio remarks in the *Merchant of Venice,* could
"cite Scripture for his purpose," if he wished.

Where, then, between the light of the individual conscience,
and the light (and rights) of the greater community, did the proper
balance lie? The question, first addressed in Church government,
evolved at once into a debate over government at large. Perhaps the
great preacher Jeremy Taylor glimpsed the answer in a sermon delivered at the opening of the Cavalier Parliament in 1661: "Both
sides pretended Scripture; but one side only can pretend to the

laws." Although the Catholic Church retained a feudal structure, most Reformed churches represented a kind of mixed monarchy, "combining the kingship of Christ with the aristocracy of elders and a democracy of lay members of the congregation." Between the Long Parliament and the Restoration, some thirty thousand political pamphlets were published in England, as the entire kingdom became a school for political theory and debate. That debate continued apace, as schemes of new government flowed from countless pens.

The ablest critic of absolute monarchy was probably John Locke, whose idea of government was based on the notion of a social contract in which the "people" consented to give up their natural liberty in order "to unite for the mutual Preservation of their Lives, Liberties and Estates." Government was thus a trust, established to serve the common good; and rulers were accountable to their subjects, holding power by their consent. At the same time, by contract, every individual was subject to the law, which was administered by the state. As for the structure of the state itself, Locke favored a mixed constitution, with an elected legislature and a sovereign, enjoying separated powers.

Locke's writings had a considerable impact on political theory throughout the English-speaking world. In time, they also spread to France. His ideas of the "social contract" were more appealing than the related ideas of Thomas Hobbes, who postulated a covenant among men to surrender their rights to a government for their own self-preservation. Without such a government, according to Hobbes, men would revert to a savage state of nature in which each struggled to master, exploit, or exterminate his neighbor in a life that was "nasty, brutish, and short." "Some coercive Power" was therefore required "to compell men equally to the performance of their Covenants, by the terror of some punishment, greater than the benefit they expect by the breach"—and that was the role of the state. They therefore surrendered "all their own power and strength" to one man or an assembly of men, authorized "to reduce all their Wills, by plurality of voices, unto one Will. . . . This done, the Multitude so united in one Person, is called a COMMON-WEALTH." The sovereign of that commonwealth did not rule by divine right, but he also could not be opposed or called to account by his subjects. For they had surrendered their will to his.

The Puritan revolution, with its chaos of popular sects—Ranters, Diggers, Muggletonians, Baptists, Anabaptists, Quakers, Levellers, Independents, Presbyterians, Fifth Monarchy Men, and so on—in conjunction with the violence of the Civil War, had bred a fear of a complete breakdown in the social order, which had threatened to revert to just that state of nature Hobbes had described. But the idea of the consent of the governed could not be dislodged. In the canons which the Church of England had drafted in the time of King James (adhering to the doctrine of divine right), we read: "If any man shall affirm that . . . all civil power, jurisdiction, and authority were first derived from the people and disordered multitude, or either is originally still in them or else deduced by their consent, naturally from them, and is not God's ordinance originally descending from Him and depending upon Him, he doth greatly err." That was in 1606, and the fact that the Church felt compelled to so state its views suggests the idea was already in the air. By the time Locke wrote, it had become the very air the people breathed.

There could be no turning back. Over the next half century, by ineluctable degrees, Parliament gradually came to terms with the political problem it faced. Ultimately, that problem might be defined as, "How to make its will the law of administrative action without itself undertaking the task of administration."

When James II, the third son of Charles I, ascended the throne upon his brother's death in 1685, he swore not to make fundamental changes in either Church or state. But he could not resist his own autocratic yearnings and (though the two need not be paired) sought to reestablish Catholicism as the religion of the realm. He revived the High Commission, forbade the clergy from attacking "Popery" from their pulpits, and placed Catholics at the head of his government and military staff. This was a great tragedy for England, where anti-Catholic bigotry had begun to subside. A Protestant rebellion under the Duke of Monmouth was brutally crushed, and Chief Justice George Jeffreys, who had become the king's instrument of legal oppression, imposed a terrible revenge on Monmouth's supporters in the "Bloody Assize." Monmouth himself was beheaded, some two hundred others were executed, and hundreds of others sold into slavery in the colonies overseas. Even one of the king's key generals recoiled at the harshness of these acts. "This marble," he reportedly cried, as he struck the chimney mantel on which he leaned, "is not harder than the king's heart."

In 1687, James issued the Declaration of Indulgence that seemed to allow freedom of worship for all, though its obvious, if covert, purpose was to enable Catholicism to regain its primary place. As one prominent Puritan told his brethren, "You are to be hugged now, only that you may be squeezed at another time." James himself said: "We cannot but heartily wish that all the people of our dominions were members of the Catholic Church." In other measures, by his interference with voting privileges, army commissions, church benefices, and university fellowships, James not only restricted the freedom of the upper classes, but endangered their privileged position, which they regarded as akin to a property right. As the Tory (or royalist) faction grew increasingly restless, the Whig or parliamentary party stood fast against his innovations to a man.

It was not long before the king's own isolation became clear—even to him. One day he asked the Duke of Norfolk to carry the sword of state before him as he went to Mass. The Duke stopped at the chapel door. "Your father would have gone farther," said the king. "Your Majesty's father was the better man," replied the duke, "and he would not have gone so far."

The alienation spread, and in 1688 a group of Whig and Tory peers covertly invited William of Orange, married to James's daughter and a champion of Protestants on the Continent, to assume the throne. William landed on the English coast on November 11, 1688, at the head of a large army, and almost at once the forces of the king collapsed. After a brief interval, James was allowed to flee to France.

William received a wildly enthusiastic welcome in the capital, but in a historic gesture, he refused to accept the vacant throne by right of arms. Instead, he insisted that he be declared king by Parliament, subject to certain conditions set forth in a Bill of Rights. At a single stroke, the monarchy of England had become constitutional, and a bill of parliamentary succession replaced hereditary right. The bill affirmed free speech, free elections, prohibited the levying of taxes or the maintenance of a standing army without parliamentary consent, and made the king subject to the law. In Locke's phrase, the title of King William III was made good "in the consent of the people." Subsequent legislation enlarged upon this settlement and ensured parliamentary control over the army with a system of courts-martial (1689); freedom of worship for most (but not all) by the Religious Toleration Act (1689), which continued the established Church as episcopal but tolerated dissenting sects; regularized the election of a Parliament every three years (1694); allowed for a free press (1695); provided for the testimony of two witnesses in all treason trials (1696); and created from the excise tax a fixed Civil List for both the Crown's household and administrative expenditures (1698). The "illegal and pernicious" prerogative courts were also condemned. In not quite the same spirit (though born of the times) the Bill of Rights included a provision prohibiting the sovereign from being a Catholic, while the new coronation oath obliged him to uphold the "Protestant reformed religion established by law."

The Bill of Rights, however, did not envision universal suffrage, nor pretend to be a statement of the natural rights of man, as would later be affirmed in the United States and France. It was a bill framed by and for "gentlemen," and as such guaranteed the freedom and rights of the nobility and the gentry against the Crown. Although it recognized the coordinate authority of Parliament in military and financial matters, aspects of royal prerogative remained: the making of war and peace, the conduct of foreign policy, and the appointment and dismissal of government ministers.

Nevertheless, the constitutional settlement is justly remembered as the Glorious Revolution in English history because it bloodlessly accomplished so much. Moreover, all of its advances took place in the face of a wholly different trend on the Continent, where centralized bureaucracies under absolute monarchs were subjecting the will of the individual to the state. Under William III and his successor, Queen Anne, England contended against the new type of Continental autocracy personified in Louis XIV, King of France. "The wars against Louis," wrote Trevelyan, "may be regarded as the ordeal by battle which demonstrated the greater efficiency of the free community over the despotic state. This result greatly astonished and impressed a world that had up till that time held a diametrically opposite theory of power. Despotism, it had been thought, was the secret of efficiency; freedom was a luxury to be enjoyed. . . . The victory of parliamentary England over despotic France was a new fact of the first order; it was the prime cause of the intellectual movement abroad against despotism in Church and State."

The English Bible fairly marks the divide. For despite Cromwell's dictatorship, by and large those who pleaded for the rights of conscience, for free discussion, and for an unrestricted press were those who held to the supreme authority of Scripture in all things. And after James II issued his Declaration of Indulgence, it was the English Nonconformists who held the balance of power and risked their own immediate freedom on behalf of the freedom of the realm. The poet William Wordsworth later suggested that the alliance of his country's revolution with the Bible had spared it the bloodshed of the French:

> *France, 'tis strange,*
> *Hath brought forth no such souls as we had then.*
> *Perpetual emptiness! unceasing change!*
> *No SINGLE VOLUME PARAMOUNT, no code,*
> *No master spirit, no determined road;*
> *But equally a want of books and men!*

The Glorious Revolution stood the test of time. From 1689 onward "no king," writes Trevelyan, "attempted to govern without Parliament, or contrary to the votes of the House of Commons, or to override the liberties of the land." Emphasis was increasingly placed upon representative government as expressed by parliamentary sovereignty, or the idea that Parliament embodied the people's sovereign will. Indeed, by the middle of the eighteenth century much of English constitutional law was already statute law which Parliament had made or affirmed. This process coincided with the exaltation of natural reason as a reflection of the divine—the other, brighter side of the Puritan insistence on the ability of each and every human being to make contact with an inner light. In his *Essay Concerning Human Understanding*, Locke wrote: "God has furnished Men with Faculties sufficient to direct them in the Way they should take, if they will but seriously employ them," for God had given reason to every man, and reason "is natural Revelation, whereby the eternal Father of Light and Fountain of all Knowledge communicates to Mankind that Portion of Truth which he has laid within the Reach of their natural Faculties." Meanwhile, Thomas Hobbes had defined a law of nature as "a precept of general rule found out by reason, by which a man is forbidden to do that which is destructive of his life." And Hugo Grotius had given the doctrine a secular sanction when he insisted on the validity of natural law "even if we were to suppose . . . that God does not exist." From such law (or laws) the created laws of society, which establish peace and security, were said to derive.

American writers cited Locke, Hobbes, and Montesquieu on natural rights and almost ritualistically invoked Locke's trinity of life, liberty, and property as the precious and inherited natural rights of all free men. They believed that political authority was, or should be, derived from the consent of the governed and that its goal was the general good. Moreover, they believed they shared in a unique political inheritance. It was their historical understanding (based on the writings of Grotius and others) that the rights they claimed by way of the English could be traced back to the Anglo-Saxons (as depicted by Tacitus in his *Germania*), who had curbed royal power by introducing a measure of representative government. That had ultimately led to England's unwritten constitution, from which (in Daniel Boorstin's summary) trial by jury, due process of law, representation before taxation, habeas corpus, freedom from attainder, the independence of the judiciary, and the rights of free speech were all derived. As described by John Adams, the English constitution was "the most perfect combination of human powers in society which finite wisdom has yet contrived and reduced to practice for the preservation of liberty and the production of happiness." By the time the American Revolution began, statute law and natural law had in some sense become equated, notably in the work (popular among the Founding Fathers) of Sir William Blackstone, whose *Commentaries on the Laws of England* began to appear in 1765.

According to Blackstone, in whom all these strands were joined, all law, including statute law, owed its validity to its conformity to natural law, which was the basis of natural rights.

∞

Whereas in England the political tradition of opposition to arbitrary government had served as the foundation for a theory of parliamentary sovereignty, in America it formed the basis of a theory of limited government. Several of the American colonies were founded during the period of constitutional conflict in England, and they carried the continuing ferment of those ideas into the New World.

The legal forms evolved. In the political life of the American colonies, local elected bodies, aspiring to their own kind of parliamentary sovereignty, came into conflict with the colonial governors, who enjoyed the aura and some of the functions of royal power. The constitutional struggles witnessed in England were rapidly recapitulated, and by 1754, the American revolutionary theorist James Otis could declare in *The Rights of the British Colonies Asserted and Proved* that those rights which the colonists seemed determined to defend could not be annulled by British authority, because they derived from a source from which the authority of Parliament itself was drawn—natural law. That notion soon acquired something like a general assent, even among those not yet prepared to sever their ties to the empire. In his *Summary View of the Rights of British America* (1774) Thomas Jefferson expressed it succinctly when he wrote that Americans considered themselves "a free people, claiming their rights as derived from the laws of nature and not as the gift of their chief magistrate," the king.

These ideas found their most inspired expression in the Declaration of Independence, which appealed to "the Laws of Nature" and "self-evident" truths. When Jefferson wrote that "all men are created equal," he was speaking from within an inherited culture that accepted the right of every man to consider all matters according to his own reason and conscience. And that right implied equality. It was (or was regarded as) a sacred right, and that is part of what resounds in the sentence "We hold these truths to be sacred and undeniable," which was Jefferson's original turn of phrase. In emulation of his document, the French Declaration of the Rights of Man and of the Citizen would assert as "imprescriptible natural rights" liberty, property, security, and resistance to oppression.

But there always remained a cross-weave to this cloth. As long as Scripture could mean as many different things to as many people as read it, the deeply thought-through conclusions of the Church down through the ages were allowed no more stature than the cloudy revelations of individual minds. And insofar as those revelations prompted actions, chaos might result. No democracy, in fact, could fail to destroy itself without some restraint imposed upon liberty—as governing action—in this sense. There had to be a frame. The great unwritten Constitution of England, and the arguably greater written Constitution of the United States, with its Bill of Rights, took the theological place in Civil Society of the Received Wisdom laid down by Church councils and preserved in Creeds.

Although Protestants and Catholics remained divided over the respective weight of Scripture and Tradition, in politics this dichotomy was, in a sense, resolved. For Law, especially common law, was an example of Tradition, in all its secular and saving grace. And like the ongoing decisions of Church councils, that law became a kind of evolving Scripture for the evolution of a free society where everyone could also think, speak, and worship as he pleased. One could almost say that the modern democratic state owed its origins in part to a defiance of Catholic dogma, but ended by adopting one of its fundamental tenets in the secular sphere.

In America it was finally established that religion required no other aid from the state than the guardianship of the rights of conscience, as true religious toleration was finally enthroned in law. After the Revolution, George Washington sent a message to the Jewish congregation of Newport, Rhode Island, affirming that the government of the United States "gives to bigotry no sanctions, to persecution no assistance." And then he movingly adapted a phrase from 1 Kings 4:25: "Every one shall sit in safety under his own vine and fig tree and there shall be none to make him afraid."

G. K. Chesterton once wrote that in breaking away from England,

> America was not thinking so much of her wrongs as a
> colony, but already of her rights as a republic. . . . The real
> case for the colonists is that they felt they could be some-
> thing, which they also felt, and justly, that England would not
> help them to be. England would probably have allowed the
> colonists all sorts of concessions and constitutional privi-
> leges; but England could not allow the colonists equality: I
> do not mean equality with her, but even with each other.
> [William Pitt, the first earl of] Chatham might have compro-
> mised with Washington, because Washington was a gentle-
> man; but Chatham could hardly have conceived a country
> not governed by gentlemen. [Edmund] Burke [the British
> statesman and political thinker] was apparently ready to
> grant everything to America; but he would not have been
> ready to grant what America eventually gained. If he had
> seen American democracy, he would have been as much ap-
> palled by it as he was by French democracy, and would al-
> ways have been by any democracy. In a word, the Whigs
> were liberal and even generous aristocrats, but they were
> aristocrats; that is why their concessions were as vain as
> their conquests. . . . [The English] did not really drive away
> the American colonists, nor were they driven. The [Ameri-
> cans] were led on by a light that went before.

That light was a biblical light, which the English Bible had given
them: the idea of the equality of man. But no one faith could claim it
as its own. It was the idea of the sacred and equal importance of
every man, as made in the image of God.

Appendix One:
Chronology

ca. 1000 B.C.   First of the Old Testament writings

3rd century B.C.   Septuagint (translation of the Old Testament into Greek)

50 B.C.   Old Testament canon established

ca. A.D. 60   Joseph of Arimathea is said to arrive in Glastonbury, England

ca. A.D. 350   New Testament canon established

405   Vulgate (translation of the Bible into Latin by St. Jerome)

597   St. Augustine of Canterbury lands at Kent

1066   Norman Invasion

1213   King John of England surrenders to the pope

1305   "Babylonian Captivity" of papacy begins

1327   Accession of Edward III

ca. 1328   Birth of John Wycliffe

1338   Hundred Years' War begins

1378   Great Schism begins

1381   Peasants' Revolt

1382   Wycliffe Bible, First Version

1384   Death of Wycliffe

1395   Wycliffe Bible, Second Version

1401	Act *De Haeretico Comburendo*
1415	Council of Constance condemns Wycliffe as a heretic and orders his bones to be dug up and burned; Jan Hus burned at the stake
1453	Fall of Constantinople to the Turks
1455	Gutenberg Latin Bible is first book printed in movable type
1488	Birth of Miles Coverdale
ca. 1495	Birth of William Tyndale
1509	Accession of Henry VIII
1516	Erasmus's edition of the New Testament
1517	Publication of Luther's theses against indulgences
1525	Tyndale's New Testament
1524–25	Peasants' War in Germany
1529	Sir Thomas More becomes chancellor of England
1530	Tyndale's Pentateuch
1533	Henry VIII marries Anne Boleyn; Thomas Cranmer becomes Archbishop of Canterbury
1534	Act of Supremacy
1535	Thomas Cromwell becomes chancellor Coverdale's Bible
1536	Suppression of the monasteries begins; Pilgrimage of Grace; Tyndale burned at the stake
1537	Matthew's Bible
1539	Act of Six Articles; Great Bible licensed
1540	Execution of Thomas Cromwell
1545	Council of Trent begins
1546	Death of Luther
1547	Accession of Edward VI
1552	Book of Common Prayer
1553	Accession of Mary Tudor
1556	Cranmer burned at the stake
1559	Accession of Elizabeth I Acts of Supremacy and Uniformity
1560	Geneva Bible
1563	Thirty-nine Articles John Foxe's *Book of Martyrs*
1568	Bishops' Bible

1582	Rheims (Douai) New Testament
1587	Execution of Mary, Queen of Scots
1603	Accession of James I
1604	Hampton Court Conference
1605	Gunpowder Plot
1609–10	Douai Old Testament
1611	King James Version of the Bible
1625	Accession of Charles I
1643	English Civil War begins
1649	Execution of Charles I
1653	Oliver Cromwell becomes Lord Protector
1660	Restoration of monarchy; accession of Charles II
1685	Accession of James II
1688	Glorious Revolution; Accession of William III

Appendix Two:
The Evolution of the English Bible

THE BIBLE BEFORE THE INVENTION OF PRINTING

1. A.D. 597–1382: Metrical paraphrases, glosses, and fragmentary translations from the Old Latin and the Latin Vulgate.
2. 1382: The Wycliffe Bible, First Version (Hereford, from the Vulgate)
3. 1395: The Wycliffe Bible, Second Version (Purvey, from the Vulgate)

THE PRINTED BIBLE

1. 1525: Tyndale's New Testament (from the original Greek)
2. 1530: Tyndale's Pentateuch (from the original Hebrew)
3. 1537: Coverdale's Bible (the first complete Bible printed in English)
4. 1537: Matthew's Bible
5. 1539: Taverner's Bible
6. 1539: The Great Bible
7. 1560: The Geneva Bible
8. 1568: The Bishops' Bible
9. 1582: The Rheims (Douai) New Testament (from the Vulgate)

10. 1609–10: The Douai Old Testament (from the Vulgate)
11. 1611: The King James or Authorized Version
12. 1881–85: Revised Standard Version

Appendix Three:
Comparative Translations

JOHN 1:1–5

An Anglo-Saxon Version, possibly by the Venerable Bede
On fruman waes word, And thaet word waes mid Gode, And God waes thaet word. Thaet waes on fruman mid Gode. Ealle thing waeron geworhte thurh hyne, And nan thing naes geworht butan him.

Thaet waes lif the [that] on him geworht waes, And thaet lif waes manna leoht; And thaet leoht lyht on thystrum, And thystro thaet ne genamon:

(In the beginning was word, And that word was with God, And God was that word. That was in beginning with God. All things were made through him, And no thing was made without him. That was life that in him was made, And that life was men's light; And that light shone in darkness, And darkness that [light] did not take.)

Tyndale
In the beginning was the word, and the word was with God: and the word was God. The same was in the beginning with God. All things were made by it, and without it, was made nothing, that was made. In it was life, and the life was the light of men, and the light shineth in the darkness, but the darkness comprehended it not.

King James Version
1. In the beginning was the Word, and the Word was with God, and the Word was God.
2. The same was in the beginning with God.
3. All things were made by him; and without him was not any thing made that was made.
4. In him was life; and the life was the light of men.
5. And the light shineth in darkness; and the darkness comprehended it not.

GENESIS 8:11

Tyndale

And the dove came to him again about eventide, and behold: There was in her mouth a leaf of an olive tree which she had plucked, whereby Noe perceived that the waters were abated upon the earth.

Coverdale

She returned unto him about even tide, and behold, she had broken off a leaf of an olive tree and bare it in her nebb. Then Noah perceived that the waters were abated upon the earth.

Geneva Bible

And the dove came to him in the evening, and lo, in her mouth was an olive leaf that she had plucked, Whereby Noah knew that the waters were abated from off the earth.

Douai-Rheims Bible

And she came to him in the evening, carrying a bough of an olive tree, with green leaves, in her mouth. Noe therefore understood that the waters were ceased upon the earth.

King James Version

And the dove came in to him in the evening; and, lo, in her mouth was an olive leaf pluckt off: so Noah knew that the waters were abated from off the earth.

EXODUS 20:1–17 (THE TEN COMMANDMENTS)

King Alfred's Anglo-Saxon Code

Drihten waes sprecende thaes word to Moyse, and thus cwaeth: Ic eam Drihten thin God. Ic the ut gelaedde of Aegypta londe and of heora theowdome. Ne lufa thu othre fremde godas ofer me.

Ne minne naman ne cig thu on idelnesse. . . . Gemine that thu gehalgie thone feste (reste) daeg. . . . Ara thinum faeder and thinre meder. . . . Ne slea thu. Ne stala thu. Ne lige thu dearnunga.

Ne saege thu lease gewitnesse with thinum nehstan. Ne wilna thu thines nehstan yrfes mid unrihte. Ne wyrc thu the gyldene godas, oththe seolfrene.

(Lord was speaking these words to Moses, and said thus: I am Lord thy God. I led thee out of the land of Egypt and its thraldom. Not love thou other strange gods over me. Not my name utter thou in idleness. . . . Mind that thou hallow the festal [sabbath] day. . . . Honor thy father and thy mother. . . . Not slay thou. Not steal thou. Not commit thou adultery. Not say thou false witness against thy neighbor. Not desire thou thy neighbor's inheritance with unright [wrongfully]. Not work thou thee golden gods, or silver.)

Wycliffe Bible, Second Version

And the Lord spake all these words: I am thy Lord God, that led thee out of the land of Egypt, from the house of servage. Thou shalt not have alien gods before me. Thou shalt not make to thee a graven image, neither any likeness of thing which is in heaven above, and which is in earth beneath, neither of the things, that be in waters under earth, thou shalt not herye [honor] tho; neither thou shalt worship; for I am thy Lord God, a strong jealous lover; and I visit the wickedness of faders into the third and the fourth generation of them that haten me, and I do mercy in to a thousand to them that loven me and keep mine hests. Thou shalt not take in vain the name of thy Lord God, for the Lord shall not have him guiltless that taketh in vain the name of his Lord God. Have thou mind that thou hallow the day of the sabbath; in six days thou shalt work and shalt do all thy works; forsooth in the seventh day is the sabbath of thy Lord God; thou shalt not do any work, thou, and thy son, and thy daughter, and thy servant, and thine handmaid, thy work beast, and the comeling [stranger] that is within thy gates; for in six days God made heaven and earth, the sea and all things that been in them, and rested in the seventh day; wherefore the Lord blessed the day of the sabbath and hallowed it. Honor thy father and thy mother, that thou be long living on the land, which the Lord and thy God shall give to thee. Thou shalt not slay. Thou shalt do no lechery. Thou shalt do not theft. Thou shalt not speak false witnessing against thy neighbor. Thou shalt not covet the house of thy neighbor, neither thou shalt desire his wife, not servant, not handmaid, not ox, not ass, neither all things that be his.

Tyndale

And God spake all these words and said: I am the Lord thy God, which have brought thee out of the land of Egypt, and out of the house of bondage. Thou shalt have none other Gods in my sight. Thou shalt make thee no graven image, neither any similitude that is in heaven above, either in the earth beneath, or in the water that is beneath the earth. See that thou neither bow thyself unto them neither serve them: for I the Lord thy God, am a jealous God, and visit the sin of the fathers upon the children unto the third and fourth generation of them that hate me: and yet show mercy unto thousands among them that love me and keep my commandments.

Thou shalt not take the name of the Lord thy God in vain, for the Lord will not hold him guiltless that taketh his name in vain.

Remember the sabbath day that thou sanctify it. Six days mayst thou labor and do all that thou hast to do: but the seventh day is the Sabbath of the Lord thy God; in it thou shalt do no manner work: neither thou nor thy son, nor thy daughter, neither thy manservant, nor thy maidservant, neither thy cattle neither yet the stranger that is within thy gates. For in six days the Lord made both heaven and earth and the sea, and all that in them is, and rested the seventh day: wherefore the Lord blessed the sabbath day and hallowed it.

Honor thy father and thy mother, that thy days may be long in the land which the Lord thy God giveth thee.

Thou shalt not kill.

Thou shalt not break wedlock.

Thou shalt not steal.

Thou shalt bear no false witness against thy neighbor.

Thou shalt not covet thy neighbor's house: neither shalt covet thy neighbor's wife, his manservant, his maid, his ox, his ass or aught that is his.

Coverdale

And the Lord spake all these words, and said: I am the Lord thy God, which have brought thee out of the land of Egypt from the house of bondage.

Thou shalt have none other Gods in my sight. Thou shalt make thee no graven image, nor any similitude, neither of it that is above in heaven, nor of it that is beneath upon earth, neither of it that is in the water under the earth. Worship them not, and serve them not: for I the Lord thy God am a jealous God, visiting the sin of the fathers upon the children, unto the third and fourth generation of them that hate me; and do mercy upon many thousands that love me and keep my commandments.

Thou shalt not take the name of the Lord thy God in vain. For the Lord shall not hold him unguilty that taketh his name in vain.

Remember the Sabbath day that thou do sanctify it. Six days shalt thou labor and do all thy work: But upon the seventh day is the Sabbath of the Lord thy God; thou shalt do no manner of work in it, neither thou, nor thy son, nor thy daughter, nor thy servant, nor thy maid, nor thy cattle, nor thy stranger that is within thy gates. For in six days the Lord made heaven and earth, and the sea and all that therein is, and rested upon the seventh day; therefore the Lord blessed the seventh day and hallowed it.

Honor thy father and thy mother, that thou mayest live long in the land, which the Lord thy God shall give thee.

Thou shalt not kill.

Thou shalt not break wedlock.

Thou shalt not steal.

Thou shalt bear no false witness against thy neighbor.

Thou shalt not lust after thy neighbor's house. Thou shalt not lust after thy neighbor's wife, nor his servant, nor his maid, nor his ox, nor his ass, nor all that thy neighbor hath.

King James Version

1. And God spake all these words, saying,
2. I am the Lord thy God, which have brought thee out of the land of Egypt, out of the house of bondage.
3. Thou shalt have no other gods before me.
4. Thou shalt not make unto thee any graven image, or any likeness of any thing that is in heaven above, or that is in the earth beneath, or that is in the water under the earth:
5. Thou shalt not bow down thyself to them, nor serve them: for I the Lord thy God am a jealous God, visiting the iniquity of the fathers upon the children unto the third and fourth generation of them that hate me;
6. And shewing mercy unto thousands of them that love me, and keep my commandments.
7. Thou shalt not take the name of the Lord thy God in vain; for the Lord will not hold him guiltless that taketh his name in vain.
8. Remember the sabbath day, to keep it holy.
9. Six days shalt thou labour, and do all thy work:
10. But the seventh day is the sabbath of the Lord thy God: in it thou shalt not do any work, thou, nor thy son, nor thy daughter, thy manservant, nor thy maidservant, nor thy cattle, nor thy stranger that is within thy gates:
11. For in six days the Lord made heaven and earth, the sea, and all that

in them is, and rested the seventh day: wherefore the Lord blessed the sabbath day, and hallowed it.

12. Honour thy father and thy mother: that thy days may be long upon the land which the Lord thy God giveth thee.
13. Thou shalt not kill.
14. Thou shalt not commit adultery.
15. Thou shalt not steal.
16. Thou shalt not bear false witness against thy neighbor.
17. Thou shalt not covet thy neighbour's house, thou shalt not covet thy neighbour's wife, nor his manservant, nor his maidservant, nor his ox, nor his ass, nor any thing that is thy neighbour's.

JUDGES 5:25–27

Tyndale

He asked water, but she gave him milk, and brought butter in a goodly dish. She caught a nail in her left hand, and a working hammer in her right, and nailed Sisera and wounded his head and pierced and went through his temples. Between her feet he bowed himself, fell down and lay still: Between her feet he bowed himself and fell. And whither he bowed himself, thither he fell brought to nought.

Bishops' Bible

He asked water and she gave him milk, she brought forth butter in a lordly dish. She put her hand to the nail, and her right hand to the smith's hammer; with the hammer smote she Sisera and smote his head, wounded him and pierced his temples. He bowed him down at her feet, he fell down, and lay still at her feet, he bowed himself and fell, and when he had sunk down, he lay there destroyed.

Geneva Bible

25. He asked water, and she gave him milk: she brought forth butter in a lordly dish.
26. She put her hand to the nail, and her right hand to the workman's hammer: with the hammer smote she Sisera: she smote off his head, after she had wounded and pierced his temples.
27. He bowed him down at her feet, he fell down, and lay still: at her feet he bowed him down, and fell: and when he had sunk down, he lay there dead.

Douai-Rheims Bible

25. He asked her water and she gave him milk, and offered him butter in a dish fit for princes.
26. She put her left hand to the nail, and her right hand to the workman's hammer, and she struck Sisera, seeking in his head a place for the wound, and strongly piercing through his temples.
27. At her feet he fell: he fainted, and he died: he rolled before her feet, and he lay lifeless and wretched.

King James Version

25. He asked water, and she gave him milk; she brought forth butter in a lordly dish.
26. She put her hand to the nail, and her right hand to the workman's hammer; and with the hammer she smote Sisera, she smote off his head, when she had pierced and stricken through his temples.
27. At her feet he bowed, he fell, he lay down: at her feet he bowed, he fell: where he bowed, there he fell down dead.

I KINGS 10:4–5

Tyndale

And when the queen of Saba had seen all Solomon's wisdom and the house that he had built, and the meat of his table, and the sitting of his servants, and the standing of his servitors and their apparel, and his butlers and his sacrifice that he offered in the house of the Lord, she was astonished.

Coverdale

When the queen of rich Arabia saw all the wisdom of Solomon and the house that he had builded, and the meats of his table, and the dwellings of his servants, and the offices of his ministers and their garments, and his butlers, and the burnt offerings which he offered in the house of the Lord, she wondered accordingly.

Geneva Bible

4. Then the queen of Sheba saw all Solomon's wisdom, and the houses he had built,
5. And the meat of his table, and the sitting of his servants, and the

order of his ministers, and their apparel, and his drinking vessels, and his burnt offerings, that he offered in the house of the Lord, and she was greatly astonished.

Douai-Rheims Bible (3 Kings, according to its order of the books)

4. And when the queen of Saba saw all the wisdom of Solomon, and the house which he had built,
5. And the meat of his table, and the apartments of his servants, and the order of his ministers, and their apparel, and the cupbearers, and the holocausts, which he offered in the house of the Lord: she had no longer any spirit in her.

King James Version

4. And when the queen of Sheba had seen all Solomon's wisdom, and the house that he had built,
5. And the meat of his table, and the sitting of his servants, and the attendance of his ministers, and their apparel, and his cupbearers, and his ascent by which he went up unto the house of the Lord; there was no more spirit in her.

JOB 14:1–2

Coverdale

Man that is born of a woman hath but a short time to live and is full of diverse miseries. He cometh up and falleth away like a flower. . . .

Geneva Bible

1. Man that is born of woman, is of short continuance and full of trouble.
2. He shooteth forth as a flower, and is cut down. . . .

Douai-Rheims Bible

1. Man born of a woman, living for a short time, is filled with many miseries.
2. Who cometh forth like a flower, and is destroyed. . . .

King James Version

1. Man that is born of a woman is of few days, and full of trouble.
2. He cometh forth like a flower, and is cut down. . . .

PSALM 23

Geneva Bible

The Lord is my shepherd. I shall not want. He maketh me to rest in green pasture, and leadeth me by the still waters. . . . Doubtless kindness and mercy shall follow me all the days of my life, and I shall remain a long season in the house of the Lord.

Bishops' Bible

God is my shepherd, therefore I can lack nothing. He will cause me to repose myself in pasture full of grass, and he will lead me unto calm waters. He will convert my soul. . . . Truly felicity and mercy shall follow me all the days of my life, and I will dwell in the house of God for a long time.

Douai-Rheims Bible (Psalm 22, according to its numbering)

1. The Lord ruleth me: and I shall want nothing.
2. He hath set me in a place of pasture. He hath brought me up on the water of refreshment:
3. He hath converted my soul. . . .
6. And thy mercy will follow me all the days of my life. And that I may dwell in the house of the Lord unto length of days.

King James Version

1. The Lord is my shepherd; I shall not want.
2. He maketh me to lie down in green pastures: he leadeth me beside the still waters.
3. He restoreth my soul. . . .
6. Surely goodness and mercy shall follow me all the days of my life: and I will dwell in the house of the Lord for ever.

ECCLESIASTES 12:1–8

Great Bible, Cranmer's Edition

Remember thy maker in thy youth, or ever the days of adversity come, and or the years draw nigh, when thou shalt say: I have not pleasure in them: before the sun, the light, the moon and stars be darkened, and or the clouds turn again after the rain, when the keepers of the house shall tremble, and when the strong men shall bow them selves: when the millers stand still, because they be so few, and when the sight of the windows shall wax dim: when the doors in the streets shall be shut, and when the voice of the miller shall be laid down: when men shall rise up at the voice of the bird, and when all the daughters of music shall be brought low: when men shall fear in high places, and be afraid in the streets: when the Almond tree shall flourish and be laden with the grasshopper, and when all lust shall pass (because when man goeth to his long home, and the mourners go about the streets). Or ever the silver lace be taken away, and or the golden band be broken: Or the pot be broken at the well, and the wheel upon the cistern: Then shall the dust be turned again unto earth from whence it came, and the spirit shall return unto God, which gave it. All is but vanity (saith the Preacher) all is but plain vanity.

Geneva Bible

1. Remember now thy Creator in the days of thy youth, whiles the evil days come not, nor the years approach, wherein thou shalt say, I have no pleasure in them:
2. Whiles the sun is not dark, nor the light, nor the moon, nor the stars, nor the clouds return after the rain:
3. When the keepers of the house shall tremble, and the strong men shall bow them selves, and the grinders shall cease, because they are few, and they wax dark that look out by the windows:
4. And the doors shall be shut without by the base sound of the grinding, and he shall rise up at the voice of the bird: and all the daughters of singing shall be abased.
5. Also they shall be afraid of the high thing, and fear shall be in the way, and the almond tree shall flourish and the grasshopper shall be a burden, and concupiscence shall be driven away: for man goeth to the house of his age, and the mourners go about in the street.
6. Whiles the silver cord is not lengthened, nor the golden ewer broken, nor the pitcher broken at the well, nor the wheel broken at the cistern:
7. And dust return to the earth as it was, and the spirit return to God that gave it.
8. Vanity of vanities, saith the Preacher, all is vanity.

Bishops' Bible

1. Remember thy maker the sooner in thy youth, or ever the days of adversity come, and or the years draw nigh when thou shalt say, I have not pleasure in them.

2. Before the sun, the light, the mood, and stars be darkened, and or the clouds turn again after the rain:
3. When the keepers of the house shall tremble, and when the strong men shall bow them selves, when the millers stand still because they be so few, and when the sight of the windows shall wax dim:
4. When the doors in the streets shall be shut, and when the voice of the miller shall be laid down, when men shall rise up at the voice of the bird, and when all the daughters of music shall be brought low:
5. When men shall fear in hie places, and be afraid in the streets, when the Almond tree shall flourish, and be laden with the grasshopper, and when all lust shall pass: because man goeth to his long home, and the mourners go about the streets:
6. Or ever the silver lace be taken away, and or the golden well be broken: Or the pot be broken at the well, and the wheel broken upon the cistern.
7. Then shall the dust be turned again unto earth from whence it came, and the spirit shall return unto God who gave it.
8. All is vanity (saith the preacher) all is but plain vanity.

Douai-Rheims Bible

1. Remember thy Creator in the days of thy youth, before the time of affliction come, and the years draw nigh of which thou shalt say: They please me not:
2. Before the sun, and the light, and the moon, and the stars be darkened, and the clouds return after the rain:
3. When the keepers of the house shall tremble, and the strong men shall stagger, and the grinders shall be idle in a small number, and they that look through the holes shall be darkened:
4. And they shall shut the doors in the street, when the grinder's voice shall be low, and they shall rise up at the voice of the bird, and all the daughters of music shall grow deaf.
5. And they shall fear high things, and they shall be afraid in the way, the almond tree shall flourish, the locust shall be made fat, and the caper tree shall be destroyed: because man shall go into the house of his eternity, and the mourners shall go round about in the street.
6. Before the silver cord be broken, and the golden fillet shrink back, and the pitcher be crushed at the fountain, and the wheel be broken upon the cistern,

7. And the dust return into its earth, from whence it was, and the spirit return to God, who gave it.
8. Vanity of vanities, said Ecclesiastes, and all things are vanity.

King James Version

1. Remember now thy Creator in the days of thy youth, while the evil days come not, nor the years draw nigh, when thou shalt say, I have no pleasure in them;
2. While the sun, or the light, or the moon, or the stars, be not darkened, nor the clouds return after the rain:
3. In the day when the keepers of the house shall tremble, and the strong men shall bow themselves, and the grinders cease because they are few, and those that look out of the windows be darkened,
4. And the doors shall be shut in the streets, when the sound of the grinding is low, and he shall rise up at the voice of the bird, and all the daughters of musick shall be brought low;
5. Also when they shall be afraid of that which is high, and fears shall be in the way, and the almond tree shall flourish, and the grasshopper shall be a burden, and desire shall fail: because man goeth to his long home, and the mourners go about the streets:
6. Or ever the silver cord be loosed, or the golden bowl be broken, or the pitcher be broken at the fountain, or the wheel broken at the cistern.
7. Then shall the dust return to the earth as it was: and the spirit shall return unto God who gave it.
8. Vanity of vanities, saith the preacher; all is vanity.

1 CORINTHIANS 13:1–2

Wycliffe Bible, Second Version

If I speak with tongues of men and angels, and I have not charity, I am made as brass sounding or a cymbal tinkling, and if I have prophecy, and know all mysteries, and all knowledge, and if I have all faith so that I move hills from their place, and I have not charity, I am nought.

Tyndale

Though I spake with the tongues of men and angels, and yet had no love, I were even as sounding brass: or as a tinkling cymbal. And though I could prophesy, and understood all secrets, and all knowledge: yea, if I had all faith so that I could move mountains out of their places, and yet had no love, I were nothing.

Douai-Rheims Bible

1. If I speak with the tongues of men, and of angels, and have not charity, I am become as sounding brass, or a tinkling cymbal.
2. And if I should have prophecy and should know all mysteries, and all knowledge, and if I should have all faith, so that I could remove mountains, and have not charity, I am nothing.

King James Version

1. Though I speak with the tongues of men and of angels, and have not charity, I am become as sounding brass, or a tinkling cymbal.
2. And though I have the gift of prophecy, and understand all mysteries, and all knowledge; and though I have all faith, so that I could remove mountains, and have not charity, I am nothing.

Appendix Four:
The King James Translators,
by Company and Assignment

FIRST WESTMINSTER COMPANY
(GENESIS THROUGH 2 KINGS)

Lancelot Andrewes: Dean of Westminster; Bishop of Chichester (1605).

John Overall: Dean of St. Paul's.

Hadrian a Saravia: Prebendary of Westminster, Canterbury, and Worcester; Vicar of Lewisham, Kent.

John Layfield: Fellow of Trinity College, Cambridge; Rector of St. Clement Danes, London.

William Bedwell: Rector of St. Ethelburga's, London.

Richard Thomson: Fellow of Clare College, Cambridge.

Robert Tighe: Archdeacon of Middlesex and Vicar of All Hallows, Barking, London.

Francis Burleigh: Fellow of Chelsea College, London.

Geoffrey King: Fellow of King's College, Cambridge; Regius Professor of Hebrew, Cambridge (1607).

Richard Clarke: Fellow of Christ's College, Cambridge; Vicar of Munster on the Isle of Thanet, Kent.

FIRST CAMBRIDGE COMPANY
(1 CHRONICLES THROUGH THE SONG OF SOLOMON)

Edward Lively: Regius Professor of Hebrew, Cambridge.

John Richardson: Rector of Upwell, Norfolk; Regius Professor of Divinity, Cambridge (1607).

Laurence Chaderton: Master of Emmanuel College, Cambridge.

Francis Dillingham: Fellow of Christ's College, Cambridge.

Thomas Harrison: Fellow of Trinity College, Cambridge.

Roger Andrewes: Rector of St. Martin's, Ongar, Essex.

Robert Spalding: Fellow of St. John's College, Cambridge; Regius Professor of Hebrew (1605).

Andrew Bing: Fellow of Peterhouse; Regius Professor of Hebrew (1608).

FIRST OXFORD COMPANY
(ISAIAH THROUGH MALACHI)

John Harding: Regius Professor of Hebrew, Oxford; President of Magdalen College (1607).

John Reynolds: President of Corpus Christi College, Oxford.

Thomas Holland: Rector of Exeter College, Oxford.

Richard Kilbye: Rector of Lincoln College, Oxford; Regius Professor of Hebrew (1610).

Miles Smith: Prebendary of Hereford and Exeter Cathedrals.

Richard Brett: Rector of Quainton, Buckinghamshire; Fellow of Lincoln College, Oxford.

Richard Fairclough: Rector of Bucknell, Oxfordshire; Fellow of New College, Oxford.

William Thorne: Rector of Tallard Royal, Wiltshire.

SECOND CAMBRIDGE COMPANY (THE APOCRYPHA)

John Duport: Master of Jesus College, Cambridge; Prebendary of Ely Cathedral.

Samuel Ward: Master of Sidney Sussex College, Cambridge.

Andrew Downes: Fellow of St. John's College, Cambridge; Regius Professor of Greek.

John Bois: Fellow of St. John's College, Cambridge; Rector of Boxworth, Cambridgeshire.

Jeremiah Radcliffe: Fellow of Trinity College, Cambridge; Vicar of Orwell, Cambridgeshire.

Robert Ward: Fellow of King's College, Cambridge.

William Branthwaite: Fellow of Emmanuel College, Cambridge.

SECOND OXFORD COMPANY
(THE GOSPELS, ACTS, AND REVELATION)

Thomas Ravis: Dean of Christ's Church College, Oxford; Bishop of Gloucester (1605); Bishop of London (1607).

Sir Henry Savile: Warden of Merton College, Oxford; Provost of Eton.

George Abbot: Dean of Winchester Cathedral; Bishop of Lichfield and Coventry (1609); Bishop of London (1610); Archbishop of Canterbury (1611).

John Harmer: Fellow of New College, Oxford.

John Perin: Regius Professor of Greek, Oxford.

Giles Thomson: Fellow of All Soul's College, Oxford; Dean of Windsor.

Richard Edes: Dean of Worcester.

John Aglionby: Principal of St. Edmund Hall.

James Montague: Dean of Worcester, succeeding Edes; Bishop of Bath and Wells (1608).

Ralph Ravens: Rector of Great Easton, Essex; Fellow of St. John's College, Oxford.

Leonard Hutten: Canon of Christ Church, Oxford.

**SECOND WESTMINSTER COMPANY
(ROMANS THROUGH JUDE)**

William Barlow: Dean of Chester; Bishop of Rochester (1605).
John Spencer: President of Corpus Christi College, Oxford (1607).
Roger Fenton: Fellow of Pembroke College, Cambridge.
Thomas Sanderson: Rector of All Hallows, London.
Michael Rabbett: Fellow of Trinity College, Cambridge.
Ralph Hutchinson: President of St. John's College, Oxford.
William Dakins: Professor of Divinity, Gresham College, London.

Appendix Five
Richard Bancroft's "Rules to Be Observed in the Translation of the Bible"

1. The ordinary Bible read in the Church, commonly called the *Bishops Bible,* to be followed, and as little altered as the Truth of the original will permit.
2. The Names of the Prophets, and the Holy Writers, with the other Names of the Text, to be retained, as nigh as may be, accordingly as they were vulgarly used.
3. The old Ecclesiastical Words to be kept, viz. the Word *Church* not to be translated *Congregation &c.*
4. When a word hath divers Significations, that to be kept which hath been most commonly used by the most of the Ancient Fathers, being agreeable to the Propriety of the Place and the Analogy of the Faith.
5. The Division of the Chapters to be altered, either not at all, or as little as may be, if Necessity so require.
6. No Marginal Notes at all to be affixed, but only for the Explanation of the *Hebrew* or *Greek* Words, which cannot without some circumlocution, so briefly and fitly be express'd in the Text.
7. Such Quotations of Places to be marginally set down as shall serve for the fit Reference of one Scripture to another.
8. Every particular Man of each Company, to take the same Chapter, or Chapters, and having translated or amended them severally by

himself, where he thinketh good, all to meet together, confer what they have done, and agree for their Parts what shall stand.

9. As any one Company hath dispatched any one Book in this Manner they shall send it to the rest, to be consider'd of seriously and judiciously, for His Majesty is very careful in this Point.

10. If any Company, upon the Review of the Book so sent, doubt or differ upon any Place, to send them Word thereof; note the Place, and withal send the Reasons, to which if they consent not, the Difference to be compounded at the General Meeting, which is to be of the chief Persons of each Company, at the end of the Work.

11. When any Place of special Obscurity is doubted of Letters to be directed, by Authority, to send to any Learned Man in the Land, for his Judgment of such a Place.

12. Letters to be sent from every Bishop to the rest of his Clergy, admonishing them of this Translation in hand; and to move and charge as many as being skilful in the Tongues; and having taken Pains in that kind, to send his particular Observations to the Company, either at *Westminster, Cambridge* or *Oxford*.

13. The Directors in each Company, to be the Deans of Westminster and Chester for that Place; and the King's Professors in the *Hebrew* or *Greek* in either University.

14. These translations to be used when they agree better with the Text than the Bishops Bible: *Tindall's* [Tyndale's], *Matthews, Coverdale's, Whitchurch's* [the Great Bible, identified by its publisher], *Geneva*.

15. Besides the said Directors before mentioned, three or four of the most Ancient and Grave Divines, in either of the Universities, not employed in Translating, to be assigned by the Vice-Chancellor, upon Conference with the rest of the Heads, to be Overseers of the Translations as well *Hebrew* as *Greek*, for the better Observation of the 4th Rule above specified.

Notes

For abbreviations used in the notes, and for full titles and other bibliographical information on books, articles, and other documents cited, the reader is referred to the Bibliography.

PROLOGUE

PAGE

12   *"formerly imprisoned"*: Hill, *The English Bible*, p. 7.
12   *"a living memory"*: Storr, *The English Bible*, p. 79.
12   *"than the greatest"*: Ibid.
12   *the deeds and thoughts*: Trevelyan, *History of England*, vol. 2, p. 135.
12   *"as wide as the waters be"*: Quoted in *The Oxford Companion to English Literature*, p. 901.
15   *"commendable promptness"*: Robinson, *The Bible in Its Ancient and English Versions*, p. 111.
15   *"tainted with Judaism"*: Ibid., p. 115.
15   *"a halo of sanctity"*: Price, *The Ancestry of Our English Bible*, p. 88.

15   *"If my occupation"*: Quoted in Phillips, *Translators and Translations,* p. 11.

CHAPTER ONE: MORNING STAR

PAGE

21   *"came in by way of Wales"*: Wild, *The Romance of the English Bible,* p. 22.

22   *"preach the Gospel"*: Mark 16:15.

22   *"Behold, the tongue"*: Quoted in Ogg, *A Source Book of Medieval History,* p. 74.

23   *"Catholic unity"*: Bede, *Ecclesiastical History of the English People,* p. 104.

23   *The pope can be judged:* Quoted in Bokenkotter, *A Concise History of the Catholic Church,* p. 112.

24   *the example it presented:* The Cambridge Medieval History, vol. 6, p. 643.

24   *"still, small"*: 1 Kings 19:12.

24   *"The preaching of the Word"*: Quoted in Stacey, *John Wycliffe and Reform,* p. 82.

26   *"by apples and drink"*: Quoted in Winn, *Wycliffe,* p. 171.

26   *"Once he had taken"*: Trevelyan, *England in the Age of Wycliffe,* p. 297.

26   *"on whom we have fixed"*: Quoted in Lupton, *Wycliffe's Wicket,* p. 38.

27   *"reared on the syllogisms"*: Stacey, *John Wycliffe and Reform,* p. 157.

27   *"second to none"*: Quoted in Workman, *John Wycliffe,* vol. 1, p. 4.

27   *"Dear God, help me"*: Quoted in ibid., p. 334.

27   *"Does the glorified body"*: Examples from Conant, *The Popular History,* p. 21.

27   *"He had an eager hatred"*: Trevelyan, *England in the Age of Wycliffe,* p. 105.

28   *"vindictive zeal"*: Quoted in Stacey, *John Wycliffe and Reform,* p. 22.

28   *"a Doctor who praised"*: Lupton, *Wycliffe's Wicket,*, p. 29.

28   *"all human activity"*: Robson, *Wycliffe and the Oxford Schools,* p. 38.

28   *"Let a man repent"*: Quoted in Lechler, *John Wycliffe and His English Predecessors*, p. 272.

29   *"as a force"*: Stacey, *John Wycliffe and Reform*, p. 7.

29   *"The house of God"*: Quoted in Lupton, *Wycliffe's Wicket*, p. 15.

29   *"spare, frail"*: Quoted in ibid., p. 13.

30   *A good man was ther:* Chaucer, *Canterbury Tales*, "The Prologue," ll. 477–90.

30   *"There are several"*: Stacey, *John Wycliffe and Reform*, p. 14.

30   *"a perfect liver"*: Quoted in Lupton, *Wycliffe's Wicket*, p. 13.

31   *"at every level"*: Quoted in Bokenkotter, *A Concise History*, p. 178.

31   *"everything could be obtained"*: Quoted in Grierson, *The English Bible*, p. 8.

31   *"The deadlock"*: Bokenkotter, *A Concise History*, p. 159.

33   *the tacit renunciation:* Hoare, *The Evolution of the English Bible*, p. 63.

33   *"the pope could draw"*: Bainton, *The Reformation of the Sixteenth Century*, p. 230.

33   *"the central bank"*: Ibid.

34   *"as far removed"*: Lechler, *John Wycliffe*, p. 44.

34   *"a receptacle of all"*: Quoted in Conant, *The Popular History*, p. 33.

35   *Let them be accursed:* Quoted in ibid., p. 7.

35   *"the exhibition"*: Ibid., p. 8.

35   *"a gloomy, isolated"*: Ibid., p. 9.

35   *"He was an esy man"*: Chaucer, *Canterbury Tales*, "Prologue," ll. 221–23.

36   *"proverbial for their effrontery"*: Hoare, *Evolution of the English Bible*, p. 85.

36   *Round many a convent's:* Quoted in Conant, *The Popular History*, p. 16.

36   *"God gave his sheep"*: Quoted in Trevelyan, *History of England*, vol. 1, p. 101.

37   *"and for this reason"*: Quoted in Conant, *The Popular History*, p. 40.

37   *"Men wonder highly"*: Quoted in ibid., p. 40.

37   *"one cope and hood"*: Quoted in Workman, *John Wycliffe*, vol. 2, p. 94.

38   *"Just so"*: Quoted in Lechler, *John Wycliffe*, p. 135.

40   *"to allow its authority"*: Trevelyan, *England in the Age of Wycliffe*, p. 43.

40   *"what masteries"*: Quoted in Lechler, *John Wycliffe*, p. 138.

40 *"Since you have much"*: Quoted in Trevelyan, *England in the Age of Wycliffe*, p. 44.

40 *"should stand"*: Cammack, *John Wycliffe*, p. 17.

40 *"contrary to reason"*: Quoted in Lupton, *Wycliffe's Wicket*, p. 89.

41 *"You put your trust"*: Quoted in ibid., p. 90.

41 *"wild with fear"*: Quoted in ibid., p. 91.

41 *"We have learned"*: Quoted in Dahmus, *The Prosecution of John Wycliffe*, p. 39.

42 *"a lad of eleven years"*: Quoted in Lupton, *Wycliffe's Wicket*, p. 92.

42 *"lawfully, in its own"*: Quoted in ibid., p. 93.

42 *"asinine stupidity"*: Quoted in ibid.

42 *"silence was imposed"*: Quoted in ibid.

42 *"to give the pope"*: Dahmus, *The Prosecution*, p. 62.

43 *"sounded poorly"*: Quoted in Trevelyan, *England in the Age of Wycliffe*, p. 85.

43 *"to the manifest forfeiture"*: Quoted in Conant, *The Popular History*, p. 38.

43 *"In this way"*: Quoted in Trevelyan, *England in the age of Wycliffe*, p. 86.

44 *"amid the wailing"*: Workman, *John Wycliffe*, vol. 2, p. 46.

44 *"cattle wandered"*: Ibid., p., 46.

44 *"insatiable avarice"*: Quoted in ibid., p. 48.

44 *"clothed in white"*: Ibid.

45 *"an abiding heretic"*: Quoted in Lupton, *Wycliffe's Wicket*, p. 100.

45 *"You will be torn"*: Quoted in ibid.

45 *"providing our mother church"*: Quoted in Workman, *John Wycliffe*, vol. 2, p. 54.

45 *"I tell you"*: Quoted in ibid., p. 56.

45 *"like a sparrow"*: Quoted in ibid.

46 *"Many noble"*: Quoted in Stacey, *John Wycliffe and Reform*, p. 31.

46 *"Some think that if"*: Quoted in Winn, *Wycliffe*, p. 124.

46 *"blessed in heaven"*: Quoted in Stacey, *John Wycliffe and Reform*, p. 49.

47 *"gorge rose"*: Trevelyan, *England in the Age of Wycliffe*, p. 179.

47 *"as wheat"*: Lechler, *John Wycliffe*, p. 274.

48 *"For no pope"*: Quoted in Stacey, *John Wycliffe and Reform*, p. 100.

48 *"Who knows the measure"*: Quoted in ibid., p. 97.

48 *"Were there a hundred"*: Quoted in Wild, *The Romance of the English Bible*, p. 41.

48 *"added a new doctrine"*: Workman, *John Wycliffe*, vol. 2, p. 51.

49 *"it is a life":* Quoted in Lechler, *John Wycliffe*, p. 273.
49 *"claimed no authority":* Stacey, *John Wycliffe and Reform*, p. 30.
49 *"a knowledge of those times":* Winn, *Wycliffe*, p. 79.
49 *"with common parts":* Quoted in Lupton, *Wycliffe's Wicket*, p. 113.
49 *"some jingle":* Stacey, *John Wycliffe and Reform*, p. 74.
50 *"the New Testament":* Quoted in Workman, *John Wycliffe*, vol. 2, p. 151.
50 *"to address himself":* Quoted in Lechler, *John Wycliffe*, p. 184.
50 *"might sweetly minister":* Quoted in Lupton, *Wycliffe's Wicket*, p. 109.
51 *"more open to":* Quoted in Moulton, *The Library of Literary Criticism*, vol. 1, p. 102.
51 *"notwithstanding that she":* Quoted in Deanesly, *The Lollard Bible*, p. 445.
52 *"Master, there is":* Quoted in Brown, *The History of the English Bible*, p. 106.
52 *"in the cradle":* Quoted in Green, *A Short History of England*, p. 255.
53 *"warmer and more exotic":* Hook, The Story of British English, p. 130.
53 *"good and cunning":* Quoted in Forshall and Madden, *The Holy Bible*, vol. 1, pp. 57-58.
56 *"phantasm":* See Lupton, *Wycliffe's Wicket*, p. 108.
57 *"Of all the heresies":* Quoted in Conant, *The Popular History*, p. 45.
57 *"to make the body":* Lupton, *Wycliffe's Wicket*, p. 107.
57 *"Who could set":* Conant, *The Popular History*, p. 45.
58 *"I believe, as Christ":* Quoted in Winn, *Wycliffe*, p. 87.
58 *"thou mayst see":* Quoted in Workman, *John Wycliffe*, vol. 2, p. 37.
58 *"What we see":* Quoted in Lechler, *John Wycliffe*, p. 344.
58 *"Yea! even irrational":* Quoted in Lechler, p. 346.
58 *"Let us accept":* Quoted in Winn, *Wycliffe*, p. 68.
58 *"animated by":* Hoare, *The Evolution*, p. 86.
59 *"the most blessed":* Quoted in Lupton, *Wycliffe's Wicket*, p. 79.
59 *"a vast floating":* Trevelyan, *England in the Age of Wycliffe*, p. 229.
60 *he was accustomed:* Quoted in ibid., p. 196.
60 *"encamped on St. Catherine's Hill":* Ibid., p. 232.
60 *"the young king":* Ibid.
61 *"Sire, if you":* Quoted in ibid., p. 233.
61 *"commutation of all":* Ibid.
61 *"If they had":* Ibid., p. 235.

61 *"Sirs, will you"*: Quoted in Fraser, *The Lives of the Kings and Queens of England*, p. 110.

62 *"Villeins ye are"*: Quoted in *Encyclopaedia Britannica*, vol. 29, p. 43.

62 *"we would have ended"*: Quoted in Lechler, *John Wycliffe*, p. 377.

62 *"wrongs by extortions"*: Quoted in Trevelyan, *England in the Age of Wycliffe*, p. 201.

62 *"Oh how happy"*: Quoted in Lupton, *Wycliffe's Wicket*, p. 83.

63 *"That the substance"*: Trevelyan, *England in the Age of Wycliffe*, p. 294.

63 *"learnt by bitter experience"*: Quoted in Trevelyan, *England in the Age of Wycliffe*, p. 294.

64 *"at the time of"*: Quoted in Workman, *John Wycliffe*, vol. 2, p. 169.

64 *"John Wycliffe, that"*: Quoted in Lupton, *Wycliffe's Wicket*, p. 170.

64 *"grievously tormented"*: Quoted in Workman, *John Wycliffe*, vol. 2, p. 330.

65 *"wearied of honors"*: Quoted in ibid., p. 332.

65 *"naked in a sack"*: Quoted in ibid.

65 *"went every where"*: Quoted in Lupton, *Wycliffe's Wicket*, p. 81.

65 *"right perfect"*: Quoted in Lechler, *John Wycliffe*, p. 441.

65 *"despised comfort"*: Quoted in Lupton, *Wycliffe's Wicket*, p. 81.

65 *"to the only life"*: Lupton, *Trodden Thyme*, p. 65.

66 *"By God, we will"*: Quoted in Cammack, *John Wycliffe and the English Bible*, p. 48.

66 *"a fruitful tree"*: Quoted in Lupton, *Wycliffe's Wicket*, p. 52.

67 *"welcomed in London"*: Lupton, *Trodden Thyme*, p. 43.

67 *"died miserably"*: Quoted in Workman, *John Wycliffe*, v. 2, p. 403.

67 *"He was humble"*: Quoted in ibid.

67 *"from county to county"*: Quoted in Lupton, *Wycliffe's Wicket*, p. 79.

67 *"costly volumes"*: Lupton, *Trodden Thyme*, p. 17.

68 *"every second man"*: Quoted in Dahmus, *The Prosecution*, p. 85.

68 *"honest men"*: Quoted in Lechler, *John Wycliffe*, p. 442.

68 *"We therefore command"*: Quoted in Robinson, *The Bible*, p. 142.

68 *"This University"*: Quoted in Lechler, *John Wycliffe*, p. 456.

69 *"it was at Cambridge"*: Lupton, *Trodden Thyme*, p. 88.

69 *"devoted its enfeebled"*: Lupton, *Wycliffe's Wicket*, p. 27.

69 *"Doctor in theology"*: Quoted in Lupton, *Wycliffe's Wicket*, p. 27.

69 *"That wretched"*: Quoted in Cammack, *John Wycliffe*, p. 64.

69 *"Christ sitting"*: Quoted in Trevelyan, *England in the Age of Wycliffe*, p. 335.

70   *"It is consecrated":* Quoted in Lechler, *John Wycliffe*, p. 453.

70   *"a man of great":* Quoted in Lupton, *Trodden Thyme*, p. 99.

71   *"preferred justice":* Quoted in ibid., p. 93.

71   *"he strove":* Quoted in ibid., p. 93.

71   *"running very fast":* Quoted in ibid., p. 99.

71   *"diseased energy":* Chesterton, *A Short History of England*, p. 129.

71   *"put a torch":* Ibid.

72   *"Come, Holy Spirit":* Quoted in Bokenkotter, *A Concise History*, p. 102.

72   *"authentic and universal pope":* Quoted in ibid.

73   *The Avon to the Severn:* Quoted in *The Oxford Companion to English Literature*, p. 901.

73   *"to taste":* Quoted in Brown, *History of the English Bible*, p. 34.

73   *"silent Protestants":* Hindley, *England in the Age of Caxton*, p. 127.

73   *"the strange":* Ibid., p. 128.

73   *"a book of the four":* Quoted in Brown, *History of the English Bible*, p. 30.

74   *"could recite much":* Quoted in ibid., p. 32.

74   *"for she knoweth":* Quoted in ibid.

74   *"I have hitherto":* Quoted in Workman, *John Wycliffe*, vol. 1, p. 9.

74   *"It is no question":* Quoted in Trevelyan, *England in the Age of Wycliffe*, p. 349.

74   *"England was not converted":* Ibid., p. 351.

75   *"the initial":* Cammack, *John Wycliffe*, p. 66.

75   *"was determined that":* Ibid.

75   *"Why else was this Nation":* Milton, *Areopagitica*, 91.

CHAPTER TWO: MARTYR

PAGE

79   *"We have now":* Foxe, *Foxe's Book of Martyrs*, p. 135.

80   *"high wild hills":* Lupton, *Tyndale the Translator*, p. 14.

80   *"like the garden":* Ibid.

80   *"right famous as":* Ibid.

80   *"the thrilling poetic":* Marius, *Thomas More*, p. 317.

80   *"how that king Athelstane":* Foxe, *Book of Martyrs*, p. 136.

80   *"by long continuance":* Ibid.

81 *"the arid and undiscerning commentaries":* Marius, *Thomas More,* p. 300.

81 *"for the man":* Chesterton, *A Short History,* p. 135.

82 *"changed the appearance":* Bacon, *The Advancement of Learning,* p. 66.

83 *"the father of English":* Hindley, *England in the Age of Caxton,* p. 225.

83 *"I was born":* Quoted in ibid., p. 227.

83 *"a good Christian man":* Quoted in ibid., p. 228.

84 *"Please explain":* Quoted in ibid.

85 *"he swept away":* Marius, *Thomas More,* p. 71.

85 *"When I listen":* Quoted in Wild, *The Romance of the English Bible,* p. 79–80.

85 *"sprang up":* Daiches, *The King James Version,* p. 142.

86 *"a divine art":* Quoted in Febvre and Martin, *The Coming of the Book,* p. 171.

87 *"It almost appeared":* Quoted in Eisenstein, *The Printing Press,* p. 300.

87 *"It is a mystery":* Quoted in ibid., p. 303.

87 *"God's highest":* Quoted in ibid.

87 *"God hath opened":* Quoted in ibid., p. 310.

87 *"laid the egg":* Quoted in Demaus, *William Tindale,* p. 27.

87 *"I laid a hen's":* Quoted in Lupton, *Tyndale the Martyr,* p. 107.

87 *"owls and bats":* Quoted in Partridge, *English Bible Translation,* p. 35.

88 *"Unsurpassed in the murkiness":* Quoted in ibid.

88 *"the safety":* Quoted in Marius, *Thomas More,* p. 263.

88 *"half of Europe":* Bokenkotter, *A Concise History,* p. 214.

89 *"not simply a":* Encyclopaedia Britannica, vol. 29, p. 51.

89 *"certain students":* Foxe, *Book of Martyrs,* p. 137.

89 *"in the common place":* Ibid.

89 *"divers great-beneficed men":* Ibid., p. 138.

89 *"waxed weary":* Ibid.

89 *Let [the student] approach:* Quoted in Wild, *The Romance of the English Bible,* pp. 86–87.

90 *"We were better":* Quoted in Foxe, *Book of Martyrs,* p. 138.

90 *"I defy the Pope":* Quoted in ibid.

90 *"He threatened me":* Quoted in ibid., p. 139.

90 *"I perceived":* Quoted in Brown, *The History,* p. 40.

91 *"a still Saturn":* Foxe, *Book of Martyrs,* p. 140.

91   *"house was full"*: Ibid.

92   *"a rare thing"*: Quoted in *Encyclopaedia Britannica*, vol. 5, p. 840.

92   *Strong be the walls:* Quoted in Harvey, *Thomas Cardinal Wolsey*, p. 9.

93   *"I will put myself"*: Quoted in D'Aubigne, *History of the Great Reformation*, vol. 3, p. 100.

93   *"limb of the devil"*: Ibid.

93   *"His Highness"*: Quoted in Hoare, *Evolution of the English Bible*, p. 144.

94   *"High and victorious"*: Quoted in Harvey, *Thomas Cardinal Wolsey*, p. 129.

94   *"a swine of hell"*: Quoted in ibid.

94   *"Since he"*: Quoted in Marius, *Thomas More*, p. 281.

94   *"Take us the little foxes"*: Quoted in D'Aubigne, *History of the Great Reformation*, vol. 3, p. 105.

94   *"Luther, the true serpent"*: Quoted in ibid., pp. 107–8.

95   *"So renowned a name"*: Quoted in ibid., p. 108.

96   *"untrue translations"*: Quoted in Hoare, *Evolution of the English Bible*, p. 122.

96   *"I took him"*: Quoted in Foxe, *Book of Martyrs*, p. 144.

97   *"during the life-time"*: Trevelyan, *English Social History*, p. 38.

97   *"there was hardly"*: Power, *Medieval People*, p. 149.

97   *"dyed in the wool"*: Trevelyan, *English Social History*, p. 36.

98   *"supported half the population"*: Daniell, *William Tyndale*, p. 15.

98   *"so skillful"*: Quoted in Dickens, *The English Reformation*, p. 70.

98   *"I do not like"*: Quoted in Rogers, *Selected Letters of Sir Thomas More*, p. 167.

98   *"A little praty"*: Quoted in Robinson, *The Bible*, p. 152.

98   *"the scourge of Luther"*: Quoted in Hoare, *Evolution of the English Bible*, p. 129.

98   *"his indiscretion"*: Rogers, *Selected Letters of Sir Thomas More*, p. 167.

99   *"whether the King"*: Quoted in Foxe, *Book of Martyrs*, p. 150.

99   *"like Mordecai"*: Quoted in Demaus, *William Tindale*, p. 113.

100 *"Rebellion never obtains"*: Quoted in D'Aubigne, *History of the Great Reformation*, vol. 3, p. 199.

100 *"I seem to myself"*: Quoted in Partridge, *English Bible Translation*, p. 36.

100 *"Now we are gathering"*: Quoted in D'Aubigne, *History of the Great Reformation*, vol. 3, p. 200.

100 *"If we are wrong":* Quoted in ibid.

101 *"to the sound of pipes":* Quoted in ibid., p. 202.

101 *"every man who wore":* Quoted in ibid., p. 197.

101 *"stab, smite":* Quoted in ibid., p. 201.

101 *"exterminate with the sword":* Quoted in ibid.

102 *"the mighty arm":* Quoted in ibid., p. 207.

102 *"Never fear":* Quoted in ibid., p. 207.

102 *"I well know":* Quoted in ibid.

102 *"Come, Holy Spirit":* Quoted in ibid., p. 208.

103 *"strip them":* Quoted in Marius, *Thomas More*, p. 141.

103 *"How far out of reason":* Quoted in Hammond, *The Making of the English Bible*, p. 92.

104 *"certain prefaces":* Quoted in Robinson, *The Bible*, p. 158.

104 *"faithfully":* Quoted in Cammack, *John Wycliffe*, p. 59.

104 *"Count it as a thing":* Quoted in ibid.

105 *"magical simplicity":* Robinson, *The Bible*, p. 160.

105 *"the consecrated dialect":* Storr, *The English Bible*, p. 69.

106 *"dreadful and penal":* Ibid.

106 *By the duty:* Quoted in Conant, *The Popular History*, pp. 85–86.

107 *"no burnt offering":* Quoted in Hoare, *Evolution of the English Bible*, p. 129.

108 *"Who?":* Edward Hall, *Chronicle*, quoted in Bruce, *The English Bible*, p. 38.

108 *"Yea, I pray thee":* Quoted in ibid., p. 39.

108 *"to stir up":* Quoted in Hoare, *Evolution of the English Bible*, p. 131.

109 *"the English Demosthenes":* Quoted in Partridge, *English Bible Translation*, p. 41.

109 *"You cannot better":* Quoted in ibid.

109 *"unspotted domestic":* Conant, *The Popular History* p. 107.

109 *"its addiction to trivia":* Quoted in Marius, *Thomas More*, p. 149.

110 *More has built:* Quoted in Lupton, *Towards King James*, pp. 49–50.

110 *"candor, justice":* Conant, *The Popular History*, p. 114.

111 *"would fain unsay":* Quoted in Conant, *The Popular History*, p. 114.

111 *"treated divers matters":* More, *Works*, vol. 3, p. 246.

111 *"scholars of standing":* Hollis, *Thomas More*, p. 150.

111 *"for every lewd":* Ibid., p. 250.

111 *I totally dissent:* Quoted in Demaus, *William Tindale*, pp. 32–33.

112 *"well known":* More, *Works*, v. 3, p. 248.

112 *"that such articles":* Ibid., p. 250.

113 *"great arch-heretic":* Ibid., p. 251.

113 *"a beast"*: Ibid., vol. 4, p. 111.

113 *"We may well rub"*: Bruce, *The English Bible*, p. 40.

114 *"it was solemnly"*: Quoted in ibid.

114 *"that I gave not"*: Quoted in Conant, *The Popular History*, p. 129.

114 *"a properly constituted"*: Partridge, *English Bible Translation*, p. 42.

114 *"organized body"*: Ibid.

114 *"Tyndale [would] make"*: Quoted in Conant, *The Popular History*, p. 127.

115 *"When our Lord"*: Quoted in Pelikan, *The Reformation of the Bible*, p. 45.

115 *"because that word"*: Quoted in Conant, *The Popular History*, p. 185.

115 *"the mighty theocracy"*: Lewis, *English Literature in the Sixteenth Century*, p. 206.

116 *The sacred writers*: See Conant, *The Popular History*, p. 129.

116 *"no society like"*: Hollis, *Thomas More*, p. 16.

116 *"By these traditions"*: Quoted in Conant, *The Popular History*, p. 119.

117 *"I call God to record"*: Letter to John Frith, quoted in Hoare, *Evolution of the English Bible*, p. 85.

117 *"with a strong"*: Lupton, *Towards King James*, p. 12.

118 *"a worshipful widow"*: Foxe, *Book of Martyrs*, p. 150.

118 *"Hans Lufft"*: Ibid.

118 *"I submit this work"*: Quoted in Conant, *The Popular History*, p. 134.

119 *"noun + of + noun"*: See Hammond, *Making of the English Bible*, p. 50.

119 *"scapegoat," etc.*: See Robinson, *The Bible*, p. 167.

120 *"Now is winter gone"*: Quoted in Lupton, *Tyndale the Martyr*, p. 91.

121 *"I beseech George Joye"*: Quoted in Bruce, *The English Bible*, p. 43.

122 *"He that judgeth"*: Quoted in Dickens, *The English Reformation*, p. 73.

122 *"feigned ordinances"*: Quoted in Conant, *The Popular History*, p. 95.

122 *"The parson sheareth"*: Quoted in ibid., p. 99.

122 *"as good the prayer"*: Quoted in ibid., p. 96.

122 *"never yet heard"*: Quoted in Greenslade, *The Cambridge History of the Bible*, p. 154.

123 *"For as Scripture"*: Sir Thomas More, *Works*, v. 1, p. 142.

123 *"Yet death shall"*: Ibid., p. 156.

123 *"It were as hard"*: Ibid., p. 170.

123 *"Where thy treasure"*: Ibid., p. 171.

123 *"a surgeon should"*: Quoted in Conant, *The Popular History,* p. 122.

123 *"And this lo!"*: Quoted in ibid., p. 133.

123 *"monotonously anxious"*: Lewis, *English Literature,* p. 174.

124 *"What! Master Doctor"*: Quoted in Foxe, *Book of Martyrs,* p. 324.

124 *"more charitably handled"*: Quoted in ibid.

124 *"faked his"*: Marius, *Thomas More,* p. 33.

124 *"urged the mayor"*: Ibid.

125 *"this is the great scab"*: Quoted in Dickens, *The English Reformation,* p. 75.

125 *"secret search"*: Ibid., p. 76.

125 *"cast off his hood"*: Quoted in ibid.

125 *lifting up our hearts:* Quoted in ibid.

126 *"in a tawny"*: Quoted in ibid., p. 77.

127 *"I would you were"*: Quoted in Fraser, *Lives of the Kings and Queens,* p. 182.

127 *"Shortly you and I"*: Ibid.

127 *"When ye had me"*: Quoted in ibid., p. 183.

128 *"whole power"*: Quoted in Conant, *The Popular History,* p. 136.

129 *"I came hither"*: Quoted in Conant, *The Popular History,* p. 144.

129 *"up to Jerusalem"*: Quoted in Dickens, *The English Reformation,* p. 80.

129 *"in so flagrant"*: Quoted in Lupton, *Tyndale the Translator,* p. 29.

129 *"sealed up his faith"*: Ibid.

129 *"Fear not"*: Ibid.

130 *"If there were in me"*: Quoted in Daniell, *William Tyndale,* p. 219.

130 *"divulging [the whole]"*: Quoted in Conant, *The Popular History,* p. 138.

130 *"This is a book"*: Quoted in ibid., p. 93.

131 *"this realm of England"*: Quoted in *Encyclopaedia Britannica,* vol. 29, p. 51.

131 *"from the beginning"*: Quoted in ibid., vol. 8, p. 315.

131 *"the slippery precipice"*: Marius, *Thomas More,* p. 363.

132 *"the heart of a true"*: Quoted in Conant, *The Popular History,* p. 152.

132 *"I perceived the man"*: Quoted in ibid., pp. 153–54.

132 *"He was a man"*: Foxe, *Book of Martyrs,* p. 146.

133   *"venerated almost":* Quoted in Conant, *The Popular History*, p.157.

133   *"the real director":* Ibid., p.158.

133   *"pointed with his finger":* Foxe, *Book of Martyrs*, p.149.

133   *"pitied to see":* Ibid.

134   *"a warmer cap":* Quoted in Bruce, *The English Bible*, p.52.

134   *"had an awful reputation":* Lupton, *Tyndale the Martyr*, p.138.

134   *"It doesn't matter":* Quoted in ibid.

134   *"The New Testament":* Quoted in Partridge, *English Bible Translation*, p.39.

135   *"The fruit that grows":* Quoted in Demaus, *William Tindale*, pp.465–66.

135   *"It is the grace":* Quoted in ibid.

135   *"with fire consumed":* Foxe, *Book of Martyrs*, p.152.

135   *"with a fervent zeal":* Ibid.

135   *"for whose sake":* Mozley, *William Tyndale*, p.323.

CHAPTER THREE: PROTESTANT, CATHOLIC, BISHOP, QUEEN

PAGE

140   *"By God!":* Quoted in Chadwick, *The Reformation*, p.112.

140   *"moved slowly across":* Ibid., p.114.

140   *"You were born":* Quoted in Dickens, *The English Reformation*, p.168.

141   *"I shall make":* Quoted in Conant, *The Popular History*, p.166.

141   *"to cut the knot":* Hoare, *Evolution of the English Bible*, p.146.

141   *"strange delicacies":* Lupton, *Myles Coverdale. Endurance*, p.52.

141   *"to raise":* Green, *A Short History*, p.344.

142   *"no less than":* Ibid., p.349.

142   *"more faithfully":* Quoted in Robinson, *The Bible*, p.212.

142   *"by the whole":* Quoted in Conant, *The Popular History*, p.164.

143   *"drank in good learning":* Quoted in Lupton, *Towards King James*, p.19.

143   *"he was one":* Lupton, *Myles Coverdale. Endurance*, p.53.

143   *"upon Easter eve":* Ibid.

143   *"with ardent soul":* Ibid., p.54.

144   *"plenteous abundance":* Quoted in Edgar, *Bibles of England*, p.141.

144 *"next unto Jeremiah"*: Quoted in Partridge, *English Bible Translation*, p. 60.

144 *"I have neither"*: Quoted in Phillips, *Translators and Translations*, p. 30.

144 *"with the sanction"*: Hammond, *Making of the English Bible*, p. 69.

145 *"ripe"*: Quoted in Robinson, *The Bible*, p. 167.

145 *"I am but"*: Quoted in ibid.

145 *"the pride of life," etc.*: See Phillips, *Translators and Translations*, p. 31.

146 *"But are there"*: Quoted in ibid., p. 56.

146 *"all the heresies"*: Quoted in Conant, *The Popular History*, p. 147.

146 *"commonly preached"*: Quoted in ibid., p. 164.

147 *Think ye not*: Quoted in Dickens, *The English Reformation*, p. 72.

147 *"Yet are ye far"*: Quoted in Conant, *The Popular History*, p. 166.

147 *"permit the use"*: Quoted in ibid.

148 *You shall receive*: Quoted in Brown, *The History of the English Bible*, p. 61.

149 *"within twelve"*: Hoare, *Evolution of the English Bible*, p. 166.

149 *"the reader might swim"*: Quoted in Edgar, *Bibles of England*, p. 150.

150 *"four great dry vats"*: Quoted in ibid.

150 *"Vivat Rex!," etc.*: See Bruce, *The English Bible*, p. 70.

150 *"laid the foundation"*: Paine, *The Learned Men*, p. 202.

150 *"the change was royal"*: Ibid., p. 133.

151 *"private or contentious"*: Bruce, *The English Bible*, p. 101.

151 *"Mine heart panted"*: See Hammond, *Making of the English Bible*, p. 84.

151 *"with exhortations"*: Quoted in Lupton, *Towards King James*, p. 141.

151 *"to avoid all"*: Quoted in Phillips, *Translators and Translations*, p. 34.

151 *"It was wonderful"*: Quoted in Brown, *History of the English Bible*, p. 67.

152 *"Here may"*: Quoted in ibid., p. 71.

152 *"thought it a pity"*: Conant, *The Popular History*, p. 181.

153 *"sinks of carnal"*: Quoted in Lupton, *Towards Kings James*, p. 135.

153 *"The lesser houses"*: Quoted in ibid., p. 135.

154 *the old religious life*: Hoare, *Evolution of the English Bible*, p. 182.

154 *"Five Wounds of Christ"*: Ibid., p. 137.

154 *"followed them":* Ibid.

155 *"It was not always clear":* Chadwick, *The Reformation,* p. 69.

156 *"I would not do":* Quoted in Elton, *Reform and Reformation,* p. 289.

156 *"very cast down":* Quoted in Lupton, *Towards King James,* p. 163.

157 *"We at no time":* Quoted in Elton, *Reform and Reformation,* p. 299.

157 *"he neither ignored":* Hoare, *Evolution of the English Bible,* p. 180.

157 *"Overseen and perused":* Quoted in Bruce, *The English Bible,* p. 71.

157 *"who had refused":* Hoare, *Evolution of the English Bible,* p. 175.

158 *"which for their":* Quoted in Edgar, *English Bibles,* p. 242.

159 *"This is my dilect":* Quoted in Dickens, *The English Reformation,* p. 136.

159 *"Wanting the power":* Quoted in Conant, *The Popular History,* p. 185.

160 *"he could not lull":* Bindoff, *Tudor England,* p. 111.

160 *"the crafty, false":* Quoted in Robinson, *The Bible,* p. 180.

160 *"disputed, rhymed":* Quoted in ibid.

160 *"I believe all":* Quoted in Conant, *The Popular History,* p. 175.

160 *"his hand in Cranmer's":* Elton, *Reform and Reformation,* p. 332.

160 *"We had all":* Quoted in ibid.

161 *"to fear God's":* Quoted in Fraser, *Lives of the Kings and Queens,* p. 190.

161 *"such wonderful proofs":* Lupton, *Myles Coverdale. Heaven,* p. 53.

162 *"abolished, extinguished":* Bindoff, *Tudor England,* p. 162.

162 *"had climbed":* Elton, *Reform and Reformation,* p. 332.

164 *"the fearful tempest":* Conant, *The Popular History,* p. 193.

164 *"her three most":* Ibid.

164 *"the cup of victory":* Bindoff, *Tudor England,* p. 173.

165 *"by adoration":* Quoted in Erickson, *Bloody Mary,* p. 389.

165 *"a virgin, helpless":* Quoted in ibid.

165 *"Touching all matters":* Quoted in ibid., p. 390.

165 *"persons undefiled":* Quoted in ibid.

165 *"It is time":* Quoted in ibid., p. 391.

165 *"the silence was such":* Quoted in ibid.

166 *"If the Mass":* Bindoff, *Tudor England,* p. 169.

166 *"the alacrity":* Conant, *The Popular History,* p. 194.

167 *"abomination":* Quoted in ibid., p. 197.

167 *"Ye see this man":* Quoted in ibid.

167 *"shifting orthodoxy":* Erickson, *Bloody Mary,* p. 452.

167 *"Young people"*: Ibid.

167 *"and only one gentlewoman"*: Ibid.

168 *"The spectacle"*: Ibid, p. 450.

168 *"as one feeling"*: Quoted in ibid.

168 *"Be of good comfort"*: Quoted in Foxe, *Book of Martyrs,* p. 309.

168 *"with a merry courage"*: Erickson, *Bloody Mary,* p. 450.

168 *"Welcome the cross"*: Quoted in ibid.

169 *"This hath offended!"*: Quoted in *Encyclopaedia Britannica,* vol. 3, p. 714.

169 *"I pray you"*: Quoted in Mozley, *William Tyndale,* p. 43.

169 *"a bad queen"*: Chesterton, *A Short History,* pp. 152–53.

170 *"This is the Lord's"*: Quoted in Fraser, *Lives of the Kings and Queens,* p. 202.

170 *"of no mingled blood"*: Quoted in ibid.

170 *"diligently to read"*: Quoted in Hoare, *Evolution of the English Bible,* p. 195.

170 *This is the jewel:* Quoted in Lupton, *Towards King James,* p. 6.

171 *"favor, lenity"*: Quoted in Bindoff, *Tudor England,* p. 235.

171 *"There is only one"*: Quoted in Weir, *Elizabeth I,* p. 54.

171 *"ropes of sand"*: Quoted in ibid.

171 *"I see many"*: Quoted in ibid.

171 *"the darkness"*: Quoted in ibid.

171 *"Babylonical Beast"*: Quoted in Hill, *Antichrist in Seventeenth Century England,* p. 33.

171 *Christ was:* Quoted in Phillips, *Translators and Translations,* p. 199.

171 *"true, natural"*: Quoted in Hill, *Antichrist,* p. 14.

171 *"I think that"*: Quoted in Weir, *Elizabeth I,* p. 55.

172 *"liking to make"*: Quoted in ibid., p. 59.

172 *"loyalty"*: Ibid.

173 *"feed on"*: Quoted in ibid., p. 60.

173 *"the use of"*: Ibid., p. 63.

173 *"She seems both"*: Quoted in ibid, p. 60.

173 *"to convert this"*: *Encyclopaedia Britannica,* vol. 18, p. 343.

174 *"the essence of"*: Hoare, *Evolution of the English Bible,* p. 201.

174 *tolerant of anything:* Ibid.

174 *"The via media"*: Eliot, *Selected Essays,* pp. 179–80.

174 *"popery and superstition"*: Hoare, *Evolution of the English Bible,* p. 189.

174 *"the holy city"*: Ibid.

174 *"new model church"*: Greenslade, *The Cambridge History of the Bible*, p. 156.

174 *"the store"*: Quoted in ibid.

175 *"God knoweth"*: Quoted in Brown, *History of the English Bible*, p. 78.

175 *"smite them,"* etc.: See Edgar, *Bibles of England*, p. 192.

176 *"cast the Great"*: Hoare, *Evolution of the English Bible*, p. 189.

176 *"worldly subtle"*: Edgar, *Bibles of England*, p. 192.

176 *"I would rather"*: Quoted in Elton, *Reform and Reformation*, p. 300.

178 *"heretical opinions"*: Quoted in *Encyclopaedia Britannica*, vol. 5, p. 914.

178 *"examine, alter"*: Quoted in ibid.

179 *"all diversities"*: Quoted in Conant, *The Popular History*, p. 214.

179 *VARIETIES IN:* Quoted in ibid.

180 *"inviolably observe"*: Quoted in ibid.

180 *"Ye that will"*: Quoted in ibid.

180 *"reverence his memory"*: Ibid., p. 218.

180 *"I will subscribe"*: Quoted in ibid.

181 *"now parted"*: Ibid., p 212.

181 *"imposed as necessary"*: Elton, *Reform and Reformation*, p. 350.

181 *"it belonged"*: Conant, *The Popular History*, p. 215.

181 *"At the beginning"*: Quoted in Levine, *Elizabeth I*, p. 81.

181 *"sorted out"*: Brown, *History of the English Bible*, p. 85.

182 *"lightness or obscenity"*: Quoted in Phillips, *Translators and Translations*, p. 147.

182 *"David took this virgin,"* etc.: See Lupton, *Towards King James*, p. 64.

183 *"By God's providence"*: Quoted in *Fathers of the English Church*, vol. 8, p. 162.

183 *"When a thing speedeth"*: Quoted in Hammond, *English Reformation*, p. 138.

184 *"it might have"*: Quoted in Edgar, *Bibles of England*, p. 195.

184 *"its circulation"*: Brown, *History of the English Bible*, p. 98.

186 *"the Pretended Queen"*: Quoted in Weir, *Elizabeth I*, p. 213.

186 *"that guilty woman"*: Quoted in ibid., p. 334.

187 *"it was declared illegal"*: Ibid., p. 335.

187 *"the corruptions"*: Quoted in Robinson, *The Bible*, p. 191.

187 *"It would be throwing"*: Quoted in Conant, *The Popular History*, p. 230.

188 *On every Sunday:* Quoted in Daiches, *The King James Version of the Bible*, p. 146. See also Lupton, *England's Word*, pp. 5–6.

189 *"because we wish":* Quoted in Partridge, *English Bible Translation*, p. 96.

189 *"not only better," etc.:* Quoted in Edgar, *Bibles of England*, p. 239.

190 *"only authentical":* Quoted in Partridge, *English Bible Translation*, p. 96.

190 *"By the fulness":* Quoted in Edgar, *Bibles of England*, p. 239.

191 *"acquisition," etc.:* See Bruce, *The English Bible*, p. 121.

191 *"inquination," etc.:* See Robinson, *The Bible*, p. 192.

191 *"To me the least":* Quoted in Lupton, *Towards King James*, p. 7.

191 *"for their genuine":* Quoted in Edgar, *Bibles of England*, p. 242.

191 *"fitly Englished":* Quoted in ibid.

191 *"darkened":* Quoted in Lupton, *Towards King James*, p. 7.

191 *"We must not imagine":* Quoted in Hoare, *Evolution of the English Bible*, p. 177.

192 *"the poor ploughman":* Quoted in ibid.

192 *"Conculcation," etc.:* See Edgar, *Bibles of England*, p. 263.

192 *"This wicked generation," etc.:* See Robinson, *The Bible*, p. 193.

194 *"confer the Latin":* Quoted in Robinson, *The Bible*, p. 193.

194 *"from every":* Hoare, *Evolution of the English Bible*, p. 203.

194 *"singed the king":* Quoted in Delderfield, *Kings and Queens of England*, p. 75.

194 *"a valueless oath":* Quoted in Hoare, *Evolution of the English Bible*, p. 205.

195 *"I have but":* Quoted in Levine, *Elizabeth I*, p. 345.

195 *"his book":* Quoted in ibid., p. 29.

195 *"she too was mortal":* Weir, *Elizabeth I*, p. 305.

196 *"the incomparable treasure":* Quoted in Harbison, *The Age of Reformation*, p. 127.

196 *"A thousand kingdoms":* Drayton, *Poetical Works*, vol. 1, p. 101.

CHAPTER FOUR: KING

PAGE

199 *"Lonely as she":* Green, *A Short History*, p. 453.

199 *"I will have no":* Quoted in ibid., p. 454.

199 *"Who but our":* Quoted in Handover, *The Second Cecil*, p. 295.

200 *"mildly like a lamb":* Quoted in Levine, *Elizabeth I,* p. 40.

201 *"I told you":* Quoted in Lupton, *Welcome Joy,* p. 183.

201 *"be-bloodied":* Quoted in Bingham, *James I of England,* p. 6.

201 *"It shall never":* Quoted in Scott, *James I,* p. 263.

202 *"great green hall":* Quoted in ibid., p. 267.

202 *"degree, priority":* Shakespeare, *Troilus and Cressida,* Act 1, Scene 3.

202 *"You cannot always":* Quoted in Green, *A Short History,* p. 401.

204 *"a due and godly":* Quoted in Opfell, *King James Translators,* p. 2.

204 *"Saul hath his":* Quoted in Lupton, *Towards King James,* pp. 108-9.

204 *"standing with his":* Quoted in Conant, *The Popular History,* p. 234.

205 *"The Church of Geneva":* Quoted in ibid.

205 *"God's silly vassal":* Quoted in Bingham, *James I,* p. 5.

205 *"the sweet-smelling incense":* Hoare, *Evolution of the English Bible,* p. 218.

205 *"as well as few":* Quoted in Opfell, *King James Translators,* p. 1.

206 *"His Majesty's":* Quoted in Lupton, *Welcome Joy,* p. 98.

206 *"no less conversant":* Quoted in Lupton, *Welcome Joy,* p. 183.

206 *"I could wish":* Quoted in Paine, *The Learned Men,* p. 83.

206 *"drink the ale":* Quoted in Fraser, *Lives of the Kings and Queens,* p. 523.

206 *"tottering gait":* Opfell, *King James Translators,* p. 5.

206 *"waddled like a duck":* Ibid.

207 *"neurotic terror":* Mathew, *James I,* p. 23.

207 *"To the most curious":* Quoted in ibid., p. 77.

207 *"lawful . . . who hath":* Quoted in ibid., pp. 81-82.

208 *"the pedantic":* Encyclopaedia Britannica, vol. 29, p. 119.

208 *"being the Blessed":* Quoted in Lupton, *England's Word,* p. 29.

208 *"their hair down":* Paine, *Learned Men,* p. 3.

209 *"Promised Land":* State Trials, vol. 2, p. 71.

209 *"without honor":* Ibid., p. 72.

209 *"It is no novel":* Ibid., pp. 73-75.

210 *"the king did wonderfully":* Quoted in Lupton, *Towards King James,* p. 110.

210 *"things pretended":* Quoted in Bruce, *The English Bible,* p. 54.

210 *"Religion is the soul":* State Trials, vol. 2, p. 77.

210 *"be suited":* Ibid., p. 78.

211 *"I was married":* Ibid., p. 84.

211 *"with my body":* Ibid.

211 *"Many a man":* Ibid.

211 *"Inasmuch as the Cross":* Ibid., p. 80.

211 *"for it was":* Ibid., p. 76.
211 *"My Lord, you ought":* Ibid.
211 *"desperate conceit":* Quoted in Opfell, *King James Translators,* p. 6.
211 *"schismatic scholars":* Quoted in ibid.
212 *"I will not argue": State Trials,* vol. 2, p. 83.
212 *"the episcopal synod":* Opfell, *King James Translators,* p. 6.
212 *"If you aim": State Trials,* vol. 2, pp. 85–86.
212 *"cried up":* Quoted in Lupton, *Towards King James,* p. 112.
213 *"where men were urged":* Quoted in Conant, *The Popular History,* p. 237.
213 *"not in the body":* Quoted in ibid.
213 *"and was kept":* Quoted in ibid.
213 "Undoubtedly your Majesty": Quoted in Lupton, *England's Word,* p. 12.
213 *"I protest my heart":* Quoted in ibid.
213 *"fly all over":* Quoted in Lupton, *Towards King James,* p. 113.
214 *"I will have none":* Quoted in ibid.
214 *"And surely if these":* Quoted in Lupton, *England's Word,* p. 12.
214 "We have kept": Quoted in ibid.
214 *"James talked much":* Quoted in ibid.
214 *"because those that": State Trials,* vol. 2, p. 80.
214 *"if every man's":* Ibid.
215 *"for the reducing":* See Lupton, *England's Word,* p. 10.
215 *"most earnest":* Quoted in Daiches, *The King James Version,* p. 64.
215 *"both for the profit":* Quoted in Lupton, *Welcome Joy,* p. 183.
216 *"most skill'd":* Quoted in Lupton, *Welcome Joy,* p. 183.
216 *"never yet seen": State Trials,* vol. 2, p. 80.
216 *"partial, untrue":* Ibid., p. 81.
216 *"Let errors":* Ibid.
216 *"I . . . move you":* Quoted in Paine, *Learned Men,* p. 11.
217 *"in their private studies":* Pollard, *Records of the English Bible,* p. 331.
217 *"so that":* Ibid., p. 332.
218 *"might have been":* Quoted in Robinson, *The Bible,* p. 199.
218 *"a great long lad":* Quoted in ibid.
218 *"addicted to the study":* Ibid.
218 *"he not only":* Quoted in Opfell, *King James Translators,* p. 30.
219 *"one of the special":* Ibid., p. 28.
219 *"an angel in the pulpit":* Quoted in Hewison, *Lancelot Andrewes,* p. vii.

219   *"taking a word"*: Quoted in ibid., p. xii.

219   *"as a Jack-an-apes"*: Aubrey, *Brief Lives*, p. 7.

219   *"Men may talk"*: Quoted in Hewison, *Lancelot Andrewes*, p. 11.

219   *"It was no summer"*: Quoted in ibid., p. 119.

219   *"The only true praise"*: Quoted in Bush, *English Literature in the Earlier Seventeenth Century*, p. 317.

220   *"still small voice"*: See Hewison, *Lancelot Andrewes*, p. xv.

220   *"a silver gilt"*: Quoted in Lupton, *England's Word*, p. 27.

220   *"with praise and affection"*: Ibid., p. 28.

220   *"What pains"*: Quoted in Paine, *Learned Men*, p. 20.

221   *"without compulsion"*: Quoted in Lupton, *England's Word*, p. 29.

221   *"beyond all other"*: Paine, *Learned Men*, p. 20.

221   *"his gravity"*: Aubrey, *Brief Lives*, p. 6.

221   *"Cannot I take"*: Quoted in Paine, *Learned Men*, p. 159.

222   *"a terrible high"*: Quoted in ibid., p. 35.

222   *"for peace and concord"*: Opfell, *King James Translators*, p. 34.

222   *"was much relied on"*: Collins, *Ecclesiastical History*, vol. 7, p. 337.

222   *"woody pine apple"*: Quoted in Opfell, *King James Translators*, p. 36.

222   *"the father"*: Ibid., p. 35.

223   *"rough sea dogs"*: Ibid.

223   *"Whilst devotion kneels"*: Quoted in Paine, *Learned Men*, p. 31.

223   *"I was requested"*: Quoted in Lupton, *England's Word*, p. 31.

224   *"the greatest English"*: Aubrey, *Brief Lives*, p. 226.

224   *"wondrous wanton"*: Ibid.

224   *Face she had*: Quoted in ibid., p. 225.

224   *"loved her infinitely"*: Ibid., p. 226.

224   *"found her"*: Quoted in ibid.

224   *"both body and mind"*: Quoted in Paine, *Learned Men*, p. 33.

225   *"that a new government"*: Opfell, *King James Translators*, p. 32.

225   *"seldom went to bed"*: Ibid., p. 36.

225   *"sit down"*: Paine, *Learned Men*, p. 41.

226   *"for a pittance"*: Lupton, *England's Word*, p. 34.

226   *"My life"*: Quoted in ibid.

226   *"an ague"*: Quoted in Opfell, *King James Translators*, p. 45.

226   *"If you do not"*: See ibid., p. 47.

226   *"train up godly"*: Ibid., p. 48.

227   *"clear and pleasing"*: Ibid., p. 47.

227   *"For God's sake"*: Quoted in Paine, *Learned Men*, p. 28.

227   *"swarms of idle"*: Quoted in ibid.

227 *"a living affection":* Quoted in Opfell, *King James Translators,* p. 47.

227 *"scores of zealous":* Ibid.

227 *"without spectacles":* Ibid., p. 48.

227 *"an excellent linguist":*Lupton,*England's Word,* p. 52.

227 *"golden key":* Paine, *Learned Men,* p. 60.

227 *"exquisite skill":* Robinson, *The Bible,* p. 199.

228 *"living library," etc.:* Quoted in Opfell, King James Translators, p. 56.

228 *"his obstinate preciseness":* Quoted in Lupton, *England's Word,* p. 72.

229 *"Neither shall":* Ibid., p. 70.

229 *"dalliance, whoredom":* Quoted in Paine, *Learned Men,* p. 24.

229 *"a gentle discretion":* Paine, *Learned Men,* p. 250.

229 *"a very skeleton":* Quoted in Lupton, *England's Word,* p. 70.

230 *"Give of none":* Quoted in Opfell, *King James Translators,* p. 59.

230 *"mighty in Scripture":*Quoted in Lupton,*England's Word,* p. 76.

230 *"I commend you":* Quoted in ibid.

230 *"drowned in books":* Quoted in ibid.

230 *"wild in his youth":* Quoted in ibid., p. 77.

230 *"reprobate heart":* Quoted in Paine, *Learned Men,* p. 48.

230 *Lo! Richard Kilbye:* Quoted in Opfell, *King James Translators,* p. 61.

231 *"at his fingers' ends":* Quoted in ibid.

231 *"There were many chosen":* See Ibid., Appendix IV, pp. 143–59.

231 *"He must not wait":* Quoted in Paine, *Learned Men,* p. 50.

231 *"famous in his time":* Quoted in Opfell, *King James Translators,* p. 62.

232 *"was a Moses":* Quoted in Paine, *Learned Men,* p. 63.

232 *"desire of preferment":* Quoted in ibid.

232 *"gasped at his pluralism":* Quoted in Lupton,*England's Word,* p. 94.

233 *"singular delight":* Allen, Quoted in *Translating for King James,* p. 133.

233 *"twelve of the hardest":* Quoted in ibid.

233 *"they liking":* Quoted in ibid., p. 135.

233 *"Many knights":* Quoted in ibid., p. 136.

233 *"they needed no help":* Ibid., p. 139.

233 *"Respectful of superiors":* Ibid., p. 140.

233 *"was careful":* Ibid., p. 147.

234 *"almost an Hebrew":* Ibid., p. 148.

234 *"books and papers":* Quoted in ibid., p. 3.

234 *"adopted"*: Quoted in Opfell, *King James Translators*, p. 78.

234 *"harsh and haughty"*: Paine, *Learned Men*, p. 51.

235 *"I would I were"*: Quoted in Allen, *Translating for King James*, p. 141.

235 *"an extraordinarily handsome"*: Aubrey, *Brief Lives*, p. 267.

235 *"always advocated"*: Lupton, *Not Unto Us*, p. 14.

235 *"have a kind"*: Quoted in Opfell, *King James Translators*, p. 83.

236 *"For the king"*: Quoted in ibid., p. 85.

236 *"One day"*: Ibid.

236 *"This of mine own"*: Quoted in Lupton, *Not Unto Us*, p. 62.

237 *"intricate figures"*: Opfell, *King James Translators*, p. 95.

237 *"Caution was given"*: Quoted in Robinson, *The Bible*, p. 200.

237 *"as little altered"*: Quoted in Conant, *The Popular History*, p. 250.

238 *"overseers"*: Quoted in ibid.

238 *"This afternoon"*: Quoted in Lupton, *England's Word*, p. 18.

238 *"each one had entered"*: Butterworth, *The Literary Lineage of the English Bible*, p. 101, quoted in Opfell, *King James Translators*, p. 39.

238 *"[brought] back to the anvil"*: See Opfell, *King James Translators*, Appendix IV, pp. 143–61.

239 *"but thirteen others"*: Quoted in Paine, *Learned Men*, p. 138.

239 *"so they could"*: Opfell, *King James Translators*, p. 39.

239 *"extract one"*: Allen, *Translating for King James*, p. 140.

241 *"most corrupted"*: Quoted in Phillips, *Translators and Translations*, p. 101.

245 *"duly paid them"*: Ibid.

245 *"would not go"*: Quoted in ibid.

246 *"the hardest part"*: Quoted in Lupton, *England's Word*, p. 102.

246 *"What then," etc.*: See Opfell, *King James Translators*, pp. 103–5; Paine, *Learned Men*, pp. 116–31; and Hammond, *The Making of the English Bible*, pp. 174–92.

247 *"a most subtle"*: Quoted in Lupton, *Not Unto Us*, p. 107.

247 *"if the words"*: Quoted in ibid., p. 75.

247 *"sharply and vehemently"*: Ibid.

248 *"all things"*: Quoted in Robinson, *The Bible*, p. 202.

248 *"a distinguished man"*: Quoted in ibid.

248 *"put the finishing"*: Quoted in Opfell, *King James Translators*, p. 104.

248 *"as reverent"*: Ibid., p. 109.

248 *"carried prelature"*: Quoted in Lupton, *Not Unto Us*, p. 79.
248 *"strange liberty"*: Quoted in Opfell, *King James Translators*, p. 105.
248 *"with frowning"*: Lupton, *Not Unto Us*, p. 80.
249 *"in came my Lord"*: Ibid., p. 81.
249 *"glorious word"*: Quoted in ibid.
249 *"is so potent"*: Quoted in ibid., p. 80.
249 *"principal Mover," etc.*: See Opfell, King James Translators, Appendix IV, pp. 143–61.
252 *"I do groan"*: Quoted in ibid., p. 111.
252 *"Look, however"*: Quoted in ibid., p. 112.
253 *"slain"*: Ibid., p. 114.
254 *"swept forward"*: Lupton, *Welcome Joy*, p. 185.
254 *"smacked too much"*: Price, *The Ancestry of Our English Bible*, p. 273.
254 *"such spectacles"*: Lupton, *England's Word*, p. 214.
254 *"its victory"*: Greenslade, *The Cambridge History*, p. 168.
254 *"To this day"*: Quoted in Paine, *Learned Men*, p. 183.
255 *"for the rhythm"*: Grierson, *The English Bible*, p. 7.
255 *stateliness and sonority*: See Storr, *The English Bible*, p. 23.
255 *"rather translated"*: Quoted in Phillips, *Translators and Translations*, p. 63.
255 *"It so happens"*: Quoted in Robinson, *The Bible*, p. 196.
256 *"antique rightness"*: Partridge, *English Bible Translation*, p. 112.
256 *"I will suffer"*: Quoted in Bruce, *The English Bible*, p. 107.
256 *"a deadly enemy"*: Quoted in Lupton, *England's Word*, p. 16.
256 *"pestered with lies"*: Quoted in Edgar, *Bibles of England*, p. 327.
256 *"The holy text"*: Quoted in Daiches, *The King James Version*, p. 156.
257 *"that hereby"*: Quoted in Conant, *The Popular History*, p. 243.
257 *"a good English style"*: Quoted in Lupton, *England's Word*, p. 11.
257 *"All true-hearted"*: Quoted in Lupton, *Not Unto Us*, p. 90.
257 *"The late Bible"*: Quoted in Phillips, *Translators and Translations*, p. 63.
258 *"peace maker," etc.*: See Robinson, The Bible, p. 193, and Storr, *The English Bible*, p. 46.
259 *"a slow, almost"*: Storr, *The English Bible*, p. 34.
259 *"private interpretations"*: Manguel, *A History of Reading*, p. 272.
259 *Blest is the man*: Quoted in Paine, *Learned Men*, p. 180.
259 *Observe the rising*: Quoted in ibid.

260 *"if everything else"*: Quoted in McAfee, *The Greatest English Classic*, p. 92.
260 *"there would be no"*: See Opfell, *King James Translators*, p. 132.
260 *"As to the situation"*: Quoted in Storr, *The English Bible*, pp. 89–90.
261 *So the Brangwens*: Quoted in Hammond, *The Making of the English Bible*, pp. 51–52.
262 *"Many attempts"*: Quoted in Paine, *Learned Men*, p. viii.
262 *"he made the revising"*: Quoted in Lupton, *Welcome Joy*, p. 186.
263 *"to sing psalms"*: Quoted in ibid., p. 187.

CHAPTER FIVE: THE COMMON WEALTH

PAGE

267 *"was made up of"*: Quoted in Delderfield, *Kings and Queens of England*, p. 871.
267 *"allowed the Reformation"*: Wright, *The Atlantic Frontier*, p. 28.
268 *"unoccupied"*: Green, *A Short History*, p. 456.
268 *"Pandora's box"*: Wright, *The Atlantic Frontier*, p. 28.
268 *"stimulated imaginations"*: Ibid., p. 32.
268 *"The mother of modern"*: Bush, *English Literature*, p. 259.
270 *"Though God"*: Quoted in Trevelyan, *History of England*, vol. 2, p. 144.
270 *"the absolute master"*: Bush, *English Literature*, p. 248.
270 *"The state of Monarchy"*: Quoted in Mathew, pp. 220–21.
270 *"the king's head Court"*: Quoted in ibid.
271 *"the father"*: Bush, *English Literature*, p. 247.
271 *"the king can do"*: More, *Utopia*, p. 101.
271 *"the king is"*: Quoted in Hill, *The English Bible*, p. 188.
271 *"in my own person"*: Quoted in Opfell, *King James Translators*, p. 7.
272 *"From this it is"*: Quoted in Paine, *Learned Men*, p. 87.
272 *"for the better discovery"*: Quoted in, Opfell, *King James Translators*, p. 123.
272 *"By the help"*: Quoted in ibid., p. 93.
272 *"If ministers"*: Quoted in ibid.
273 *"most bitterly"*: Scott, *James I*, p. 291.
273 *"revolt in the Low Countries"*: Quoted in ibid.
273 *"in his own"*: *Encyclopaedia Britannica*, vol. 3, p. 44.1

274   *"lions under the throne"*: Quoted in Mathew, p. 230.

274   *"When an act"*: Quoted in ibid., p. 235.

275   *"right and due," etc.: Encyclopaedia Britannica*, vol. 29, p. 58.

276   *"the gabble and indecorum"*: Quoted in Green, *A Short History*, p. 486.

276   *"he might be"*: Quoted in ibid.

276   *"to that time"*: Quoted in ibid., p. 488.

276   *"I will grant"*: Quoted in ibid., p. 489.

277   *"He has broken"*: Quoted in ibid.

278   *"The Gospel"*: Quoted in ibid., p. 494.

278   *"a capital enemy"*: Quoted in ibid., p. 495.

278   *"had enlarge[d] itself"*: Quoted in ibid., p. 494.

279   *"Few sources"*: Hill, *The English Bible*, p. 77.

280   *"popular Bible reading"*: Ibid., p. 15.

280   *"faith in plain Scripture"*: Quoted in ibid., p. 15.

280   *"Either we must"*: Quoted in ibid.

280   *"move [the people] to rise"*: Tyndale, *The Obedience of a Christian Man*, p. 163.

280   *"The art of Printing"*: Quoted in Eisenstein, *The Printing Press*, p. 303.

280   *"Scripture doth"*: Quoted in Paine, *Learned Men*, p. 153.

281   *"the common life"*: Quoted in Hill, *The English Bible*, p. vii.

281   *"to justify"*: Ibid.

281   *"that neither"*: Quoted in Storr, *The English Bible*, p. 8.

281   *"We ought rather"*: Quoted in Hill, *The English Bible*, p. 62.

281   *"Earthly princes"*: Quoted in ibid., p. 59.

282   *"had died like"*: Quoted in Mathew, *English Works of Wycliffe*, p. 227.

282   *"Egyptian tyranny"*: Quoted in Hill, *The English Bible*, p. 114.

282   *"All must acknowledge"*: Quoted in Paine, *Learned Men*, p. 151.

282   *"Great deliverance"*: Quoted in ibid., p. 91.

283   *"This is the Lord's"*: Quoted in ibid.

283   *"O Lord God"*: King, *English Reformation Literature*, p. 410.

283   *"God revealed"*: Quoted in Hill, *The English Bible*, p. 265.

283   *"Truth is compared"*: Patrick, *The Prose of John Milton*, pp. 334–37.

284   *"I have neither"*: Quoted in Green, *A Short History*, p. 531.

284   *"like the feudal": Encyclopaedia Britannica*, vol. 29, p. 333.

284   *"Nimrod"*: Quoted in Hill, *The English Bible*, p. 218.

284   *"a king cannot"*: Quoted in *Encyclopaedia Britannica*, vol. 3, p. 113.

285 *"a second Moses":* Quoted in Hill, *The English Bible*, p. 113.

285 *"a second Jeroboam":* Quoted in ibid., p. 114.

285 *"overborne":* Green, *A Short History*, p. 461.

285 *the Church had been:* Ibid., p. 587.

286 *"awful":* Chesterton, *A Short History*, p. 169.

286 *"If power without":* Quoted in Carleton, *Charles I*, p. 350.

286 *"I am as much":* Quoted in Burton, *Cromwell*, p. 99.

287 *"That which one":* Chesterton, *A Short History*, pp. 127–28.

287 *"Let a man":* Quoted in Sutherland, *English Literature in the Late Seventeenth Century*, p. 298.

288 *"the labor of":* Quoted in ibid., p. 299.

288 *"To say that God":* Quoted in Green, *A Short History*, p. 601.

288 *"The Puritan iconoclast":* Hoare, *The Evolution of the English Bible*, p. 249.

288 *"Both sides pretended":* Quoted in Hill, *The English Bible*, p. 423.

289 *"combining the kingship:* Ibid., p. 172.

289 *"to unite for":* Quoted in Sutherland, *English Literature in the Late Seventeenth Century*, p. 361.

289 *"Some coercive Power":* Quoted in Bush, *English Literature*, p. 254.

290 *"If any man shall":* Quoted in Green, *A Short History*, p. 472.

290 *"How to make":* Ibid., p. 602.

291 *"This marble":* Quoted in ibid., p. 645.

291 *"You are to be":* Quoted in *Encyclopaedia Britannica*, vol. 29, p. 65.

291 *"We cannot but":* Quoted in ibid.

291 *"Your father would":* Quoted in Green, *A Short History*, p. 649.

292 *"The wars against Louis":* Trevelyan, *History of England*, v. 2, p. 147.

293 *France, 'tis strange:* Quoted in Storr, *The English Bible*, p. 14.

293 *"no king":* Trevelyan, *History of England*, v. 2, p. 273.

294 *"God has furnished":* Quoted in Sutherland, *English Literature*, p. 345.

294 *"a precept":* Quoted in *Encyclopaedia Britannica*, vol. 8, p. 559.

294 *"even if":* Quoted in ibid.

294 *"the most perfect":* Quoted in Beloff, *The Debate on the American Revolution*, p. 10.

295 *"a free people":* Quoted in Beloff, *The Debate on the American Revolution*, p. 34.

296 *"gives to bigotry":* Quoted in Brookhiser, *Founding Father*, p. 147.

297 *America was not:* Chesterton, *A Short History*, pp. 200–1.

Bibliography

Allen, W. (ed.) *Translating for King James.* Kingsport, TN, 1969.

Alter, R., and F. Kermode. *The Literary Guide to the Bible.* Cambridge, MA, 1987.

Anderson, C. *Annals of the English Bible.* London, 1845.

Anderson, G. K. *Old and Middle English Literature from the Beginnings to 1485.* New York, 1962.

Arber, E. *The First Printed English New Testament.* London, 1871.

Armitage-Smith, S. *John of Gaunt.* London, 1904.

Arrowsmith, R. S. *Prelude to the Reformation.* London, 1923.

Aston, M. "Lollardy and Reform." *History,* 49, 1964, 149–70.

Aubrey, J. *Brief Lives.* Ed., O. L. Dick. London, 1949.

Avis, F. C. "Book Smuggling into England During the Sixteenth Century." *Gutenberg Jahrbuch* (1972), 180–87.

———. "England's Use of Antwerp Printers, 1500–1540." *Gutenberg Jahrbuch* (1973), 234–40.

Bacon, Sir Francis. *The Advancement of Learning.* New York, 1952.

Bainton, R. H. *Christendom.* New York, 1966.

———. *Erasmus of Christendom.* New York, 1969.

———. *Here I Stand: A Life of Martin Luther.* New York, 1950.

———. *The Reformation of the Sixteenth Century.* Boston, 1952.

Baldwin, T. W. *William Shakespeare's Small Latine and Lesse Greeke.* Urbana, 1944.

Bale, J. *Brief Chronicle of Sir John Oldcastle*. Parker Society, vol. 36, London, 1902

Barlow, W. *The Summe and Substance of the Conference, which, it pleased his Excellent Maiestie to have with the Lords, Bishops, and other of his Clergie, (at which the most of the Lordes of the Councell were present) in his Maiesties Priuy-Chamber, at Hampton Court. January 14, 1603.* London, 1604.

Barnstone, W. *The Poetics of Translation: History, Theory, Practice.* New Haven, 1993.

Barr, J. *The Semantics of Biblical Language.* New York, 1960.

Baumer, F. Le Van. *The Early Tudor Theory of Kingship.* New York, 1966.

Bede, the Venerable. *Ecclesiastical History of the English Church and People.* London, 1955.

Beloff, M. *The Debate on the American Revolution, 1761-1783.* London, 1963.

Bennett, H. S. *English Books and Readers, 1475 to 1557.* Cambridge, 1969.

Bernard, G. W. "The Fall of Anne Boleyn." *English Historical Review* 106 (1991), 584-610.

———. "The Fall of Anne Boleyn: A Rejoinder." *English Historical Review* 107 (1992), 665-74.

Bewer, J. A. *The Literature of the Old Testament.* New York, 1944.

Biblia Vulgata. Salmantica, 1946.

Bindoff, S. T. *Tudor England.* Baltimore, 1950.

Bingham, C. *James I of England.* London, 1981.

Binns, J. *Intellectual Culture in Elizabethan and Jacobean London.* London, 1990.

Black, M. H. "The Printed Bible." *The Cambridge History of the Bible: The West from the Reformation to the Present Day.* Cambridge, 1963, 408-75.

Blake, N. F. *Caxton and His World.* London, 1969.

Bokenkotter, T. *A Concise History of the Catholic Church.* New York, 1979.

Bone, G. "Tindale and the English Language." In S. L. Greenslade (ed.), *The Work of William Tindale.* London, 1938, 50-68.

Boorstin, D. *The Americans: The Colonial Experience.* New York, 1958.

Bosworth, J. and G. Waring (eds.). *The Gospels: Gothic, Anglo-Saxon, Wycliffe, and Tyndale Versions.* London, 1907.

Bowker, M. *The Henrician Reformation.* London, 1984.

Brenton, Sir L. C. L. *The Septuagint with Apocrypha: Greek and English.* London, 1986.

Brigden, S. *London and the Reformation.* Oxford, 1989.

Brook, S. *The Language of the Book of Common Prayer.* London, 1975.

Brookhiser, Richard. *Founding Father.* New York, 1998.

Brown, J. *The History of the English Bible.* Cambridge, U.K., 1912.

Browne, Sir Thomas. *A Letter to a Friend.* London, 1656.

Bruce, F. F. *The English Bible: A History of Translations.* London, 1961.

Buddensieg, R. *John Wiclif: Patriot and Reformer.* London, 1884.

Burnet, G. *The History of the Reformation in England.* Ed., Nicholas Pocock. 7 vols. London, 1865.

Burton, B. *Thomas Cromwell.* London, 1982.

Bush, D. *English Literature in the Earlier Seventeenth Century.* Oxford, 1962.

Butterworth, C. C. *The English Primers (1529-1545): Their Publication and Connection with the English Bible and the Reformation in England.* Philadelphia, 1953.

———. *The Literary Lineage of the English Bible.* Philadelphia, 1941.

Butterworth, C. C. and A. G. Chester. *George Joye, 1495?-1553.* Philadelphia, 1962.

Cadbury, H. J. *The Making of Luke-Acts.* London, 1958.

Callus, D. A. (ed.). *Robert Grosseteste, Scholar and Bishop.* Oxford, 1955.

Cambridge Medieval History, vol. 6. Cambridge, U.K., 1955.

Cameron, E. *The European Reformation.* Oxford, 1991.

Cammack, M. M. *John Wycliffe and the English Bible.* New York, 1938.

Capes, W. W. *The English Church in the Fourteenth and Fifteenth Centuries.* London, 1903.

Capgrave, J. *The Chronicle of England.* Ed., F. C. Hingeston. London, 1858.

Carleton, C. *Charles I. The Personal Monarch.* London, 1983.

Catto, J. I., and R. Evans (eds.). *The History of the University of Oxford, II: Late Medieval Oxford.* Oxford, 1992.

Cavendish, G. *Thomas Wolsey, Late Cardinal, His Life and Death Written by His Gentleman-usher.* London, 1973.

Chadwick, H. *The Early Church.* Middlesex, 1967

Chadwick, O. *The Reformation.* Middlesex, 1964.

Chambers, R. W. *Thomas More.* London, 1935.

Chapman, J. *Notes on the Early History of the Vulgate Gospels.* Oxford, 1908.

Cheetham, N. *A History of the Popes.* New York, 1982.

Chester, J. L. *John Rogers*. London, 1861.

Chesterton, G. K. *A Short History of England*. London, 1917.

Childs, E. *William Caxton: A Portrait in a Background*. London, 1976.

Churchill, W. *History of the English-Speaking People*. New York, 1956.

Clebsch, W. A. *England's Earliest Protestants, 1520–1535*. New Haven, 1964.

Collins, J. *Ecclesiastical History*, vol. 7. London, 1852.

Colwell, E. C. *The Study of the Bible*. Chicago, 1937.

Conant, H. C. *The Popular History of the Translation of the Holy Scriptures into the English Tongue*. New York, 1880.

Constant, G. *The Reformation in England*. 2 vols. London, 1942.

Cotton, H. *Editions of the Bible and Parts Thereof in English*. Oxford, 1852.

———. *The 1535 Bible of Miles Coverdale*. London, 1838.

Craig, H. *The Literature of the English Renaissance, 1485–1660*. London, 1962.

Dahmus, J. H. *The Prosecution of John Wycliffe*. New Haven, 1952.

Daiches, D. *The King James Version of the Bible*. Chicago, 1941.

Daniell, D. *Let There Be Light: William Tyndale and the Making of the English Bible*. British Library Exhibition Pamphlet. London, 1996.

———. *William Tyndale: A Biography*. New Haven, 1994.

Danielou, J., A. H. Couratin and J. Kent. *Historical Theology*. Baltimore, 1969.

Darlow, T. H., and H. F. Moule (eds.). Revised, A. S. Herbert. *Historical Catalogue of Printed Editions of the English Bible, 1525–1962*. London, 1968.

D'Aubigne, J. H. M. *History of the Great Reformation of the Sixteenth Century*. 3 vols. New York, 1843.

Davis, J. F. *Heresy and Reformation in the South-East of England, 1520–1559. Royal Historical Society Studies in History*, no. 34, London, 1983.

Deacon, R. *William Caxton: The First English Editor*. London, 1976.

Deanesly, M. *The Lollard Bible and Other Medieval Biblical Versions*. Cambridge, 1920.

———. "Vernacular Books in England in the Fourteenth and Fifteenth Centuries." *Modern Language Review*, 15 (1920), 349–58.

Delderfield, E. R. *Kings and Queens of England*. New York, 1971.

Demaus, R. *William Tindale: A Biography*. London, 1904.

DeMolen, R. L. (ed.). *Essays on the Works of Erasmus*. New Haven, 1978.

Devereux, E. J. *The English Reformation*. London, 1989.

———. *Reformation and Society in Sixteenth-Century Europe*. London, 1966.

———. *Thomas Cromwell and the English Reformation*. London, 1959.

Dickens, A. G. *The English Reformation*. London, 1964.

———. *Reformation and Society in Sixteenth-Century Europe*. London, 1966.

———. *Thomas Cromwell and the English Reformation*. London, 1959.

Dodd, C. H. *The Bible and the Greeks*. London, 1935.

———. *The Bible Today*. Cambridge, MA, 1968.

Dowling, M. "Anne Boleyn and Reform." *Journal of English History*, 35 (1984), 30–46.

———. "A Woman's Place? Learning and the Wives of Henry VIII." *History Today*, June 1991, 38-42.

Drayton, M. *Poetical Works*. London, 1899.

Duffield, G. E. (ed.). *The Work of William Tyndale*. London, 1964.

Dugmore, C. W. (ed.). *The Interpretation of the Bible*. London, 1944.

Duhamel, P. A. "The Oxford Lectures of John Colet." *Journal of the History of Ideas*, 14 (1953), 493–510.

Edgar, A. *Bibles of England*. London, 1889.

Eisenstein, E. *The Printing Press As an Agent of Change*. London, 1979.

Eliot, T. S. *Selected Essays*. New York, 1950.

Elton, G. R. *Reform and Reformation: England, 1509-1558*. Cambridge, MA, 1977.

Encyclopaedia Britannica. 15th edition. Chicago, 1988.

English Historical Documents: V, 1485-1558. Ed., C. H. Williams. London, 1967.

Erasmus of Rotterdam, Desiderius. *Erasmus: Enchiridion Militis Christiani: An English Version*. Ed., A. M. O'Donnell. Oxford, 1981.

Erickson, C. *Bloody Mary*. New York, 1978.

Faludy, G. *Erasmus of Rotterdam*. London, 1970.

Farrar, F. W. *History of Interpretation*. London, 1886.

Fathers of the English Church. Vols. 4 and 8. London, 1809 and 1812.

Febvre, L., and H.-J. Martin. *The Coming of the Book: The Impact of Printing, 1480-1800*. London, 1976.

Fernald, J. C. *Historic English*. New York, 1921.

Fines, J. *Biographical Register of Early English Protestants, 1525-1558*. 2 vols. London, 1980 and 1987.

Finucane, R. C. *Miracles and Pilgrims: Popular Beliefs in Medieval England*. London, 1977.

Fisher, John. *The English Works of John Fisher.* Ed., J. E. B. Mayor. London, 1876.

Fiske, J. *The Critical Period of American History.* Boston, 1889.

Forshall, J., *John Purvey's Remonstrance Against Romish Corruptions.* London, 1851.

Forshall, J., and F. Madden (eds.). *The Holy Bible: Made from the Latin Vulgate by John Wycliffe.* 4 vols. Oxford, 1850.

Foxe, John. *The Acts and Monuments of John Foxe.* 8 vols. Ed., J. Pratt. London, 1877.

———. *Foxe's Book of Martyrs.* Springdale, PA, 1981.

Fraser, A. *Mary Queen of Scots.* New York, 1970.

———. *The Six Wives of Henry VIII.* London, 1992.

———. (ed.). *The Lives of the Kings and Queens of England.* Los Angeles, 1975.

Fuller, T. *Works.* Vols. 1–3, *Church History of Britain;* vols. 4–6, *History of the Worthies of England.* London, 1840–1842.

Gairdner, J. *Lollardy and the Reformation in England.* 4 vols. London, 1908–1912.

Gardner, J. H. *The Bible As English Literature.* New York, 1907.

Gilbert, G. H. *Interpretation of the Bible.* New York, 1908.

Gleason, J. B. *John Colet.* Berkeley, 1989.

Goodspeed, E. J. (trans.). *The Apocrypha.* New York, 1959.

———. *The Making of the English New Testament.* Chicago, 1925.

Gordon, C. H., and G. A. Rendsburg. *The Bible and the Ancient Near East.* New York, 1965.

Grant, R. M. *A Short History of the Interpretation of the Bible.* New York, 1948.

Greaves, R. L. *The Puritan Revolution and Educational Thought.* New Brunswick, 1969.

Green, J. R. *A Short History of England.* London, 1886.

Greenslade, S. L. *The Cambridge History of the Bible.* Cambridge, U.K., 1963.

———. *The Work of William Tindale.* London, 1938.

Grierson, Sir H. *The English Bible.* London, 1933.

Gruber, L. F. *The Truth About Tyndale's New Testament.* St. Paul, 1917.

Gwyn, P. *The King's Cardinal: The Rise and Fall of Thomas Wolsey.* London, 1990.

Haigh, C. *The English Reformation.* London, 1987.

———. *English Reformations: Religion, Politics and Society Under the Tudors.* London, 1993.

Hammond, G. *The Making of the English Bible*. Manchester, U.K., 1982.

———. "William Tyndale's Pentateuch: Its Relation to Luther's German Bible and the Hebrew Original." *Renaissance Quarterly*, 33 (1980), 351–85.

Handover, P. M. *The Second Cecil*. London, 1959.

Harbison, E. H. *The Age of Reformation*. Ithaca, 1955.

Harpsfield, N. *The Life and Death of Sir Thomas More*. Ed., E. V. Hitchcock. London, 1932.

Harvey, N. L. *Thomas Cardinal Wolsey*. New York, 1980.

Heath, P. *The English Parish Clergy on the Eve of the Reformation*. London, 1969.

Herbert, R. "The Way of Angels." *Parabola*, vol. 14, no. 2, May 1989, 77–86.

Hewison, P. E. *Lancelot Andrewes: Selected Writings*. Manchester, 1995.

Hill, C. *Antichrist in Seventeenth Century England*. London, 1990.

———. *The English Bible and the Seventeenth-Century Revolution*. London, 1993.

Hindley, G. *England in the Age of Caxton*. New York, 1979.

Hoare, H. W. *The Evolution of the English Bible*. New York, 1901.

Hollis, C. *Thomas More*. Milwaukee, 1934.

Hook, J. N. *The Story of British English*. Dallas, 1974.

Hook, W. F. *Lives of the Archbishops of Canterbury*. Vols. 1 and 2. 1860 and 1863.

Hudson, A. "Debate on Bible Translation." *English Historical Review*, January 1975, 1–18.

Hunt, E. W. *Dean Colet and His Theology*. London, 1956.

Innis, G. S. *Wycliffe: The Morning Star*. Cincinnati, 1907.

Ives, E. W. *Anne Boleyn*. Oxford, 1986.

———. *Factions at the Court of Henry VIII*. London, 1972.

———. "The Fall of Anne Boleyn Reconsidered." *English Historical Review*, 107 (1992), 651–64.

Jean, G. *Writing: The Story of Alphabets and Scripts*. New York, 1992.

Johnson, J. *Tudor Gloucestershire*. Gloucester, 1985.

Jones, E. *The Origins of Shakespeare*. Oxford, 1977.

Karpman, D. M. "William Tyndale's Response to the Hebraic Tradition." *Studies in the Renaissance*, 14 (1967), 110–30.

Kennedy, G. A. *Classical Rhetoric and Its Christian and Secular Tradition from Ancient to Modern Times*. Chapel Hill, 1980.

Kenyon, F. G. *Our Bible and the Ancients' Manuscripts*. London, 1895.

Ker, J. *The Psalms in History and Biography*. New York, 1886.

Kermode, F. (ed.). *The Selected Prose of T. S. Eliot.* New York, 1975.

King, J. N. *English Reformation Literature: The Tudor Origins of the Protestant Tradition.* Princeton, 1982.

Knox, D. B. *The Doctrine of Faith in the Reign of Henry VIII.* London, 1961.

Lawton, D. *Faith, Text, and History.* Charlottesville, 1990.

Lechler, P. *John Wycliffe and His English Predecessors.* London, 1878.

Lehmberg, S. E. *Sir Thomas Elyot: Tudor Humanist.* Austin, 1960.

Letters and Papers, Foreign and Domestic, of the Reign of Henry VIII. Ed., J. S. Brewer, J. Gairdner, R. H. Brodie et al. 21 vols. London, 1862-1932.

Levine, J. M. (ed.). *Elizabeth I.* Englewood Cliffs, 1969.

Lewis, C. S. *English Literature in the Sixteenth Century, Excluding Drama.* London, 1954.

———. *The Literary Impact of the Authorized Version.* London, 1950.

Lloyd Jones, G. *The Discovery of Hebrew in Tudor England: A Third Language.* Manchester, 1983.

Locke, John. *Essay Concerning Human Understanding.* New York, 1954.

Loserth, J. *Wiclif and Hus.* Trans., M. J. Evans. London, 1884.

Lovett, R. *The Printed English Bible, 1525-1885.* London, 1894.

Lupton, L. *England's Word.* London, 1993.

———. *Myles Coverdale. Endurance.* London, 1979.

———. *Myles Coverdale. Heaven.* London, 1980.

———. *Not Unto Us.* London, 1994.

———. *Towards King James.* London, 1990.

———. *Trodden Thyme: Lollard Aftermath.* London, 1985.

———. *Tyndale the Martyr.* London, 1987.

———. *Tyndale the Translator.* London, 1986.

———. *Up to Hampton Court.* London, 1992.

———. *Welcome Joy.* London, 1988.

———. *Wycliffe's Wicket.* London, 1984.

Luther, Martin. *Three Treatises.* Philadelphia, 1973.

Lyte, H. C. M. *History of the University of Oxford.* Oxford, 1886.

MacCulloch, D. *Thomas Cranmer: A Life.* New Haven, 1996.

Mallet, C. E. *History of the University of Oxford,* 2 vols. Oxford, 1924.

Manguel, A. *A History of Reading.* New York, 1996.

Manning, B. L. *The People's Faith in the Time of Wycliffe.* London, 1919.

Marius, R. *Thomas More: A Biography.* London, 1985.

Mathew, D. *James I.* London, 1967.

Matthew, F. D. *The English Works of John Wycliffe.* London, 1880.

Mayor, J. E. B. *English Works of John Fisher.* London, 1876.

McAfee, C. B. *The Greatest English Classic.* New York, 1912.

McBrien, R. P. *Lives of the Popes.* San Francisco, 1997.

McConica, J. K. *English Humanists and Reformation Politics under Henry VIII and Edward VI.* London, 1965.

McCusker, H., and G. Walker. *Plays of Persuasion: Drama and Politics at the Court of Henry VIII.* Cambridge, MA, 1991.

McGiffert, M. "William Tyndale's Conception of Covenant." *Journal of Ecclesiastical History,* 32 (1981), 167–84

Merriman, T. B. *Life and Letters of Thomas Cromwell.* London, 1902.

Meyer, C. S. "Henry VIII Burns Luther's Books, 12 May 1521." *Journal of Ecclesiastical History,* 9 (1958), 173–87.

Moller, J. G. "The Beginnings of Puritan Covenant Theology." *Journal of Ecclesiastical History,* 14 (1963), 46–67.

Mombert, J. I. *A Handbook of the English Versions of the Bible.* New York, 1890.

———. *Tindale's Pentateuch.* New York, 1884.

More, Thomas. *The Complete Works of St. Thomas More.* Vols. 3, 4, 5, 6, and 8. New Haven, 1969–81.

———. *Utopia.* New York, 1949.

Moulton, C. W. *The Library of Literary Criticism.* Vol. 1. Buffalo, 1901.

Moulton, W. F. *The History of the English Bible.* London, 1911.

Mozley, J. F. *Coverdale and His Bibles.* London, 1953.

———. "The English Enchiridion of Erasmus, 1533." *Review of English Studies,* 20 (1944), 97–107.

———. *John Foxe and His Book.* London, 1940.

———. *William Tyndale.* London, 1937.

Myers, L. M. *The Roots of Modern English.* Boston, 1966.

Norton, D. *A History of the Bible As Literature,* vol. 1. Cambridge, 1993.

Oberman, H. A. *Luther: Man Between God and Devil.* New Haven, 1989.

Ogg, F. A. *A Source Book of Medieval History.* New York, 1972.

Opfell, O. S. *The King James Translators.* London, 1982.

Owst, G. R. *Literature and Pulpit in Medieval England.* Cambridge, 1933.

Oxford Companion to English Literature. Oxford, 1967.

Paine, G. S. *The Learned Men.* New York, 1959.

Partridge, A. C. *English Bible Translation.* London, 1973.

Pastor, L. *History of the Popes.* London, 1899.

Patrick, J. M. (ed.). *The Prose of John Milton.* New York, 1967.

Pattison, T. H. *The History of the English Bible.* London, 1894.

Pelikan, J. *The Reformation of the Bible: The Bible of the Reformations.* New Haven, 1996.

Phillips, H. L. *Translators and Translations.* Anderson, IN, 1958.

Pineas, R. "More Versus Tyndale: A Study of Controversial Technique." *Modern Language Quarterly,* 24 (1963), 144–50.

———. "William Tyndale: Controversialist." *Studies in Philology,* 60 (April 1963), 117–32.

———. "Willam Tyndale's Use of History as a Weapon of Religious Controversy." *Harvard Theological Review,* 55 (1962), 121–41.

Pollard, A. F. *Cardinal Wolsey: Church and State in Sixteenth-Century England.* New York, 1966.

Pollard, A. W. *Records of the English Bible.* Oxford, 1911.

Poole, R. L. *Wycliffe and the Movements for Reform.* Oxford, 1889.

Power, E. *Medieval People.* New York, 1960.

Price, I. M. *The Ancestry of Our English Bible.* New York, 1956.

Prickett, S. (ed.). *Reading the Text: Biblical Criticism and Literary Theory.* Oxford, 1991.

Puttenham, G. *The Arte of Englishe Poesie.* Eds., G. D. Willcock and A. Walker. Cambridge, 1936.

Rex, R. "The English Campaigns Against Luther in the 1520's." *Transactions of the Royal Historical Society,* 5th series, 39 (1989), 85–106.

Robinson, H. W. *The Bible in Its Ancient and English Versions.* Oxford, 1954.

Robinson, J. M. (ed.). *The Nag Hammadi Library.* San Francisco, 1978.

Robson, J. A. *Wycliffe and the Oxford Schools.* Cambridge, MA, 1961.

Rogers, E. F. *Selected Letters of Sir Thomas More.* New Haven, 1961.

Routh, E. M. G. *Sir Thomas More and His Friends.* London, 1934.

Rummel, E. *Erasmus' Annotations on the New Testament: From Philologist to Theologian.* Toronto, 1986.

Saul, N. *Richard II.* New Haven, 1997.

Scarisbrick, J. J. *The Reformation and the English People.* London, 1984.

Schoenbaum, S. *William Shakespeare.* New York, 1977.

Schwarz, W. *Principles and Problems of Biblical Translation: Some Reformation Controversies and Their Background.* Cambridge, 1955.

Scott, O. J. *James I.* New York, 1976.

Seebohm, F. *The Oxford Reformers John Colet, Erasmus and Thomas More: Being a History of Their Fellow-work.* London, 1867.

Sheppard, G. T. *The Geneva Bible: The Annotated New Testament 1602 Edition.* Cleveland, 1989.

Shirley, W. W. (ed.). *Fasciculi Zizaniorum Magistri John Wycliffe. (A Bundle of Tares of Master John Wycliffe.)* London, 1858.

———. *Catalogue of the Extant Latin Works of Wycliffe.* Revised, J. Loserth. London, 1924.

Skeat, W. W. (ed.). *The New Testament in English (John Purvey's Revision).* Oxford, 1879.

Smart, J. D. *The Interpretation of Scripture.* Philadelphia, 1961.

Smeeton, D. D. *Lollard Themes in the Reformation Theology of William Tyndale.* Vol. 6, *Sixteenth-century Essays and Studies.* Ed., C. G. Nauert. Kirksville, MO, 1984.

Smith, G. *The United States: Political History, 1492-1871.* New York, 1901.

Smith, H. M. *Pre-Reformation England.* New York, 1938.

Smith, H. P. *Essays in Biblical Interpretation.* Boston, 1921.

Stacey, J. *John Wycliffe and Reform.* Philadelphia, 1964.

Stanier, R. S. *Magdalen School: A History of Magdalen College School.* Oxford, 1940

Stapleton, T. *The Life and Illustrious Martyrdom of Sir Thomas More.* Fordham, 1966.

Starkey, D. (ed.). *Henry VIII: A European Court in England.* London, 1991.

State Trials, vols. 1 and 2. Ed., William Cobbett. London, 1809.

Steinberg, S. H. *Five Hundred Years of Printing.* London, 1974.

Stevenson, F. S. *Robert Grosseteste.* London, 1899.

Storr, V. F. *The English Bible: Essays by Various Writers.* London, 1938.

Strype, J. *Ecclesiastical Memorials.* 3 vols. London, 1821.

———. *Memorials of Archbishop Cranmer.* 2 vols. London, 1812.

Sturge, C. *Cuthbert Tunstall: Churchman, Scholar, Statesman, Administrator.* London, 1938.

Sutherland, J. *English Literature in the Late Seventeenth Century.* New York, 1969.

Sylvester, R. S. and G. P. Marc'hadour (eds.). *Essential Articles for the Study of Sir Thomas More.* Hamden, CT, 1977.

Talon, H. *John Bunyan.* London, 1956.

Thomson, J. A. F. *The Later Lollards, 1414-1520.* Oxford, 1967.

Thomson, S. H. "The Philosophical Basis of John Wycliffe's Theology." *Journal of Religion,* XI (1931), 86-116.

Trapp, J. B. "Erasmus, Colet and More: The Early Tudor Humanists and Their Books." *The Panizzi Lectures, 1990.* London, 1991.

Trevelyan, G. M. *England in the Age of Wycliffe, 1368-1520.* London, 1899.

———. *English Social History*. London, 1943.

———. *History of England*. Vol. 2. London, 1926.

Trousdale, M. *Shakespeare and the Rhetoricians*. London, 1982.

Tyndale, William. *The Beginning of the New Testament Translated by William Tyndale 1525: Facsimile of the Unique Fragment of the Uncompleted Cologne Edition*. Ed., A. W. Pollard. Oxford, 1926.

———. *The New Testament of Our Lord and Saviour Jesus Christ*. New York, 1837.

———. *The Obedience of a Christian Man*. Parker Society. Cambridge, U.K., 1848.

Tyndale's New Testament. Modern spelling edition. Prepared by D. Daniell. New Haven, 1989.

Tyndale's Old Testament. Modern spelling edition. Prepared by D. Daniell. New Haven, 1992.

Ullmann, W. *The Origins of the Great Schism*. London, 1948.

von Ranke, L. *History of the Popes, Their Church and State*. 3 vols. Translated, E. Fowler. New York, 1901.

Walker, G. *John Skelton and the Politics of the 1520s*. Cambridge, 1988.

———. *Plays of Persuasion: Drama and Politics at the Court of Henry VIII*. Cambridge, 1991.

Weir, Alison. *Elizabeth I*. London, 1998.

Warnicke, R. M. *The Rise and Fall of Anne Boleyn*. Cambridge, U.K., 1989.

Weiss, R. *Humanism in England During the Fifteenth Century*. Oxford, 1957.

———. *The Spread of Italian Humanism*. London, 1964

Westcott, B. F. *A General View of the History of the English Bible*. London, 1905.

Wheeler Robinson, H. (ed.). *The Bible in Its Ancient and English Versions*. London, 1940.

Wild, L. H. *The Romance of the English Bible*. New York, 1929.

Williamson, G. A. (ed.). *Foxe's Book of Martyrs*. Boston, 1965.

Willoughby, H. R. *The First Authorized English Bible and the Cranmer Preface*. Chicago, 1942.

Winn, H. E. (ed.). *Wycliffe: Select English Writings*. London, 1929.

Wolf, A. *William Roye's "Dialogue Between a Christian Father and His Stubborn Son."* Vienna, 1874.

Wood, A. *Athenae Oxoniensis*. Oxford, 1848.

———. *The History of Antiquities of the Colleges and Halls of the University of Oxford* [Annals]. 2 vols. Ed., J. Gutch. London, 1786–90.

Workman, H. B. *John Wycliffe: A Study of the Medieval Church.* 2 vols. London, 1926.

Workman, S. K. *Fifteenth Century Translation as an Influence on English Prose.* Princeton, 1940.

Wright, C. K. *Bunyan As a man of Letters.* Folcroft, PA, 1916.

Wright, L. B. *The Atlantic Frontier.* New York, 1951.

Index

About the Author

Benson Bobrick earned his doctorate in English and Comparative Literature from Columbia University, and is the author of six previous books, including *Angel in the Whirlwind: The Triumph of the American Revolution, East of the Sun: The Epic Conquest and Tragic History of Siberia, Fearful Majesty: The Life and Reign of Ivan the Terrible,* and *Labyrinths of Iron: Subways in History, Myth, Art, Technology & War.* His books have been translated into German, Spanish, Italian, Russian, Dutch, Chinese, and Japanese. He lives in Vermont.